ON OUR DOORSTEP

Craig Collie is the author of the highly acclaimed *The Path of Infinite Sorrow* and *Nagasaki*, as well as *The Reporter and the Warlords* and *Code Breakers*. He is a TV producer-director by background and was head of TV Production at SBS.

ON OUR DOORSTEP

When Australia faced the threat of invasion by the Japanese

CRAIG COLLIE

ALLEN&UNWIN
SYDNEY • MELBOURNE • AUCKLAND • LONDON

First published in 2020

Allen & Unwin
83 Alexander Street
Crows Nest NSW 2065
Australia
Phone: (61 2) 8425 0100
Email: info@allenandunwin.com
Web: www.allenandunwin.com

NATIONAL LIBRARY OF AUSTRALIA
A catalogue record for this book is available from the National Library of Australia

ISBN 978 1 76063 228 1

Maps by Mapgraphics
Set in 12.75/17 pt Adobe Garamond Pro by Midland Typesetters, Australia
Printed and bound in Australia by Griffin Press, part of Ovato

10 9 8 7 6 5 4 3 2 1

MIX
Paper from responsible sources
FSC www.fsc.org
FSC® C009448

The paper in this book is FSC® certified. FSC® promotes environmentally responsible, socially beneficial and economically viable management of the world's forests.

CONTENTS

Acronyms		vii
Maps		xi
Chapter 1	Grazing gazelles	1
Chapter 2	Unstoppable	23
Chapter 3	Gibraltar of the East	57
Chapter 4	Frontier town	92
Chapter 5	Great and powerful friends	133
Chapter 6	Home fires burning	163
Chapter 7	Expendable	200
Chapter 8	Watchers of the north	223
Chapter 9	Night of the midgets	260
Chapter 10	The turning tide	299
Chapter 11	The invasion of Australia	333
Acknowledgements		347
Notes		349
Bibliography		375
Index		395

ACRONYMS

ABC	Australian Broadcasting Commission
ABDA	American-British-Dutch-Australian
AIF	Australian Imperial Force
ALP	Australian Labor Party
ARP	Air Raid Precautions
ASDIC	Anti-Submarine Detection Investigation Committee
AWA	Amalgamated Wireless (Australasia)
AWC	Advisory War Council
BHP	Broken Hill Proprietary Company Limited
CBD	central business district
CCC	Civil Collaboration Column, Civil Construction Corps
CGS	Chief of General Staff
CMF	Citizen Military Force
DCA	Department of Civil Aviation
DoI	Department of Information
ES&A	English Scottish & Australian (bank)
GHQ	General Headquarters

GI	enlisted member of US armed forces (originated as abbreviation for galvanised iron in US Army supply records)
HQ	Headquarters
IED	improvised explosive device
IGHQ	Imperial General Headquarters (Japan)
IJA	Imperial Japanese Army
IJN	Imperial Japanese Navy
JCS	Joint Chiefs of Staff (US)
KLM	*Koninklijke Luchtvaart Maatschappij* (Royal Dutch Airlines, literally Royal Aviation Company)
mph	miles per hour
MSB	Maritime Services Board
NAOU	North Australia Observer Unit
NAWU	North Australian Workers' Union
NCO	non-commissioned officer
NEI	Netherlands (Dutch) East Indies
NSW	New South Wales
NT	Northern Territory
NTSRU	Northern Territory Special Reconnaissance Unit
NWA	Northwestern Area
PhD	Doctor of Philosophy
PIB	Papuan Infantry Battalion
PM	Prime Minister
PMS	postmaster's
PO	post office
POW	prisoner of war
PR	public relations
PS	postscript
RAAF	Royal Australian Air Force

RAF	Royal Air Force
RAN	Royal Australian Navy
RASC	Royal Army Service Corps
RSL	Returned and Services League
RSSAILA	Returned Sailors', Soldiers' and Airmen's Imperial League of Australia
SWPA	South West Pacific Area
UAP	United Australia Party
USAAF	United States Army Air Forces
USAFFE	United States Army Forces in the Far East
USSR	Union of Soviet Socialist Republics
VAOC	Volunteer Air Observer Corps
VC	Victoria Cross
VDC	Volunteer Defence Corps

MAPS

Map 1	Japanese advance through Malaya, December 1941–January 1942	43
Map 2	Japanese invasion of Singapore, 8–15 February 1942	71
Map 3	New Britain: lines of retreat from Rabaul, January–February 1942	231
Map 4	Solomon Islands: observation posts of Allied coast watchers, 1942	234
Map 5	Northern Australia: disposition of Australian surveillance groups, NTSRU and NAOU, 1942–3	239
Map 6	Sydney Harbour: key positions of Allied and Japanese vessels, 31 May–1 June 1942	270

Chapter 1

GRAZING GAZELLES

> 'I can't understand the mentality of the Australian people. One day they are in a panic (about the war) and the next they want more race meetings. When things looked bad in New Guinea, morale sagged; now things are better everybody will probably want Christmas off.'[1]
>
> John Curtin, Prime Minister of Australia, off the record, 6 October 1942

In December 1941, the Japanese military launched strikes at several points around the Pacific Ocean and southeast Asia. An attack by Japan was not a surprise, but Japan's new enemies were unprepared for its extent or its enterprise. Rolling south over the following weeks, the juggernaut seemingly had Australia in its sights. Not for the first time, Australians—the government, the military, the people—believed themselves under threat of invasion, but for the first time the threat felt imminent. The lingering uncertainty and what to do about it produced a range of responses from alarm to nonchalance. Sober assessment sat like a stranger somewhere in the middle.

Although Australia has not been invaded by a foreign power since 1788, it persuades itself from time to time that another invasion is just around the corner. In the colonial era, as an outpost of the British Empire, it had to live with the possibility of military action by Britain's enemies and rivals. The French had arrived at Botany Bay a week after the First Fleet and, with this in mind, Governor Arthur Phillip set up fortifications around Sydney Cove and lookouts near the entrance to Sydney's harbour.

To the south, a second colony had been established at Van Diemen's Land (now Tasmania), and it moved quickly to counter the menacing French. On arrival, Lieutenant-Governor David Collins decided protection was needed in case France sent a warship up the Derwent River. In 1804, two ships' cannons were set up on an earthwork redoubt overlooking the port of Hobart Town, growing as a resupply station on the trade routes of the British Empire.[2]

Captain Roger Kelsall of the Royal Engineers was sent out to Hobart Town in 1833. Declaring the port undefended, he devised a network of fortified batteries with interlocking firing arcs.[3] No course could be plotted up the river that was at any point not in range of a shore gun. The cost was prohibitive with the British Empire temporarily at peace, but work started nonetheless with convict labour. Over the next 45 years, five batteries were built, but they were never called on to repel an invasion force.

That Governor Phillip's fortifications and lookouts on Sydney Harbour were insufficient became clear one night in 1839. Under cover of darkness, two American naval ships slipped unnoticed into Port Jackson and dropped anchor in Sydney Cove. The town awoke the next morning to find foreign warships had been able to enter the harbour undetected. It wasn't a threat—these were ships of the Wilkes Antarctic expedition—but it could have been.

'If [we had been] enemies,' Charles Wilkes wrote, 'it would have been in our power before daylight to have fired all the Shipping and store houses, laid the town under contribution and departed unhurt.'[4]

It's a warning that has infused strategic thinking on home defence ever since, first of Australia's colonies, then its federation. Typically Australian, it has jumped without much logic back and forth between panic and complacency.

A continuing concern was that any war involving the Mother Country would spill over to an attack on its colonies. Whenever England was threatened, a series of scares prompted work on harbourside fortifications, but they were seldom finished before the scare subsided, and were often left half built. Start, dawdle, defer. Start, dawdle, defer. It was a repeating cycle. Public unease at Wilkes' ships evading the notice of Sydney's harbour defences prompted fortification of the mid-harbour rock island called Pinchgut, but work ground to an unfinished halt after a few years.

By the late 1850s, the gold rushes of inland New South Wales and Victoria had created a new source of invasion fear. The unprecedented wealth flowing from Australia's goldfields caused authorities to worry about raids by foreign ships intent on plundering the colony's gold reserves. Rumours ran of likely attacks by American pirates, coupled soon after with a fear that with the outbreak of the American Civil War, the North might declare war on England and her colonies for aiding the Southern states.

Neither pirates nor Union Army materialised on the distant continent's lonely shores, but meanwhile a new threat had emerged. In Europe, a dispute with Tsarist Russia had escalated into the Crimean War. Governor Sir William Denison ordered a reinforcement of Sydney's harbour gun emplacements in response and a resumption of work on Pinchgut. Renamed Fort Denison, the island fort was finally completed in 1857, but by then its armaments were largely obsolete and the Crimean War was over.

The colonial administration in Victoria was also persuaded that the Russian navy posed a threat. Captain Peter Scratchley, having served in the Crimean War, was sent by the War Office in London to advise on fortifications for Melbourne. He recommended batteries at the entrance to Port Phillip Bay and inside at Williamstown and Sandridge, as well as a floating battery and a fort on piles in Hobsons Bay. Proposals for batteries, towers and forts were costed and, despite the fear of war with the United States, almost all were abandoned.[5] The Victorian colonialists thought British sea power was sufficient protection against invasion. They had greater concern about 'a sudden attack with a view to plunder' by 'some dashing fellow in command of an enemy's frigate, or a privateer', but had no particular plan to counteract this.[6]

By the late nineteenth century, Britain had withdrawn its garrisons from all its Australian colonies, leaving them to fend for themselves. The colonies' governments ordered assessments of the possibility of major attacks and what was needed to resist them, without any thought that they might be an occupation force themselves. All that could be envisaged by the inquiries was small-scale naval raids from French, Russian or American bases around the Pacific Ocean. A royal commission determined nonetheless that batteries should be built at five points on Sydney Harbour. Visiting English writer Anthony Trollope was shown the new fortresses.

'There was much martial ardour,' he commented, 'and a very general opinion that "they" would have the worst of it.'[7]

But 'they' never came.

With the turn of the century, a new threat emerged. Previously, potential invaders had been rival colonial powers with familiar objectives and cultures, but this had changed. Now, a fear of the Other was driving the threat to Australia's shores. It started with Chinese drawn to the gold rushes of New South Wales and Victoria. There had been incidents of anti-Chinese violence on many of the goldfields, like at Lambing Flat in 1860, with the public and newspapers increasingly agitated. By 1888, all Australia's colonies had enacted laws excluding further Chinese immigration. In the newly federated nation, these would give birth to White Australia, a policy given gristle with the *Immigration Restriction Act* of 1901.

The drive for federation was built on the perceived need for national security. Its most imposing advocate, Sir Henry Parkes, toured the colonies giving speeches that warned of the threat posed by 'the countless millions of inferior members of the human family who are within easy sail of these shores', and the menace of China, 'a barbarous power, which is so rapidly creating armies and a formidable navy, that it is sufficient at all events to awaken the intelligent attention of reflecting men'.[8]

The issue had taken on a more xenophobic, indeed racist, tone. The modus operandi of invasion was envisaged differently too. No longer would the invader come barging into a harbour protected by untested fortifications. Parkes told the 1891 convention for the federation constitution there was evidence that China and other Asian nations were awake to the power of their immense population. They could move stealthily into 'some thinly populated portion of the country', he said, 'where it would take immense loss of life and immense loss of wealth to dislodge the invader'.[9] These were people so Other that they could infiltrate uninhabitable parts of the continent and make themselves at home.

What grew in the public imagination, fuelled by politicians' rhetoric, was some sort of military showdown along racial lines.

T.T. Ewing, an Australian Protectionist Party MP, thought the White Australia policy might provoke Asian retaliation. 'Between the white and the yellow man there is racial hatred,' he opined. 'They are destined to be enemies for all time.' Ewing predicted a future with 'the greatest storm which the world has ever seen when the white man eventually in these latitudes faces the yellow man in deadly war'.[10] He would later become Minister of Defence.

Australia's military leaders might not have put it so vehemently, but they were in partial agreement with their future minister. Captain William Creswell, Director of the Commonwealth Naval Forces, feared Japan or China could conspire with one of the European powers. 'The very immensity of our lands,' he warned, 'opens up the chance of co-operation. German, Jap and Chinese colonies could be carved out of the North and West of Australia.'[11] The targets, again, were not Australia's fortified harbours, but the remote expanses of the continent, unsettled and undefended. Australia's settlers had clung to its coastal areas, awestruck by the continent's lonely interior. Now they feared that others were not so daunted by those forbidding parts.

One nation in particular emerged as the main threat in the region. From the close of the nineteenth century, Australia worried about the intentions of an industrialising Japan looking for an outlet for its manufactured goods, and eyeing China as the natural market. That meant Japan taking on the Western colonial powers there, demanding an open trading door. After Admiral Heihachirō Tōgō's crushing defeat of Russia's Baltic Fleet in 1905, the Japanese were not going to be easily fobbed off.

In 1923, the British announced that a naval base would be built at Singapore, consolidating its authority in the region and serving to blunt Japanese ambitions there. Construction of the base didn't start for five years, held up by a change of government in Britain. There were further delays during the reclamation of a mangrove swamp, due to heavy rainfall and the British refusing to allow a customary ceremony to appease the spirits in a *keramat* (sacred place) tree on the site of the planned dry dock. After an outbreak of malaria among the workmen and three British officials dying, Chinese labourers raised funds to pay for the rites, and work on the base resumed.[12]

In the aftermath of the First World War, Australia had no confidence in its defence being assured by either the League of Nations or Washington agreements limiting naval expansion. Allies during the war, the Japanese had been browbeaten by America and Britain into accepting warship restrictions at the Washington Naval Conference in 1922. The battlecruiser *Ibuki* had even transported Australian troops to Gallipoli, but Australia's military strategists viewed Japan as 'the only potential and probable enemy'. Japan could land troops almost anywhere on the Australian coast it wished, they concluded, and keep them supplied.[13] What to do about it became an issue in federal parliament. The Labor opposition argued that the country should prepare for its own defence. The Nationalist government, led by Prime Minister Stanley Bruce, was persuaded by Britain that only the naval force promised with the planned base at Singapore could ensure Australia's security. The Mother Country was determined to keep a tight grip on defence of its 'possessions'.

The political arm wrestle drew in the military. In 1926, Colonel Henry Wynter, a rising star of the Australian Army, expressed concern at the government's reliance on the British, whose defence structure was primarily for the security of Great Britain. In Wynter's view, 'Australia should provide in her own territory, within the area which is defensible by her local air and land forces, a first class naval base.' He argued this should be in addition to, not a substitute for, the Singapore base.[14]

Colonel John Lavarack, another army rising star, put a similar view in the 1930s, shortly before a visit to Australia by Sir Maurice Hankey from London's Committee of Imperial Defence. The visitor from England told the Australian military it would be reliably protected by the naval base at Singapore, still under construction eleven years after it was announced, and Australia's army should be reduced in size. Army chief, General Julius Bruche, tartly commented that Hankey's views were to be respected, but the Australian government had its own military advisers.[15]

It did, but the Minister of Defence, Sir Archdale Parkhill, relied more on the views of Imperial passers-by like Hankey. By so doing, he kept an English rather than Australian perspective. It was early days in the parting of those two perspectives.

The Australian focus remained on Japan, although a lone bureaucratic voice suggested the danger was not so real. Edmund Piesse, Director of the Pacific Branch of the Prime Minister's Department, expressed the view that the Royal Navy was inadequate for Australia's defence needs, and its own capacity needed to be increased. Conceding it was likely Japan would 'extend her Empire towards Australia', Piesse argued that was 'far short of saying that she plans to annexe Australia. For that there is scarcely any evidence; and . . . it would seem most unlikely that she has any such plan.'[16]

This was a minority view at a time when Australia was reassessing its defence needs. It had reduced its armed forces in the two decades that followed the First World War, putting its faith in a lasting peace after the War to End All Wars. The pool of experience in soldiers who returned from the war was thought to make up for the reduced number in the military, but after the never-ending carnage of the First World War less than half had been battle-fit by the time of demobilisation and all were now entering middle-age.

By the end of the 1930s, the region's security apple cart had been upset. Japan had moved into Manchuria and subsequently spread its tentacles into China. As long feared, Japan was looking to dominate Asia and squeeze out the European colonial powers. Under threat was Australia's sense of security, which came from having the British fleet in Singapore (ignoring the fact that it wasn't actually there), the French in control in Indochina, the British in Malaya, the Americans in the Philippines and the Dutch in the East Indies. Colonialism ensured political stability and the natural order of things, the brutality of colonising powers being neither here nor there. The long-feared rise of Asian power came as a powerful psychological shock.

Australia's Labor Party leader, John Curtin, had pushed defence as an issue in the 1937 election with little electoral response, but he was convinced nonetheless that Australia would face a challenge from Japan in the foreseeable future. It seemed set on a collision course with Britain and, with the prospect of simultaneous wars in Europe and Asia, there was a suspicion Britain might abandon its interests in Asia. Having dismissed Curtin's election call for increased defence spending, Prime Minister Joe Lyons did just that after the election. The defence budget doubled in 1938, responding mostly to the looming German threat to Mother England. However, rebuilding couldn't take place overnight. On the eve of the Second World War the Australian Army was dangerously inexperienced, its equipment obsolete and in short supply.

When war began in Europe, Australians seemed numbed by the news. On 3 September 1939, a Sunday, the English Prime Minister Neville Chamberlain's speech was relayed live through local radio stations. Unlike the excitement of 1914, the public mood was sadness and resignation. The broken men who had returned from the War to End All Wars were still in the public memory, indeed were still part of the lives of many. 'The news provoked tears and revived memories among mothers, fathers, and others who had lost close relatives in the last war,' Melbourne's *Argus* noted.[17]

A crowd gathered at the *Age* office for a special edition with the Chamberlain announcement.[18] The calls of newspaper sellers rang from the streets. Four thousand Melburnians converged on Flinders Street railway station, but unlike 1914, there were no flags, no impromptu demonstrations of patriotism or Empire songs, no speeches.[19] At the nearby suburb of Richmond, the Union Jack and the Swastika hung side by side in the almost-deserted German Club. Two policemen watched the club from a street corner a hundred yards away.[20]

Authorities took steps to thwart spies, infiltrators, saboteurs . . . and air raids, despite their improbability. Ambulance services were prepared for large-scale rescue work, their vehicles equipped with two-way wireless telephones. A military guard was placed over Kingsford Smith Airport and all merchant ships entering Sydney Harbour were to be inspected and searched. Entry to the port was permitted in daytime only and vessels failing to stop were in danger of being fired on. Radio transmission was forbidden in all Australian harbours, with Customs sealing the wireless room in ships on arrival.[21] Amateur wireless enthusiasts in the cities and towns were ordered to cease operations and dismantle their equipment.[22]

The notion that the country was soon to be attacked went into overdrive. Sydney's State cinema was showing a 'special film' before the main feature, a few days after war was declared. Called *The Warning*, the British-made film showed 'what to do if your country is bombed'.[23] It would be some months before even England was threatened with bomb attack.

Margaret Maxwell was nine years old at the time, living in a town on the Murray River. 'As soon as war was declared, they put a guard on the Swan Hill bridge and my father was one of them,' she recalls. 'There was Dad and somebody else with a gun marching up and down on the bridge and the other side, in New South Wales, was just the Hay Plains and there was nothing (there).'[24]

Ren deGaris has similar memories: 'They felt very keenly there might be an invasion at that stage. They even put a guard on the Millicent [South Australia] powerhouse—which was two diesel engines with about 60 horsepower.'[25]

For a young girl in Sydney's suburbs, the new war was a nuisance. 'My parents became glued to the radio,' says Yve Jeanneret. 'My brother and I . . . he was two years older than me . . . we were just a little bit irritated that we had to remain quiet and not say a word throughout these news broadcasts. So that was my very first feelings about it.'[26]

Expectation was rife but unclear. When there was no reply to his challenge, a militia guard at Vacuum Oil Co on Sydney's harbour foreshore fired a warning shot at a man in a launch flashing his torch to another boat. Two men were brought to shore as more guards and a police squad car rushed to the scene. The men turned out to be Italian fishermen signalling that there was no Fisheries inspector about.[27]

The simmering tension in the days leading up to the outbreak of war had found foreigners a useful escape valve. A Footscray man, charged with assaulting a motorist a week before, told the court he'd been reading war stories and thought the motorist was German. He was put on a good behaviour bond and told to 'abstain from intoxicating liquor'.[28] On the night before the war was declared, a stone had been thrown through the window of a German community leader's shop in Sydney.[29]

The declaration of war didn't seem to ease the animosity. Sydney's Commissioner of Police announced, 'It has come under my notice that some misguided persons have been visiting the shops of the subjects of Greece and Italy, and making unworthy and unwarranted remarks.' Police were directed to discourage antagonism towards Greeks and Italians 'who are the subjects of nations most friendly to the British Empire'. Italy at the time was going through the pretence of neutrality.[30] The same protection wasn't offered to Germans living in Australia. They were being rounded up and interned.

Before the war, Australia's part-time militia met one night a week at local drill halls or parks. At annual camps, they exercised and handled rudimentary weapons. Late in 1938, the militia force was authorised to double to 70,000, but recruiting proved difficult with little public respect for these chocolate soldiers, or 'chockos', as they were known in the expectation they would melt in the heat of battle. The Defence Act gave the Menzies government the power to conscript men for home defence, so the militia was expanded with compulsory recruiting, mixing earlier part-time volunteers with new full-time conscripts. It wasn't a comfortable mix.

With war declared, Robert Menzies announced a 'special force' of 20,000 to be enlisted for service at home or abroad as the 2nd Australian Imperial Force, the 1st AIF having fought in the First World War. By law, the militia with its conscripts could only fight on Australian soil, but the AIF had volunteered and could be sent overseas. While public sentiment for sending an expeditionary force to the European war was growing, political leaders had to keep an eye on the increasing regional belligerence of Japan to the north, even though that country had not at this stage entered the war. The politicians were conscious that Australia had no standing army, no tanks or modern warplanes, and insufficient ships to stop an invasion fleet. Australia was some distance from Japan, but even more distant from Britain's protection.

Disinclined to send Australian troops away until the Pacific region was more secure, Menzies' hand was forced when New Zealand matched Canada's commitment to the European war.[31] When he announced on 29 November that the newly formed 6th Division AIF would join the British Empire's fighting forces, the *Age* asked whether Australia should be deprived of 'the flower of her young manhood in what shortly may be the hour of her direst need'.[32] It was an oblique reference to the dark cloud of Japan.

General Thomas Blamey was appointed commander of the 6th Division over the more senior—although three years younger—General Gordon Bennett. A veteran of the First World War, Blamey had been Victorian Police Commissioner between the wars and had come out of retirement to chair the government's Manpower Committee. Blamey was a clear-thinking, forceful personality, but confrontational and ruthless, seldom inspiring loyalty or trust. Nonetheless, the politicians Robert Menzies and Richard Casey and Defence secretary Frederick Shedden were convinced Blamey was a better choice than Bennett, who had a prickly temperament and a tendency to act outside orders. The command would be subordinate to British generals and Bennett had been scathingly critical of British as well as Australian officers.[33]

Recruiting for the new force had begun in October, but only a trickle of men was enlisting. The government had tried to keep the nation calm, encouraging 'business as usual'. The prime minister's wife, Pattie Menzies, joined the campaign, urging women to 'carry on home life as usual. No good can come of spreading alarming rumours or of making unnecessary changes in our ordinary way of living.'[34]

This advice did not inspire a stampede of enlistments by anyone not on the list of 'reserved' occupations. A further disincentive was the general perception that recruits were 'five-bob-a-day murderers' drawn from the ranks of the unemployed.[35] The exception to this recruiting apathy was the air force. In the dawning technological age, there was widespread expectation that warfare of the future would be conducted in the air. The RAAF was rushed with recruits. Although it only wanted 170 men, two thousand applied in Melbourne alone, and by March 1940, 11,500 had applied as aircrew. Only 184 were selected for training.[36]

Ignoring their geographical isolation, Australians feared devastation might be coming from the skies. The author Russell Braddon had enlisted at this early stage. 'The first thing they did with us at Victoria Barracks,' he says, 'was to ship seven or eight heroic youngsters like myself to a racecourse with instructions we were to guard it against Nazi parachutists who were due to land imminently.'[37]

State governments were given responsibility for Air Raid Precautions (ARP). Men over 45 and women were recruited as ARP wardens to advise what was to be done and make sure it was carried out. Air-raid drills and shelters, first aid, firefighting, the rescue of 'gassed' people and evacuation drills were all on the agenda. A first aid and decontamination post was set up in Melbourne's Brighton, lectures on gases and ARP given to residents in Sydney. School windows were taped so they couldn't shatter; pupils practised evacuation and were lectured about gases.

Initially the wardens took their role seriously, perhaps too seriously, wearing arm bands and helmets and carrying gas masks, rattles and whistles. Sydney's first air-raid siren test took place in February 1940. Drowned by traffic, few heard it.[38] Enthusiasm slowly turned to indifference, with concerns that ARP activities were increasing anxieties, not calming them. The expected air raids didn't materialise, however, and Australians lost interest in the European war, at a standstill during the freezing northern winter.

Some wardens felt foolish and ceased to pay Air Raid Precautions much attention. The public began to see ARP as a joke, although the organisation itself continued to urge gas-proofing rooms, building air-raid shelters in the garden and shatter-proofing windows. One Darlinghurst flat-dweller commented, 'The instructions I have are that, in the case of a bombing raid all are to walk down to the ground floor. In the case of a gas attack all are to go to the top floors. What happens in the event of a bombing raid with gas is best left to the imagination.'[39]

News from Europe deteriorated in mid-1940. After months of inaction on the Maginot Line, the German army advanced rapidly through the Ardennes forest to France and the British army was evacuated from Dunkirk. Italy opportunistically entered the war. On 17 June, France surrendered.

At the same time, bogged down in its incursions into China, Japan was trying to cut off supply lines from Western powers to the defending forces there. The Vichy government had taken over colonial rule of French Indochina and agreed hesitantly to allow Japanese troops into the country's north to block access to Yunnan province. Japanese diplomatic pressure had forced the closure of the Burma Road. The Australian government and its military advisers watched developments with concern, but this went unnoticed by the general public, distracted by the disturbing turn of events in Europe.

Sixteen-year-old Robert Brown was training in Brisbane at that time to be a teacher. 'We heard of the emperor [of Japan] from time to time,' he says, 'and that was about all. As far as the politics of the country was concerned not much of that seemed to seep out … to where I was, anyway.'[40]

To ten-year-old Yve Jeanneret, the Japanese were part of another universe. 'My image of them is that they were strange little people with slanty eyes that spoke a language I didn't understand and that was it,' she says.[41]

'Made in Japan' was stamped on goods in the cheaper stores. 'We looked on Japan as a second-rate nation,' says Gulgong farmer Bill Graham, 'right from the end of the First World War. If something was made in Japan it was inferior—tools, for instance, and any of their mechanical work—it was all second-rate.'[42]

Yve Jeanneret's toys were like that. 'I always thought they were cheap and nasty. You know, they broke easily. They didn't ever last.'[43]

Australians didn't take the Japanese seriously as a military threat. They were small, short-sighted people, not very good at sport. They couldn't possibly pose a military threat. Their crushing defeat of the Tsar's Baltic Fleet was long forgotten. In any case, any military challenge that might come from elsewhere would be blocked by the impregnable British fortress of Singapore, dubbed 'the Gibraltar of the East' by new British Prime Minister Winston Churchill. The island's northern boundary was the Strait of Johore. Beyond it, the mangrove swamps and dense jungle of the Malay Peninsula were considered impenetrable by a large attacking force. Any attempted invasion of Singapore would have to be from the south and seaborne. It would face massive 15-inch guns pointing in that direction, protecting the island's naval base and airfields.

The base had finally opened in February 1938, on Singapore's northside. Eleven thousand guests had witnessed the inauguration by Governor Sir Shenton Thomas, with a parade of 42 naval ships and a low flypast of 64 aircraft. The King George VI Dock was then the largest dry dock in the world, but that didn't mean it was operational. It needed four more years of construction to be completed.[44]

No Eastern Fleet had been assembled. Instead, the Royal Navy would be sent if Singapore was under attack, while the RAF protected the naval base and the army protected the airfields. Any attackers would be held at bay until the British Fleet came steaming out from wherever to save the day.

That was the mantra anyway. The 'Singapore strategy' was built on naval strength that wasn't there, outmoded ideas of Malaya's impenetrability, and air and land defences that were deficient. Few asked themselves whether Britain would be able to spare any of its navy while it was embroiled in a war in Europe that wasn't going well. Even fewer wondered why a Japan set upon invasion of Australia would divert to attack Singapore. Why not head directly to the target?

Britain's military hierarchy saw the defence of Malaya's airfields as central to its Far East strategy. The Argyll and Sutherland Highlanders, an infantry regiment recruited from the cities and highlands of Scotland, were sent out there, along with Indian reinforcements, arriving piecemeal through 1940 and 1941. The Indian soldiers had little general training and none of it in jungle warfare, having expected to be fighting, like the Australians, in the Middle East. Officers commanding the rapidly expanded Indian Army were mostly English, unfamiliar with jungle terrain, unsure who they might be fighting and some with little fluency in the language of their troops.[45]

In June 1940, Britain asked Australia to send a division to Malaya. The response was that this was not possible. A later British proposal to transfer the 6th Division from the Middle East was similarly rejected.[46] Australian soldiers preferred to go to the fighting they were preparing for, rather than carry out garrison duty somewhere else.

Events soon overtook the Australian government. When a plane crashed on landing in Canberra on 13 August, Cabinet lost three of its ministers and the Australian Army lost its Chief of General Services, General Brudenell White. Criticised for weak leadership, Menzies had already lost a seat in a recent by-election. Not prepared to risk three by-elections, he called a general election for 21 September.

Menzies was trapped between widespread apathy about the war in faraway Europe, where Australian soldiers were not yet fighting, and a press critical of Australia's war effort. In a swing against his United Australia Party (UAP), it lost five seats and was able to hold on to government only with the support of two independents.

War continued to threaten the Pacific, even if the Australian public was blasé about it. Australia's military chiefs advised their government that 'in the absence of a Main Fleet in the Far East, the forces and equipment available in this area for the defence of Malaya are totally inadequate to meet a major attack by Japan'.[47] Australia offered Britain a brigade—some 4000 troops from the 8th Division—to be located temporarily in Malaya until it could be relieved by Indian troops.

Australia's military capacity at that time was divided between the Middle East and the defence of Australia. All of its well-trained forces were occupied overseas at a time when the nation's leaders were getting jittery about home security. The garrison troops that remained behind were judged to be of generally poor fighting quality, many of them returned soldiers from the previous war. Army intelligence appraisal was that 'there are some very fine soldiers among them, but also many of the type who in civilian life could be described as unemployable'.[48] They would make up a significant part of the Malaya force.

Menzies went to England in February 1941 to protest Britain's poor defences in Singapore, but he found the proximity to British decision-making and the attention he received from the English press seductive. The AIF's 6th Division had overwhelmed the Italian fortress at Bardia in Libya, pushing on westward to capture Tobruk and Benghazi. Italy's army was in tatters and the spotlight in London was on Australians.

Churchill told Menzies he was certain of American participation in any war with Japan and that President Roosevelt was determined to stamp out Nazi Germany.[49] The British PM conveniently ignored the widely held belief that the American public needed an incident before it would accept going to war.

Some of Churchill's initial gloss was wearing thin. Menzies noted he was not a good listener and had no use for expert or local opinion. Churchill's oratory was inspiring, but a two-edged sword. To Menzies, his 'real tyrant is the glittering phrase—so attractive to his mind that awkward facts may have to give way'.[50] It was the beginning of reservations by successive Australian governments about the great war leader's candour.

The 6th Division was withdrawn to Greece by the Allied leadership to help repel a German invasion, its initial job apparently done. General Blamey and Prime Minister Menzies both regarded the operation as risky, but agreed after British assurances muffled the prospect of defeat. Outnumbered and without air cover, the defenders were driven back and evacuated to Egypt and Crete after two weeks of fighting.

In London, Menzies was lauded for speaking out against appeasement of Japan. He was told by Britain's political and military hierarchy that Singapore would be heavily reinforced with fighter aircraft and that, in the near future, the Admiralty would advise which ships would come to the Far East. At the same time, there appeared to be British doubts about whether such measures were really necessary. 'The Jap is reported here as a poor airman', Menzies wrote home, and British admiral Sir Tom Phillips told him his fleet was happy to attack even with numerically only 60 per cent of the Japanese naval strength.[51] Like the Australian public, Britain's senior servicemen had a low assessment of Japan's military capacity.

While Menzies was still in Britain, basking in its stately surrounds, dimmed ever so slightly by war, the tide was moving against him back home. Opposition leader Curtin put to a Sydney union convention that Australia's position had become as vulnerable as Britain's. Australia should continue to provide Great Britain with food and other necessities, he told the crowd, but it was no longer appropriate to send soldiers to the war in Europe. It was crucial to prevent any back-door entrance to Singapore.[52]

With whispers that Japan would soon enter the war, Australia's War Cabinet met for what the press dubbed a 'crisis meeting'. It didn't resolve much because there wasn't much to resolve as long as Japan made no obvious move. Japan's consul-general assured Australia that any grievances between the two countries could be solved by peaceful negotiation. Acting PM Arthur Fadden declared the Far East 'critical but not alarming', whatever that meant.[53] It made a good headline.

Robert Menzies returned to Australia in May after four stimulating months as part of the British War Cabinet, but he didn't endear himself to many people, relating the high opinion the English held of him and complaining of having to return to 'play party politics'.[54] He would soon be relieved of that burden.

Shortly before Menzies returned, Japan signed a Neutrality Pact with the Soviet Union, easing the need to garrison its empire in Manchuria and freeing it to deploy forces further south. In July, 50,000 Japanese troops moved into southern Indochina. Roosevelt responded by freezing all Japanese assets in the US and placing an embargo on exports to Japan, principally oil and scrap metal. Britain, its empire and the Dutch East Indies followed suit. In quick time, Japan had lost three-quarters of its overseas trade and 90 per cent of its oil supplies.

Australians put to one side their low opinion of Japan's industrial and military capacity and began to fret about the region's growing instability. To large chunks of the public, Menzies was 'Pig Iron Bob', a nickname given to him in 1938 when, as Attorney-General, he had taken a hard line on Port Kembla wharfies' refusal to load pig iron for export to Japan. The nickname returned in the changing climate. Never popular, Menzies lost support in his own party and resigned. Country Party leader Fadden became prime minister on 29 August 1941, having entered Cabinet only five months earlier.

The likable but inexperienced Fadden struggled with his new role in a disorganised coalition. Labor looked like the only party capable of the stability and leadership required in such uneasy times. On 3 October, the two independents voted against the government and Fadden resigned as prime minister. John Curtin was invited by the Governor-General to form government.

Although a tense and austere man, sometimes over-sensitive to criticism, Curtin was respected as a person on both sides of parliament. Percy Spender, from the other side, would write of him years later as 'a kindly, warm-hearted man, despite a rather prim and somewhat cold appearance, he was an outstanding wartime leader'.[55]

In this he was fortunate—or wise—enough to form a partnership with Frederick Shedden, whom he inherited as his secretary of the Department of Defence Co-ordination. Shedden became Curtin's right-hand man, his main adviser on strategy, emphasising reliance on the United States and the need to maintain Australian sovereignty. It was a partnership that would play significantly throughout the coming war.

As prime minister, Curtin made only minor changes in policy regarding the European war. He and Menzies had never been diametrically opposed on that. The differences were more of style and emphasis. Curtin had never met Churchill and didn't feel beholden to him when he became prime minister. Unlike Menzies, he didn't aspire to be like him.

Menzies had been concerned with protecting British commercial interests in the region, refusing an American request to use Australian airfields to cross the Pacific. Curtin, more concerned with his country's future protection, offered permission for US military aircraft to land in Australia in his second week as prime minister, ensuring an air route between Hawaii and the Philippines. Britain was informed of this, but not consulted.

General Blamey returned to Australia in November to consult with the new government. Never one to hold back for reasons of diplomacy, he expressed surprise at the complacency of his countrymen in a time of regional tension. Australians at home, he declared, were like 'a lot of gazelles grazing in a dell on the edge of the jungle, while the beasts of prey are working up toward you, apparently unseen, unnoticed'.[56] A letter in *The Bulletin* of 3 December countered, 'In this year alone the press, backed by the Government, has reported a crisis in the Pacific no fewer than eleven times. The first of these reports was received by the country at face value; the second and third with suspicion; the rest with apathy, if not with downright disbelief.'[57]

The timing of the letter wasn't great. It would only take a few more days for the uncertainty to resolve itself.

Chapter 2

UNSTOPPABLE

Pearl Harbor wasn't, as is widely believed, the opening salvo in the war with Japan. That honour, if that's what it is, goes to Kota Bharu. The Imperial Japanese Army's (IJA) plan was to land an invasion force on the northeast Malayan coast, where Australian airmen and Indian infantry were stationed, and capture the airfield there. They would use it as a base to provide air cover for detachments landing concurrently at Pattani and Songkhla on the east coast of Thailand. This force would invade Malaya through its northwestern state of Kedah with air cover from Kota Bharu. Japan had pressured the Thai government to allow its troops to pass through Thailand. Unlike their comrades landing on the Malayan coast, this force didn't anticipate any serious opposition until they got to the Thai–Malay border.

Malaya was earmarked as part of Japan's vision of a Greater East Asia Co-Prosperity Sphere. The European imperialists were to be replaced by Japan as the dominant colonial power in Asia in the pursuit of building an empire and gaining access to valuable resources. Malaya produced 58 per cent of the world's rubber and 38 per cent of its tin.[1] This was an attractive drawcard, as it had been for Britain over a century before. Pushing on to capture Singapore would provide a valuable military base for the Japanese as well as undermining Britain's authority in the region.

Aware of the possibility of Japanese attack, the British had spent 1941 setting up beach defences along Malaya's east coast, the northern coastline guarded by India's 9th Infantry Division, the southern by the Australian 8th Division. The British also had a plan, codenamed Matador, for a pre-emptive strike into southern Thailand, if necessary, to delay an enemy attack coming from that direction until the main British force arrived.[2] They were unaware of the arrangement with Japan for its troops to pass unopposed through Thailand. By the same token, the Thais had not been notified of the British contingency plan. Indeed, the British ambassador in Bangkok had signed a non-aggression pact with Thai Prime Minister Phibun.[3]

In advance of launching their attack in southeast Asia, the Japanese had cultivated a network of agents drawn from a group of disaffected Malayans calling themselves the Tortoise Society. Japan also picked up intelligence from Japanese, Korean and Formosan businessmen and tourists, and by their own embassy staff. Leading up to invasion, the Japanese had provided financial support to the Malay pro-independence movement, Kesatuan Melayu Muda (Young Malays Union), in return for information about British troop movements and strengths.[4]

On 4 December 1941, while a naval air contingent was heading towards Pearl Harbor, a Japanese invasion force from General Tomoyuki Yamashita's 25th Army steamed out from Hainan Island, off China's south coast. The convoy was joined as it moved south by a flotilla with additional troops that had been sheltering in Indochina's Cam Ranh Bay. Two days later, an Australian Lockheed

Hudson aircraft, on reconnaissance patrol from Malaya, spotted the convoy.

At first Flight Lieutenant Johnny Ramshaw reported three ships. Fifteen minutes later he saw a much larger group. There were at least 25 transports, his radioman messaged to Kota Bharu, escorted by a battleship (actually a heavy cruiser), five cruisers and seven destroyers. Ramshaw's estimation was that they were heading for either neutral Thailand or the Malay Peninsula.[5] It was a sighting as significant as it was unsurprising.

The chief of Britain's Far East Command, 63-year-old Air Chief Marshal Sir Robert Brooke-Popham, had been given authority to decide if Operation Matador should be activated without the need to refer first to London. But it was still British policy to avoid war if possible and, with the fleet turning north, it was plausible it was heading to an anchorage on the western seaboard of Cambodia and not Thailand or Malaya. The autonomy of Brooke-Popham, who had a habit of falling asleep at meetings, was somewhat illusory. Free to make his own decision as long as it was the decision London would have made, he put his forces in Malaya—nearly 90,000 troops, 158 obsolete aircraft and no tanks—on full alert and ordered continued surveillance of the Japanese convoy.[6]

Hudsons from two Australian squadrons tried to shadow the ships over the day, but low cloud and heavy rain made it difficult. Aware of planes in the vicinity, the invasion fleet had changed direction to disguise its destination, steaming into the Gulf of Siam. British planes were ordered to conduct further patrols, but the stormy monsoonal weather prevented the planes taking off.

On the same day, 6 December, Admiral Thomas Hart, commanding officer of America's Asiatic Fleet, held discussions in Manila with his British counterpart, Sir Tom Phillips. An American naval officer came into the conference room with the message that an Australian reconnaissance plane had sighted a large convoy of warships and merchantmen coming around the bottom of French Indochina. It was a convoy whose make-up was typical of an invasion force. Sensing the long-anticipated move of Japan into open war, Admiral Phillips ordered the battlecruiser *Repulse* to cancel its planned trip to Darwin and return immediately to Singapore. The American admiral instructed four US destroyers in Borneo to head for open sea.

Next morning, the Japanese convoy split into two forces. The fleet heading north remained hidden under low cloud, but its more southerly counterpart was spotted by a Catalina on RAF patrol. A floatplane took off from one of the Japanese ships and attacked the flying boat from the rear, damaging its radio. The Catalina was shadowed by the floatplane for 25 minutes until five fighters arrived, shooting down the patrol plane and killing its Australian pilot, Flying Officer Patrick Bedell, and his crew of seven.[7] They were the first Allied casualties of the Pacific War, some seventeen hours before the first torpedo bomber hit Pearl Harbor.

Poor visibility continued and aerial patrols lost sight of the Japanese fleets until late afternoon. Mysteriously, no reports were coming in from the Catalina that had left in the morning. Finally, as nightfall was setting in, search planes spotted the warships about 120 kilometres out from Songkhla in southern Thailand and heading south. Far East Command called a conference for 10.30 that night in Singapore's Naval Base War Room. Still hesitant to launch Operation Matador, the aging Brooke-Popham decided to delay the operation, at least until morning. It was enough time to allow events to overtake him.

Just after midnight, an Indian patrol on one of Kota Bharu's beaches made out three shadowy shapes about 3 kilometres out to sea. They were the Japanese transport vessels *Awagisan Maru*,

Ayatosan Maru and *Sakura Maru*, dropping anchor and preparing to land over 5000 troops. These were elite soldiers, already hardened by several months of harsh jungle training and fighting in China. While they were loaded on landing craft, amid heavy rain and crashing waves, the escorting warships began their softening-up bombardment of the shore. It was not yet 12.30 a.m. on 8 December 1941. Across the Pacific, Japan's carrier-borne bombers were still 90 minutes away from Pearl Harbor.

In the rough seas and strong winds some of the small boats capsized, and several soldiers drowned. By the time the first wave of landing craft was heading for the beach in towed lines of three or four barges, the defence had opened up intense artillery and machine-gun fire from pillboxes and trenches. The fire was so heavy that Japanese soldiers had to lie on the floodlit beach, half in and half out of the water, unable to raise their heads. When they grabbed an opportunity to move forward, they did so over the bodies of comrades who'd already tried that.[8]

It wasn't particularly favourable terrain for an amphibious landing. The narrow beach was split by two estuaries leading to the mouth of the Pengkalan Chepa River through a maze of creeks, lagoons and swampy islands. Two kilometres inland was Kota Bharu airfield and the main road. The shoreline was fortified with land mines and barbed wire, with covering fire from two pillboxes. A field battery was further back, adjacent to the airfield.

This wasn't yet an attack on Australia, but the Indian defenders were at the needle-point of Australia's fear of invasion. Through the jungly scrub on the edge of the beach they could see a ribbon of sprawled men, making their opportune moves, scuttling like crabs. On the water, approaching lines of barges brought in more invaders.

The first waves had been pinned down until vicious hand-to-hand fighting forced a breach in defences on the south bank of the main estuary. The attackers were able to move in and disable the two pillboxes and their supporting trenches. The Indian sepoys defending them began to fall back from their untenable positions to the edge of the airfield.

As soon as the naval shelling of the shore had begun, crews at the Australian air base at Kota Bharu were wakened and briefed to attack the Japanese fleet at their doorstep. Seven Hudsons took to the air from the grass airstrip, each armed with four 250-pound bombs. Continuous heavy rain and a thick blanket of cloud hanging over the sea compelled the aircraft to swoop in at low level amid intense anti-aircraft fire. The prime targets were the three troopships. The largest, *Awagisan Maru*, sustained two direct hits in the first run. After more bombing strikes and strafing by machine-gun fire, the transport was left burning and sinking. *Awagisan Maru* had the distinction of becoming the first Japanese ship to be sunk by enemy action in the Second World War. One of the Hudsons, piloted by Johnny Ramshaw, who'd spotted the convoy first two days earlier, returned to base so quickly that his copilot, Don Dowie, was still smoking the cigarette he'd lit before take-off.[9] No. 1 Squadron RAAF had made its mark in the opening exchange of the coming war.

Worried about the damage already inflicted and expecting another aerial assault, the Japanese escort's fleet commander sought permission to withdraw his ships, but General Hiroshi Takumi, who was commanding the invasion army, needed to reinforce his troops. The fleet remained off the shore, with black smoke drifting across it from fires on the transport ships.[10]

The air base had meanwhile re-armed its Hudsons. Leading the second attack, Ramshaw flew in at masthead height and dropped bombs around an escort warship. Pulling out after the strike, he was hit with anti-aircraft fire and crashed. Soon after, a similar fate befell Lieutenant John Leighton-Jones' plane, hit while strafing the Japanese beachhead and crashing into one of the troop barges. Sixty Japanese soldiers still on board were killed, along with Leighton-Jones and his crew.

The RAAF No. 8 Squadron, stationed halfway down Malaya's east coast, received a signal from Kota Bharu, and three of their Hudson bombers were airborne by first light. They were able to inflict only minor additional damage on the Japanese fleet which, soon after, was given permission to withdraw. Fires were burning on all three troopships, but only *Awigasan Maru* was left behind. In the Australian squadrons, two planes had been shot down and a further three badly damaged. Only five of the original ten Hudsons from the two squadrons were still airworthy.

Ramshaw and Dowie were the only survivors of their plane crashing into the sea, both thrown through its Perspex roof. Ramshaw was badly burned with two broken limbs; Dowie's spine was broken. For a while, they called out to each other through the inky, squally night, but eventually Ramshaw went silent. Dowie grabbed an unmanned prau, a small Indonesian boat, as it floated past and drifted with it for two days until he was picked up by a Japanese armed patrol boat. By May 1943, he was working on the Burma Railway, his spinal injury having healed.[11]

On that opening day of the Pacific War, General Takumi had three infantry battalions ashore by mid-morning, despite the strong initial defence accounting for some 15 per cent of his landing force. Over 300 Japanese were killed at Kota Bharu, but it wasn't the main landing point, merely the one that was the most strongly defended. A greater number of troops came ashore up the coast in southern Thailand, along with tanks and vehicles. They landed at Pattani from five transports in rough seas on a muddy sea bed, and further north from ten troopships at Songkhla. Both were opposed by Thai infantry and police until Prime Minister Phibun could be located to sign an armistice. Fighting ceased in the morning and a few hours later, Japanese aircraft flew into the airfield at Songkhla.

While the main invasion force consolidated in Thailand, RAF bombers from further afield in Malaya were sent during the morning for an all-out effort against the invasion fleet's ships at Kota Bharu. They arrived to find the fleet had been withdrawn. Flying on to Pattani, where a British patrol had earlier sighted the larger expeditionary force, they were met by Japanese fighters. Hurriedly dropping bombs around the ships at Pattani, without inflicting much damage, the British airmen hotfooted back to their bases to find they'd stirred up a hornets' nest.[12] All the airfields in northern Malaya were attacked repeatedly through the day by Japanese bombers with fighter escorts coming from Thailand's southern airstrips.

The accuracy of Japanese aerial bombing came as a shock to its recipients. The attackers would avoid serious damage to airfield surfaces, preserving them for their own future use. Instead, Zero fighters attacked British planes as they landed or took off. The defenders might have been less surprised if they'd seen intelligence reports on the Zero's performance that were gathering dust at Far East Air Command in Singapore.[13] By the evening of 8 December, the British had lost 60 of their 110 aircraft in northern Malaya. The surviving planes were withdrawn to Singapore.

That afternoon, the Kota Bharu airfield came under attack from the ground as well as the air as the Japanese neared its perimeter. Returning after a short absence, the base commander found the place in flames and staff preparing to leave. Wing Commander Noble ordered his staff to remain, having found the enemy was not yet at the perimeter. The respite was short-lived. Japanese troops were penetrating between British positions in the dying light. When the transport ships reappeared off the beach soon after dark, the defenders faced isolation by freshly landed enemy units. Approval was given by Far East Command to withdraw during the night.[14]

The defence forces continued to pull back over the next couple of days, demolishing whatever might be useful to the enemy on road or railway as they went. The air base followed suit, with the last of the serviceable Hudsons flying off to Singapore. Australian ground crew and base headquarters staff packed what they could into trucks, which took them to the rail line at Kuala Krai and thence by train to Singapore. By midnight, troops and guns had been evacuated from the airfield and it was in Japanese hands. The British had stationed troops in Malaya primarily to protect the airfields. Their purpose had already been lost in the northeast within 24 hours.

The Japanese entered the town of Kota Bharu the next day, 9 December. Villagers had dug trenches and lay low for a few days. When they emerged, the beaches were covered with corpses, some already swollen and rotting. Within two weeks, the assault force had moved on, but some villagers had noticed among the Japanese officers a man called Kawasaki. They recognised him from before the war. Riding a bicycle around local villages at that time, selling shrimp rice crackers, he had spoken fluent Malay.[15] Unobserved by the villagers' colonial masters, the invaders had been doing their homework.

After a meeting of the War Cabinet in Melbourne on Friday 5 December, John Curtin was leaving his office in Victoria Barracks to get a train to Canberra. With him were a few cronies from the press who were going to walk up to Spencer Street station with him. Defence secretary Fred Shedden appeared and took the prime minister to one side. The whispered conversation and the look on Curtin's face indicated something serious had happened. Shedden departed and Curtin told the gathered group, 'I'm sorry. I've misled you, gentlemen. I'm not returning to Canberra tonight after all.' He didn't elaborate.[16]

The War Cabinet reconvened for half an hour to be told the Allies had received a report of a Japanese expeditionary force that had come from Indochina. This was not the Malaya invasion fleet, which hadn't been sighted at that stage, but another Japanese assault force, this one heading in the direction of the Philippines.

After the meeting, Curtin returned to the Victoria Palace Hotel, a temperance hotel in Little Collins Street he habitually stayed at when in Melbourne. He retired to his small, shabby sitting room, 'crowded with aspidistras and palms and the press, the air blue with cigarette-smoke', and explained the reason for the reconvened meeting to the newsmen with him.[17]

Curtin stayed in Melbourne over the weekend, to be on hand if reports of any further developments came in . . . and they did. Over the next two days, reports came from the RAAF patrols out of Kota Bharu of another force, possibly heading to Thailand or Malaya. It was unsettling news, but might at least resolve the uncertainty they had been living with for some time.

At 5.45 a.m. on Monday, 8 December, Curtin's press secretary, Don Rodgers, woke him at the hotel. The government's short-wave monitoring service had picked up news that Japanese aircraft had attacked the US Pacific Fleet at Pearl Harbor and the American airbase in the Philippines.

'Well, it has come!' said Curtin, a note of resignation in his voice and perhaps some relief.[18] The guessing game was over.

Prime Minister Curtin spoke to the nation on ABC radio at 7.30 p.m. 'Men and women of Australia,' he said, 'we are at war with Japan.'

'We here, in this spacious land where, for more than 150 years, peace and security have prevailed, are now called upon to meet the external aggressor. The enemy presses from without,' he continued, finishing with an echo of T.T. Ewing. 'We Australians have imperishable traditions. We shall maintain them. We shall vindicate them. We shall hold this country and keep it as a citadel for the British-speaking race and as a place where civilisation will persist.'[19]

The War Cabinet had met at eleven that morning. An Admiralty message that had been received overnight was read out: 'Commence hostilities against Japan repeat Japan at once.' A report had come from China that the Japanese were attempting to land troops from five ships at Kota Bharu. Nothing was known about how that attack was progressing; no information was coming from command headquarters at Singapore. That island had been bombed overnight and had lost its cable connection with Australia. The only detail known of the night's events was from American short-wave radio and that was concerned only with the bombing raids on Hawaii and the Philippines.[20]

Alerted by radio and word of mouth, crowds gathered outside the *Age* office in Melbourne. A bulletin had been posted with news of the Pearl Harbor attack. Morning papers had reported the convoys steaming into the Gulf of Siam, but went to press too early for what followed. The *Sydney Morning Herald* had taken comfort in the strengthening of Singapore with the arrival of 'a powerful British fleet'.[21] News of subsequent events was circulated in shouts and quiet conversations in shops and on the streets. A cyclist with a window-cleaning ladder on his shoulders called out to men on the footpath, 'The Japs are at us!'

The landing at Malaya was a blank page. A public mood had developed, a sense that the cards were now on the table, but it was a response to Pearl Harbor rather than Kota Bharu. A band played martial music during lunch hour at Melbourne's Town Hall. The radio played 'The Yanks Are Coming', a popular song from the First World War, and crowds responded with 'Australia Will Be There', sung by Australian soldiers as they marched into battle at that time.[22] There was a lot of heat, but not much light.

With little awareness of the unfolding catastrophe in Malaya, Australians didn't see Pearl Harbor having much direct relevance to them. 'I think it was generally felt that was something the Yanks had to look after,' says Bruce Acland, a civil aviation radio operator posted to Darwin, 'and while it was very sad and that sort of thing, it was something that belonged to America. Very remote. I couldn't see in any way that it affected me.'[23]

'It was not particularly threatening to life in Australia,' recalls Robert Brown, the Brisbane trainee teacher, 'but we considered it to be a very dirty trick. That didn't improve our attitude to the Japanese at all.'[24]

Japanese nationals were quickly rounded up from their homes in Sydney's well-to-do suburbs. A crowd waited in Martin Place while police raided the Yokohama Specie Bank. When eight smiling men were brought out, some in the crowd hissed and booed as the detainees bowed before entering the car. All the Japanese submitted quietly and were handed over to military authorities. Victoria could find only twenty Japanese nationals state-wide to intern. Two arrested in Canberra were described as 'dangerous fanatics'.[25]

The War Cabinet knew little more than the public at this stage, unaware that Australians had already been killed in this new war. It agreed that a state of war existed against Japan, but that was more in support of America. However, the government moved to an escalated, more localised war footing. Convoy sailings were to start immediately. Coastal lights were to be turned off, except where navy-controlled. Urgent action was needed to deal with an industrial dispute at Darwin's wharves. Australia's military chiefs of staff were instructed to advise the forms and likelihood of attack, defences necessary and preparedness to meet them, now that they were at war with Japan.[26] Apprehension of an increased threat of invasion permeated the Australian government, even with uncertainty about how this might take place.

Not enough was yet known to see important differences between the attacks on Hawaii and Malaya. Pearl Harbor was a raid in which the target was bombed and the planes flew home. Kota Bharu was an invasion—the attacking force intended to stay there. More to the point for Australians, Malaya was on the way to Australia, Hawaii was not.

By afternoon, the press was catching up. 'JAPANESE ATTACK ON MALAYA AND HAWAII: GREAT NAVAL AND AIR BATTLES IN PROGRESS' headlined Sydney's *Daily Mirror*.[27] There was detail about Pearl Harbor, much of it wrong: an aircraft carrier and four Japanese submarines sunk, paratroopers dropped on Hawaii. America had lost 'one old battleship' and a destroyer at Pearl Harbor. About the Malaya assault, there was an 'attempted landing' at Kota Bharu, but the report gave no clue to how that battle was proceeding.

By holding off until morning, Air Marshal Brooke-Popham had put Operation Matador on the back foot. By then, aerial patrols were finding the enemy had landed and was operating from Thai airfields. It was too late for any dynamic, pre-emptive move. Instead, the Far East Command had to settle for harassing the expected Japanese advance. An Indian mobile detachment was sent north across the border at 5.30 p.m. along the road to Songkhla to delay the advance, a feeble remnant of Matador's enterprising counter-attack. This unit, with anti-tank guns, was immediately set upon by Thai constabulary.

Progress in the overcast conditions and failing light was difficult. Thai snipers intentionally let Indian scouts through to fire on the mobile unit following them. Clearance teams too came under fire on road obstructions. As darkness fell, the Indian detachment halted for the night only a few kilometres into Thailand, frustrated with their rain-soaked bivouac and the watered-down version of Matador.

Shortly after 9 p.m., an approaching rumble could be heard, with light beams flickering in the middle distance. Growing louder, it burst into a roar as a column of some 35 Japanese vehicles came reverberating down the main road, headlights blazing and with tanks at the front. The first two tanks were taken out, but Japanese infantry jumped smartly from their trucks and moved noiselessly around the Indian flanks. Ill-equipped for a dogfight in the dark, the defenders withdrew through their own rear positions.[28]

The next day, Australia's press 'knew' how the battle was proceeding. Japanese ships had attempted to land troops in northern Malaya. According to the *Sydney Morning Herald*, 'All the ships covering the invasion eventually retired at full speed and the few troops left on the beach were heavily machine-gunned.'[29] Singapore sources advised that 'Japan's first surprise attack on Malaya has failed . . . it was a splendid testing of the defences in this area.'[30]

Was it now? By the time the *Herald*'s readers received this reassurance, Kota Bharu airfield was in Japanese hands and no British warplane remained in northern Malaya. Japan's fleet had retired because its job was done. As usual, truth was the first casualty.

'Equally unsuccessful,' continued the *Herald*, 'has been Japan's first bombing raid on Singapore.' It's not clear what yardstick of success the *Herald* used for such raids, but over sixty people were killed in that one. All were either Indian or Chinese.[31]

These were times of innocence and ignorance, with the Japanese regarded as physically inferior, their manufacturing as ludicrously inept. 'I can remember what an outrageous thing we all thought it was, Japan attacking a power like America,' recalls Brian Loughry, a Sydney schoolboy at the time, 'Initially we thought it was almost a comedy that they'd even attempt such a thing.'[32]

But attempt it they had. It took a while for Australia's newspapers to acknowledge they had done so successfully. Still, the citadel of impregnable Singapore and its 'powerful British fleet' would halt their advance.

When word came through of the Japanese landing at Kota Bharu, Admiral Phillips ordered the hastily assembled Force Z to intervene. A modern battleship, *Prince of Wales*, a First World War era battlecruiser, *Repulse*, and an escort of four destroyers, one of them the Australian *Vampire*, made up this 'powerful British fleet'. The aircraft carrier *Indomitable* had been intended to join them in Singapore until it ran aground in Jamaica. Force Z was the best Churchill could do to appease Curtin's concerns about British commitment to Singapore as a bulwark of southeast Asia. Churchill and his advisers had doubts about Singapore's impregnability, but kept that to themselves.

Sir Tom Phillips had been appointed commander-in-chief of the British Eastern Fleet only a week earlier, and his task force was far from battle-ready. *Prince of Wales* had an advanced anti-aircraft system, but the heat and humidity of the tropics had made its radar, driving its anti-aircraft fire, inoperable. As well, the force's air cover was thin, having lost its carrier-borne support and with aging fighters making up the region's aircraft.

Although he concluded his two capital ships couldn't supply sufficient muscle to crush the Japanese fleet, Phillips felt an obligation to go on the offensive with the prospect of Malaya being overrun. He elected to go ahead without air cover, believing his ships could protect themselves against air attack and underestimating the fighting abilities of the Japanese.[33] No. 453 Squadron RAAF with veteran Brewster Buffalo fighters was standing by at Singapore for a call to provide cover, if the need arose.

Force Z sailed from Singapore at 5.10 p.m. on 8 December, aiming to attack the invasion fleet at Songkhla on the 10th. Frequent rainstorms and low cloud concealed the British flotilla from aerial reconnaissance for the first part of the journey, but at 2 p.m. on the second day, it was observed by a Japanese submarine that shadowed the ships for five hours. Notified of the approaching force, Admiral Jisaburo Ozawa ordered his warships to escort their emptied troopships back to Cam Ranh Bay in Indochina.

Navy seaplanes began shadowing the British task force in the late afternoon. Having spotted the enemy patrol, Phillips realised he had lost the element of surprise and, without air cover, the balance was tipped too strongly against him. He cancelled the operation and ordered his force to return to Singapore.[34]

A radio message was sent to Phillips during the night that the Japanese were believed to be landing at Kuantan, not far off Force Z's return course. Deciding to hamper the new incursion, Phillips diverted his force to Kuantan but, as he didn't advise Singapore, no air support was activated. After sunrise, a reconnaissance aircraft was catapulted from *Prince of Wales* to report on the offensive at Kuantan. Nothing could be seen: no invasion, no evidence there had ever been one. The reported landing was flawed intelligence. To make matters worse, Force Z was sighted by a scout plane, which radioed the British flotilla's location to a squadron already out searching for it.[35]

Spotted by submarine the previous afternoon, Force Z had been observed returning south. Squadrons from three Japanese air bases—about 90 aircraft—took off in pursuit but, unaware of the diversion, they searched too far south. There had been no Japanese landing at Kuantan, so no reason for them to expect the British ships to divert there. However, alerted by the scout plane, they now knew where to go and arrived in force an hour later. As they were running short of fuel, each bomber attacked *Repulse* on arrival, in a hasty and uncoordinated fashion. All but one bomb missed, with that bomb exploding in the marine mess and causing little serious damage and few casualties.

A second attack didn't appear to fare much better. Of some two dozen torpedoes, mostly launched at *Repulse*, only one hit a British ship, but it was ultimately catastrophic. *Prince of Wales* was struck on one of its propellers, bending the shaft. The twisted propeller, still turning, ruptured the ship's hull and sea water flooded into the engine room, causing the battleship to lose speed and list to port.

Having dodged nineteen torpedoes, *Repulse*'s luck ran out. It was attacked on both sides and hit by at least four missiles. The crew were ordered to abandon ship immediately, but *Repulse* listed and sank in just six minutes with heavy casualties.

Prince of Wales had been hit on its starboard side by three torpedoes. It fought on, but its list prevented its gun barrels from lowering sufficiently to fire effectively at low-flying bombers. The ship started capsizing to port; it rolled over and sank at 1.20 p.m., nearly taking with it the destroyer *Express*, which had moved cautiously alongside to pick up abandoning crew.[36]

Alerted by *Repulse* an hour after the attack started, a squadron of RAAF Buffalos arrived from Singapore as *Prince of Wales* went down. The Japanese attack planes had already gone. Spread below the Australian airmen was an extraordinary canvas: hundreds of men, clinging to bits of wreckage in water heavily covered with oil, and being picked up by what remained of Z Force. Admiral

Phillips had gone down with his flagship, one of 840 navy personnel lost, along with two of the Royal Navy's capital ships that had been sent to the Far East.[37]

Flight Lieutenant Tim Vigors RAF, in charge of No. 453 Squadron on that day, told a London newspaper, 'Every man waved and put up his thumb as I flew over him. During that hour I had seen many men in dire danger waving, cheering and joking, as if they were holiday-makers at Brighton waving at a low-flying aircraft. It shook me, for here was something above human nature.'[38]

The next morning, the Australian press was reporting the loss of the two ships with reasonable accuracy, questioning how a most modern British warship could be sunk, and noting it could hardly have been caught unawares. It was an early sign to the general public that the Royal Navy might not provide the protection imagined. As some consolation perhaps, Sydney's *Daily Mirror* declared all was quiet at Kuantan, indicating the invasion attempt had been defeated.[39] It hadn't occurred to the *Mirror* that it was quiet because no invasion had been staged there.

The *Sydney Morning Herald*, updating on the fighting at Kota Bharu, claimed only 200 of Japan's 5000 troops there had actually reached shore and then dispersed into the jungle. Japanese ships had withdrawn, leaving men on the beaches subject to withering fire. RAAF crews had 'returned to Singapore after making magnificent efforts to prevent landings on the beaches', but were reluctant to talk of their heroic deeds. Datelined Singapore, 11 December, this was three days after the defenders had abandoned Kota Bharu and left the invaders in control of the airfield.

The paper was prepared to concede that the Japanese fighting ability might have been underestimated. 'All people who have seen examples of Japanese bombing,' said the *Herald*, 'agree that there is not much wrong with the Japanese eyesight or bomb sight.'[40]

Curtin tried to instil a sense of determination in the public with a national broadcast. 'Enemy striking-power in the air has given to the enemy an initial momentum, which only a maximum effort can arrest,' he said. 'Nobody worries about being a few goals down at half-time.'[41] It would turn out to be more like the opening minutes of the first quarter.

The War Cabinet met on 11 December to digest news of the British warships. Chiefs of staff of the three services presented an 'appreciation' of the position their country now found itself. The attack on Malaya 'might well be a first step in the Japanese plan for a major attack on Australia', their advice ran. 'The possibility of a direct move on Australia via the islands to the north and north east must now be considered.' The necessary forces should be mobilised urgently to thwart any attempt at invasion.[42] That should have been their aim a year before, as military historian David Horner has commented.[43]

A further meeting the next day approved a call-up of 114,000 more men and increased forces in Darwin, Port Moresby and Timor. The War Cabinet decided not to reinforce Rabaul as insufficient troops were available to repel an invasion force. The existing garrison would stay there as a forward observation line. Better for the public to see the enemy fight for territory than to abandon it to them.[44]

Australia had asked Britain's chiefs of staff for their assessment of the position in the Far East. Less uneasy than their Australian counterparts, the British declared events were moving too quickly for a general review, but concluded there was not 'any immediate large-scale threat'. Underlining Britain's priority, they added, 'We must not forget that Germany is still the main enemy.'[45]

Churchill had offered a similar view to Curtin a couple of days before, cabling that 'Australia will face nothing more serious than air raids'. Privately, Churchill complained that the Australians were 'jumpy about invasion', putting it down to lack of fortitude coming from 'bad stock'.[46]

The invaders had already advanced into the northern Malay state of Kedah. Indian infantry were set up in positions waterlogged by the constant rain, putting up barbed wire in a rush, laying anti-tank mines and quickly running out phone cables, but the defences were spread thinly and the attack was able to punch a hole in them. The defenders were soon in full retreat with the Japanese advancing so rapidly that forward patrols on motorcycles were sometimes driving through retreating columns.[47]

That set the pattern as the Japanese moved down the Malay Peninsula. Lieutenant General Arthur Percival, commanding British army forces in Malaya, established defensive lines at strategic points down the peninsula, hoping to stall the enemy until infantry reinforcements and new RAF squadrons could get to Singapore from Britain. Percival's defensive lines would last about ten days before the Japanese broke through. Each time, the British forces fell back to a new defensive line, which would halt the onslaught for a short time only.

The belief in London that Malaya was all impenetrable jungle was woefully out of date. Roads were now built, and jungle had been cleared for rubber and palm plantations. Railway lines ran through the western side of the peninsula. The invasion force advanced along the well-sealed roads, initially attacking defensive positions from the front. At the same time, enemy troops moved around in uncleared jungle. The restricted vision of dense vegetation and tree-filled plantations allowed flanking to go undetected. Defenders found themselves encircled and having to fight their way out.

As the Indian forces withdrew along with British forces defending western Malaya, they left behind large amounts of

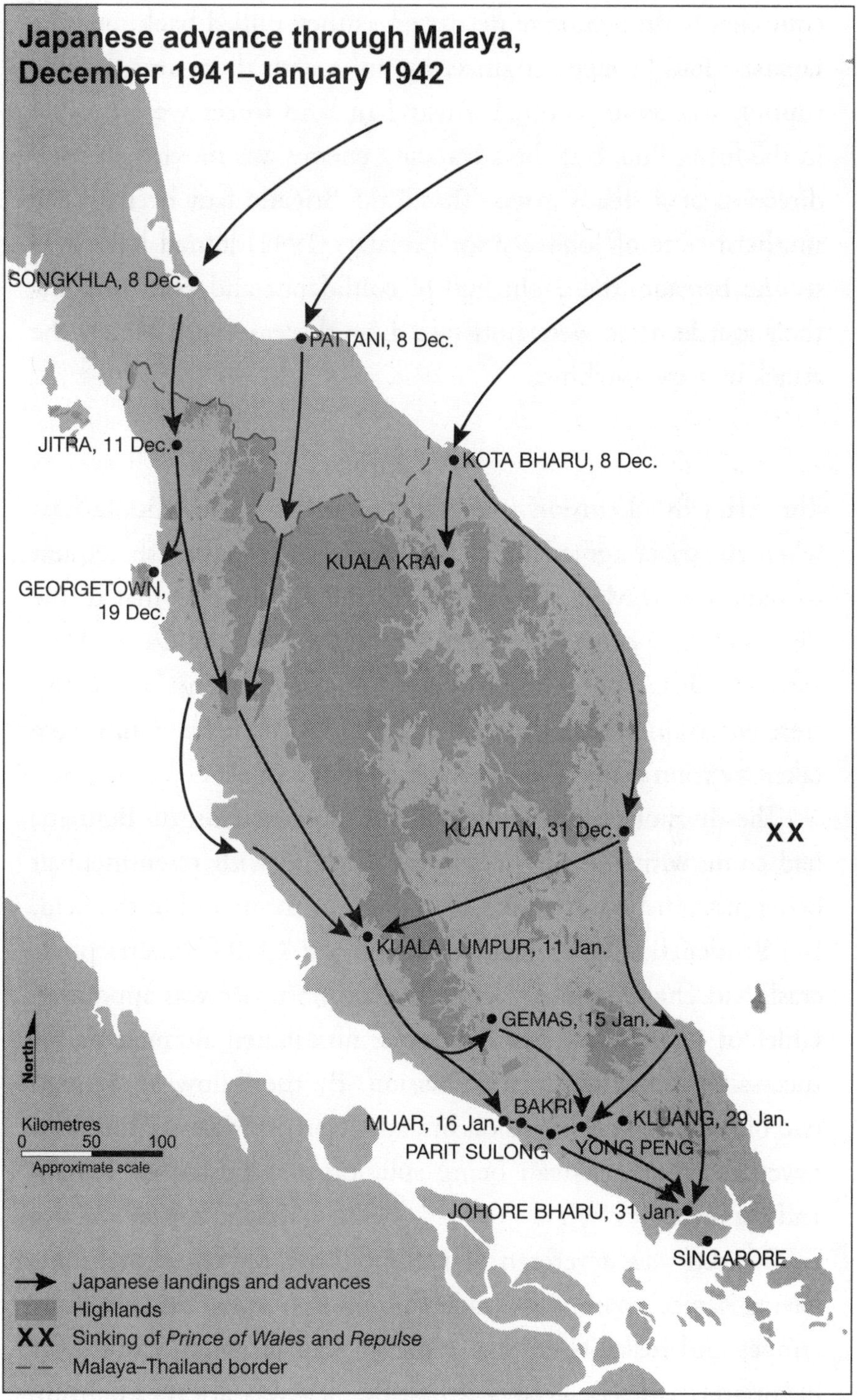
Japanese advance through Malaya, December 1941–January 1942
SONGKHLA, 8 Dec.
PATTANI, 8 Dec.
JITRA, 11 Dec.
KOTA BHARU, 8 Dec.
KUALA KRAI
GEORGETOWN, 19 Dec.
KUANTAN, 31 Dec.
XX
KUALA LUMPUR, 11 Jan.
GEMAS, 15 Jan.
BAKRI
MUAR, 16 Jan.
KLUANG, 29 Jan.
PARIT SULONG
YONG PENG
JOHORE BHARU, 31 Jan.
SINGAPORE
North
Kilometres
0 50 100
Approximate scale
Japanese landings and advances
Highlands
XX Sinking of *Prince of Wales* and *Repulse*
Malaya–Thailand border

equipment. Bridges were destroyed as they pulled back, but the Japanese had brought engineering units with them and the disruption was soon rectified. Australian land forces were not yet in the firing line, but the advancing enemy was moving in their direction at a steady pace. The 22nd Brigade had been in the southern state of Johore since February 1941, joined later by a second brigade, the 27th. Full of confidence and keen to show their mettle, they were undeterred by the ease with which the attack was approaching.

The AIF's 8th Division was being trained for the Middle East when Australia agreed in December 1940 to a British request to station it in Malaya instead. Over 5000 men, the first of the division's three brigades, arrived in Singapore on the *Queen Mary* early in 1941. While officers stayed at Government House and were entertained with drinks at Raffles Hotel, lower ranks were taken by train across the causeway to Johore.[48]

The division's commander, Major-General Gordon Bennett, had come with the garrison force, seething with resentment at being previously overlooked for a division command in the field. But Brudenell White's death in the August 1940 Canberra plane crash had changed that. General Vernon Sturdee was appointed Chief of General Staff and Sturdee nominated Bennett as his successor commanding 8th Division. By the following August, two of the three 8th Division brigades were in Malaya. The third never got there, instead being split up and posted to Rabaul and Darwin.

Bennett was a veteran of Gallipoli and the Western Front, having served there with leadership and courage. But his short temper and inability to take criticism had led First World War historian Charles Bean to note that Bennett was 'always a fighting leader of his men, but always quarrelling with the men beside him [his fellow officers]'.[49] After a year in Malaya, Bennett's argumentative nature had led to strained relations with British commanders and with his own staff, particularly the commander of the first contingent to Malaya.

Brigadier Harold Taylor, a Sydney analytical chemist, had known Bennett from the militia before the war, but that counted for nothing. Bennett had expanded his Division HQ and insisted everything go through it, so that Taylor was inundated with orders for training exercises, some of them confusing and contradictory.

Taylor was a Military Cross holder from the First World War. When he sought clarification of one exercise, Bennett took umbrage. As the interference grew, Taylor took that up with Bennett and was accused of trying to take control of the AIF in Malaya. After a mix-up in a map-reading exercise—either Taylor misread the map or he wasn't given a map reference code—Bennett planned to sack his brigade commander. Then he changed his mind.[50]

While this drama was unfolding, Taylor's 22nd Brigade was being trained for local conditions. Before the decision to send them to Malaya, it had been preparing for desert fighting. The Australian Army's textbooks, tactical methods, equipment and clothing had been developed for a European war, but everything was different here. Desert camouflage on vehicles had to be painted over. The men were spooked by the eerie silence and limited vision under the jungle canopy, and by their exaggerated fear of its flora and fauna. Most were out of Australia for the first time. Raised on Hollywood depictions of the terrifying African jungle, they now had to become 'jungle-minded'.[51]

Guided by Major Charles Anderson, a South African with East African jungle experience from the First World War, an astute training regime was devised. The men were taken into bushland to learn from Sakai tribesmen and other Malays about living and moving in such conditions. It was 'impossible to see the sun through the leaves high above, as the trees grow close together', one soldier noted in his diary. 'We could not move off the track as the trees had vines growing over them.'[52]

Up to their thighs in mud in marshy ground with swamp snakes and leeches, the men suffered tropical diseases and infections requiring hospital treatment. Training in a hot, humid, jungle-covered country began to pall. The men came to despise the climate, the terrain, the vegetation and their own inaction. They developed a hatred of Malaya and their own standing as a garrison force.

'I only wish I could get out of this country and over to the Middle East where those dirty damn Huns are,' another soldier wrote home. 'I really don't think the Japs will have a go.'[53]

Their frustration wasn't helped by a *Women's Weekly* article early in the year. Well-intended, no doubt, it described troops training, but it included stories and pictures of 'the glamour of the East'. The men started getting letters from wives and girlfriends asking what they were 'doing towards the war effort'.[54] This fed into their later disenchantment with their lot in the war.

Immersed in their growing resentment, the troops in Johore were woken one night by bombers flying overhead, followed by distant gunfire and explosions. It was 8 December and Japanese aircraft were attacking Singapore. By dawn, their past frustration had been replaced by excitement and enthusiasm. Training and defence preparations were intensified. Men were placed on guard at key locations.

The Pacific War had started. What they had trained for had finally arrived, and the men of the 8th Division and their leaders were confident they would acquit themselves well.

Through the month of December, the Japanese juggernaut swept across southeast Asia and the western Pacific. Guam was seized on the 10th and Wake Island on the 23rd. Japan had invaded Burma, British North Borneo and Hong Kong, in addition to the campaigns under way in Malaya and the Philippines. Hong Kong fell on Christmas Day.

On 23 December, Britain's chiefs of staff had advised Australia that the US was unlikely to provide naval support in the Pacific and 'we ourselves can *not* provide a balanced fleet at Singapore at once. Therefore unsound to send capital ships there at present'.[55]

Churchill had promised Menzies in April that Britain would send an aerial armada in the absence of the long-promised fleet if the Japanese attacked Singapore. The London planners had already pooh-poohed Singapore's estimated need of at least 582 aircraft. Singapore, London responded, takes 'too pessimistic a view . . . The Japanese have never fought against a first-class Power in the air and we have no reason to believe that their operations would be any more effective than those of the Italians.'[56]

Three hundred and thirty-six front-line aircraft would be sufficient, they said. As it turned out, London had badly underestimated the Japanese and the 336 aircraft never came anyway.[57]

Three days before the British chiefs' advice was received, Curtin cabled Churchill, then in America, that Singapore's reinforcements were 'utterly inadequate'.[58] Australian troops on the island were facing a similar fate to those in Greece and Crete, outnumbered and without adequate air cover. Churchill responded that the promised aircraft were on the way, though they were well short of 336. Fifty-one Hurricane fighters would soon be packed in crates and shipped to Singapore.[59]

Australia's political and military leaders had grave doubts about Britain's commitment and ability to play a significant role in the Pacific War while it was entangled in Europe. Although

America's contribution had been largely directed at protecting its own interests in the Philippines, it was seen as at least having the capacity to expand its role.

With this in mind, Curtin wired US President Franklin D. Roosevelt and Churchill on 25 December, suggesting, 'Should United States desire we would gladly accept United States command in Pacific Ocean area.'[60] Churchill was spending four weeks in Washington with the president, developing a plan to win the war in Europe. He didn't appreciate an implication the British Empire might lack solidarity.

Two days later, Melbourne's *The Herald* published the speech the prime minister would be giving on New Year's Day. It was a pep talk to get the public onside for the constraints of wartime. Curtin began by making a point he'd been hammering, on Defence secretary Shedden's advice, since Japan joined the war. 'The war with Japan is not a phase of the struggle with the Axis powers, but is a new war,' he insisted.

However, it was a statement in the middle of the speech that attracted attention at the time, and whose significance has been much discussed by historians and political commentators ever since.

'Without any inhibitions of any kind,' the Australian prime minister said, 'I make it quite clear that Australia looks to America, free of any pangs as to our traditional links or kinship with the United Kingdom. We know the problem that the United Kingdom faces. We know the constant threat of invasion. We know the dangers of dispersal of strength, but we know too, that Australia can go and Britain can still hold on.'[61]

The speech didn't go unnoticed. It shocked many Australians who thought of themselves as an antipodean British community. Curtin was accused by conservative politicians Robert Menzies and Billy Hughes of turning his back on Britain. The speech's 'harsh tones' were attacked by Churchill as ungrateful and impudent. He threatened to broadcast to the Australian people over Curtin's head.[62] Even Roosevelt got in the act. He's said to have told the Australian minister in Washington that the statement 'tasted of panic and disloyalty'. If it was to ingratiate Australia with the United States, he reportedly advised, it would have the opposite effect.[63]

It didn't. Curtin had made two statements—one privately to the Allied leaders, the other very public. These brought about their desired effect. By the following week, ABDA (American-British-Dutch-Australian) Command was set up to prosecute the war against Japan. Roosevelt nominated as commander of ABDA the English general Archibald Wavell, who had managed to defeat the Italians in North Africa. Neither the Australians nor the Dutch were consulted about the appointment.

The British suspected America regarded the war with Japan as a lost cause for the time being, and they may well have taken that view. Certain events, however, would overtake the decision and vindicate Curtin's position.

While the command re-structure was taking place, the Japanese were driving down the plains west of Malaya's jungle-covered highlands. More troops landed on the east coast, cutting through the mountains of Pahang to join the main thrust or pushing down the eastern seaboard.

The aging Air Marshal Brooke-Popham resigned his Far East Command post, and was replaced by General Wavell, who flew into Singapore on 8 January to take over the new force. As ABDA Command had absorbed Far East Command into its broader operation, Wavell would be stationed in Java, not Singapore. He met with General Percival, who had been commanding Britain's forces in Malaya, and who was optimistic the British could hold Johore until February, then flew on. Three days later, the Japanese entered Kuala Lumpur, which had been used as the main supply base for the Indian III Corps.

Indian units in western Malaya had been pushed back 600 kilometres in a month of unequal fighting. Disheartened and drained, they began withdrawing through Australian lines to Johore on 11 January 1942. Watching this, Gerald Veitch of the ambulance corps noted in his diary, 'Every one of them was absolutely exhausted, the drivers going to sleep at the wheel, most of the officers having been killed.'[64]

The Australians moved forward to new defensive positions, alive with anticipation. For a month, General Bennett had been planning a series of ambushes, but he now had to adjust these to a new command structure set up by General Percival. The Australian 22nd Brigade had been moved by Percival to the eastern side of the state under a British commander. Bennett was to lead the newly created Westforce, made up of 15,000 men from his 27th Brigade and the Indian 45th Brigade. The balance of British defenders made up Eastforce on the other side of the Malay Peninsula, under the Indian III Corps commander, General Lewis Heath.

Twenty men and one officer from Westforce moved forward on 13 January to Gemencheh Bridge, 11 kilometres west of the town of Gemas. Setting up either side of a long cutting through thick bushland just east of the wooden bridge, they were to remain there until the enemy appeared, possibly two or three days away. They placed explosives under the bridge, and left intact the bridges further along the road, to give the impression of a panic retreat that might make the advancing Japanese over-confident and careless. The rest of the Australian battalion lay in wait back down the road to Gemas.

At about four the next afternoon, the waiting men heard approaching voices. Across the bridge and bursting into the cutting came the front end of the enemy on the move, hundreds of soldiers laughing and chattering on bicycles, looking more like a picnic party than an advancing army. Rifles were tied across their handlebars. As they passed below, Australian fingers tightened around triggers and Mills grenade pins. It was a frozen moment.

The Australian soldiers lying in wait allowed some of the cyclists to pass through and out the other side. With several hundred still packed in the cutting, the bridge behind them exploded. Bicycles, bodies and pieces of bridge were flung in the air with a roar. A dense column of smoke and fragments shot skywards. At the same time, machine-gun and rifle fire poured into the cutting from both sides. Grenades rolled down the slope. Panic set in with the surprised Japanese, shouting and screaming, climbing over fallen comrades and buckled cycles, unsure which way to go with their retreat closed off.[65]

After twenty minutes of mayhem the ambush withdrew, but the Japanese were already amassing along the road. The Australians had to work their way back through the jungle in failing light and with occasional skirmishes with enemy patrols.

The Japanese repaired the bridge in six hours and started moving tanks in. As they rumbled towards the main battalion force in the morning, six of their front group of eight were destroyed by anti-tank gun fire. Other tanks moved in and soon the Australians had to pull back to the town, where the battalion's headquarters came under dive-bomber attack. After a day of fighting in Gemas, the battalion withdrew to avoid becoming encircled.

Flushed with the initial success at Gemencheh Bridge, General Bennett told the *Singapore Times* his men would stop the Japanese and put them on the defensive.[66] To prevent a flanking move by the enemy, he put two Indian battalions, mostly teenagers half-trained for desert fighting, on the banks of the Muar River, down the coast west of Gemas.

Japan's elite Imperial Guards captured barges moored at the mouth of the river and crossed unnoticed during the night of 15 January. At dawn, the outflanking force surprised and routed Indian defenders on the south bank, isolating those on the north bank. By noon the town of Muar was under attack from both sides, with an air raid destroying the brigade headquarters there. The sun set with both the town and the harbour in Japanese hands and the remnants of the Indian brigade retreating down the coast to Bakri, the young sepoys leaderless with virtually all their officers killed.

Attempts to recapture Muar failed. With both Australian and Indian commanders killed, the South African, Charles Anderson, assumed command of all units around Bakri. His first order was to break out of Bakri and pull back to Yong Peng.[67]

Taking field guns and lorries, the encircled force started down the road to the junction town with the Australian infantry at the front singing 'Waltzing Matilda' and the Indians as rearguard. They fought through a succession of roadblocks set up with broken-down vehicles, each obstruction attacked desperately with mortars, gunfire and grenades. Colonel Anderson himself led a bayonet charge that broke through one roadblock.

Casualties mounted and the wounded were piled on lorries laden with diminishing ammunition. After 24 hours of slow, determined progress, they reached the bridge over the Parit Sulong River to find it guarded by a machine-gun post set up by the flanking enemy.[68]

Attempts to dislodge the post were driven back by tanks, artillery and air attack. A wireless message came through that a relieving force was coming from Yong Peng, but it was an English brigade that had arrived at Singapore a week before after three months on crowded troopships. With only rudimentary training, it was unable to make any impact on the new Japanese line.

At dusk, Anderson radioed Bennett for an air strike at dawn on the bridge guards and an air drop of food and morphine. The division commander's reply, 'Look up at sparrowfart', was designed to be incomprehensible to enemy signallers who might pick it up.[69]

Anderson sent two ambulances carrying the critically wounded to the bridge, with a truce flag and a request to pass through to Allied lines. When he refused the Japanese demand that the rest of the party surrender, the wounded could not continue, but were allowed to return. The ambulances, however, were held on the bridge as a roadblock, with the threat that any attempt to move them would be met with gunfire. Under cover of dark, two men crept through to the vehicles and released their hand brakes so they rolled quietly back off the bridge; then they turned the engines on and drove them under gunfire back to their position.

At first light, two RAF biplanes dropped food and medicine. RAAF Buffalos bombed the Japanese bridge post with little effect, while enemy tanks and troops attacked the British column. Anderson put the seriously wounded in one ambulance, which was driven at high speed across the bridge. It got to the other side before machine-gun fire killed the driver and the truck could be seen from a distance overturning into a ditch.[70]

When it became clear that the attempted relief had failed, Anderson took the only option remaining to him. At 9 a.m. on 22 January, six days after the Indian brigade had been driven out of Muar, he ordered a retreat. After the men had destroyed their field guns, lorries and equipment, all who were capable of moving dispersed in groups through the jungles and swamps east of Yong Peng to try to reach their own lines, leaving 150 immobile wounded behind with voluntary attendants.

Of the men of the Indian brigade and two Australian battalions—over 4000 in total—500 Australians and 400 Indians managed to reach British lines. The wounded left behind were not so lucky. Apart from a handful who escaped, they were massacred by the Japanese after being taunted with buckets of water out of reach. The Australians were machine-gunned and their bodies set alight; the Indians were beheaded with samurai swords.[71]

The public was kept informed by the Australian press of its military's actions in Malaya with greater reliability than the bare and sometimes wildly inaccurate reporting of the Kota Bharu landing. Great play was made of the ambush at Gemencheh Bridge and the heroics of the withdrawal from Bakri. Articles included reports coming from Tokyo radio, mostly accurate at that time. Generally in wartime journalism, when your side is doing well, you report it accurately; when it isn't, you don't.

Newspapers were reporting every day an enemy that had moved further south. The Australians were moving back each day after initial stern resistance. The press didn't shy away from the word 'withdraw', although it implied this was tactical withdrawal. Fight and flight. Allied troops were constantly described as outnumbered.

It was valiant and, like Pearl Harbor and North Africa, it was far away. Japan's successes in Malaya didn't raise the spectre of invasion in the minds of ordinary Australians in the way they worried the country's political leaders and military, whose warnings the public largely ignored. There was always Singapore.

'We always thought of Singapore as the impregnable Far Eastern base of the magnificent British navy, which was the greatest navy in the world to us,' says Robert Brown. 'I had a poster of the British navy ship by ship.'[72]

Air Raid Precautions continued as they had for over two years without air raids seeming even remotely likely. None of it was taken seriously, except by ARP wardens with their helmets and whistles. *The Australian Women's Weekly* reported in January 1942 that a survey of 60 waterfront homes in Sydney found that half had no permanent blackout provisions, twenty had bought material for blackouts but had not installed it, and only four had shatter-proofed their windows. Thirty-three had sand and shovels for fires, 25 had sand but no shovels, and one said they'd wait until Singapore fell before they did anything.[73]

Malaya was a world away, the domain of Tarzan jungle books, but for the British soldiers there it was brutal reality. The Japanese were continuing to advance on three fronts in western Johore. Eastforce was holding its position on the eastern side of the state, but flanking from the west threatened to infiltrate behind and isolate it. Eastforce was withdrawn to maintain a line with Bennett's Westforce.

Reinforcements from Australia, Britain and India were arriving, but they were too late and too inexperienced to save Malaya. On 27 January, Wavell gave Percival discretion to pull back to Singapore if he thought it advisable. Knowing the troops still in Malaya were not strong enough to stall the enemy advance, Percival ordered a complete withdrawal across the Johore Strait.

After dark on a clear night with a full moon, the last of Malaya's defenders began crossing the strait over the kilometre-long road and rail bridge known as The Causeway. After all troops were across, The Causeway would be detonated in two places, one to wreck the steel lock system that allowed ships through, the other to blow a gap in its main section.

The movement of troops and equipment was haphazard. An 8th Division staff officer, Major John Wyett, worried that the bridge might be blown up prematurely, cutting off men and transport. Investigating, he found English sappers had mined the lift-bridge.

The British sergeant in charge told Wyett he would detonate it at midnight.

'It'll be at least five or six hours before the last troops get across,' said Wyett.

'I can't help that,' responded the sergeant. 'My orders are to blow it up at midnight and that's what I'll be doing.'

'Then I'm giving you an order to not carry out the detonation.'

'I don't take orders from Australians,' said the increasingly truculent sergeant, adding an ironic, 'Sir!'

Wyett pulled out his service revolver. 'If you won't take orders from me, maybe you will from this.'

The sergeant stared at the firearm, lost for a response, then shrugged and shuffled off.[74]

Towards dawn, the last Bren carriers and trucks moved across the still-intact bridge. Finally, rearguard troops crossed from Johore in formation, a dramatic 'first light' march. Two Australian battalions, along with British infantry group the Gordon Highlanders, passed through a guard of the Argyll and Sutherland Highlanders at the northern end of The Causeway. The Argylls, now reduced to 250 men, followed through in the dawn light, played in by their regimental pipers. The British had made a hash of the defence of Malaya in so many ways, but they could still do military ceremony impressively.

At 8.15 a.m. on 31 January, one explosion destroyed The Causeway's lock system, then another blew a 20-metre gap in the bridge.[75] The Japanese would have to find some other way of getting to Singapore.

Chapter 3

GIBRALTAR OF THE EAST

Fortress Singapore was something of a charade, a symbolic gesture that masked a decade of bumbling. Its large naval base, still under construction in 1940, was the centrepiece of Britain's Singapore strategy, the undertaking to dispatch its main fleet if its possessions in Asia came under attack. As far back as 1934, Australia's senior army officers had concluded that Japan was unlikely to challenge British interests unless Britain was distracted elsewhere, but the Australian government preferred to accept Britain's hollow assurances.[1] No matter how unrealistic, it was preferable to providing for Australia's own defence.

The assumption that Singapore was vulnerable only to seaborne attack on its southern shore had been tested in 1936 by the British army commander in Malaya, Major General William Dobbie, in an exercise in Malaya's east coast jungle. It revealed that an invading force could be landed there to attack Singapore from the north. It could be protected from air defence by monsoonal cloud cover.[2]

Supported by his then chief of staff, Colonel Arthur Percival, Dobbie proposed a line of defences across southern Johore and along the northern coast of Singapore. When Singapore Governor Sir Shenton Thomas refused to cooperate, the War Office agreed to assist if the budget was slashed. That was sufficient to start clearing jungle and building machine-gun pillboxes in Johore, but when Dobbie retired in 1939, the project was abandoned and the pillboxes gradually disappeared under the jungle.[3]

British military planners calculated the 'period before relief', the time for the fleet to get to Singapore, as 42 days.[4] By 1939, the Admiralty was conceding that if Britain was threatened in Europe the Mediterranean would take priority over the Far East. It promised nonetheless to send 'a strong fleet' to the Far East, if necessary, although it couldn't guarantee timing or size of that fleet.

Menzies responded to this guarded undertaking that his government might conclude that 'in the event of war, Great Britain might not be able to defend her overseas possessions' and asked for 'some supplementary and reassuring statement for use here'. British Prime Minister Neville Chamberlain complied, insisting Britain still intended to send a fleet to Singapore, but if the fight was not as previously envisaged, the fleet size would depend on when Japan entered the war and the losses sustained.[5] Menzies didn't question that woolly pledge any further.

When war did finally start in Europe, the period before relief had become 180 days. Churchill, then First Lord of the Admiralty, claimed Singapore was a well-defended fortress, which could only be subdued after a four- or five-month siege by an army of at least 50,000 men. Japan was unlikely to try, he said, but if it did, the Royal Navy would come to the rescue.[6]

Singapore's defence planning was plagued by feuding between its army and air force commanders and within its civilian administration. The feuding became so toxic that London decided to appoint a commander-in-chief for the Far East. As it was no longer intended to station a fleet at Singapore and the RAF would be required to repel invaders initially, an RAF officer was chosen for the new position.

Tall, unkempt and with a reddish moustache, Air Chief Marshal Brooke-Popham was in the twilight of his military career. Born Henry Robert Moore Brooke, he had added Popham to his name after an admired relative.[7] With a high-pitched voice and giggling laugh, he was not an imposing figure. Little knowledge of modern warfare and a conviction that Japanese soldiers weren't up to the mark didn't help.

The new commander-in-chief had inherited a chaotic command, under-resourced and fractured in structure. His authority was limited to army and air force, while the transient naval units in the region reported directly to the Admiralty in London. The RAF had only 88 aircraft in the Far East, half of them obsolete. Brooke-Popham saw his role as not making waves, commenting when he was appointed that 'our job in the Far East is not to press for facilities that cannot be given'.[8]

'We can get on all right with Buffalos out here,' he later remarked. 'Let England have the super-Spitfires and the hyper-Tornados. Buffalos are quite good enough for Malaya.'[9] The American Brewster Buffalo fighters would soon be shown to be disastrously outclassed by Japan's Zero.

In February 1941, Brooke-Popham flew to Australia to pacify its War Cabinet while General Bennett and his 22nd Brigade were settling into southern Malaya and Menzies was in London complaining about Singapore's defences. The Far East commander met Fadden and Curtin, at the time acting prime minister and opposition leader respectively. He assured the War Cabinet of Churchill's promise of a battle fleet if Singapore was attacked, of the Buffalos committed to Singapore, and that the impenetrable terrain of Malaya made a land attack improbable. No one in the War Cabinet questioned these assertions.[10]

General Dobbie's former chief of staff, Arthur Percival, returned to Singapore in May after three years with General Staff in Britain, already promoted to lieutenant general. Appointed commander of the British army in Malaya, Percival had been a highly regarded staff officer, with a reputation as uncompromising against the IRA during Ireland's Troubles.[11] But, like Brooke-Popham, he didn't look the part. A tall, gangling man who habitually wore an old-fashioned pith helmet, Percival had a toothbrush moustache, buck teeth and a receding chin.[12] None of that relates to military skill, but he was untried as a senior commander and had neither the drive nor the ruthlessness necessary.

Percival's problems were compounded by the attitude of the Indian III Corps commander, Lieutenant General Lewis 'Piggy' Heath. Two years older and promoted earlier than Percival, the Indian-born Heath objected to taking orders from his new superior officer. Heath's domineering personality overawed Percival, who had difficulty establishing his own authority.[13] The new commander had problems as well with the War Office in London, which was often slow or inflexible in its decisions. Percival anticipated the Japanese would use tanks—correctly, as it turned out—but the War Office refused his request for a tank regiment. All Britain's tanks had gone to Russia, after the German invasion, or to the Middle East.

Meanwhile, General Bennett had put a deferential battalion commander, Brigadier Duncan Maxwell, in command of the recently arrived 27th Brigade, comprising three battalions. As Bennett preferred, Maxwell had come through the militia, not the regular army. He had been a doctor in civilian life.

Bennett tended to see conspiracies everywhere, and word of this reached General Vernon Sturdee, Australia's chief of army staff. He came out to Malaya to see for himself and was told by the senior medical officer that Bennett was in reasonable health, but not robust for his age, easily tired and feeling strain unduly. In the medico's view, General Bennett was too old for active service in the field.[14]

Sturdee asked Percival his opinion, got a hedged response, and procrastinated. Soon after, Percival granted Bennett's request for a defined area of responsibility, giving him the states of Malacca and Johore to defend. Bennett moved his command headquarters to Johore Bharu, the state capital, where he cultivated a friendship with the Sultan of Johore. The 68-year-old sultan gave the Australian commander gifts of expensive Scotch and allowed him to flirt with his young Romanian wife.[15] At that time, the sultan was under observation by Singapore Special Branch, and reportedly held pro-Nazi views despite his £250,000 contribution to Britain's war effort.[16]

Brooke-Popham returned to Melbourne in October to brief the new prime minister and address Australia's Advisory War Council. Brimming with optimism, he advised that Singapore now had five squadrons of Buffalos, 'superior to the Japanese and well-suited for work in Malaya'.

'What's happened with the 336 aircraft London thought necessary to defend Burma, Malaya and Borneo?' Curtin asked him.

'There are 180 aircraft in hand, including seven Catalinas in Ceylon,' was the reply.

Curtin was unimpressed.[17]

Within a week of landing an invasion force in Thailand and at Kota Bharu, the Japanese had an iron grip on northern Malaya. By then there was nothing a British fleet could do to save Singapore. The invasion force had already crossed the sea and was well established on land, out of reach of the Royal Navy. The Singapore strategy was rudely exposed as a fallacy. Malaya's jungles were not impenetrable. Whenever the fleet did arrive, it would be too late. As it happened, it never came.

Ten Hudson bombers were never going to prevent the Japanese landing at Kota Bharu. After that landing and with his force still a month away from engagement with the Japanese, General Bennett was complaining to Australian Army headquarters in Melbourne that there was not enough air cover for the army to operate without harassment from enemy aircraft. 'I fear another Crete,' he wrote.[18]

For some time after that, while the invaders concentrated on the land battle, Singapore was subjected to only occasional bomber raids. Speed was key to the Japanese drive down Malaya, which allowed no time for British forces to regroup. However, from the beginning of January, air attacks on Singapore became more frequent with raids every night and by mid-month daytime raids as well, increasing in frequency and intensity as the Japanese moved inexorably nearer to the island state. With little in the way of fighter defence or anti-aircraft fire to disturb the raiders, civilian casualties increased steeply.

Reinforcements were on the way, but these were ground troops, not the aircraft—bombers and fighter cover—so desperately needed. Late in January, 1900 Australian soldiers and 7000 from India arrived, but the reinforcements were seriously underprepared for battle against a formidable enemy. Part of Britain's 18th Division was already in Malaya, retreating with other British forces. The rest arrived on 5 February while General Percival was marshalling his defences for the expected Japanese assault on Singapore.

Singapore's extremes of wealth and poverty lived side by side in its steamy heat. As the Japanese pushed swiftly down the Malayan peninsula, European refugees arrived by train while military casualties poured into this crowded mixing pot by truck. Expats lived out of suitcases in temporary accommodation. A curfew and martial law had been established, and there was some sort of rationing.

Reports reached Singapore at the end of January of a gloomy prediction of their fate by Churchill in the House of Commons.[19] After that, long lines of alarmed citizens gathered at the port, many booked to Ceylon (now Sri Lanka) on empty returning troopships.

Those who stayed, dined in restaurants or went to cinemas and dance halls as if nothing had changed. Raffles Hotel offered a nightly dinner dance in its blacked-out ballroom, the orchestra playing from 8 p.m. to midnight.[20] Outside, in Chinatown, entire streets had been levelled by bombing, with corpses buried in mass graves or left under rubble as the retreating Australian, Indian and British troops streamed onto the island.

General Percival had 85,000 troops at his disposal, although 15,000 were non-combatants in transport, medical and administrative units. His 70,000 combat soldiers included the 10,000 recent reinforcements, inexperienced and mostly barely trained.[21] Percival estimated Japanese strength in Malaya at 150,000 and 300 tanks, relying largely on exaggerated estimates by unit commanders and intelligence officers made during the Japanese advance.[22] General Yamashita had in fact only 30,000 men with a light tank brigade in support,[23] but they were well trained, battle-hardened and well led.

Now cradled on the island, Percival's troops were spread thinly right around its 120 kilometres of coastline, covering all possible avenues of Japanese attack, including a seaborne assault on Singapore's southern shore, once believed the only feasible approach. Percival expected the Japanese, consolidating in Johore across the strait, would most likely land on the island's north side, east of The Causeway in the vicinity of the naval base.[24] The British 18th Division, the freshest of his available forces, was deployed there by Percival under General Heath's command, along with his Indian III Corps. They were fresh because they were newly arrived, but the 18th Division troops were undertrained. It was a brigade from that division that had been unable to rescue Colonel Anderson's column retreating from Bakri.

Percival ignored staff advice that the Japanese would be more likely to cross the Strait of Johore at its narrowest section, west of The Causeway, where there was a river mouth to provide cover for launching troop barges. This was also the view of ABDA's commander, General Wavell, but Wavell had earlier made a tactical suggestion that proved flawed. This time he deferred to his field commander Percival's local knowledge.[25] Percival would later argue that 'the object of the defence was not to hold Singapore Island, but to protect the Naval Base'.[26] It's not an argument that stands much scrutiny.

With a Japanese landing on Singapore imminent and no fleet at the base, the naval dockyard was closed down on 30 January, its staff shipped to Ceylon. British troops took up defensive positions around the abandoned base. Tossed papers cluttered its precinct, food and ammunition were found in the stores and half-eaten meals had been left on tables in the mess hall. The giant floating dock had been scuttled, but was only half-submerged. Equipment and cranes were being demolished by an army team.

General Percival deployed the Australian 8th Division west of The Causeway, a long frontage of inlets, tidal flats and mangrove swamps. Behind that was jungle broken by creeks. General Bennett put his two brigades either side of the Kranji River, over a kilometre wide at its mouth. But this created an unequal spread of the two: Brigadier Taylor's 22th Brigade was to defend 16 kilometres of this difficult coastline west from the Kranji, while Brigadier Maxwell's 27th Brigade covered a mere 4 kilometres between the river and The Causeway to its east.

Bennett considered moving one of Maxwell's three battalions across the Kranji. But that would elevate Taylor, putting him in command of four battalions, and the two were barely on speaking terms. So Bennett shelved the idea.[27]

The setting up of defences was problematic for a number of reasons. The men arrived to find no preparation by Malaya Command of the positions they were to defend against an enemy gathering on the opposite shore. To cover the length of coast allocated, defence posts had to be set up hundreds of metres apart, with patrols covering the space between. Mangroves restricted the posts' fields of fire. Bennett came forward from his headquarters set up in the middle of the island and worried about the vulnerability of the gaps; but he made no protest to his commanding officer, General Percival, and he didn't go forward again.

On top of that, there were morale issues with the Australians. Gordon Bennett had puffed up the physique and training of Australian soldiers to reporters after the successful ambush at Gemas three weeks earlier. Since then, his battle-weary troops had backed off through a series of 'fight and flight' engagements until they withdrew over The Causeway. Their bravado had been badly dented. Now they were setting up in unprepared positions to defend a naval base that was empty and burning.[28]

Soldiers are trained to not ask questions, but sometimes this can't be avoided. If any had asked themselves what they were defending in Singapore, they might have concluded they were fighting to save nothing more than an abandoned symbol of British power.

The Australian battalions, depleted by fighting in Johore, had been built up in numbers with the 1900 reinforcements that had arrived a fortnight before. These were seriously undertrained, some having embarked for Malaya a week after they'd enlisted in Martin Place. Many had not been taught bayonet fighting, or ever seen a Bren gun, or handled a sub-machine gun. A few had never even handled a rifle.[29]

'They were not only almost useless,' says a unit leader from the 22nd Brigade, 'but actually a positive menace to anyone near them and to any commander who expected his orders to be carried out.'[30]

Percival had ordered the Australians to position along the shoreline with little defensive depth. There were two points where rivers narrowed the access behind Taylor's troops: a 4-kilometre neck between the headwaters of the Kranji River (to the north) and the Berih River (to the west); and behind it a 10-kilometre gap between the Kranji and the Jurong River (to the south). Taylor asked Bennett to approve a recce of the Jurong line, but he got no response.[31]

Bennett's chief of staff, Colonel Jim Thyer, had actually inspected the line and given a map of it to his commander. 'He told me it was a defensive line,' Thyer recounted, 'and went into a tantrum about the withdrawal complex.'[32]

Harold Taylor instructed his battalion commanders that if their defences were overwhelmed, they should fall back to the Kranji–Berih line and attempt to hold the attack there. It's unlikely he let Bennett know of this instruction. Percival would later claim that Taylor should have held on and waited for reserves to counter-attack, but the English general had little in reserve after spreading his defenders around the entire island.[33]

Taylor's men prepared their defensive positions mostly at night to avoid the increasing artillery and air attacks. They quickly used up the barbed wire allocated to them, then found most of what was still in the ordnance store earmarked for the northeast shore, where Percival anticipated the Japanese would land.

After constant Japanese shelling, the three Singapore airfields were abandoned by the RAF, which moved to Sumatra, leaving only a few Hurricanes on Kallang field on the island's south as frontline defence. General Yamashita then ordered his gunners to destroy the oil tanks at the naval base and the Shell tanks at Kranji so their contents couldn't be released into the strait and fired to impede the Japanese attack. Soon black smoke was rising from ruptured tanks and oily soot rained down on the colony.

Probably unaware that Percival had already decided the assault would come from there, the Japanese set about to deceive the defenders into believing that the northeast shore was where they would launch their attack. From 5 February, they concentrated artillery fire on that quarter and drove empty trucks in and out of a dummy camp set up opposite. Four hundred Japanese troops in noisy motorboats occupied Ubin Island in the middle of the strait on that side. Percival cabled Wavell in Java, 'Present indications show main enemy strength north of Ubin.'[34]

On 6 February, Yamashita moved his headquarters near to the Sultan of Johore's palace, confident the British Army would be reluctant to shell the palace. From his operations room in the five-storey Moorish tower of the Johore Municipal Building he could observe Allied positions. Australian gunners could see Japanese officers moving in the tower, but Bennett refused permission to fire at them, either because he had undertaken not to damage his friend's palace or because Percival had ordered rationing of ammunition in anticipation of a three-month siege. Possibly one was a convenient excuse for the other. Some of the Australians took unauthorised pot shots at the tower anyway.[35]

The following night, two Australian patrols crossed the strait and saw lines of field guns 50 metres apart and a large field kitchen. The kampongs (villages) had been cleared of livestock and civilians, although the patrols saw very few troops. More significantly, no landing craft were sighted. However, the Japanese had been bringing armoured barges and collapsible craft down by truck from Kota Bharu and Thailand. While the patrols snooped around the shoreline, these boats were up creeks and rivers with troops busily preparing them.[36]

The Japanese had conducted their own patrol on the Australian side, noting that soil in the drained sections of mangrove scrub was firm enough for landing. Like the Australian patrols, they weren't seen, although footprints in the soil were spotted after they had gone.[37]

Japanese artillery began a ferocious bombardment of the 22nd Brigade's positions from dawn on 8 February. Casualties were light because the defenders were spread wide, but this was the first taste of heavy shellfire for many of the reinforcements. A cacophony of shell explosions continued all day, jumping around the Australian positions. The din and uncertainty of where the next would land was more than some could endure. On top of that, morning showers turned into a deluge until early evening. The men were wet, cold and miserable in water-filled slit trenches. An Australian request that an artillery unit be moved west was refused. Malaya Command didn't want any weakening of defences where the attack was expected.

Percival had pressured Bennett to order the patrols from Taylor's sector, possibly prompted by the footprints on the shoreline. At midday, he visited Bennett's headquarters, some 15 kilometres back from the front line, but the patrol's report didn't come through until mid-afternoon.[38] Although evidence of troop concentration had been noted and the enemy was bombarding the sector, no landing craft had been observed. General Percival stuck doggedly to his original assessment and concluded that the bombardment was a feint that would continue for a couple of days, then switch to the east side in preparation for the expected amphibious attack. The Australians would just have to endure the distraction.

A week earlier, on 1 February, General Percival had spoken to the colony in a radio broadcast. 'Our task is to hold the fortress until help can come, as assuredly it will come,' he insisted. 'Any of the enemy who sets foot in our fortress must be dealt with immediately.'[39]

It was a mix of wishful thinking and empty bluster. The only help that was coming was the undertrained reinforcements then arriving. There were no aircraft on the way nor any suggestion there would be. The truth was that the Allied leadership had given up on Singapore with no expectation that it could be held . . . or even that it should be.

On 19 January, the new commander-in-chief, General Wavell, had advised Churchill from Java that the Gibraltar of the East, with no permanent fortifications facing Johore, could not withstand a siege.[40] The British chiefs of staff suggested it might be better to sabotage the naval base and concentrate on the defence of Burma. Burma was a barrier to Japan's pathway to India, whereas Singapore no longer seemed to be a barrier to much at all. The Americans didn't regard Singapore as important, instead wanting Burma defended as the supply route to China.

A shocked Churchill—he'd only recently assured Curtin that Singapore could be held for some time—confided to the British War Cabinet that Singapore might be lost and that Burma had become critical to Britain's regional defence. The Australian minister resident in London, Earle Page, was present at the meeting and reported to the Australian government, incorrectly, that Churchill was planning to withdraw from Singapore.[41] Although evacuation had been discussed, no plan arose from that. Churchill's proposal was diversion of British reinforcements to Burma, then on the way to the Far East.

Australia's attention at that time had turned to its own territories. In New Guinea, Rabaul was invaded by the Japanese on 23 January and Bougainville had come under attack. On radio that night, Army minister Frank Forde warned it was the first time in history Australian territory had been attacked and that in time the Australian mainland would also be targeted.[42] Despite the distraction of Rabaul, an emergency meeting of Australia's War Cabinet in Curtin's absence discussed Page's report and drafted a protest cable, to which External Affairs minister Bert Evatt added, 'After all the assurances we have been given, the evacuation of Singapore would be regarded here and elsewhere as an inexcusable betrayal.'[43] Taken aback by the vehemence of the response, Churchill allowed the reinforcements to continue to Singapore. General Percival was oblivious to his leaders' weakening interest in the island's fate.

Night fell on Singapore, clear and moonless. By the time the dark came on 8 February, the downpour had stopped. The moon wouldn't rise until early morning. Arthur Percival might have been convinced the enemy would mount its attack elsewhere on the coast, but the Australians had been enduring the barrage all day with some trepidation. At around eight-thirty, in a lull in the bombardment of their positions, the defenders could hear a murmur of engines across the water from Johore. Tiny moving dots could be discerned against the darkened far shore. They grew larger, eventually recognisable as landing craft.

A fleet of about 150 barges and collapsible boats had fanned out from the mouth of the Skudai River for the six-minute journey across the Strait of Johore. This was the first of four

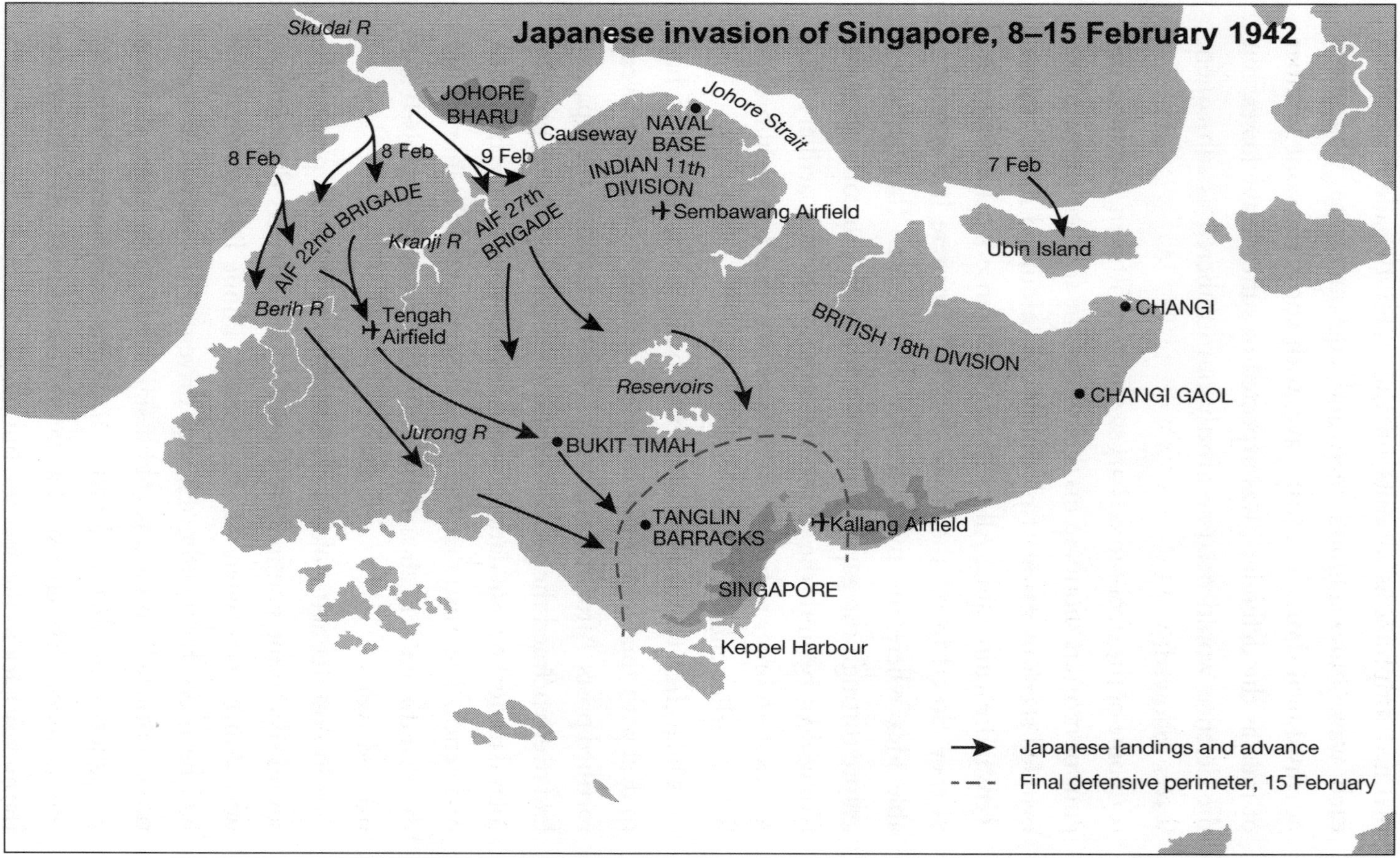

Japanese invasion of Singapore, 8–15 February 1942
Skudai R
JOHORE BHARU
Causeway
NAVAL BASE
Johore Strait
INDIAN 11th DIVISION
Sembawang Airfield
8 Feb
8 Feb
9 Feb
7 Feb
AIF 22nd BRIGADE
AIF 27th BRIGADE
Kranji R
Berih R
Tengah Airfield
Ubin Island
CHANGI
BRITISH 18th DIVISION
CHANGI GAOL
Reservoirs
Jurong R
BUKIT TIMAH
TANGLIN BARRACKS
Kallang Airfield
SINGAPORE
Keppel Harbour
Japanese landings and advance
Final defensive perimeter, 15 February

planned amphibious assaults on the 22nd Brigade's positions, each wave moving 4000 men and equipment to Singapore's northwestern shore. The first wave, with about the same number of men as the defenders, was expected to suffer heavy losses, but the defence would become greatly outnumbered as subsequent waves followed.

Some of the steel-hulled barges, carrying 50 men, had machine guns or mortars mounted on their bow. The smaller boats, in two coupled sections made of plywood with moulded rubber joints, were more vulnerable. All came under intense machine-gun fire as they closed in on the shore, but the Japanese had a reasonable idea where the fixed defence posts were. They streamed ashore through the gaps with little artillery fire to contend with. Concealed behind the front-line posts, defence artillery had received no order to fire. Their field phone lines had been broken by the earlier enemy barrage.[44]

Once they reached the shelter of mangroves, the attack had to deal with the lesser threat of mobile patrols operating between fortified posts. After fierce fighting for about an hour, the Japanese had overwhelmed the pockets of thinly spread resistance, pushing inland under cover of dark and vegetation, bypassing the front line of defence. The Australians fell back to set up a patchy line around the abandoned Tengah airfield, the withdrawals disorganised and panic-driven.

Gordon Bennett woke in his bungalow at about 11 p.m. to the sound of distant gunfire. He rang the headquarters duty officer, who didn't know what was happening. Phone lines to the front had been cut by shellfire. He was driven to the division's operations room, where he was told a signal had come through from Brigadier Taylor that the Japanese had landed and were penetrating the defences. Bennett issued an order to counter-attack and drive the enemy back to the beaches, but the phone line had gone dead.[45]

Fighting continued through the night. The Australians were pushed back, with heavy casualties, often bypassing other groups trying to drop back. After midnight, an isolated Taylor ordered his battalions to withdraw to the Jurong line. In the retreat through unfamiliar jungle at night, many became confused and dispirited. Groups wandered leaderless away from the battle front, saying they'd had enough.

As the sun rose on 9 February, Australian soldiers emerged from the jungle of western Singapore, covered in soot and swamp mud. Many were only partly dressed; some had left their weapons behind. Panic and demoralisation had replaced Aussie self-assurance. They trudged in the morning light down Bukit Timah Road towards Singapore city, military police unable to stop them. It wasn't easy to tell who were regrouping and who were deserting.[46]

The Japanese had landed 13,000 troops on the northwest shore during the night and a further 10,000 after sunrise.[47] Yamashita had moved the bulk of his force across the strait but Percival, with his exaggerated estimate of enemy strength, believed significant numbers were being held in reserve for the speculated northeast landing. Still reluctant to weaken his defence on that side, he was prepared to release to Bennett's command only an Indian brigade, badly mauled in Malaya and held in reserve in the centre of the island.

The west of the island was swarming with Japanese, but people in the city were confident they would be driven off. While parts of the city had been heavily bombed, the commercial area, including Raffles and waterfront warehouses, was still intact and conducting business much as normal. Duncan Maxwell, his 27th Brigade headquarters 10 kilometres back from his own front line but close to Bennett's headquarters, was not so sanguine. Concerned about Japanese penetration on his left flank, he sought to pull back on that side, but Bennett refused to sanction it.

Although the bullnecked Maxwell was an imposing figure at 6 feet 3 inches (1.9 metres), he was getting rattled. During the day, he sacked two of his three battalion commanders with whom he didn't get on. The Japanese had ominously opened an artillery barrage around The Causeway and continued it throughout the day, but Maxwell still believed his main threat was from the enemy already landed. He told Colonel Thyer, Bennett's chief of staff, that resisting the Japanese attack on Singapore would lead to senseless slaughter and he was going to Percival to urge surrender. Thyer told him he should speak to Bennett first. It's not known if Maxwell did, but it seems unlikely.[48]

Certainly Maxwell went to Percival and told him that, being a doctor, he knew a patient would die when his or her whole body was in collapse. There was no point fighting to save the life of Singapore, he said—it would be a waste of men's lives. Percival wasn't greatly interested in this metaphorical discussion and sent the Australian back to his post.[49]

Maxwell returned and told his officers that if the Japanese landed additional troops in their sector, they were to destroy the fuel depot on their side of The Causeway and withdraw to a line between the river and the main road south.

At about 7.30 that night, a battalion of Imperial Guards—maybe 800 men—crossed from the Skudai River mouth to the opposite shore, a pincer movement to connect with the force that had landed the night before. The beaches in this sector, defended by Maxwell's 27th Brigade, had not been reconnoitred by the Japanese. As a result, many of the attackers found themselves stranded on tidal flats or lost in swamps. As the machine-gun posts there were closer to each other than in the previous night's landing, Japanese casualties were heavy.

Maxwell ordered the destruction of any oil-storage tanks that had escaped the Japanese artillery barrage. When a truck carrying explosives and detonators was destroyed by shellfire on the way to the depot, valves on the tanks were opened. Oil ran into creeks and, ignited by a spark, flowed blazing towards the disembarking enemy.[50] Mortars, machine guns and burning bodies were a nightmare for the assault force, but General Yamashita refused the unit commander's request to withdraw. The Imperial Guards had insisted that, as an elite force, they should mount a separate attack, and the general wasn't going to let them escape the consequences.[51]

Although his men were frustrating the Japanese attack, Maxwell stuck to his original plan, ordering a withdrawal at midnight once the oil depot had been destroyed. As the defence fell back, the enemy took control of the beaches, allowing armoured units to be ferried across. An effective defence was coming badly unstuck.

The officer Maxwell had appointed that morning pulled his unit back further than his commander intended and took a second battalion back with him, exposing the left flank of the adjacent Indian division. Bennett wasn't told until 5 a.m. that the Japanese had landed overnight at Kranji. That advice was passed on to Percival, who was told half an hour later that the 27th Brigade had withdrawn. The defence was in tatters. Each unit that withdrew exposed the flank of another and the Japanese infiltrated the space. Neither Bennett nor Percival was getting current reports, but the Australian troop numbers were falling.

Told of his Indian division's exposure, General Billy Key demanded 27th Brigade re-occupy its position. That wasn't possible, Bennett told him. There were now insufficient Australian troops in the sector to do that. Key directed his own reserve unit to occupy the 27th Brigade positions.[52] When the attempt was driven back, Key fumed. 'If Maxwell was a British officer,' he said, 'I would place him under arrest.'[53]

On the morning of 10 February, General Wavell flew in from Java and met with Percival at Bennett's headquarters. His self-esteem bruised, the Australian commander had scant knowledge of Taylor and Maxwell's troop movements and showed no inclination to go forward and find out.[54] Wavell next conferred with the Indian Corps commanders Heath and Key, returning to be told that Taylor's men had been pushed back from the Jurong line. Wavell ordered a counter-attack to recover the line. A three-stage offensive was devised by Percival and passed to Bennett to implement.[55] It was a shambles.

Bennett forgot to pull back a battalion he'd sent forward before he got Percival's plan. While waiting for the order to advance, the unit was crushed as the Japanese drove forward with tanks ferried across from Johore. The counter-attack was scattered by the advancing enemy and came to nothing.

That evening Wavell received a cable from his prime minister. 'The defenders must greatly outnumber Japanese forces who have crossed the straits, and in a well-contested battle they should destroy them,' Churchill insisted. 'There must be at this stage no thought of saving the troops or sparing the population. The battle must be fought to the bitter end at all costs. Commanders and senior officers should die with their troops. The honour of the British Empire and of the British Army is at stake.'[56] It says it all.

Wavell drafted an order to Percival paraphrasing the contents of the cable. He flew back to Java first thing the next morning, and never set foot in Singapore again. Percival, for his part, passed on Wavell's order to his two senior generals, Heath and Bennett, instructing them to convey the 'gist' of the message to all ranks. 'In some units the troops have not shown the fighting spirit which is to be expected of men of the British Empire,' Percival commented. 'It will be a lasting disgrace if we are defeated by an army of clever gangsters many times our inferior in numbers.'[57]

Most of the unit commanders refused to pass on this message to their men.

The defence of Singapore was unravelling, with deserters becoming increasingly conspicuous. Bennett reported to Malaya Command HQ that 600 Australian troops had been picked up and returned to their units, but, by the third day of the incursion, returning them had become impractical.[58] Morale was low and the deserters drunk and aggressive.

'Hundreds of these soldiers, Australians mainly, sprawled all over the road, drunk,' recalls one Singaporean. 'They broke into shops opposite the Orchard Road Market. They were looting the place for food and liquor. And they were drinking it straight from the bottle, smashing the bottles all over the streets.'[59] Estimates by those there are that about 80 per cent of this out-of-control horde was Australian. The soldiers who bore the brunt of the Japanese onslaught were also Australian.[60]

The British leadership decided to pull out some men, all Britons, with sufficient experience in jungle warfare to train future recruits. Along with rescued sailors and the few remaining airmen, they were taken to the cruiser HMS *Durban*, which arrived secretly in the dead of night. *Durban* was escorting a convoy taking civilian evacuees to the town of Batavia (now Jakarta) in Java. While the convoy waited in the channel, small boats carrying British and Australian deserters came out and forced themselves on board.[61]

The cargo ship *Empire Star*, still berthed at Keppel Harbour, had also been instructed to evacuate women, children and approved personnel, including Australian army nurses. As the civilians crowded onto the gangway in the afternoon, marauding deserters came barging through in small packs, pushing a path for themselves with rifle butts. Some shinned up mooring ropes. Small groups of deserters had been persuaded to leave other smaller boats to make room for civilians, but the British guards on the wharf decided against confronting this unruly armed mob, which was in a dark and truculent mood.[62]

Empire Star and another merchant ship, *Gorgon*, left Singapore at night, escorted by HMS *Durban*. The convoy was attacked repeatedly by Japanese bombers. Under gunfire, Australian nurses attended to 30 casualties from the attacks. On reaching Batavia, the deserters were taken off and arrested. *Gorgon* went on to Fremantle, where its 45 deserters on board were taken away under armed guard.[63]

Those still on Singapore island were facing an increasingly desperate prospect. Driving back from Taylor's forward headquarters that night, Bennett's staff officer, Major Charles Moses, came across enemy tanks blocking the road. Getting away on foot from the shootout that followed and picked up by a passing Bren carrier some time later, Moses got back in an adrenaline-charged state to the Australian command centre.[64]

Lancashire-born and ex-British Army, Moses had come to Australia after the First World War, selling real estate and cars before joining the Australian Broadcasting Commission as a sports announcer. By the time the next war started, 42-year-old Moses was General Manager of the ABC.

After a shower, shave and breakfast, the former radio executive ran into Lieutenant Gordon Walker, Bennett's aide-de-camp, in the operations room. Resolve had been planted in Moses' mind by the night's drama. He told Walker he could see no outcome in Singapore other than capitulation, and he was not intending to be taken prisoner.

'It would be marvellous if we could get the general away too,' said Walker. Later, he told Moses that Bennett was all for trying to escape if he found himself free to do so.[65]

Japanese planes continued to add to the mayhem in Singapore, coming in formations of 27, those at the front spitting machine-gun fire while behind bombers dropped their payload. There was little protection on the ground, no proper bomb shelters. The public made do with sandbagged trenches and filthy drains.

Clouds of sooty smoke, rising from burning oil tanks and warehouses full of rubber, drifted lazily across the sky. Enemy aircraft flew below this layer and dropped behind British lines a few red-and-white tubes with fluttering ribbons. Inside each was a message from General Yamashita to 'British High Command', an invitation in English to 'give up this meaningless and desperate resistance', otherwise 'I shall be obliged, though reluctantly from humanitarian considerations, to order my army to make annihilating attacks on Singapore'.[66]

Yamashita was bluffing. He had a problem. His numerical weakness ruled out any drawn-out battle; he was also running out of supplies, and particularly out of ammunition.[67] To preserve bullets, some advances had already been conducted with bayonets drawn rather than with rifle fire. Time was getting critical for the Japanese commander.

But he didn't get the response he wanted. Indeed, he didn't get any response at all. Percival got his orders from London and, whatever might have been his personal view, he had no discretion to act on circumstances as he saw them.

Percival cabled General Wavell in Java. 'Have received letter from Commander of Japanese Army asking for surrender of fortress. Letter was dropped by air. Have no means of dropping message so do NOT propose to make reply which would of course in any case be negative.'[68]

Yamashita had no option but to press on with his attack. Having now to contend with tanks, Percival decided to set up a defensive perimeter around the city. This largely unfortified, 45-kilometre line was a last-ditch Allied defence, still only four days after the Japanese had first crossed to Singapore. Defenders were pulled back from the eastern and southern shorelines, many of them British soldiers who had not yet faced the enemy on the island. A division was left to defend reservoirs in the centre, Singapore's only water supply after detonation of The Causeway had severed the pipeline from Johore.

Within Percival's perimeter, Gordon Bennett had set up a separate Australian perimeter around Tanglin Barracks and moved the remnants of the AIF into it. Australian gunners were instructed to fire only in defence of their own perimeter. The Johore Volunteer Engineers, placed under Bennett's command, were ordered to take up positions guarding the Australian rear. The Johore commander refused and received no more orders.[69]

Without telling Percival, Bennett cabled Canberra advising, 'Wavell has ordered all troops to fight to the last. If enemy enter city behind us will take suitable action to avoid unnecessary sacrifices.'[70]

Harold Taylor's 22nd Brigade was badly depleted, reduced to 800 infantry from the 3400 of four days before. Casualties accounted for some of the losses, but the major loss was from men missing, either from desertion or wandering lost in the unfamiliar jungle. Exhausted, the 52-year-old brigade commander collapsed that afternoon after a confrontation with Bennett. He asked one of his battalion leaders, Colonel Arthur Varley, to take command while he caught up on sleep.

The next day, Bennett promoted Varley to brigadier, relieving Taylor of his command and sending him to hospital. But this wasn't out of concern for his officer's welfare.[71] After the war Bennett wrote, 'I have never forgiven myself for not sending him home when I originally decided to', referring to his intention, which he never followed through, of sacking Taylor in 1941.[72]

A million people had crammed into the British-held area within Percival's perimeter. A hellish nightscape pulsed in

Singapore, with the glow and crackle of fires everywhere. The stench was inescapable—burning and decaying bodies, of burning rubber and oil, of cordite. An air raid demolished shop-houses in Orchard Road. A petrol station exploded, throwing two cars in the air. Dead and dismembered bodies were everywhere, along with shrieking and groaning. Cratered streets were blocked by rubble and abandoned vehicles. Singapore was a city in collapse.

General Percival met with his senior commanders the next afternoon. It was Friday the 13th. With Bennett in support, Heath proposed surrender to minimise civilian casualties. Percival was considering a counter-attack instead.

Heath commented, 'The last counter-attack was a complete fiasco. There are no fresh troops now.'

'There are other things to consider. I have my honour to consider and there is the question of what posterity will think of us if we surrender this large army and valuable fortress.'

'You needn't bother about your honour,' Heath said. 'You lost that a long time ago in the north.'

Percival was taken aback by this slight, yet he let it go. He said instead that the troops must fight on, but he'd cable Wavell for the discretion to decide when resistance no longer had any purpose.[73]

Wavell would not budge. 'You must continue to inflict maximum damage on enemy as long as possible,' he cabled back. 'Your action in tying down enemy and inflicting casualties may have vital influence in other theatres. Fully appreciate your situation but continued action essential.'[74]

Yamashita had moved his headquarters to the Ford motor factory on the island. He had been told the British forces were digging in around the city, and worried that Percival planned a protracted campaign, expecting reinforcements. He ordered a sea search to intercept any convoy on the way, knowing he didn't have the resources for a long siege. On the night of 14 February, the Japanese pressed the perimeter, but they couldn't break through it.

In the morning, Percival was advised that the city's water was pouring out of broken pipes. The Japanese had driven the defence back from the reservoirs, but didn't cut off the supply. It wouldn't last more than a day anyway.

The Japanese attacked a Malayan unit adjacent to the Australian perimeter set by Bennett within Percival's perimeter. With the Australian artillery instructed by Bennett not to fire in their support, the Malays were soon overrun. The next line of defence, an Indian unit, exchanged gunfire while it fell back, retreating into the Alexandra Hospital grounds. The Japanese attacked the hospital in the early afternoon. A man approaching with a white flag was killed on the spot with a single bayonet thrust. The intruders stormed buildings, killing doctors and nurses and soldiers undergoing treatment. Male staff and patients were bound and bundled into small rooms to be later bayoneted.[75]

At four o'clock on the morning of 15 February, General Wavell was woken with a cable from Churchill, who had modified his position. He now left Wavell and Percival to judge when nothing could be gained by fighting on. Wavell passed on to Percival the instruction to fight on if damage could be inflicted on the enemy, but he now had discretion to cease resistance if he was satisfied that was no longer feasible. He added that, before any ceasefire, those wanting to escape should be allowed that opportunity, a considerable retreat from the instruction to fight to the death.[76]

A conference of senior officers was called for 9.30 a.m. at Fort Canning, Percival's headquarters inside Singapore city. Bennett went by truck, worried that a staff car might be recognised from the air. After some time convincing the fort guards of his identity, the general walked through the iron doors and along a hallway of locked rooms. The staff in Fort Canning—known to the Australians as 'Confusion Castle'—usually communicated by phone.

Percival summarised to his generals the position they were at: overnight infiltration of all sectors by the enemy; food and ammunition running low; water supply critical. The options of immediate counter-attack or surrender were discussed, the debate getting heated with recrimination.

'We should do what we should have done two days ago,' said Heath. Bennett agreed. A week before, Heath had argued there were too many generals in Malaya Command and had proposed that he and his pregnant wife be evacuated to India.

'The commander-in-chief's orders then were to continue at all costs,' replied Percival.

'How can Wavell command this battle from Java?'

With all agreeing that a counter-attack was pointless, General Percival agreed to surrender. He would request a ceasefire at four that afternoon. Until agreement was reached with the Japanese, resistance was to continue.[77]

In the relieved chatter that followed this decision, Bennett said, 'How about a combined attack to recapture Bukit Timah?' Bukit Timah was the town in the middle of the island where Bennett's headquarters were initially located.

The suggestion was met with stunned silence, no one sure if it was a serious proposal or an example of wry Australian humour. Bennett was the only Australian in the room. After a pause, talk resumed about conditions in Singapore, as if he hadn't spoken.[78]

Later that morning, three men drove up Bukit Timah Road: Brigadier Terence Newbigging, a Percival staffer; Major Cyril Wild, a former Shell subsidiary executive; and Hugh Fraser, Singapore's Colonial Secretary. When they got to a Japanese-manned roadblock, they took a Union Jack and a white flag from the car and walked 600 metres into Japanese-occupied territory.

Stopped by a patrol that took their pistols, the Japanese-speaking Wild explained that they were there on behalf of General Percival to see General Yamashita.

After waiting tensely in a villa for about an hour, a colonel arrived with a letter outlining conditions for surrender. The British were to lay down their arms and remain in position. Percival was required to meet with Yamashita in person; the Japanese general would not deal with envoys. The British party was given a large Japanese flag to fly from Singapore's tallest building, the Cathay, if Percival accepted the conditions and was coming to meet with his counterpart.[79]

The Japanese flag hung from the Cathay building for ten minutes at about 3.30 p.m.[80] Shortly after, two cars drove up Bukit Timah Road to the front line bringing General Percival, Brigadier Kenneth Torrance, his chief of staff, and Newbigging and Wild with their two flags. The four British officers were driven to Yamashita's headquarters at the Ford factory, where they sat in a small room on one side of a table opposite six Japanese officers. The two generals sat in the middle facing each other. Surrounding them were Japanese camera crews, photographers and journalists.

After a protracted discussion, Yamashita agreed to allow a thousand British soldiers to retain their arms so they could police looting until they were relieved by the Japanese. Hostilities were to cease at 8.30 p.m.; surrender was to be unconditional. Percival signed the only copy of the surrender document, which was retained by the Japanese. The two generals stood and shook hands.[81] The British party returned to their lines numbed by the competing emotions of relief and failure.

At the meeting, Wild had noticed a Japanese staff officer's map of Singapore, with blue marks suggesting a thrust east of Bukit Timah Road. It was highly likely it was planned for that night. If successful, it would have split the city's defences in two.[82]

That afternoon, three Australian pilots escaped in battered Hurricanes from Kallang airfield after a speedy patch-up job by ground staff.[83] The constant whistle of artillery shells continued into the evening, spouting dust and debris. High-level bombers unloaded through a hail of anti-aircraft fire, dive-bombers roared over rooftops; then at 8.30 p.m. the guns stopped and there was silence. No voices, only the crackle of spot fires.

Russell Savage was there, one of the AIF gunners. 'I couldn't believe we were surrendering,' he says. 'We were still a good fighting unit, so why had the fighting stopped? Rumours were coming in that troopships were arriving with reinforcements and that Hurricanes had been landed in crates and were being assembled. We didn't know there was no chance of assembling anything.'[84]

Even after the surrender, there were men mooching around the shoreline trying to escape in small boats. In the city, many of the soldiers and civilians just went to sleep. It was all over.

The next morning, General Percival was told that Gordon Bennett had escaped from Singapore. According to Bennett's chief of staff, Jim Thyer, 'He just went off the handle.'[85]

Three nights before the surrender of Singapore, Charles Moses had filled a water bottle with brandy and a haversack with supplies in preparation for his escape bid with Gordon Walker and Bennett. In the morning he went looking for a guide and a boat. By 15 February, he was still negotiating through his Chinese contact to get the boat.[86]

Bennett returned from Percival's conference that morning with news of the intention to surrender and issued an order for all ranks to stand fast 'so the spirit of the ceasefire is not destroyed by foolish action'.[87] A mass escape attempt might draw retaliation.

He instructed all soldiers to be issued with fresh clothing, new boots and two days' rations. A list of the men was to be compiled and handed to the enemy to be forwarded to the Australian government so families could be advised.[88]

Bennett then toured the Australian lines with Moses and Walker. The troops were still full of fight, taking the capitulation badly. Some wept with exhaustion at the news. The men were told the exact time of the ceasefire was being negotiated, but they could oppose any Japanese advance up to that time. Instructions were issued about where arms were then to be dumped.[89] Told that escape was permitted but only after hostilities ceased, some of the men started packing for that. Some lost heart partway through the process, resigned to their fate.

On returning to his headquarters, Bennett found that Percival was meeting with the Japanese. He began destroying his private papers. When he heard the surrender had been signed, he told his senior officers he was intending to escape, explaining that he could pass on lessons learnt in fighting the Japanese and pull strings on behalf of the men about to be taken prisoner.[90] He gave no indication to these men about to be taken prisoner of what strings these might be.

Moses and Walker returned at about ten o'clock that night with their Chinese fixer. Bennett handed command of the 8th Division to the officer next in seniority, artillery commander Brigadier Cecil 'Boots' Callaghan, and slipped out into the night. Weak with malaria, Callaghan was not impressed with this unwelcome promotion.[91]

With his commander gone, Major John Wyett went to Bennett's quarters to ensure nothing sensitive had been left behind. He found bottles of expensive whisky, a gift from the Sultan of Johore, poured himself a drink, then smashed the bottles. An envelope marked 'Not for Australia' contained photos of Bennett and the sultan's Romanian wife, which Wyett later described as 'compromising'. He destroyed the photos and left.[92]

The three escapees and their guide made their way in Bennett's staff car through deserted, cratered streets to the waterfront east of the city. They arrived to find their guide's friend's house reduced to rubble and his boat missing. Japanese officers were said to be nearby. Determined and desperate, the trio's best hope was to commandeer a sampan. Walker stripped off, swam out to a group of sampans beyond the jetty and found one he could row. He pulled it back to the wharf.[93]

They were just about to leave when eight men from the Malayan Volunteers, the local militia, came striding onto the jetty. The Australians cautiously agreed to let them on the boat. Diaries of two Volunteers, an accountant and a mines inspector in civilian life, describe a slow chaotic progress: rowing was difficult in a sampan with eleven men on board; Bennett screamed 'like a young girl' that the Japanese might see Walker standing naked in the boat.[94]

Bumping into boats in the misty night, they came upon a Chinese junk floating towards them. Scrambling aboard, they found the owner smoking opium with his two crewmen. Three British soldiers had already swum out to the vessel. Soon after, two more dragged themselves on board, threatening to shoot if resisted.

By the time the captain was persuaded to sail, he had 21 uninvited passengers. Bennett wanted to go to Malacca, where he said he had friends, but he was ignored. The *tongkang*[95] meandered through a chain of islands, then across to Sumatra. By night it would anchor at fishing poles, becalmed one day while Japanese planes flew overhead. It was nerve-racking for everyone except, it seemed, the skipper.[96]

Four days after they had set out, an RASC (Royal Army Service Corps) motor launch came by. Bennett identified himself to the launch captain, and successfully argued for his party to be transported. The three Australians left without a word to their companions of the previous few days and were taken to Padang in West Sumatra.[97] It was the end of an undignified journey for the irascible general, but his slide from glory was not finished.

When Gordon Bennett arrived in Sydney following his escape, he was feted by the press, Australian and English, for his boldness. After he met with the War Cabinet, Curtin was full of praise, although that might have been more politically driven than sincere. Army minister Frank Forde had already expressed surprise that Bennett spoke to the press days before making any contact with army headquarters.

Bennett's escape drew a mixed response in Australia. The belief was either that he brought valuable lessons in fighting the Japanese, or he left his troops to become prisoners of war. Bennett was loudly critical of the conduct of the Malayan campaign, of British leadership and of the low morale of Indian troops. Snubbed by the military hierarchy, he was promoted to a command in Perth. A Japanese invasion was then thought still possible, but he never again led troops in battle.[98]

At the end of the war, General Percival was repatriated and accused Bennett of unlawfully vacating his command. Blamey convened a military court of enquiry. It found Bennett not justified in handing over his command.[99]

Bennett always found more support from his men than from his fellow officers. There was sufficient agitation on his behalf for the new prime minister, Ben Chifley, who took office in July 1945, to appoint a Royal Commission in November that year into the circumstances of Bennett's escape. While not questioning Bennett's personal courage, Justice George Ligertwood reached the same conclusion: that Bennett's action had been unjustified.[100]

Two anecdotes perhaps best illustrate the ambivalence about General Gordon Bennett. When the freed 8th Division soldiers arrived in Sydney after the war, some hung a sign over the side of their ship saying, 'We want Bennett'.[101] On the other hand, his former troops, in POW camps for the remainder of the war, called their running shoes 'Gordon Bennetts'.[102] The first anecdote is in an uncritical authorised biography of the general; the second in a book by an English war historian highly—and perhaps obsessively—critical of Australian ill-discipline in Singapore and Bennett's leadership. These two stories are drawn from the same cohort of men. The first source provides a photo in support; the second doesn't attribute a source. The shoes might well be an example of droll POW humour. It's always hard to tell with Australian soldiers.

The retreat from northern Malaya to the fall of Singapore took 70 days. At the end of the campaign, 130,000 British soldiers had been taken prisoner, 80,000 of them on surrender at Singapore and 15,000 of those Australian soldiers.[103] Although Australia provided only 13 per cent of British ground forces, they accounted for 73 per cent of soldiers killed in combat, a total of about 1800 men.[104] Many of the prisoners of war remained in Changi Prison on the island. Others, including Australians, were taken in 'hell ships' as forced labour on the Burma Railway, Sandakan airfield in Borneo and other Japanese wartime enterprises.

It was widely expected by Australians, including the soldiers themselves, that troops would be evacuated, as at Dunkirk. Anger grew at the perception of another Gallipoli-style debacle by the English. In fact, there isn't much comparison with Dunkirk, only 65 kilometres from England with the Royal Navy commanding the sea and the RAF able to challenge the Luftwaffe.[105] Singapore, on the other hand, is nearly 4000 kilometres from Perth, and the Japanese controlled both the sea and the air around it.

Prime Minister Curtin called Singapore 'our Dunkirk', escalating the fear of invasion and emphasising the need for both vigilance and austerity by Australians. 'The fall of Singapore opens the Battle of Australia,' he proclaimed. 'Protection of this country is no longer that of a contribution to a world at war, but the resistance to an enemy threatening to invade our own shore. What the Battle of Britain required, so the Battle for Australia demands.'[106]

'We are now faced with the defence of our own land at home rather than abroad,' the *Sydney Morning Herald* responded. 'All our resources must be harnessed to the best possible use in the national struggle for survival. What remains of the "carnival spirit" which General Blamey condemned must be ruthlessly abolished.'[107]

Its editorial two days after the surrender blasted the lazy complacency of the Singapore strategy. 'There have been few more serious miscalculations in all British history than those which have led up to the fall of Singapore,' it said. 'Its real causes are to be sought in the attitude of mind which produced the constant official assurances on behalf of the highest Service officials in the Empire that Singapore was virtually impregnable . . . we have been taught to rely on a naval Maginot Line which the Japanese rapidly unmasked and outflanked.'[108]

Within a few days of Singapore's surrender, the Australian press was offering further reasons for the failure there. A *Sydney Morning Herald* correspondent offered his views of the causes: poor intelligence, senior command not facing facts during the campaign, insufficient air support, and lack of appropriate training for many of the troops.[109] *The Times* rep in Singapore noted that during the campaign the 'Asiatic population' had remained spectators, 'not greatly interested in continuing British rule'.[110] It was an early indication of a regional realignment that would follow the war.

'There was a lot of talk about being betrayed in a way,' recalls Josie Clements, a thirteen-year-old Sydneysider at the time. She hadn't been very conscious of the war until Singapore fell. 'I think it was more when they were all captured in Singapore. I remember my brother had a friend that was captured by the Japanese, was in Changi.'[111]

Stationed in Darwin, halfway to the fallen British colony, civil aviation radio operator Bruce Acland was conscious of its significance. 'I felt Singapore would hold out,' he recalls. 'After all, Singapore was a naval base of the British Empire and I had no feelings of the Japanese coming any further. Then views started to change. And as the Japanese progressed further and further south, and it wasn't taking very long, there became a general awareness around Darwin that we'd better look out for ourselves.'[112]

Chapter 4

FRONTIER TOWN

Darwin was a place where very few wanted to be, a frontier outpost cut off from the rest of Australia except by a dirt track to Alice Springs. By the early 1940s it had become a military town. A garrison was brought across from Thursday Island in 1932 to protect an oil-storage depot being built to support the naval base at Singapore. Troops were housed at Vestey's abandoned meatworks until barracks were built at Larrakeyah. Soon, service personnel and workers on defence contracts began moving in, installing coastal guns to defend the tanks against sea attack. Nothing protected them from air attack.

In 1938 work began on an air force base, but it progressed so slowly that when No. 12 Squadron RAAF arrived a year later, it too was housed at the meatworks and its planes flew out of Darwin's civil airport at Parap.

By mid-1941, the new base was operating a few kilometres further out of town, but the RAAF had grown quicker than its backup. It had no fighter aircraft, using instead the Wirraway, an armed training plane. At that time, Darwin had thirteen Wirraways and eighteen of the newly arrived Hudson bombers to oppose any attack. Seven hundred air crew were stationed at the base, without effective leadership training and no staff support to speak of.[1]

The enemy in Darwin and its surrounds was not the Japanese, but boredom and the risk of 'going troppo'. The duties were monotonous; loneliness and depression were rife; the climate was hot and stifling. There was little to do off duty. Soldiers resented being garrisoned in Darwin. They were the 23rd Brigade, recruited in Tasmania and Victoria and diverted from joining General Bennett in Malaya. Enlisting in the army to fight overseas, they were doing work they considered the militia could do. In April 1941, after four months in Darwin, frustration erupted in a brawl at a boxing event, followed by riots that weekend. Hotels, cafes and shopfronts were smashed and looted.

Punishments for the outburst were light, mostly cancellation of some leave, as the military looked for ways to head off a repeat performance. Attention was given to better recreational facilities. Home leave was increased to six weeks, creating a new problem. As navy ranks hadn't gone on the rampage, they didn't get the additional home leave. The feeling was that the army rewarded its men for causing trouble, while navy men got nothing for not joining in.[2] A pattern of poor decisions had begun.

Darwin had long been a town of unsealed streets with scattered government buildings, stores and houses. At one end of Cavenagh Street was Chinatown, tightly packed with stores and dwellings, laundries and gambling dens. The town's rich racial mix included Chinese-Australians, who owned most of the general stores, and Japanese, involved in the pearling industry.

Defence spending from 1938 gave Darwin instant prosperity. Business area streets were sealed, kerbed and guttered;

construction boomed; wages were high and jobs plentiful. But despite the growth, Darwin was still at heart a Wild West town.

Bob Heppel arrived in October 1941 as an eighteen-year-old gunner. 'I patronised the "Ins and Outs" gambling games at Cavenagh Street,' he recalls. 'These would be rooms filled with men and smoke, people were shoulder to shoulder, and the place stank of sweat, grog, and stale smoke. There was heaps of money around. In fact, the place was awash with money, mostly from contractors who were building the defence installations.'[3]

At first, the civil aviation worker Bruce Acland played 'Ins and Outs', a form of poker, at the Chinatown tables a few times. After realising he couldn't afford to continue playing the card game, he'd watch the games without joining in. 'There were, as we would call them today, wharfies. There were post office staff, there was general business staff, there were government officials,' he says. 'It was a bit stuffy at the top, at the time, and it was a bit rough down at the bottom, but there was a lot of in-between.'[4]

The increased population put pressure on electricity and water supply, and resulted in rationing and service breakdowns. Petrol shortages led to queues at service stations, with vehicles left in line overnight. Even worse in a thirsty town, beer came fortnightly by ship from the eastern states, but it couldn't meet the increased demand from the military presence. Servicemen were banned from restaurants and cafes, adding to their frustration.[5] Everything was the fault of either 'Abbott' or the 'wharfies', depending where you sat socially and politically.

The son of a magistrate and educated at the patrician King's School in Sydney, Aubrey Abbott had tried a number of careers without much success before entering federal parliament for the Country Party in 1929 and becoming Minister for Home Affairs in the Bruce–Page government. He had been appointed Northern Territory administrator in 1937.

Now in his mid-fifties, Abbott was aloof and socially conscious—charming and affable with his social equals, standoffish and snobbish with others. Although he'd developed close relations with the Territory's pastoralists, townsfolk regarded him as insensitive and arrogant. Administering with no council and no formal access for residents, he found several local groups to clash with . . . or they found him.[6]

Darwin's wharf labourers had a reputation for irresponsible militancy. Highly unionised and belligerent, they were poorly paid for work that was hot and difficult. Mick Ryan, a North Australian Workers' Union (NAWU) official, conceded that 'no man who could earn a living in the south would ever stay in Darwin voluntarily'.[7] They may not have been the cream of the nation's workforce, but working conditions were poor. Government stalling meant the port's equipment was outmoded, the control of cargo was managed inefficiently by four bodies and the superintendent of wharf labour was a frail, retired captain who the wharfies ignored.[8]

Unloading on the L-shaped jetty was cumbersome. To cope with the high tidal range, and with single fuel and water pipes, ships constantly shuttled back and forth between wharf and anchorage. The jetty turned too sharply for a locomotive to negotiate, so railway trucks were instead manhandled in the tropical heat onto a turntable operated by donkey engine.[9]

A series of industrial disputes between the NAWU and defence contractors led to the military labelling the union a 'subversive organisation' with communist connections. The army joined with Abbott, long critical of the wharfies, in calling for the use of troops to work on the wharves but successive federal governments, both UAP-Country and Labor, would not support this.

By late 1941, the strikes and friction were continuing. The harbour had become congested with American ships, with captains used to good facilities. Military pressure on the government increased. The War Cabinet sent its minister for labour and national service, the firebrand left-winger Eddie Ward, to Darwin in January to come up with a solution. He persuaded the NAWU to agree to shifts of up to twenty hours to speed up unloading and for 160 men to be flown in from the south. It would not prove to be a good move for the newcomers.[10]

It wasn't just with the wharfies that Aubrey Abbott was at loggerheads. In June 1940, with Australia at war in Europe and Japan a threat, particularly to the north, the administrator agreed to form a civil defence unit, including ARP (Air Raid Precautions). Operating diligently but without any legal authority, the new body wasn't widely welcomed. Residents were irritated by registers and weekly checks on movements by people they saw as interfering busybodies.

After a year of negativity, a civil defence report complained of the public's 'cheap jibes' and refusal to fill out forms, of the lack of equipment and 'hopeless' air raid warning system.[11] The report was shown to a local newspaper, drawing a rebuke from Abbott that they were courting Canberra retaliation . . . but Canberra habitually took no notice of Darwin.

On 11 December 1941, shortly after Pearl Harbor, Darwin's air-raid sirens sounded on a moonless, overcast night. People spilled out into darkened streets, a soldier broke a shop window and smashed a light left on, and hundreds huddled on the beach. A lone bugle was heard at Larrakeyah Barracks. Two hours later, the 'All Clear' sounded.[12] There had been no raid, nor any likelihood of one. Darwin was then out of range of Japan's air bases.

Civil Defence asked Abbott to declare a state of emergency. He wouldn't, fearing public panic, but asked Canberra to authorise evacuation of non-essential civilians. The War Cabinet approved, and on 16 December the administrator issued an order for compulsory evacuation of women and children 'as soon as possible, except women required for essential services'. A notice was sent to every Darwin householder, advising who was to go, what they could take (one suitcase, two blankets and eating utensils) and to be ready to leave on 24 hours' notice. Pets had to be destroyed, poultry to remain as a back-up food source. Vehicles and personal possessions were to be left behind. Some residents motored south; but part of that journey, between Adelaide River and Katherine, was hazardous with the wet season starting. Most left by ship.[13]

The American luxury liner *President Grant*, taking evacuees from the Philippines to Brisbane, was diverted to Darwin to pick up 225 women and children. They were the lucky ones, mostly allocated first-class cabins. An unlucky 542 were evacuated on the troop-carrier *Zealandia*, joining 300 sick troops and Japanese internees already on board. Guards threw luggage overboard if it was over the 15-kilogram weight limit. Two hundred more internees were loaded at Thursday Island. The ship was hot, filthy and without fresh food. Four-berth cabins were overcrowded. Internees were kept in the hold under armed guard, Chinese families kept on an open deck. All the while, there was a fear of mines laid by Japanese submarines.[14]

The *President Grant* was a one-off. Evacuation by ship continued in conditions similar to those on the *Zealandia* until mid-February, by which time half the population had left. Only 2000 people remained in Darwin. Of them, 63 were women in ostensibly essential services, two were small girls hidden by their parents, and 35 were part-Aboriginal girls who had been brought from Bathurst Island, north of Darwin.[15]

On 16 February, Abbott learned that the postmaster's wife and daughter were still in Darwin, working as a telephonist and in the library. Five more women were working on the post office switchboard.

'Train your telegraph messengers to operate the switchboard,' Abbott told the postmaster, Hurtle Bald.

'Then who will deliver the telegrams?' said Bald.

Abbott said they could be picked up at the post office, and Bald agreed without enthusiasm to send the women away. He didn't attach any urgency to doing it.[16]

Many of those who stayed behind resisted ARP's advice to dig slit trenches, either because it was sweaty work in the tropical climate, or because they didn't believe Darwin would be attacked, or both. The wardens had no power to enforce blackouts, either, and continued to press Abbott for legal standing, something he could have granted by local ordinance. He chose instead to send an urgent request to the Interior minister for full powers under National Security Regulations. That was 30 December 1941. For seven weeks he got no response.[17]

ARP volunteers were meanwhile given grudging training by the army. 'All we ever did was present arms and [learn] how to pull a .303 to pieces,' says Reg Weston. 'I don't know whether they thought we were going to present arms to the Japs or what!'[18]

By late January the wardens had had enough. They wrote to the administrator, threatening to resign in three days' time unless they could be given the authority they said they needed to carry out their function. Having received no reply from Abbott by 26 January, the ARP wardens resigned en masse, advising the prime minister by telegram. Some of the wardens continued to work unofficially on Air Raid Precautions. False alarms had continued, but the possibility of a genuine raid was looming ominously.[19]

Once the Pacific War started, a sense of foreboding had seeped into the temper of the town. Darwin's planes were moved desperately back and forth to try to stall Japan's spreading empire.

Sent to Rabaul, Ambon and Timor, those not shot down ended up back in Darwin.

'The Air Force boys that we danced with, they were screamingly funny, some of them,' says Toni Mooy, who worked in Darwin's army records office. 'They'd be there and then they wouldn't. They'd fly off in their antiquated planes to Timor and a lot of them didn't come back. Nobody said anything but you knew damn well a plane had gone down.'[20]

By February 1942, Singapore was on the verge of collapse. Air Commodore George Jones inspected the Darwin base and reported a lack of urgency in its staff. Planes parked close to each other for convenience were an attractive target for air attack. Little use was made of camouflage, an ammunition store invitingly white. Australia's first radar unit, set up north of Darwin, had no antenna installed.[21]

Unnoticed by Jones, an RAAF wireless group was working on the upper floor of an old building next to base headquarters. It had been sent up from Melbourne a few months before and was intercepting Japanese coded radio messages to send back to Melbourne. Darwin's RAAF officers had no idea why the unit was there, nor did they care. It had been given accommodation, as requested, and was ignored thereafter.[22]

In the middle of the night of 14 February, a convoy of five transport ships carrying supplies, equipment and troops to reinforce Timor left Darwin with the cruiser USS *Houston* and an aging destroyer, USS *Peary*, for protection. They left without air cover as fifteen Kittyhawks coming from South Australia had not turned up. By morning the convoy was being shadowed by a Japanese flying boat, which dropped bombs without causing damage and left. *Houston* radioed for fighter support and a Kittyhawk that had just arrived came out. Engaged in a dogfight with three enemy flying boats, it was shot down after forcing one of them to ditch.

Ten of the overdue American planes had by then arrived in Darwin, all with inexperienced pilots apart from their leader, Major Floyd Pell. In the late afternoon and early morning, they ran sorties out across the Timor Sea, operating near the limit of their range and returning to Darwin without sighting anything. Shortly after they had gone, 45 Japanese bombers attacked the convoy in two waves, inflicting limited damage and casualties. ABDA (American-British-Dutch-Australian) Command in Java suspected an enemy carrier and support fleet was lying in wait and ordered the convoy back to Darwin.[23] That risked drawing unwanted attention to Darwin.

The military's command structure in Darwin was a dog's breakfast. The role of North-Western Area Command, under Air Commodore Douglas Wilson, was to coordinate the three services, but it was plagued with friction between service heads. With no building of its own, NWA Command Headquarters was stationed in the RAAF Operations building. The RAAF station head, Wing Commander Sturt Griffith, had been there for only two weeks, and found NWA officers often overruled him, posting men in and out of his unit without consultation. Responsibilities in the two groups seemed to be duplicated, not complementary, so that Griffith had little effective authority in an air base where he was supposedly commander.[24] At that time, the Darwin area was under the Allies' ABDA Command, not Australian command.

On 18 February, three days after the fall of Singapore, Wilson was in Java with USAAF general George Brett, trying to resolve communications difficulties between ABDA and Darwin.[25] Group Captain Frederick Scherger was temporarily in command at NWA Headquarters. Captain Penry Thomas was Naval Officer-in-Charge, Darwin, a martinet and ongoing source of friction in Darwin's Defence Coordination Committee. Major General David Blake was commanding officer of the 7th Military District, based at Larrakeyah Barracks.

Barbed-wire entanglements had been erected along the beach and concrete machine-gun posts built and manned, but a lack of vigilance held sway at command level. Despite the convoy having been pulled back, Air Commodore Wilson or ABDA Command thought for some reason Java was a better place than Darwin for him to monitor what was unfolding. Sixty-five warships and merchant vessels were packed into the centre of Darwin Harbour that day. Even with an attack anticipated, Captain Thomas didn't see a need to move them apart.[26]

Darwin's air defence wasn't going to save him either if an attack was imminent. There was a disabled P-40 Kittyhawk at the RAAF base, and five Wirraways stored under camouflage netting, awaiting repairs. The only serviceable Wirraways, nine of them, were kept at Batchelor airstrip, 100 kilometres away.[27] The rest of the American Kittyhawks were being sent on to Timor.

The convoy returned on the morning of 18 February. *Houston* left for Java that afternoon, but *Peary* and the five transports remained. To many in the town, the return of these ships indicated a large Japanese fleet somewhere in the Timor Sea, posing the very real possibility of an attack, perhaps invasion.[28] After Malaya, New Britain, and Singapore a few days before, was it now Darwin's turn?

It was. Four aircraft carriers—the same four that had launched the Pearl Harbor attack—had left the naval base at Palau in the western Pacific on 15 February. Early on 19 February the Japanese naval force was in position in the Timor Sea. Cloud, following a cyclone earlier in the month, had provided cover, but on this cloudless morning the sun shone brightly through the humid air.

At six o'clock, a floatplane flew undetected over Darwin. Two hours later, aircraft started taking off from carriers turned around into the wind. It took twenty minutes to get all 188 aircraft into the air: 36 Mitsubishi A6M 'Zero' fighters, 81 Nakajima B5N 'Kate' light bombers and 71 Aichi D3A 'Val' dive-bombers. Commodore Mitsuo Fuchida led the attack as he had at Pearl Harbor.[29]

The formation skirted around Darwin to attack the harbour and town from the southeast with the morning sun low behind them.[30] A US Navy Catalina, on its way to patrol near Ambon, was sighted and shot down by a Zero, its radio destroyed before it could alert base.[31] Nor did a warning come from navy coast watcher Jack Gribble on Melville Island, north of Darwin. He saw the planes at 9.15 a.m., but without his codebook didn't report it.[32]

However, a warning did come from Father John McGrath, a Catholic missionary on adjacent Bathurst Island. Another volunteer coast watcher, he too saw the massed aircraft in the distance and sent a message by teleradio, received at the AWA (Amalgamated Wireless Australasia) station in Darwin.

'I have an urgent message,' the voice said. 'An unusually large air formation bearing down on us from the northwest. Very high. Identity suspect. Visibility not clear.'

'Message received,' came the response. 'Stand by.'

There was no time for standing by. Planes were approaching and McGrath dashed for shelter. A group of Zeros screamed in, machine-gunned the village and destroyed a Beechcraft plane standing by the airstrip. McGrath's radio hut was also a casualty. No further report came from the mission.[33]

An hour and a half earlier, six RAAF Hudsons had returned to Darwin with evacuees from Timor. Without adequate identification, they were fired at by the Fannie Bay anti-aircraft post.

It set an unfortunate precedent, and they weren't the only local planes in the air that morning. The ten American Kittyhawks had left at 9.15 for Timor, but the combination of a storm and low cloud around Koepang and the inexperience of the pilots resulted in USAAF Operations calling them back after twenty minutes.[34]

The AWA operator who received McGrath's call at 9.35 a.m. wrote it down as, 'Big flight of planes passed over going south very high.' He sent it immediately to RAAF Operations, where the duty controller reported it to Area Command. The controller had decided it was probably the Kittyhawks returning from their aborted mission and passed his guess on with McGrath's message.[35] Responsible for activating the air-raid alarm, Area Command was without its acting chief, Group Captain Scherger, who was driving into town to meet a visiting senior officer. It was more expedient for those on duty to accept the controller's speculation than risk another false alarm.

It was a fair guess a missionary might regard ten aircraft as a 'big flight' and might not be able to distinguish between south and southwest bearings of distant planes. On the other hand, a Japanese attack was widely anticipated and the Kittyhawks' flight path should have been too far from Bathurst Island to be seen. The number of false alarms right up to that morning no doubt influenced the decision to not rush into sounding the alarm. It was a tragic judgement that compounded.

A warning also came from No. 1 Wireless Unit RAAF, next door to Operations. An intercept officer there had picked up increased radio traffic, possibly between enemy aircraft and aircraft carriers, which could indicate an operation under way. This intelligence was conveyed to the next building, but as the wireless unit's activities were secret and no one at the base knew they were intercepting Japanese signals, base personnel had no idea what had prompted the warning. They gave it little credence.[36]

Finally, both Bruce Acland at the civil airport at Parap and a battery commander at Nightcliff, north of the town, watched a dogfight in which a Kittyhawk was shot down with the pilot parachuting. On hearing gunfire and explosions, Acland sent out the emergency signal 'Q-Q-Q', meaning 'air raid in progress'. He locked up his code machines and cipher books, switched off the power and headed for shelter.[37] Nightcliff's officer meanwhile phoned RAAF Operations and asked if enemy planes were known to be in the area. 'If this is a raid, we know nothing of it,' he was told.[38]

At nearby Casuarina Beach, Trooper Burns on lookout saw the massed planes and came running to his sergeant with news that 'the Japs are here'. Sergeant McDonald asked how he knew they were enemy planes. 'They've got bloody great red spots on them,' spluttered Burns.[39]

McDonald phoned army headquarters shortly before ten o'clock, but events overtook his call. By then, someone at Area Command had seen the approaching planes.

Darwin's air-raid siren sounded at 9.58 a.m. as the first wave of high-altitude pattern bombing swept out of the sun and over the harbour. Zeros were already engaging in dogfights with the returning Kittyhawks and had attacked the minesweeper HMAS *Gunbar* as it was leaving the harbour, but a concentrated bombing attack was looming.[40] Twenty-seven bombers came in each wave, groups of three in V formation, the groups themselves set out in a V pattern. It was clearly not a false alarm this time.

Merchant navy radio operator Phil Chapman noted in his diary, '. . . suddenly discern right above us, 27 heavy Jap bombers in perfect formation, scramble into trench then hell lets loose. Screaming of bombs and terrific cracks and explosions, earth shudders, trench seems to spin wildly, sand bags open up and rubble pours in, stench of explosives and thick smoke and dust everywhere.'[41]

The first strike hit the right-angled elbow of the wharf, tearing out a section of the structure and tossing a locomotive, six railway trucks and men into the sea. A shed on the wharf, where workers were having their morning smoko, was demolished and the men inside killed instantly. Oil pipelines running along the wharf were broken, the oil spilling into the harbour and igniting. Wharfies and ships' crew, cut off on the outer jetty, jumped into the water to find themselves covered in oil and struggling to avoid pools of burning fuel.[42]

Meanwhile, the returning P-40 Kittyhawks were dealing with Zeros that had come directly to Darwin after strafing Bathurst Island. Floyd Pell, the group leader, had ordered five of the P-40s to patrol while the other five landed at the RAAF airfield. As the patrol aircraft climbed through gathering cloud, Robert Oestreicher, one of the pilots, spotted an enemy plane diving from 2000 feet (600 metres) above him. 'Zeros! Zeros! Zeros!' he radioed.

The Americans scattered with Zeros chasing them, the dog-fights seen from Nightcliff and Parap. Two pilots were shot down and killed. One Kittyhawk managed to land, its wounded pilot leaping out and running to a slit trench. Another came down into the sea after its pilot had parachuted to safety. Only Oestreicher stayed in the air, climbing into cloud cover, where he stayed until the attack was over.

Pell was standing by his aircraft when Oestreicher's radio call came through. He ordered the five landed planes to drop their belly tanks and get back in the air. It proved to be a futile gesture. Pell and another pilot were attacked during take-off, and killed. The remaining three pilots got into the air before they too were attacked, two bailing out and surviving, the third crash-landing and somehow crawling from the wreckage.[43]

The air battle was a sideshow. A second V formation of bombers flew over the town, while dive-bombers and fighters followed the first wave over the port. The new attack targeted the government block, a short distance from the wharf. When they realised what was happening, townspeople rushed to slit trenches or huddled against beachside cliffs. Some just found somewhere to shelter in their building.

Aubrey Abbott had told his staff to take cover under his office in the event of an air raid. When the siren sounded, Abbott and his wife, their servants and his staff headed there. A concrete floor on reinforced concrete pillars seemed a reliable refuge. As soon as they got there, a bomb burst 15 metres away.

'Mortar, concrete, grit fell, bruising and blinding us. The whole structure cracked and moved down over us and the most terrible screams filled the air,' Hilda Abbott described the experience. 'The noise was so terrific that nothing was distinguishable—our guns, their guns, bombs—it was all just enormous and terrible.'[44]

The blast had snapped the pillars and lifted the concrete floor. Only a steel strongroom door holding up one corner of the floor prevented them all from being crushed to death. As it was, Daisy Martin, a young Aboriginal maid, was killed under a concrete block and a groundsman was pinned by his leg. Abbott and his driver tried to extricate the trapped youth while the others hurried in shock and fear down the cliff face to shelter there.[45]

Reg Rattley, a phone mechanic, had asked his foreman that morning, 'What do you think of our chances today?'

'We're going to get it in the neck,' was the reply.[46] The Timor convoy's return would be too tempting a target for the Japanese.

When the siren sounded soon after, Rattley went to a slit trench that had been dug in the postmaster Hurtle Bald's garden nearby.

It was already quite crowded with the Bald family and telephone and postal workers, so Rattley headed back to the exchange. Iris Bald had run home from her workplace to be with her parents. A junior postal clerk had given her his place in the trench and run across to shelter under the cliff. Just before the siren, Bald had commented to a policeman, 'I wonder if today will be the day.'[47]

For the postmaster, it was. A direct hit demolished the shelter, the bomb falling into the trench and exploding, killing its nine occupants instantly.

Bruce Acland, out at Parap airfield, was more fortunate. 'I sheltered down below the wall of one of the tin huts,' he recounts. 'And then I really woke up to what strafing was all about. I heard a roar of an aircraft and a row of holes appeared just above my head.'[48]

He threw himself into a slit trench, landing on top of two of his colleagues. Ted Betts had been shaving in his pyjama pants when Fred Riley pointed out a formation of planes approaching. They raced to the nearest trench, Betts with face half-lathered, Riley with only a towel around his waist. After Acland tumbled on top of them, they were joined by their supervisor wearing only shoes and a tin hat. He'd been in the shower.[49]

The air everywhere was full of smoke and noise and dust and the smell of cordite. Bomb explosions were deafening, aircraft screaming low. Dive-bombers swarmed, and predatory Zeros darted around at tree-top level, the pilots' faces visible from the ground. Anti-aircraft fire was intense but ineffectual.

Anti-aircraft posts set up around Darwin had responded immediately to the attack, but the gunners had fired live rounds only twice before, both times across the path of Hudsons without proper identification, never in the fury of battle. The new experience of 40 to 80 rounds a minute was deafening and disorienting. The guns generally shot below or behind their targets. To preserve ammunition, they hadn't been calibrated with live rounds, and fuses on heavy anti-aircraft shells timed differently in the tropical heat.[50] Lewis and Vickers machine guns weren't much better, unable to reach the high-flying bombers.

Dive-bombers and fighters flew on to the civil and military airfields, already subjected to high-altitude bombing. Bombs poured into the RAAF's hangars and workshops. Strafing machine guns cut across buildings, smashing radio sets and an emergency power generator, setting an oil store on fire and putting the few planes on the ground and a fire engine out of commission. An ammunition magazine was burning, its contents soon exploding as if it was cracker night. Lewis guns, mounted on improvised wooden stakes, and rifles were the only opposition, but it was on the harbour that most of the damage was done, most lives lost.

Seeing the planes approaching, USS *Peary*'s skipper had ordered its engines on and anchor up. The destroyer was heading to the harbour entrance when it was pounced on by dive-bombers. Struck five times, *Peary* sank slowly at the stern while moving forward 'like a hunted deer trying to escape while shot in the hindquarters'.[51] One bomb had hit its ammunition store. The delayed explosion disintegrated the ship in a burst of flame shooting upwards some 30 metres. *Peary* slid into the harbour, its guns still blazing at its attackers. Crew who had managed to jump overboard found themselves surrounded by burning oil.[52]

Berthed at the wharf, the cargo ship *Neptuna* had been transferring depth charges and explosives to HMAS *Swan*, tied alongside. Shortly before the attack, *Swan* had dropped its lines and moved away. A bomb hit *Neptuna*'s saloon, where crew were sheltering; another hit a hold filled with timber, starting a fire that was soon burning out of control. Crew, including 62 Chinese seamen, and wharfies were ordered by the skipper to abandon the blazing ship, still with 200 tonnes of depth charges and TNT in its holds. With the adjacent wharf cut off the men swam to shore, some dying in the attempt, unable to avoid the drifting pools of burning fuel.[53]

The hospital ship *Manunda*, a converted passenger liner, was ignored for 15 minutes before it was attacked by a dive-bomber. A bomb fell through the decks before exploding, killing twelve people, scattering broken glass and turning a grand piano into twisted wire. Fires broke out but were eventually extinguished. *Manunda* had large red crosses on its funnel and deck. Either the pilot ignored them or, coming in at a low angle, didn't see them.[54]

Halfway into town to meet the air marshal, Group Captain Scherger heard anti-aircraft gunfire. Stopping, he saw the Japanese air armada. He turned around and tore back to the base. Barely inside the main gate, a Zero's strafing run just missed his car as the plane screamed over the top. Scherger sprinted over to nearby long grass and lay there until the attack was over.[55]

'It was all over in less than 30 minutes,' recalls Bob Heppel, the young gunner. 'I didn't have time to be frightened during the raid, and the reaction afterwards was one of sheer exhaustion. We just sat down in our pit. Then we started to get frightened. We realised that there would be more raids, and you wondered whether you would survive the next one.'[56]

The 'All Clear' sounded ten minutes after the last Japanese plane had disappeared. Civilians and servicemen were already taking small craft out on the harbour to rescue bodies from the fiery sea. Some were pulled from the flames, badly burned, and taken to Darwin Hospital. The dead were placed on a handcart and taken to the hospital mortuary.

Much of the emergency work was carried out by ARP wardens ignoring their own strike, along with other volunteers pitching in. Working on a service launch for flying boats when the planes arrived, John Waldie took the boat and a deckhand out while the attack was still under way. The pair were still picking up men, 30 to the boatload, and pulling crowded lifeboats into shore well after the raid ended.[57]

A continuous rumbling came from the burning *Neptuna*, glowing red alongside the wharf. Eventually it exploded with a ferocity that shook the town. Smoke and flames climbed in a column, billowing high over the ship. Pieces of decking were thrown into the air while *Neptuna* rolled over and sank.[58]

After the 'All Clear', Acting Area Commander Scherger found three undamaged Hudsons and ordered a search for the enemy's carriers somewhere out in the Timor Sea. Scherger instructed Batchelor airfield to arm its Wirraways and American A-24 dive-bombers and stand by for when the carriers were located.[59]

At the same time, a telephone engineer, Harry Hawke, had been to the badly damaged telephone office, rescued a Morse key and relay, taken them up to the Lands and Survey Office, which had emergency power and telegraph lines, and sent a message down the line to Alice Springs 40 minutes after the raid ended.

'We have just had bombing raid which appeared centred on & near postal buildings causing much damage & several lives lost many injured,' the message read. 'Cursory inspection reveals post office & PMs residence completely wrecked. Cannot locate postmaster but saw bodies what appears be his daughter & female telephonists . . . the scene of destruction at PO is most nerve wracking.'[60]

By grim contrast, some Territorians refused to be inconvenienced any more than necessary. A road gang had watched the raid from a secluded spot on The Esplanade, then resumed work laying drainage pipes when the raid ended. Stopping for lunch, they returned complaining they couldn't get a meal.[61]

Others too were picking up the pieces after the attack. The Department of Civil Aviation (DCA) operations building at Parap was a mess. The ceiling fan was dangling, the walls crumbling in places. Transmitter lines were open but there was no power. Bruce Acland went to AWA's coastal radio station and was sending a damage report to head office in Melbourne when a shout went out that more planes were coming.[62]

Two hours after the morning raiders arrived, a lookout on the depot ship HMAS *Platypus* saw a new air attack approaching from the northwest, a formation of 27 heavy bombers. *Platypus* sounded the air-raid siren and army headquarters advised RAAF Operations that they appeared to be heading for the air base.[63]

They were right. The bombers ignored the town and flew straight to the military airfield. At the same time, a second force, also of twin-engine bombers in V formation, came in from the opposite direction. Both came from newly established air bases on occupied islands in the Dutch East Indies, one from Celebes, the other from Ambon.[64] Flying across each other at different altitudes in perfect formation as if a star attraction at an air show, they released a pattern of bombs. Having swept once over the base, each formation circled around and came in from the opposite direction.[65]

These bombs were bigger than those in the earlier raid, each exploding with a deafening roar and a flash of yellow flames, sending out a violent pressure wave and hurling concrete, metal and wooden debris in all directions. Pandemonium ruled for those on the ground. Storage buildings and workshops, barracks and mess halls and the military hospital were all badly damaged.[66]

Most of the civilians working at the air base had not been allocated trenches or steel helmets. One of them, Bob Andrew, was caught in the open when the bombing started. 'You just lay low and hoped there wasn't a bomb with your name on it,' he recalls.

'Like most things in war it was the luck of the draw. There were two or three fellas killed near where my mate and I decided we'd better lie down.'[67]

It was all over in little more than 20 minutes. They had arrived, meted out precision devastation and disappeared. Miraculously, only six more were killed in the second raid, this time all on the ground. Thirty aircraft were destroyed in the two raids.

Casualties were already being pulled from rubble or plucked from the harbour along with other survivors before the second raid. Steel boats ventured into flaming water for rescue work. The oil would continue burning for a day or two, high tides carrying the slick onto the foreshore. Bodies were washed ashore or in among the mangroves, where some were eaten by crocodiles. The death toll could never be calculated with certainty.

Some of the injured were taken on board the hospital ship *Manunda*. Most were transported to one of the five hospitals in Darwin, which were all short of equipment and medical supplies. Many of the injured were badly burnt, their peeling skin smeared with fuel oil. The oil was cleaned off under general anaesthetic and the burns covered with sterile Vaseline on gauze. The X-ray machine at the army hospital had been disabled in the attack, leaving medicos to assess fractures by touch. There were no supplies for blood transfusions. Medical officers improvised treatment, working through the day and into the night. When emergency batteries ran down, they worked under torchlight.[68]

Outside on the streets of Darwin people bustled about taking stock of the attack. They had anticipated its arrival, but its ferocity was unexpected. The devastation was most pronounced on and around the harbour, where most of the casualties occurred, and at the air force base. Apart from the cluster of government buildings, the town itself was relatively unscathed, the army barracks virtually untouched. There was no obvious panic, no screaming or yelling or fighting to get hold of a car. People were moving around in Darwin's streets, disorderly and directionless in many cases, but not panicked.

As administrator, the highest civil authority in the Territory, Aubrey Abbott dithered, expecting the military to take control. Although a follow-up invasion seemed likely, General Blake saw no reason to take charge as army chief; instead, he visited his coastal batteries, and after that, toured the town.[69] The senior military commander in Darwin, Group Captain Scherger, remained at the ravaged RAAF base, just out of town. Nothing came of his planned counter-attack. Communications had been destroyed in the second raid, and without ground-to-air radio the Hudsons couldn't report any sightings they might make.[70]

After the second attack, Bruce Acland and his DCA workmates loaded a transmitter and a receiver onto their utility and drove out to the RAAF base. They found its signals station deserted, the transmitter room door wide open. There were no communications people about.[71]

Men at the base were mostly technical personnel, ground crew. The few with weapons had little idea how to use them and didn't fancy their chances against the Japanese marines expected any time soon. Already, the sight of two pilots bailing out had triggered a rumour that paratroops were landing.

Returning to Area Command from his abandoned counter-attack, Scherger was told by his base commander that, with a further raid expected and the warning siren smashed, the men would be fed off the base. Wing Commander Griffith gave a verbal order for all men to move half a mile down the main road, then half a mile inland to be fed there. It was a detailed instruction begging to be distorted in passing from person to person, and that's what happened.[72]

RAAF mechanic Murry Lawson describes his experience on the day: 'An order came to go down the road a mile, then another mile and regroup there. Some of us did that and there was no one there.'[73] Half a mile had become a mile. He says his group went back to the base. Most didn't.

The air force men interpreted the order as one not to regroup but to 'go bush'. The specifics of the order got lost in the absence of any coherent leadership, lost in a rumour that the base was being abandoned, lost in the need to get away. Officers and non-commissioned officers (NCOs) joined the other ranks moving down the Stuart Highway, merging with a civilian exodus already heading south. Some got lifts with army trucks.

One RAAF officer saw a clearly rattled Sturt Griffith driving around the base in a staff car. 'I asked him what we should do,' he recalls. 'He held up his hands and drove off.'[74]

Eventually, late in the afternoon, Griffith worked out what had happened and ordered the men be brought back. A few officers who hadn't left went into the bush and brought back those stragglers they could find. Some had hidden in the bush near the base, coming out in the evening to eat. Many continued walking and hitchhiking south, camping by the side of the road.[75]

The DCA radio operators had gone on to the main transmitter at the location known as Eleven Mile, hooked their receiver into it and opened a watch for civil aircraft in the area. Later, three RAAF operators arrived and opened their own watch.

The attack of 19 February 1942 was the first time a war had reached Australia. A newspaper poll shortly before had found over half of Australia believed a Japanese invasion was possible—not just a raid, but an invasion.[76] In the reverberations of the second attack, rumours spread through Darwin that an invasion would follow, that the two air raids were softening up the town for a landing in force. Singapore had fallen four days before and the Dutch East Indies was coming under Japanese control. Again, why wouldn't they press on to Darwin?

There wasn't a comprehensive Air Raid Precautions plan to deal with an attack like this: Aubrey Abbott had overridden much of its planning in the previous couple of months. But what he did attend to immediately, in case the place was going to be invaded, was the evacuation of all remaining women, the few old men and the wounded. The chief ARP warden was tasked with overseeing the process. A train was to be brought to Parap station to take evacuees south. Police were to ensure orderly departure. On his way to army headquarters for assistance, Abbott saw cars queued at a petrol station. He put a stop to further sales.[77]

The expectation that the Japanese might land the next day and slaughter whoever was still in Darwin festered in the collective mind, both civilian and military. Police patrols, ARP wardens and army officers were telling civilians to leave town. Some insisted martial law had been proclaimed. 'Every man for himself' became the driving force amid a breakdown of military control and rumours the army was evacuating. People fled, leaving half-finished drinks and untouched lunches, beds unmade, doors wide open.

Reg Weston was an army contractor, driving trucks. 'I thought, well I'm not going to stay here and be shot or taken prisoner, there wasn't much future in that,' he says. 'We had nothing to fight with. I had one .303, being in the VDC [Volunteer Defence Corps]. That was the only rifle between four of us.'[78]

No longer the short-sighted manufacturers of fragile toys and Mickey Mouse tools, the Japanese were now ruthless, bloodthirsty fanatics, well armed and remorseless. The shopkeepers and clerks of Darwin were not going to stay and confront such unequal odds. There was only one way out of town: road and rail ran south for 500 kilometres to the Larrimah railhead. The remaining 1000 kilometres to Alice Springs were by road only, boggy in many places from monsoonal downpours.

By early afternoon, men were streaming down the Stuart Highway by whatever means available. Not a stampede as many have since described it, but certainly an exodus, which is not the same thing. A few possessions clutched under their arms or stowed on vehicles, they left on foot, horse or bicycle, in cars or lorries if they still had fuel. A road grader had nine men clinging to its side; an ice-cream vendor had a box of block ice still strapped to the front of his bicycle. A night cart would later follow them, carrying official documents.[79] The destination of this surreal cavalcade was the army rest camp at Adelaide River, 110 kilometres away. The human river included servicemen, both Australian and American, officers as well as enlisted men. The exodus would come to be disparagingly called the Adelaide River Stakes, when it was later characterised as a panicked dash for safety.

Half the population left Darwin that afternoon or soon after. About a thousand stayed behind. From a temporary office he set up in police headquarters, the Territory's administrator ordered a cafe be taken over and set up as a food kitchen for those civilians still in town. A team was sent out to scour shops and cafes for suitable food left behind, which volunteers cooked up in a huge stew. By 4 p.m., meals were being served for the shipwrecked and the homeless.[80]

The people designated by Abbott for evacuation were brought by army truck to Parap, where a freight train of flat-top rail trucks and cattle trucks was standing by. Mattresses and sheets, taken from Darwin Hotel, had been brought to the railway station, and a Parap shopkeeper offered clothes and food from his store. A man from Civil Defence issued passes to designated people who boarded and looked for a spot to settle down with what personal belongings they'd been allowed to bring with them.[81]

Before long, young men began arriving, pushing roughly past the women. Their numbers grew and police, unable to control the developing chaos, called for armed protection. Two military police arrived and fired into the ground around the troublemakers. That problem subsided, but not the resolve to leave.[82]

Late in the afternoon, a shout went out to take cover from a coming air attack. The train pulled out abruptly, only half-full but with its intended passengers on board, and began its 30-hour crawling journey to Larrimah. All Darwin's women, apart from army nurses, were evacuated that day. The air raid turned out to be another false alarm.[83]

Back in the town, Sergeant Major Macarthur-Onslow of the Provost Corps (military police) had barged into police headquarters, drunk and brandishing a revolver. 'Martial law has been proclaimed,' he said, although it hadn't. 'You have to take orders from us!'[84]

In the vacuum, the provosts prowled the streets of Darwin. With the authority of uniform and revolver, they threw their weight around, threatening civilians with their guns, a law unto themselves throughout the afternoon and evening.

Macarthur-Onslow spent the latter part of the day at Parap railway station, where he and other provosts who had been drinking fired indiscriminately over the heads of people milling about, although none were causing any real trouble.[85] Macarthur-Onslow and Lieutenant Pye, another drunken provost, egged each other on. Pye was second-in-command of Darwin's Provost Corps.

Abbott sent the judge, Thomas Wells, to Parap to investigate reports of trouble there. 'Macarthur-Onslow was there. He was even drunker than usual,' Wells says. 'He was pretty bad, and most of the Provost Corps, as far as I could see, were all in a pretty bad state.'[86]

At dusk, Pye and Macarthur-Onslow moved down to a picket turning cars back to ease the pressure expected to be building at Adelaide River. The two began stopping cars and trucks by shooting out their headlights. When eventually they returned to their command base, both were arrested by Pye's immediate superior, and subsequently court-martialled.[87]

It wasn't an isolated incident. In the absence of leadership, spot fires sprang up. With civilians having left Darwin and unlikely to return, servicemen had been sent to look for materials needed for the war effort. Supplies from the south had always been unreliable and insufficient. Goods and equipment left behind in homes and businesses could be put to good defence use. Food that would otherwise perish was also scooped up but, as evening fell, 'defence use' took on a looser meaning. It began to include home furniture and personal belongings taken to command rooms and living quarters.

Men, mostly army and a majority of them from the Provost Corps, started looting liquor shores. Through the night the looters rampaged. Stuff was taken for personal gain and things that weren't of interest were just vandalised for the sake of it. Crystal glassware was smashed, favourite knick-knacks broken, drawers emptied on the floor, photos and papers torn up. Clothes the men wouldn't wear were ripped up or thrown to one side. Commanders in the camps near town made no attempt to control the plunderers.[88]

After the first attack, the Abbotts had returned to Government House, shaken but recovering their poise. A Civil Defence official informed Hilda Abbott all women, including her, should be evacuated as soon as possible. She packed clothes and left in the official car just before the second raid, with her cook, a chauffeur and two maids. A policeman was detailed to drive them to Adelaide River.

Hilda Abbott was perceived by Territorians as haughty; but she would win some approval for roughing it, sleeping on a tarpaulin in an Adelaide River garden, then travelling by train to Larrimah in an open goods wagon under canvas. The remainder of the journey to Alice Springs by army truck was no more comfortable.[89]

Aubrey Abbott returned to Government House around 2.30 p.m. Noting the cellar doors had been forced, he sent in a policeman with a torch to see if his liquor was still there. It was, so Constable Leo Law was instructed to pack it into a police car and take it to Flagstaff House, General Blake's residence. Abbott assisted for a short time before returning to his temporary office.[90]

Superintendent Alan Stretton of Darwin Police was instructed to provide a sergeant and two constables to pack and remove 'government property' to be taken to Alice Springs. There were fifteen police in Darwin; the administrator had commandeered four of them. He wanted his crockery, glassware and silverware packed, and told the sergeant to get a police truck. When Sergeant Littlejohn returned to say no truck was available, Abbott settled for packing the belongings in readiness for when one was. By the time packing was completed, it was getting dark. The packed goods were left overnight with a constable on guard while Abbott took his silverware and a coffee service with the liquor to the general's house, where he would stay that night.[91]

After dinner with Blake, Abbott met with Darwin's four bank managers. When the raid started, bank staff had moved tills and cash boxes into strongrooms before going to shelter. Staff of

ES&A Bank and a customer had stayed in the strongroom during the attack, jamming the door open with a ledger.

Anticipating further attacks, the administrator instructed the managers to move cash and records out of Darwin that night. Abbott had suggested one manager escort them to Alice Springs; but the Commonwealth Bank's manager insisted each of them should escort his own bank's property, ensuring at the same time their evacuation from the danger zone. Cash, securities, bonds and scrip worth hundreds of thousands of pounds were loaded in pitch dark on a three-ton truck and taken to the railway station at Parap. Bank staff remained in Darwin with no instructions; the managers were assured by Abbott that their people would be evacuated within 48 hours.

The 1500-kilometre journey to Alice took five days on a flat-top rail truck and an open army truck; the four managers carried revolvers, for which they had had no training, and took turns to sleep. On arrival, the four banks set up new branches in Alice Springs wherever they could find office space. The Commonwealth Bank took over a large cell in a disused gaol. The ES&A Bank eventually moved to Adelaide and operated its Darwin office from there.[92]

Darwin Hospital's chief medical officer had asked the army to provide a surgical team, but none arrived. Instead, after midnight, the army's senior medical officer ordered all patients to be transferred to its new hospital at Berrimah, 15 kilometres away. The doctors believed patients were better left where they were, but this was overruled by the military, who feared that Larrakeyah Barracks, located near the hospital, would be bombed in the morning.

Three hundred civilian and service patients were carried out on stretchers during the night, loaded on ambulance trucks and taken to Berrimah. One, taken directly from the operating theatre, vomited all the way. Four of the ambulances were used as emergency surgeries. The new hospital was soon overcrowded.

Military hospitals had also been built inland in the Territory at Adelaide River and Katherine, although they then had little food and no beds, linen or other necessities of a functioning hospital. Less urgent cases were transferred further south to these two facilities while Darwin's abandoned homes were searched for the needed materials.[93]

Some patients still remaining at Darwin Hospital and some serious cases at Berrimah were transferred to the battered *Manunda* to be evacuated to Fremantle. The ship left just before midnight on the day after the raid. By the time it got to its destination six days later, nineteen of the patients had died and been buried at sea.[94]

The army wasn't just moving hospital patients; it was also moving itself. Infantry started surreptitiously leaving Larrakeyah Barracks before dawn, and General Blake let it be known in the morning that he'd decided to move the army back from the shoreline. If Japanese forces landed behind a neck on the Darwin promontory known as The Narrows, they could isolate the town and its defenders. By the following day all troops, apart from anti-aircraft gunners, had left Darwin. Rumour had become fact.[95]

Blake set up an Advanced Command in a camp in the bush at 22 Mile, 35 kilometres down the road from Darwin, with a Rear Command at Coomalie Creek, 60 kilometres further on. Dropping the defence front line back past The Narrows left all unarmed civilians still living and working in the town, including Bruce Acland, in a potential battle zone . . . along with the military's supplies. There was a depot at Adelaide River, but most supplies were still kept in town at the former Vestey's meatworks. Trucks went forward each day for rations.

The army needed more men. A road block had been set up at Adelaide River and, as civilian refugees drifted down, they were stopped and assessed medically. About 500 went through this procedure, with over 250 called up for military duty. The rest continued south by rail and road.

While Darwin emptied of servicemen, the civilians still in no-man's-land were busy cleaning up the devastated town, assisted by surviving wharfies and merchant seamen marooned there. A foreman went to the RAAF base to recover the Public Works grader and found it had been driven to Adelaide River.[96]

Civil Aviation's Ted Betts took a team with gear from Eleven Mile down to Katherine to set up their main communications station. Acland and two others stayed in Darwin and set up an emergency station in a Chinese shop in Parap, using an aircraft transmitter and a receiver powered by batteries.[97]

An army officer warned Acland they were expecting an invasion. 'Darwin's a sort of peninsula,' the radio operator recounts, 'and we were told there was a line drawn at a point just a little bit down the track . . . and that was going to be their first line of defence. "We'll give you as much warning as we can, but if you don't hear, or get past that barrier in time, well, too late, son!"'[98]

Bodies were decomposing on the shore, food was rotting, homeless dogs and cats prowled and howled at night. Aubrey Abbott returned to Government House in the morning after the raid to supervise packing. He found soldiers had raided his pantry and held a dinner party in his home. Military ribbons had been carelessly left behind. On his way out, the administrator said to Superintendent Stretton, 'You'd better arrange to get the body of Mary [Daisy] Martin out.'[99] She was the maid crushed in the bomb blast.

The expected invasion never came, but the looting continued. Provosts made little attempt to impose law and order and some led marauding groups. Unoccupied houses were raided by souvenir-hunting servicemen. Before long, those still in Darwin were coming home to find their place comprehensively turned over. Most of the looted property initially went to Australian and American military camps. Later, when shipping operations resumed, goods would be taken in army lorries to sell to sailors at the wharf.

John Selman's house was only slightly damaged in the raid, but he returned from work the next night to find handles had been broken off his knives and forks, drawers pulled out and smashed against a glass door, a wedding dress torn to pieces.[100] Evacuated to Adelaide, 71-year-old Florenz Blesser left behind books, annotated flora and fauna specimens and photographic plates, collected over 50 years. They were thrown out of his house, trampled and destroyed.[101]

On 21 February, all of the Northern Territory north of Alice Springs was put under military control, although it continued under civil law. Judge Wells remained in Darwin with judicial powers, while Aubrey Abbott and the Territory's administration were relocated to Alice Springs. General Blake appointed one of his officers, Major Anderson, as Darwin mayor.[102] In his new civic role, Anderson issued 'licences to loot'. Although they didn't reduce the indiscriminate nature of much of the looting, they did enable some of its victims to be later compensated by the government.

When Ossie Jensen, an electrician, returned to his shop, he found soldiers loading his batteries onto an army truck.

'What do you think you're doing?' he asked.

'You'll get paid,' he was told and was shown a 'chit' authorising them to take away anything the army might need. Jensen received a cheque in payment a few months later.

He wasn't so lucky with his three utility trucks, commandeered by army officers as staff cars. After Jensen joined the army, one of the officers gave him a lift. He pointed out the truck they were in was actually one of his.

'It might've been,' said the officer. 'It's the army's now!'[103]

Jensen didn't get paid for his trucks as they had been taken without anyone going to the trouble of getting a 'licence to loot'.

An ABC mobile unit had sent out a message in the first few minutes of the raid that an attack was under way. Shortly after, the broadcaster shut down. In the aftermath of the raid, Harry Hawke was soon working his patched-up system in the Lands and Survey Office, and DCA had its team operating at Eleven Mile. The navy, its radio station damaged, set up a makeshift cable office for military traffic. Some of that information was passed on to government.

The Australian government's Advisory War Council met in Sydney on 19 February and debated the fate of the AIF 7th Division, then at sea returning from the Middle East. The issue was whether it should be landed at Burma, as Churchill proposed, or brought back to Australia as the government wished. The meeting broke for an air raid practice in the Commonwealth Bank building. On their return, Minister for Supply and Shipping Jack Beasley announced, 'The Japs have bombed Darwin! That settles it!'[104]

John Curtin, absent from the meeting and in Sydney's St Vincent's Hospital for a few days, issued a statement from hospital. 'Australia has now experienced physical contact of war within Australia,' it said. 'The extent of the raid and the results of the attack are not yet known. Though information did not disclose details of casualties, it must be obvious that we have suffered.'[105]

The next day, Minister for Air Arthur Drakeford issued a press release with some details. There were two raids, the statement said, bombing and machine-gunning the township, wharves and shipping and the RAAF base. Damage and casualties were understated, possibly deliberately but it's possible also that the military was withholding this detail from its government.[106] Chief of Air Staff Charles Burnett flew to Darwin on 22 February, reporting back that twelve servicemen had been killed. He made no mention of civilian casualties, looting or the exodus.[107]

The press relied initially on government communiqués, but soon had access to other sources. Radio messages were picked up overnight. The next morning, Brisbane's *Courier-Mail* was telling the story of the American pilot Robert Oestreicher's escape into the clouds. The same paper had access the following day to eye-witness accounts from passengers on a Qantas flying boat that had escaped damage in the raid and flown to Townsville.[108]

On 21 February the *Courier-Mail* detailed the attack formation and the post office deaths, but understated damage and casualties, quoting instead another Drakeford communiqué that there was 'no vital damage to Darwin air stations' and that Australian planes had attacked the raiders with no reported damage in combat.[109] The Qantas passengers would have known the death toll was dramatically higher than the nineteen acknowledged, and known of damage to the wharf, of *Neptuna* exploding and probably of devastation of the two airfields. There was no mention of looting or the exodus in the report either, but looting was in its early stages when they flew out and those evacuees were unlikely to be critical of people leaving by a different route.

Reporting for the Melbourne *Herald*, Darwin journalist Douglas Lockwood wrote a story about the raid as soon as it was over and took it to the telegraph office. He found there was no longer a telegraph office. Jumping on a flat-top truck on the train to Katherine the next day, Lockwood sent his story from the post office there. It was never printed, although *The Herald* could draw on its details within restrictions imposed by the chief censor.[110] A few days later, the prime minister would acknowledge publicly that information about the Darwin raid was being limited for national security. 'I do not propose to inform [the enemy] of the degree of success or failure which marked the attack,' he explained.[111]

Newspapers offset this limited information with calls to arms, probably with encouragement. The Curtin government saw an opportunity to mobilise a wavering public to the war effort, regardless of its own assessment of the likelihood of Japanese invasion. There was both a real fear and an insurance policy in play.

The *Sydney Morning Herald* announced that 'opening shots in the Battle of Australia were fired on the mainland yesterday'.[112]

'The Government regards the attacks as most grave and makes it clear that a severe blow has been struck on Australian soil,' Melbourne's *Age* added.[113]

The *Newcastle Herald* was equally strident in its editorial that day: 'The falling of bombs on the Australian mainland will destroy whatever shred of complacency lingered in this country. It will cause no dismay and raise no doubts. If it underlines the very real peril in which the whole of Australia now stands, that will but steel the resolution of the people to defend their homeland.'[114]

The Adelaide *Advertiser* pumped up the rhetoric even more. 'The noise of Japanese bombs bursting in Darwin cannot be ignored,' it editorialised, 'if Australia is not to share the fate of the enemy-occupied countries of this war-torn world.'[115]

In contrast, the *Courier-Mail* had an anonymous 'War Commentator' assessing Japan's strategy as 'to close in upon Java and to cut the supply lines by which reinforcements can reach the Dutch. An essential part of the plan to encircle Java would, therefore, be the neutralisation of Darwin.'[116] This writer saw the raids as a prelude to invading Timor, which proved to be the case. There was no mention of invading Darwin or anywhere else in Australia.

Administrator Abbott cabled the Department of the Interior in Canberra on 24 February with the message, in part, 'Darwin now normal and essential services in hand.' The next day he cabled, 'Darwin quite normal', and a day later, 'Everything normal'. He would later claim he didn't want news of looting to leak out.[117]

On 27 February, Abbott changed his tune, reporting confusion after the raid, 'greatly accentuated by unauthorised actions by various service sections, including Provost Corps. Discipline was very bad, men were drunk . . .' He estimated 300 killed, including ship's crew. None of this was released to the press.[118]

What got out to the public via the embargoed press was a mishmash of the Darwin bombing. Snippets of heroism and suppression of the worst were spiced up with wild rumours that came and went: Darwin was in flames; thousands had been killed; Japanese aircraft disguised with American markings had bombed hospitals; soldiers were shooting looters and deserters; the Japanese were heading for Sydney.

Yesterday's rumours were replaced by today's whispers. In truth, the public had at best a patchy knowledge of the attack. Curtailing news about Darwin had the advantage for the government of covering its failure to prepare for it, the failure of military leadership in response to it, and the Territory administration's bungling and confusion.

The fear of invasion was boosted in some sections of the public, brooding about the consequences of such a calamity, while others continued in their belief that it would somehow turn out fine, as it always did. As Swan Hill schoolgirl Margaret Maxwell put it years later, 'I always felt we'd win because we won the other war, and I was brought up on that.'[119]

In Sydney, eleven-year-old Yve Jeanneret had followed the conversations of her parents, glued to the radio as the Japanese moved closer. 'I think it really hit home with the bombing of Darwin,' she says. 'My parents became more engrossed and more apprehensive. They're on our shores! I suppose by then I was listening to the radio too.'[120]

For other Australians in the populated parts, the unpreparedness was a matter of some concern, but Darwin was still a long way away. No one actually went there. 'We thought of Darwin as a very remote part of Australia,' says the Brisbane teacher Robert Brown. 'We thought mainly of cattle-raising and that sort of thing in the Territory. We hadn't thought of Darwin as the protective outpost.'[121]

The Japanese invaded Timor on 20 February, the day after they bombed Darwin, and landed at three places in Java a week later. For a fortnight there was no further attack on Darwin, neither air raid nor attempt to land an invasion force. The respite was used by the remaining population to prepare for meeting an attack when it did come. That was not going to be achieved overnight.

Four days after the Darwin bombing, a muster at the RAAF base revealed 278 men still missing. After a couple of weeks, most of the officers and men had come back from the bush and some order was being restored at the base. Construction was accelerated on an order dating back to before the attack, to develop ten new aerodromes in the north of the Territory.[122]

For a month, there was no fighter cover for Darwin. In mid-March, a squadron of USAAF Kittyhawks arrived, then two more squadrons a month later. By then, 60 fighters were defending the north. The newly developed radar was operational at Dripstone Caves, north of Darwin, giving 30 minutes warning of approaching attacks. Although it was initially treated with scepticism, its reliability changed attitudes. By the end of 1942, there were six radar posts.[123]

After the attack, there was only enough ammunition for the twelve Vickers machine guns to fire for five minutes. 'Had the expected landing occurred, the battle would have been short and disastrous,' says gunner Rex Ruwoldt. 'All we could do was sit here and wait for it to happen.'[124]

On 4 March, the Japanese did come back. Nine Zeros from a captured airfield in Timor strafed the RAAF station, damaging its control tower. With no casualties, the attack was minor compared to a raid the day before on Broome, the remote pearling town in northwestern Australia.

Broome had become a stopover for military planes and flying boats shuttling between the Dutch East Indies and Perth as Japan's grip around Java tightened. Believed to be beyond the range of Japanese planes, as it was until the capture of Timor, the town had no anti-aircraft guns and no fighter cover. By late February, Broome was overflowing with refugees and military personnel. People slept where they could, waiting for connecting flights.

The morning of 3 March was warm and sunny, with sixteen Qantas and KLM flying boats moored on Broome's Roebuck Bay. Some of these aircraft were over a kilometre out from shore; others were sitting on mud, waiting for the tide to rise. Women and children evacuating from the Dutch colony had slept overnight on board.

Nine Zeros appeared over the bay at 9.30 in the morning, sweeping in low to attack the moored planes with machine-gun and cannon fire. The bay was soon ablaze from aviation fuel. Women and children not killed in the gunfire escaped from burning planes into the fiery sea. A Liberator evacuating wounded

Americans from Java had just taken off after refuelling and was shot down off Cable Beach.

The strike on Roebuck Bay was over in fifteen minutes. An undamaged refuelling tender moved around the burning surface rescuing survivors, while the Zeros moved on to Broome's airfield. Six bombers and transports standing there were hit and left in flames. The attackers had gone by 10.30, leaving no operational aircraft and killing at least 88.[125]

Human remains began washing up on the beach of Roebuck Bay. Dutch aircrew, having spent the night on shore, refused to help bury the dead. According to Broome journalist Cyril Longmore, they went into a 'curious apathy' and, along with Australian officials, 'went down to the hotels and drank beer all afternoon'. A convoy left town, heading for Perth; but it was forced back, the roads impassable after recent heavy rain.[126]

With stories circulating about the Darwin attack, Curtin wanted to issue an authoritative statement about casualties. Consulting with service chiefs of staff, he was advised that it was not in the national interest, giving the enemy valuable information and setting a precedent.[127] Graphic details of the Darwin raid were kept from the public until December 1942, when they were included in the Australian War Memorial's annual publication, *Soldiering On*.[128]

The Darwin and Broome attacks marked the beginning of nearly two years of Japanese air raids on Northern Australia's mainland and offshore islands. The targets ranged from Exmouth Gulf in the west to Townsville in the east, and as far inland as the 300 kilometres to Katherine. There were 97 air attacks in that time, but none were a prelude to invasion, and none matched the scale of the first attack, the only one by carrier-borne aircraft. At that time, Darwin was thought by the Japanese to be a major Allied base.

Mitsuo Fuchida, who led the attack, would comment after the war, 'It seemed hardly worthy of us. If ever a sledgehammer was used to crack an egg, it was then.'[129] On the other hand, an RAAF officer said with disgust at the time, 'A hundred Japs armed with frying pans could have occupied Australia that day.'[130]

On 3 March, twelve days after the Darwin raid, Justice Charles Lowe was appointed to head a royal commission into circumstances connected with the attack, and to recommend changes necessary to meet a future attack. A judge in the Supreme Court of Victoria, Lowe conducted hearings during March in Darwin—while looters still roamed the streets outside—and Melbourne, before submitting a first report on 27 March and a briefer supplementary report on 9 April. The gist of his findings was that Darwin suffered from a lack of military and civil leadership, and that its defences were inadequate. Few came out of his report with much credit.[131]

The report was not made public until after the war, and transcripts of the commission's testimony remained secret until 1977. Service chiefs were given access to the reports but not the transcripts. Its findings on the number of fatalities appeared in the Melbourne *Herald* on 30 March 1942.[132] Lowe found 240 people had been killed in the attack, although he speculated the actual number might be nearer 300. Amid claims that the government had been suppressing the truth, Curtin explained to the nation that national security precautions prevented an earlier statement of numbers killed and shipping losses, which would then have been of value to the enemy.

The 'panic evacuation' south ran through the rumour mill and grew as a post-war story, fuelled by the catchphrase 'Adelaide River Stakes' and a speech made in Darwin by Paul Hasluck, then

Minister for Territories. He labelled 19 February 'the anniversary of a day of national shame'.[133]

It's a harsh judgement when invasion by a large and brutal force was thought imminent and civilians were advised by authorities to leave town. They responded much as people anywhere would have, but perhaps not with the unruffled composure and laconic stoicism Australians sometimes imagine of themselves. As Territory historian Alan Powell has put it, 'The people of Darwin performed no worse than other human beings in similar situations; the real problem might be that they performed no better.'[134]

Chapter 5

GREAT AND POWERFUL FRIENDS

A little after midnight, early in March 1942, Frank Green was heading home after a marathon session of the House of Representatives, where he was Clerk of the House. Walking by the fence of The Lodge, the prime minister's official residence in Canberra, he slipped through a gap in the wire. The Lodge had no guard in those days, but Green wasn't just passing by. An old Perth friend of John Curtin, he had been told by the PM's driver that Curtin hadn't slept for several days, instead spending the night pacing about the grounds of The Lodge. Frank Green decided to investigate and see what he could do about it.

He found the prime minister roaming the moonlit garden, feverishly puffing on a cigarette and fiddling with its holder, as if a messenger was expected any moment.

'Jack, you should get some sleep.'

The two stood in silence on the lawn for a while. Then Curtin said, 'How can I sleep while our men are out in the Indian Ocean . . . surrounded by Jap submarines?'

Green tried to talk him into going to bed, but Curtin would have none of it, instead agreeing to go to The Lodge's kitchen with his friend and share a convivial pot of tea. Not a great deal was said. There wasn't much to be added to the fellowship of two men who'd known each other a long time. When the pot was finished, Green went home to bed and Curtin continued pacing in the Canberra night air.[1]

John Curtin was particularly on edge because he was grappling with the outcome of a cable war with Winston Churchill. In an operation spread over a couple of months, 64,000 AIF troops were being transported from the Middle East, across the submarine-infested Indian Ocean, to defend their homeland against the anticipated Japanese invasion. Their destination was Australia only because their country's leader had insisted his government would determine where its troops were deployed, prevailing over his desperate and sometimes duplicitous British counterpart. Now that they were heading home at Curtin's insistence, he felt personally responsible for the danger faced by the 70 ships making the journey. That was in John Curtin's nature.

Curtin and Churchill, their respective nation's wartime leaders, came from starkly different backgrounds. In contrast to the patrician English prime minister, the Australian was the son of an Irish immigrant who had been a low-ranked policeman eventually cashiered out of the force with arthritis and syphilis.[2] Moving between rented houses, Jack Curtin had left school early, but educated himself after work, developing a passion for socialism and Australian Rules football. Working as a journalist, mostly on union newspapers, he was an inspiring soapbox orator on Melbourne's Yarra Bank and soon became involved with the Australian Labor Party. He had been unexpectedly elected leader of the faction-ridden ALP in 1935 and had managed to pull it together as a cohesive political force.

Dealing with depression, nervous stomach ailments and periodic bouts of alcoholism throughout his life, he found sanctuary in family life, settling eventually with his wife and two children in a red-brick bungalow at Cottesloe in Perth. The fervent idealist switched between optimism and melancholy. He was not a man for risqué banter and his swearing was mild at its worst; but he was not a wowser, and he was notably congenial and tolerant.

Jack Curtin often doubted his own ability, but when he became prime minister—and became John Curtin—he showed the decisiveness, imperturbability and self-confidence widely believed to be lacking in him. Nonetheless, he wore his heart on his sleeve, taking as a personal burden the impact of decisions he made. The pressure of his battle of wills with the British leader between January and March 1942 may have shored up his nation against the expected invasion, but it would have a lasting impact on his health.

John Curtin's sleepless nights had their origins almost a year before this. In the overlapping of the wars, forces committed to one part of the world had become necessary in another. In mid-1941, before the war with Japan began, Tobruk had been the only battlefield where British forces were successfully resisting the Germans. Held grimly by the AIF 9th Division—the renowned 'Rats of Tobruk'—the town's defenders were close to exhaustion. The AIF's 6th Division was recuperating after being driven out of Greece and Crete; and its 7th Division was fighting the Vichy French in Syria and Palestine.

General Thomas Blamey, Australia's Middle East commander, argued that Tobruk's defenders should be relieved, and that the AIF should operate as a single force and not be spread across the Middle East and North Africa. Menzies put that to Churchill, who rejected it as mere political expedience to mollify the

Australian electorate.[3] When Menzies was replaced as Australia's prime minister, his successor, Arthur Fadden, reiterated the request. Sensing a greenhorn leader, Churchill urged Fadden to 'weigh very carefully the immense responsibility which you would assume before history by depriving Australia of the glory of holding Tobruk till victory was won'. When Fadden rejected his argument, Churchill curtly replied, 'Orders will at once be given in accordance with your decision.'[4]

It typified Churchill's relationship with his colonial counterparts: he viewed their forces as being at his disposal. When his plans were resisted, he would work at wheedling his way around the objections. When Japan entered the war, nearly all of Australia's forces were at the English leader's disposal anyway. The Royal Australian Navy (RAN) was in the Mediterranean; the RAAF trained in Canada and operated from Britain. Apart from the 8th Division, the AIF was in the Middle East. What remained of the army in Australia was mostly part-time militia, the Citizen Military Force (CMF).

Pearl Harbor brought America fully into the war, which was welcomed by both Churchill and Hitler. The Führer anticipated the Japanese would tie down the US forces so he could defeat the Soviet Union before America could concentrate on Europe. Churchill's aim was to divert the Americans from the Pacific, concerned that a German victory in Russia would push on through Iran to the Indian Ocean and link with the advancing Japanese. On 15 December 1941, Churchill instructed his chiefs of staff to look at transferring Australia's 6th Division from the Middle East to help resist the Japanese in Malaya and reduce the need for American forces there.[5]

Relying on advice from his three military chiefs of staff, two of them seconded from Britain, Curtin made a counter proposal. A British division was then at sea off South Africa, he pointed out, and it could get to Singapore before any troops pulled out of the Middle East.[6] In the end, the British troops were reluctantly diverted to Singapore and 1800 raw recruits were sent from Australia to reinforce the AIF 8th Division in Malaya.

By the close of 1941, Churchill was again proposing the relocation of Australian troops from the Middle East to either India or Singapore. Meeting in Melbourne on 31 December, the Advisory War Council opposed sending them to India, but recommended agreeing to a transfer to the Far East, if requested. Three days later, the British government formally requested the transfer of two AIF divisions, the 6th and the 7th, to the newly formed ABDA Command in the Dutch East Indies. On 5 January, Curtin's War Cabinet approved the mass movement of Australian troops and their equipment across the Indian Ocean.[7]

Much of Churchill's strategic thinking in the Far East was directed towards ingratiation with the Americans and enlisting their support for 'beat Hitler first'. At the same time, his belief in the unlikelihood of a Japanese invasion of Australia was probably genuine. Churchill could afford to be wrong on this, but it was not a risk the Australian leader was prepared to take with the Japanese moving inexorably in his country's direction. The two men struggled to prevail in determining the deployment of Australia's forces.

Curtin was conscious that Britain might have to abandon its support for Australia if things got worse in Europe. He remarked in a letter to his wife, Elsie, in Perth, 'The war goes very badly and I have a cable fight with Churchill almost daily. He has been in Africa and India and they count before Australia and New Zealand. The truth is that Britain never thought Japan would fight and made no preparations to meet that eventuality.'[8]

In mid-January 1942, the first convoy of eight small freighters left Port Tewfik at the bottom of the Suez Canal, carrying some smaller units of the AIF's 7th Division.[9] While they steamed towards Colombo for refuelling, Britain's military heads discussed evacuating Singapore, unnerved by ABDA commander General Wavell's pessimism about its ability to be defended. An option was to sabotage the naval base and concentrate on the defence of Burma, diverting Singapore's reinforcements there. Churchill canvassed this with his Defence Committee, prompting the letter by External Affairs minister Bert Evatt in Curtin's name, protesting against such an 'inexcusable betrayal'. Although the Australians, already crossing the Indian Ocean, were not mentioned specifically, they might well have been included in the diversion plans.

That proposal was stalled, but Earle Page, Australia's minister in Britain, reported home that 'Churchill went off the deep end about Australians generally and said if they were going to squeal he would send them all home.'[10] Bluster Churchill never intended to carry out, this wouldn't have helped relations with the Australian PM. Churchill probably imagined Page would keep it to himself.

Curtin returned the barb in a radio broadcast on 26 January. 'No single nation can afford to risk its future on the infallibility of one man,' he said, 'and no nation can afford to submerge its right of speaking for itself because of the assumed omniscience of another.'[11]

With relations between Britain and Australia strained, the ocean transfer continued as planned. The converted liner *Orcades* left Port Tewfik unescorted on 1 February, carrying an advance infantry unit of 3400 men and a machine-gun battalion, but without their vehicles, guns or stores. That equipment, along with 10,900 further troops, had left on a convoy of small freighters two days earlier. While this convoy crawled to Bombay (now Mumbai) at 10 knots, *Orcades* moved at twice that speed, rapidly overtaking it and heading for Colombo.[12]

In the days that followed, 17,800 more troops were boarded on various ships to disembark at Bombay and wait there for the smaller vessels to take them the rest of the way to the Dutch East Indies. They eventually left Bombay on 13 February for refuelling at Colombo en route. Some, like the fast American tourist liner *Mount Vernon*, went directly to Colombo, its 4600 Australian troops packed on folding iron bed frames in three-deep rows in the cargo hold.[13]

The Australian commander, General John Lavarack, had flown ahead to Java to confer with ABDA's commander-in-chief, General Wavell. He took issue with Wavell's plan to spread Australian troops across the East Indies, half the 7th Division to be deployed in Java, half in Sumatra. The convoys bringing the AIF from the Middle East had been instructed to offload their troops that way.

The fighting quality of Australians is doubled if they fight side by side, Lavarack insisted to deaf ears. Blamey alerted Curtin from Cairo that the British were trying to scatter Lavarack's command.[14]

While the Australian government was dealing with this issue, another arose. By early February, with the British driven out of Malaya and Japanese forces poised to attack Singapore, Lavarack was advising General Vernon Sturdee, his chief in Melbourne, that the Dutch defences were inadequate. Without control of sea or sky, Java and Sumatra couldn't be held. Meanwhile, the freighters of the first convoy had separated into two groups and docked at those two islands.[15]

On 15 February, *Orcades* berthed in South Sumatra at Oosthaven. Troops disembarked to find Japanese paratroops had already landed and were 20 kilometres away. Men from the first convoy had been told to destroy their equipment and reboard their vessels.[16] Those from *Orcades*, their equipment still out on the ocean, also reboarded and reached Batavia (now Jakarta) two days later. Wavell rejected Lavarack's plea for the under-equipped soldiers to stay on their ship at Batavia, insisting 2000 be landed to defend aerodromes.[17] RAF and RAAF crew were taken on board in their place, and the AIF men ended up in POW camps when Java fell three weeks later.

On the day *Orcades* arrived at Sumatra, Singapore surrendered to the Japanese and the Australian chief of general staff (CGS) phoned John Curtin with the army's view that the returning troops should be brought back to Australia, along with the 9th Division still in the Middle East. Over the green Secraphone (the then state-of-the-art scrambler phone), Vernon Sturdee read out Lavarack's assessment and added that, even if Java held on, it wasn't a suitable base for an Allied counter-offensive. Australia, he argued, should be built up as the base for this campaign, with British and American soldiers joining the returning AIF.[18]

Singapore had fallen. The invasion of Australia loomed in Curtin's mind as a distinct possibility. After agonising about it overnight, he cabled Churchill with his CGS's advice and suggested the AIF, then scattered across the Indian Ocean, be diverted to Australia. The tone of this message was not demanding—perhaps with hindsight it should have been—asking only that this be considered if it was agreed the troops should not proceed to the East Indies.[19]

Even while insisting troops from *Orcades* be landed, Wavell viewed sending the AIF to Java as a 'risk unjustifiable from a tactical and strategical point of view'.[20] It should be diverted to the new priority, Burma. His advice was tabled at Churchill's Pacific Council in London, which decided Australia's 7th Division should now go to Rangoon. Earle Page, representing Australia on the council, agreed despite Curtin's cable.

Page wrote to Curtin reporting the council's decision. He recommended agreeing with it without mentioning he had already done that. Only the 7th Division could reach Rangoon in time to keep the Burma Road open, he argued, ignoring or unaware that the division's artillery and supplies were on other ships.[21] The Japanese at the time were advancing rapidly on Rangoon; but the defence of that city was in tatters, with desertions and tensions between Indian and Burmese defenders.

Churchill was bombarding Curtin from several directions on the issue of Burma's vulnerability. The Americans had always regarded the Burma Road as more strategically important than Singapore. Prompted by Churchill, Roosevelt asked the Australian government, through Richard Casey, its representative in Washington, to send two divisions to Burma or India if the United States would send 60,000 troops and equipment to Australia in March.[22]

The Americans didn't see their troops as being there to defend Australia, however. General George Marshall, the US Army's chief of staff, had already decided it was the most suitable base for the planned counter-offensive and that would be their main purpose. Defending Australia would be incidental to that.

Curtin cabled Page that the government was unlikely to change its mind. 'If you have not already done so,' he said, 'you should act at once to ensure that convoy should not (repeat not) be committed to Burma.'[23] Later in the day, the PM addressed a war loan rally in Martin Place. An hour after that, John Curtin was in Sydney's St Vincent's Hospital with gastritis from prolonged nervous strain. He was there for the next two nights.[24]

The cross-party Advisory War Council, meeting in Sydney on 19 February without the prime minister, considered Page's recommendation. Churchill had given assurances that air support for Burma was 'already in train', although it wasn't. In a debate that got acrimonious, Opposition members of the AWC supported the London decision, arguing that the Burma Road was vital to Chinese resistance to the Japanese.[25] High Commissioner Stanley Bruce had pitched in from London. Even if the Australians failed in Burma, he argued, the positive effect on Chinese morale justified their participation.[26]

The counter-argument was that Burma was on the verge of defeat and Australian soldiers without weapons or transport couldn't change that. They would end up prisoners of war, like their compatriots in Singapore, instead of defending their homeland.

News of the bombing of Darwin disrupted the debate, but the competing arguments were weighed up soon after by the government's War Cabinet. Curtin was not there again, but had made his views known. Cabinet reviewed the discussion and confirmed that the AIF should return to defend Australia against Japan's anticipated invasion.

External Affairs minister Bert Evatt drafted a cable to Page in Curtin's absence, to advise the British government that 'because NEI [Netherlands (Dutch) East Indies] is now ruled out as the agreed destination of the AIF, it should now come to Australia with the greatest possible expedition'.[27] Earle Page cabled on 20 February that the destination had not been changed to Burma and convoys had been instructed to sail to Australia.

Not fully recovered, Curtin discharged himself prematurely from St Vincent's so he could be taken to Canberra for a secret joint sitting of parliament. 'The enemy's successes to the north-west and northeast of Australia have brought the enemy to our very gates,' he told it, 'and Australia is now face to face with the likelihood of enemy attacks in force on our own shores.'[28]

At 9 p.m. that same night, Winston Churchill ordered the Admiralty to tell the troopships nearest to Burma to turn north.[29] He then cabled an appeal to Curtin that the Australian force was the only one that could get to Rangoon in time to prevent its capture.

Churchill was prepared to pull out all stops to extract Curtin's agreement, but he didn't reveal he had instructed ships to be diverted. Instead, he claimed he had put the British 18th Division in Singapore instead of Burma at Australia's insistence—it was actually heading for Egypt before its diversion—and that a refusal to agree might have 'a very grave effect' on Roosevelt's support.[30]

'I need an immediate answer,' Churchill ended the cable. 'I trust you will give the most careful consideration to the case I have set before you.'[31]

Having just been told the Japanese were 65 kilometres from Rangoon, Australia's War Cabinet met to consider Churchill's request. Landing troops there seemed an exercise in futility; the outcome could only be more Australian POWs.[32] Cabinet adhered to its original decision and Churchill was duly informed. 'I have received your rather strongly worded request at this stage, though our wishes in regard to the disposition of the AIF in the Pacific theatre have long been known to you,'[33] Curtin cabled. Australia's decision stood.

A bombshell response from Churchill confirmed all Curtin suspected about the British prime minister. 'We could not contemplate,' it ran, 'that you would refuse our request and that of the President of the United States for the diversion of the leading Australian division to save the situation in Burma. We knew that if our ships proceeded on their course to Australia while waiting for your formal approval they would either arrive too late at Rangoon or even be without enough fuel to go there at all. We therefore decided that the convoy should be temporarily diverted to the northward. The convoy is now too far north for some of the ships in it to reach Australia without refuelling.' Churchill continued that this gave Curtin an opportunity to change his mind, otherwise 'the Australian division will be returned to Australia as you wish.'[34]

Curtin was aghast. At best this was arrogant and imperious, at worst calculating and duplicitous. These were men's lives Churchill was playing with, pieces on a chessboard to appease his American allies with no realistic assessment grounding his strategy. It was all about gestures, sacrifices (by someone else) and currying favour.

With some of the vessels now needing to go back to Colombo for refuelling in order to reach Australia, the insistence on troops returning home was no longer straightforward. These ships and the men in them would be exposed to an extended threat of submarine attack. Curtin had cabled Roosevelt after his previous response to Churchill, confirming the Australian decision, explaining that his country with its small population—'the only white man's territory south of the equator'—was now directly threatened.[35] Roosevelt had not taken issue with this, but Churchill had thrown a firecracker into their midst.

John Curtin felt boxed in. He needed to give himself air and space. Strolling in the Majura hills on Canberra's north side, along dirt tracks snaking through old woodland and open forest of casuarina, yellow box and red gum, his thoughts crystallised in the softening glow of the late summer afternoon. As so often, he had to weigh up issues and risk for a nation in peril, his only company brightly coloured parrots and screeching cockatoos. He'd taken a stand against Churchill and the British military, against the American president and Opposition members of his own Advisory War Council. In support of his determination were Australia's War Cabinet and its army. He could not retreat from that stand.

At 5.45 p.m., invigorated by his ramble in the hills, Curtin wrote to Churchill, firing from both barrels. 'It appears you have diverted the convoy towards Rangoon,' he led off, 'and had treated our approval to the vital diversion as merely a matter of form. By doing so, you have established a physical situation which adds to the dangers of this convoy, and the responsibility for the consequences of such diversion rests on you.'[36]

He wasn't finished.

'Australia's outer defences are now quickly vanishing and our vulnerability is completely exposed,' he continued. 'With AIF troops we sought to save Malaya and Singapore falling back on the Netherlands East Indies. All these northern defences are gone or going. Now you contemplate using the AIF to save Burma. All this has been done as in Greece without adequate air support. We feel a primary obligation to save Australia not only for itself but to preserve it as a base for the development of the war against Japan. In the circumstances it is quite impossible to reverse a decision which we made in the utmost care and which we have affirmed and reaffirmed.'[37]

Churchill finally gave up the fight. 'Your convoy is now proceeding to re-fuel at Colombo,' he replied that night. 'It will then proceed to Australia, in accordance with your wishes.'[38]

Japanese submarines and German raiders prowled the Indian Ocean. While Winston Churchill was relieved of the tussle over Burma's defence, having run out of options, John Curtin carried a heavy emotional load and sleepless nights from his dogged insistence, until all ships reached haven in Australia. It was on one of these nights that his old Perth mate Frank Green tried to persuade him to go to bed . . . to no avail.

The first to dock was the converted tourist liner, *Mount Vernon*, at Adelaide on 9 March. Soldiers of the 6th and 7th divisions continued arriving throughout March in dribs and drabs. Over nearly three months, the 70 vessels carrying troops, equipment and vehicles safely crossed the Indian Ocean. Japanese submarines had sunk four American ships and one British, but no troopship, in this massive operation.

Late in March, scheduled trains on the Trans-Continental line and in South Australia were cancelled, to allow troops to be dispersed from Fremantle and Adelaide across the continent for leave at home before redeployment. Many went next to New Guinea.

The AIF's return was announced publicly, 'in accordance with the agreed plan of the allies'. Newspapers headlined 'The Boys are Back'.[39] Another obstacle to Japanese invasion had been put in place and an even greater one was in the early stages of being set up. Major changes were under way as part of Australia's preparation to confront a rampant enemy. Ring out the old; ring in the new!

John Curtin's sleepless nights were over . . . for the time being.

The United States was talking to the Curtin government about expanding its presence in Australia even before Japan entered the war. Wearing civilian clothes to avoid attracting attention, General Lewis Brereton of the US Army Air Force was in Australia in November 1941 to discuss a plan to fly B-17 Flying Fortresses and other large warplanes to the Philippines via northern Australia and Port Moresby. The American government offered US$18 million to upgrade airfields across the north, but events moved too fast to fully implement that plan.[40]

After Pearl Harbor, George Marshall's deputy, General Dwight Eisenhower, argued that the Philippines defence couldn't hold out and Australia should be developed as a USAAF base, building on the existing use of airfields. Marshall agreed, raising it on the agenda of December's Washington Conference of American and British military leaders.[41]

The US Joint Chiefs of Staff (JCS) approved the proposal, but American troops had arrived in Australia anyway the day the conference began. A convoy carrying 4600 troops to reinforce the Philippines garrison was diverted to Australia because of the American colony's uncertain prospects. Arriving at Brisbane on 22 December, the unit set up headquarters in Lennon's Hotel, with its men in camps on Brisbane racecourses.[42]

Richard Casey, Australia's representative in Washington, kept contact with the Americans and their visitors at the conference. Although Churchill had persuaded Roosevelt that the Allies' priority was to 'beat Hitler first, then deal with Japan', it was agreed that Australia must be held. Casey picked up that Roosevelt was keen to set up a regional command under US direction in the Pacific. The Australian recommended his government pre-empt the move by suggesting it.[43]

Curtin duly cabled Roosevelt and Churchill while they were together in Washington. 'Should United States desire we would gladly accept United States command in Pacific Ocean area', the Australian prime minister offered.[44] There was no immediate response to his overture, but the possibility continued to lurk in strategic planning in the Pacific.

Meanwhile General George Brett arrived in Brisbane on 28 December, appointed commander of all US forces in Australia. A few days later, he moved headquarters to Melbourne. Personnel started arriving from the United States soon after, building airfields in Townsville in Queensland and Deniliquin, the NSW Riverina town close to the Victorian border, with no public acknowledgement and censorship to ensure there was no mention in the press.

An acquaintance of military historian Michael McKernan related to him an incident in January 1942, while her father was away at the war. After helping her mother and brother put up blackout screens in their Melbourne home, she heard the tramp of marching feet. It wasn't the familiar metallic sound of Australian soldiers. She wondered if they were British or American, or even Japanese, but no one in the house dared look outside. They were actually Americans marching along Dandenong Road to a camp at Caulfield Racecourse, but this family had no idea American soldiers were in the country.[45] Huge camps soon sprung up in parklands, schools and sports grounds in Melbourne and Brisbane; there for all to see, but the press continued to appear not to have noticed.

By February, it was clear that the US forces in the Philippines were doomed, despite the earlier optimism of their commander, General Douglas MacArthur. Marshall agreed with Eisenhower's proposal to expand the base in Australia by committing ground troops to its defence. On 14 February, after consultation with the host nation, the US Joint Chiefs ordered the 41st Infantry Division to Australia.

On 25 February, the ill-fated ABDA Command was dissolved, having overseen the loss of Malaya and Singapore, and left Java, Sumatra and Burma as inevitable further losses. General Wavell moved to India, the left flank of a defensive screen conceived as running from India to Australia. Taking responsibility for the right flank, the United States proposed setting up a South West Pacific Area (SWPA) Command in Australia. Its brief was to halt the southern advance of the Japanese and to prepare for a counter-offensive to recover captured territories. Someone had to lead the new force and the general chosen was Douglas MacArthur, the embattled American commander in the Philippines, a tireless self-promoter with an uneven military record.

MacArthur was a born showman. Dismissed by a *Time* journalist as a ham actor,[46] he provoked a wide range of responses, from adulation to loathing. Two assessments by officers working with him in SWPA Command tell much the same story. To subordinate General George Brett he was 'a brilliant, temperamental egoist; a handsome man, who can be as charming as anyone who ever lived, or harshly indifferent to the needs and desires of those around him. Everything about Douglas MacArthur is on a grand scale; his virtues and triumphs and shortcomings.'[47]

A British liaison officer characterised MacArthur as 'shrewd, selfish, proud, remote, highly-strung and vastly vain. He has imagination, self-confidence, physical courage and charm but no humour about himself, no regard for truth, and is unaware of these defects. He mistakes his emotions and ambitions for principles.'[48]

To John Curtin, Prime Minister of Australia, he provided a strength and a liability—a strength because he ensured American support and supply, a liability because it required some sacrifice of Australia's sovereignty. But the first more than outweighed the second.

Raised in a Texan military family—in the Civil War his father had been a Unionist captain who rose to lieutenant general—Douglas MacArthur graduated top of West Point Military Academy's class of 1903. After a stint at the War Office's Bureau of Information, where he was the US Army's first press officer, he fought at the Western Front, rising at the age of 38 to brigadier general. After the First World War, MacArthur was assigned to the Philippine Islands, beginning his long association with that American colony. He quelled a 1924 army mutiny there and, on returning to Washington, was involved in dispelling 'Bonus Army' protests. Conservatism became ingrained in his political outlook. Strongly anti-Communist, he developed a driving belief in America's destiny in the Asia-Pacific region.

Doug MacArthur was unorthodox for a military man. He wore a Japanese kimono at his desk and smoked with a jewelled cigarette holder. He had lunch with his mother each day when he was stationed in Washington, and read military history books in the evening, feeding a love for historical trivia and a penchant for convoluted, archaic language. He would refer to himself as 'MacArthur', hiring staff to promote his public image.[49] Admirers lauded his 'intelligence', but he had little intellectual depth, just a good memory and a repertoire of quotes and anecdotes.[50]

For some time, MacArthur's private life was discordant. After living with his ailing mother, he married at the age of 42 a socialite heiress, Louise Cromwell Brooks. Five years later, they divorced. Soon after, as the US Army's chief of staff, he installed a mistress, the teenage Filipina actress Isabel Rosario Cooper, in a Washington hotel. When the press threatened to expose the relationship in 1933, MacArthur gave her money and a ticket back to the Philippines.[51] She used the money, but not the ticket.

MacArthur was appointed Military Advisor to the Philippines Government in 1935. Sailing to Manila with his mother on the SS *President Hoover*, he met another socialite, Jean Faircloth, at 37 twenty years his junior. With his mother dying soon after arriving in Manila, MacArthur married for the second time and his private life finally took on some order. Devoted to Jean, they had a son, Arthur, to whom he was equally as devoted.[52]

American concern at an increasingly bellicose Japan prompted the recall of MacArthur to active duty in July 1941 as commander of US Army Forces in the Far East (USAFFE) and local forces in the Philippines. Washington's strategy, in the event of a major invasion, had been to withdraw garrison units to the Bataan Peninsula and defend only the harbour near Manila until relief arrived. MacArthur changed that, planning to hold the entire main island, Luzon, and use his Flying Fortresses to sink the invading armada. 'We'll stop them on the beaches,' he declared. That resolve would soon be put to the test.

A signalman listening to a California radio station was the first US Army person in the Philippines to hear of the Pearl Harbor attack. Richard Sutherland, MacArthur's chief of staff, was told and he notified his boss at 3.30 a.m. local time. MacArthur was stunned, having confidently told all and sundry there would be no war until April at the earliest. Now in mental paralysis, he remained in his office, communicating only through Sutherland.[53]

His air force commander, Lewis Brereton, proposed bombing Japanese bases in Formosa (now Taiwan), but was refused permission through Sutherland. By 8 a.m., Brereton had ordered his B-17s into the air without bombs, to avoid being an easy target for enemy bombers. They were still airborne when Brereton managed to talk directly to MacArthur and got the authority he sought. The B-17s were brought back to Clark Field to be armed, but within fifteen minutes a Japanese air attack descended on the US base, wrecking half the warplanes standing alongside the runway.[54]

Two days later, an amphibious force landed Japanese troops on the beaches of northern Luzon. They weren't stopped. The US Asiatic Fleet's submarines failed to sink any vessels of the invasion force, which was met with little opposition from the Filipino Army. The nation's army folded within 48 hours. By 14 December, the Asiatic Fleet and its commander, Admiral Thomas Hart, had left Manila for Java, and General Brereton's remaining bombers had withdrawn to Australia.[55]

While the Japanese pushed relentlessly towards Manila, MacArthur clung to the view that all of Luzon could be held, calling for an immediate US offensive in the Philippines and assuring his troops a relief force was on the way. But his strategy had spread the defences too thinly. By 23 December, the general had no choice but to order a retreat to Bataan.

Supplies that had been moved forward were abandoned in the confusion. MacArthur transferred himself, his family and his General Headquarters (GHQ) to the island of Corregidor in Manila Bay.[56] In the nearly three months he was on the fortified island, during which his troops were desperately holding off the enemy, he visited Bataan just once, prompting jaundiced soldiers' songs about 'Dugout Doug'.[57]

Back home, however, Douglas MacArthur was America's first war hero. A day seldom passed without a press release telling of heroic resistance in the Philippine jungle, victories in fictitious battles. Mostly they were written by and featured MacArthur. While Washington struggled to get supplies and reinforcement through the Japanese blockade, MacArthur lashed out at the lack of assistance he was getting. Political forces antagonistic to Roosevelt grabbed their opportunity, castigating the government for assisting the British and the Russians but not doing enough for the 'Lion of Luzon'. This helped protect MacArthur's career and would incidentally benefit Australia in the Pacific War.[58]

When the Allied leaders decided to replace ABDA Command with an American-led command based in Australia, public and political pressure dictated General Douglas MacArthur should be its commander-in-chief. The shortcomings of his leadership in the Philippines were largely unknown in Washington at the time and the Allies needed MacArthur as a symbol. Eisenhower's objection, that MacArthur's 'love of the limelight' might undermine 'more complicated situations', was overruled.[59]

When told that the JCS and the president wanted him to leave Corregidor for Australia to take command of Allied forces in the region, MacArthur insisted on a direct order from the president. He didn't want it to appear he'd abandoned his men. On 22 February, Roosevelt gave that order. MacArthur delayed his response before agreeing, insisting his departure should be at his timing. Nothing more was heard for over a fortnight until, in a lull in the Japanese offensive, MacArthur suddenly announced his intention to leave on 15 March, when the submarine USS *Permit* was due to arrive at Corregidor.[60]

Japanese naval patrols in the vicinity had increased, suggesting a radio message noting the commander's planned departure had been intercepted by the enemy. MacArthur decided to leave immediately, by PT-41 torpedo boat on the night of 11 March. Marshall had authorised only Sutherland to leave with the Philippines commander, along with Mrs MacArthur, their son and his Cantonese *amah* (nurse), but thirteen senior staff officers left with them, leaving General Jonathan Wainwright in command with no experienced support.[61]

The party arrived two days later at Mindanao, still in the Philippines. They were to be taken to Australia by Flying Fortress bombers, but there was only one crippled plane on the muddy plantation airfield. When three more B-17s arrived—they were what was left of those that had got away from Clark Field—MacArthur refused to fly in 'dangerously decrepit' aircraft, demanding 'the three best planes in the US or Hawaii'.

Coordinating the evacuation from Australia, General Brett could only offer navy B-17s from Townsville, but MacArthur was not prepared to be 'rescued' by the US Navy. The issue was resolved by transferring the planes to the USAAF and then sending them to Mindanao.[62]

At midnight of 17 March, two B-17s arrived from Australia with sulphur drugs, quinine and cigarettes, landing on an airstrip lit by flares at each end. The senior pilot told the evacuating party most of its luggage could not be carried on the return trip. Space was at such a premium that MacArthur sat in the radio operator's seat and Sutherland was wedged into a bomb bay.[63]

MacArthur would later tell the press their planes were pursued by enemy fighters during the flight and narrowly escaped bombers when they landed at Batchelor airfield, south of Darwin.

Dick Graf, a wireless operator on one of the aircraft remembers it differently, describing the flight as uneventful, never under threat.[64]

A third B-17 left Batchelor that day for Mindanao with more emergency supplies and returned with the rest of the MacArthur party and its offloaded luggage. According to Ralph Knox, a serviceman helping load the planes, it was filled with 'footlockers, crates of clothing and fur coats, pipe tobacco, several straight back chairs, little Arthur MacArthur's toys, one rocking chair and two particularly heavy mattresses'. It could have been better used to evacuate American nurses, he says.[65]

Meanwhile, in relative safety on Australian soil, MacArthur's thoughts drifted to his new command. Asking an American officer stationed at Batchelor about the build-up of troops in Australia, he was told, 'So far as I know, sir, there are very few troops here.'

MacArthur murmured to Sutherland, standing alongside, 'Surely he's wrong.'[66]

The Australian government was not told Douglas MacArthur was coming until he touched down at Batchelor airfield. General George Brett, then-commander of US forces in Australia, telephoned John Curtin and read out a letter prepared in Washington.

'The President of the United States has directed that I present his compliments to you and inform you that General MacArthur, US Army, has today arrived in Australia,' Brett recited. 'In accordance with his directions, General MacArthur has now assumed command of all US Army forces here. Should it be in accord with your wishes and those of the Australian people, the President suggests it would be highly acceptable to him and pleasing to the American people for the Australian government to nominate General MacArthur as the Supreme Commander of all Allied forces in the South West Pacific.'[67]

Curtin called a meeting of the War Cabinet that day. It was in immediate and enthusiastic agreement, insisting Curtin cable Washington and London as Roosevelt proposed.

The cable started, 'General Douglas MacArthur, having arrived in Australia, the Commonwealth government desires to nominate him as Supreme Commander of Allied forces in this theatre. His heroic defence of the Philippine Islands has evoked the admiration of the world and has been an example of the stubborn resistance with which the advance of the enemy should be opposed.'[68]

MacArthur couldn't have written it better.

His appointment was made public and Australian newspapers could finally acknowledge the presence of Americans. 'It is gratifying to be able to announce that there are very substantial American forces in Australia,' Curtin was quoted. 'We will not be left quite alone.'[69]

Meanwhile, MacArthur was busy trying to find the best way out of the Northern Territory. His staff officers were flying on to Melbourne, but the general, with a wife and son exhausted by the journey, had decided his family would get there by rail. Young Arthur was being fed intravenously and Jean refused to fly any further. The American commander demanded a motorcade to the next railway station, to be told that it was Alice Springs, a thousand miles away over unsealed track.[70] They flew instead, once more by B-17, and slept that night on a hotel verandah.

The next day the family set out for Adelaide on a special three-coach wooden train pulled by steam locomotive, the carriages furnished with lengthwise hardboard seats. When the train stopped at one point for sheep farmers wanting medical assistance, MacArthur mistakenly thought they wanted a speech from him.[71]

His expectation was met the following afternoon with the train reaching Terowie, a pioneer town 220 kilometres north of Adelaide where the railway line changed to a wider gauge. As the

American war hero stepped from his carriage, a huge cheer went up from gathered townspeople and passengers on a nearby waiting train. MacArthur saluted the crowd, made a short speech and inspected a guard of honour of local soldiers under the command of a First World War veteran.

'The President of the United States ordered me to break through the Japanese lines and proceed from Corregidor to Australia for the purpose, as I understand it, of organising an American offensive against Japan,' he told the crowd. 'I came through and I shall return.'[72]

Ridiculed by troops left behind in the Philippines, 'I shall return' became the catchcry of the Allied cause. It had been coined by Sutherland back in Corregidor as 'We shall return', but a local journalist remarked that while they felt the United States had let them down, Filipinos still trusted MacArthur. The slogan was changed accordingly. Washington instructed MacArthur to change it back, but it never was.[73]

In Adelaide, the MacArthurs were met by staff officer Dick Marshall. He'd come from Melbourne to advise there were only 25,000 American troops in Australia, mostly air corps and base staff, considerably less than the new commander had imagined. Outside on the station concourse, crowding civilians and soldiers were held back by police. Responding to a request for a press statement, MacArthur scrawled a version of his Terowie 'I shall return' speech on the back of an envelope, and the MacArthur entourage moved on.[74]

On the morning of 21 March, over 6000 cheering Melburnians overflowed from Spencer Street station as the Adelaide Express pulled in. Douglas MacArthur stepped from his private carriage wearing a light tropical uniform and gold-braided cap. Leaning on a walking stick, he shook hands with waiting military chiefs and government and civic representatives. The general was officially welcomed to Australia by its Army minister, Frank Forde. A hero's welcome for a commander withdrawn from the front line was provided by a guard of honour of 360 US Army engineers and an Australian Army band.

MacArthur directed that newsmen should be allowed through the cordon of soldiers on the platform, and spoke to them briefly before getting into a black Wolseley with 'USA-1' plates. After a few metres, the car stopped and the celebrity soldier stepped out for photographers. MacArthur and his family were then driven—with his wife and son taken in a separate car—to the Menzies Hotel, where they would occupy the entire sixth floor.

People thronged outside in William Street, sitting on cars and in trees.[75] They were still there an hour later, maybe a thousand of them, when MacArthur left to visit the Governor of Victoria. Australia wouldn't see something like this again until the Beatles came, more than twenty years later.

With the dark cloud of Japanese invasion hanging over them, the arrival of Douglas MacArthur was a tonic to the Australian press and public. The excitement of his dashing style and showy leadership generated adulation in newspapers and magazines, and was lapped up by their readers. The MacArthur family was news, whatever it did, with the press following wife Jean and young Arthur on their excursions to Melbourne's shops.[76] But it was the assurance of American support and its military muscle that most cheered Australians.

'General MacArthur is not only America's outstanding soldier,' the *Sydney Morning Herald* enthused, 'but ranks first among the commanders who have fought against the Japanese. He will speak clearly and directly to political leaders, as he has done before.'[77]

Brisbane's *Courier-Mail* put it more simply: 'The arrival in Australia of General Douglas MacArthur . . . is stirring news, the best news Australians have had for many a day.'[78]

MacArthur was pure theatre, equally as arrogant and devious as Churchill; this time Curtin didn't fight it, he used it.

The two met in Canberra at Parliament House on 26 March, a marriage of convenience, as one historian has described it, between 'the drab, socialist politician and the colourful, conservative general'.[79] MacArthur's orders were to 'hold the key military regions of Australia as bases for future offensive action against Japan', to halt the Japanese advance towards Australia and to attack shipping between Japan and its new conquests.[80] This was music to John Curtin's ears, providing the military presence needed to resist Japanese invasion. His side of the compact was to use the obligation to an ally to extract resources for MacArthur from America's military coffers, in competition with the demands of 'beat Hitler first'.

'Mr Prime Minister, we two, you and I will see this thing through together', the press release quoted the general. 'You take care of the rear and I will handle the front.'[81]

MacArthur addressed the Advisory War Council later that day. His first step, he said, was to secure Australia, and then prepare a counter-offensive towards the Philippines. The Japanese might try to set up airfields in northern Australia or New Guinea, but he doubted that they would invade Australia.

'The spoils here are not sufficient to warrant the risk,' he said bluntly.[82]

The American waxed more lyrical the next day, speaking to the Australian Parliament. 'There is a link between our countries which does not depend upon written protocol, upon treaties of alliance, or upon diplomatic doctrines,' he proclaimed. 'It goes deeper than that. It is that indescribable consanguinity of race which causes us to have the same aspirations, the same hopes and desires, the same ideals and the same dreams of future destiny.'[83]

That evening at a Parliament House banquet, he pulled out all stops. 'We shall win or we shall die, and to this end I pledge you the full resources of all the might and power of my country and all the blood of my countrymen'.[84]

In fact, Australians would initially provide the blood. They would provide for some time the bulk of the armed forces of South West Pacific Area. They would be commanded by an American general under instruction from Washington. However, the Australian Cabinet would not agree to a US proposal that MacArthur be given carte blanche to move Australian troops outside Australia. It was quickly dropped from the agreement setting up SWPA. Australia would decide, on advice, when and where its troops would go.[85]

Douglas MacArthur assumed leadership of SWPA on 18 April and set about establishing his command structure. Marshall had encouraged him to include Australians and Dutch in his senior staff, but the new commander replied that there were no qualified officers available, notwithstanding that three Australian divisions had been fighting in the Middle East.[86] The matter hadn't actually been raised with General Blamey, who had returned from the Middle East to be the Australian Army's commander-in-chief back home and became the only Australian MacArthur appointed to senior staff of SWPA. The rest were Americans, all but three having come with him from the Philippines.

MacArthur surrounded himself with servile officers, who were aware of his vanity and inflexibility and indulged it. Known as the 'Bataan gang', they lacked combat experience, resulting in poor planning and intelligence-gathering, panic-stricken responses and placing unrealistic demands on field commanders, who at first were mainly Australians. Most of MacArthur's senior officers were billeted at the Menzies Hotel and stayed aloof from the others when off duty. A large round table was set aside by the hotel for US personnel, but the next day a sign appeared: 'This table reserved for members of General MacArthur's party.' MacArthur, however, ate in his suite alone or with his family.[87]

At one stage, Blamey asked for American officers to be added to his forces. Aware that Australian staff officers were more experienced than their American counterparts, MacArthur warned Washington that poor-performing officers would be 'a black eye for US when placed with experienced and capable Australian officers'.[88] The general could play a different tune when it suited him.

With the arrival of MacArthur, the process of wartime decisions by the Australian government changed significantly. Cabinet was replaced by the Prime Minister's War Conference as the strategic decision-making body, made up of only three people: Curtin, MacArthur and Defence secretary Fred Shedden. Ministers and military leaders were called to their meetings as required.[89]

At first appearance, the Australian government had handed sovereignty to a foreign power and that's true to some extent, but it was a calculated gamble. Australia saw itself threatened with invasion and doubted its ability to repel that unaided. An American commanding Allied forces committed the United States to defending Australia. In any case, Australia's sovereignty had long been compromised. Its armed forces were habitually headed by officers from the British military. The chiefs of the RAN and RAAF at that time were both seconded from Britain. Only the Australian Army was led by an Australian.

While naval and air force defences might have been predominantly American, ground troops were Australian. MacArthur accepted he needed Australian government approval for matters affecting the Australian people or deployment of Australian forces. The US Army wasn't decisive in SWPA. Blamey's command under MacArthur was more substantial than it had been with the British in the Middle East or for Australians under Wavell. Australian troops were never put in as hopeless a position as the British had put them in Greece, Crete and Singapore . . . and, had Churchill prevailed, in Burma too.

The US provided strategy, modern warplanes and equipment, airpower and some sea transport; Australia provided a base, much of the food, clothing and facilities for the forces, and ground troops with combat experience. Curtin and MacArthur worked in tandem. The interests, plans and ambitions of each depended on the other: Curtin to protect Australia, MacArthur to defeat the Japanese.

Together, they got 'beat Hitler first' gradually watered down: America's Joint Chiefs committed more to SWPA than they ever intended. For all his idiosyncrasies, MacArthur relieved the Australian of some of the burden of war leadership. His presence reassured Australia it would not be abandoned by its allies.

Curtin was not MacArthur's puppet. Theirs was a relationship of complimentary political interests and mutual understanding. The Australian may have had a high personal regard for the American, or seen him merely as key to Australia's security; it's hard to tell. Curtin may have looked to America with public enthusiasm, 'without any inhibitions of any kind', but in private conversation he was mostly critical of America's war leaders and policies.[90]

The press and the public, however, were transfixed by MacArthur. John Hinde was sent to cover his first Melbourne press conference. 'People just needed something new. And of course MacArthur was the new thing we got,' Hinde says. 'I was strangely reassured by this magnificent figure that MacArthur cut. He was very tall and good-looking and he had this sloppy cap and lots of braid and a corn cob pipe that he loved and chewed on and actually smoked and he had absolute confidence in himself and what he was going to do.'[91]

Sydney schoolgirl Yve Jeanneret had a preteen's perception. While her parents looked on him as a saviour, her view was coloured by her unbridled admiration of American film stars.

'I had a number of idols and General MacArthur joined their ranks,' she says. 'He looked so strong and glamorous in his wonderful uniform . . . in my eyes large enough and sufficiently impressive to lead us out of any mess.'[92]

The Yanks were here! The US Army's 41st Division had arrived in Melbourne in early April and gone into camp up the highway at Seymour. The arrival of American troops and the return of the AIF from the Middle East enabled forces to be moved to Darwin and Port Moresby, previously thinly defended, and for Townsville to be reinforced. Ever since the Darwin raid in February, Australia had been conscious of how open its northern frontier was to enemy attack with non-existent defence over much of the 5000 kilometres of coastline there. Military strategists weighed up how vigorously the north could and should be defended against the feared invasion, and how best to cover that wide open door.

The arrival of American troops in Australia had an impact far wider than its military value, however. They were different and conspicuous, and changed the fabric of civilian life in Australia in ways that would never be reversed.

Chapter 6

HOME FIRES BURNING

The response of ordinary Australians to war and the possibility of being invaded progressed in three stages. After war was declared in Europe, the early burst of public energy soon receded. People lost interest in a war temporarily at a standstill, too distant anyway to feel a serious threat. Civilian restraints were introduced, in imitation of those in Britain, but soon they weren't taken seriously. There was no expectation of being greatly troubled at home by the Germans.

When it entered the war, Japan introduced a more plausible menace. However, the United States was seen by Australians as Japan's main target. In any case, although young Australians were fighting in Malaya—or soon would be—Singapore was the citadel that would prevent the Japanese from coming within striking distance of the Australian homeland. Then, over five days, that reassurance collapsed. The Gibraltar of the East capitulated with alarming ease and Darwin was bombed with a force big enough to suggest an invasion would follow.

For whatever reason, the invasion didn't follow, but it seemed only a matter of time. Air strikes against military targets in northern Australia were becoming frequent. There was no reason to think they wouldn't work their way down to the more populated southern states, in particular the industrial hub of Newcastle–Sydney–Port Kembla.

Aircraft range at that time restricted Japan's raids by land-based aircraft to a northern arc from Exmouth Gulf to Townsville, but the continent to the south could still be attacked from aircraft carriers, as Pearl Harbor and Darwin had been, or from airfields captured in northern Australia.

After Pearl Harbor, Air Raid Precautions (ARP) began to be taken seriously again and official indifference and public apathy receded, although not completely. There was a war on, with competition for scarce resources. ARP wardens complained of continuing lack of equipment; in one instance, a post of twelve men had only one tin hat and one telephone among them. As they were volunteers, wardens were expected to provide their own meals on duty, pay their own fares to get there and put their own stamps on official letters.[1]

ARP training intensified; it included an eerie walk with a mask through a caravan filled with gas. Despite their country's geographical isolation, Australians feared a conflagration of bombs and gas from the skies.

From the outset the larger cities prepared themselves for air attack. Brick aprons were built around key buildings and sandbags were stacked around shop windows and doors. Glass was lattice-taped to reduce shattering. Some shops had large sheets of 3-ply over their windows, with square holes cut so passers-by could look in at the window display. In Brisbane, mains were laid along Elizabeth Street to pump water from North Quay for fighting fires from incendiary bombing.[2]

These measures sometimes had unwanted consequences. Sandbags would split, spilling out onto the pavement. Sand heaps dumped on the streets to put out fires became sand pits attracting kids and animals. Matches and cigarette butts were tossed into buckets of sand put in hospitals for the same purpose.

State governments had been advocating trenches and pillboxes as air-raid shelters since 1939, and four concrete shelters had been built on Sydney's Domain to show civilians how backyard models should look.[3] Little notice was taken until war erupted in the Pacific. Suddenly, building public shelters became a high priority. The New South Wales government decreed shelters should be provided immediately in all buildings with more than 30 people. The next day, newspapers reported a shortage of materials and labour to carry this out. Even without the shortage it would have taken twelve months to fulfil.[4]

Nonetheless, with some ingenuity, an assortment of spaces was converted to shelters. The day after Pearl Harbor, the state's National Emergency Services minister, Bob Heffron, pointed out Sydney's underground railway system could be made available. The unused sewer tunnel in the southern suburb of Oatley could accommodate over 50,000 people,[5] ignoring the difficulty of getting them in there. Railway tunnels dug in the 1920s for the still-unbuilt Eastern Suburbs line could provide shelter for 20,000 at St James underground station. The RAAF moved its local command centre into part of that tunnel, behind bomb-blast curtains.

Shelters were many and varied. Smaller shelters were built at points around Sydney: one at Eveleigh Rail Yards for its workers, another built into the foot of a cliff near Luna Park for amusement park staff.[6] In Brisbane, brick pillboxes were jerry-built in the middle of city streets. The size of two small rooms, they allowed just enough space either side for cars to squeeze past.[7]

Trench-digging intensified. Schools, factories and city parklands, including the lawns around Melbourne's Shrine of Remembrance, were pitted with open trenches. The zig-zag excavations, up to

2 metres deep and over a metre wide at the top, were lined with sandbags and sheets of iron. Earth banks ran along both sides.

Lawns and gardens were also dug up for backyard shelters, mostly slit trenches covered with galvanised iron or old planking. One home shelter in Melbourne's Prahran was a partly buried delivery van,[8] while many inner-suburban families with small backyards were expected to huddle beneath a sturdy kitchen table.

The Australian Women's Weekly provided a guide to the public for dealing with air raids. Turn glasses and bowls upside down, it advised, so splintered or powdered glass doesn't get in them. Keep warm saline eyebaths handy in case of persistent gas. Shelter in a hallway or under a table in case of falling glass or debris, and take with you a cushion, rug and radio or book. Cover an incendiary bomb with sand after it stops splattering, shovel it into a bucket of sand and take it out to the garden as if it were a redback spider.[9]

In the Australian population, there were those who worried about the prospect of Japanese bombs raining down, and there were those who didn't. And there were those who had some concern, but not enough to do much about it. The *Border Morning Mail* expressed disappointment that only fifteen men volunteered to dig trenches at Albury's sportsground, 'yet hundreds devoted the afternoon to sport and sleep or sought pleasant companionship in hotels and elsewhere'.[10]

Despite assurances by their prime minister and the press that it was real, the belief of Australians in their imminent peril ebbed and flowed. When describing the bombing of Darwin as the 'opening shots in the Battle of Australia', the *Sydney Morning Herald* proclaimed: 'We may as a people have needed some such grim development to awaken us finally to the realities of war. Too many have regarded the ARP practices, in one of which Sydney was engaged yesterday while bombs were actually falling on Darwin, simply as a nuisance.'[11]

Cities started testing their air-raid procedures at the end of 1941, predictably exposing teething problems. In Darwin, people waited on the streets to see the Japanese planes.[12] Sydney's air-raid shelters were found to be inadequate, with people standing twenty deep outside the entrance to Wynyard station. Adding to the confusion, fire engines were racing to a Pitt Street cafe blaze just as the air-raid siren stopped.[13] In Albury, a plane was coming from Wagga Wagga to give a sense of realism to the first trial, but it was delayed. A train whistle was mistaken for the 'All Clear' and the town had returned to ordinary business by the time the 'air-raid' started.[14]

Melbourne's tests went more smoothly, with some 2000 people evacuated from a busy city section in two minutes. Women arrived from a beauty parlour with hair in curlers and face packs, while another woman refused to leave a cafe until she'd finished her coffee. Two visitors from Singapore ignored the siren, saying they were used to air raids.[15]

The trenches had their own problems as they continued to be put to little use. They became improvised urinals and in garrison towns were used by servicemen for sex. In Queensland, slit trenches filled with water, then mud, toads and mosquitoes. A Cairns schoolboy at the time, Allen Tucker recalls trenches full of red slippery mud where he and his barefoot mates played.[16] Generally, throughout Australia, winter rains filled the trenches with mud, and in summer mosquitoes bred there.

Melbourne's *Argus* summed it up in a short piece of doggerel:

There's a trench in our backyard,
With water it is brimming,
What shall we do in our backyard?
Breed ducks, or just go swimming?[17]

National emergency officialdom took steps to ensure enemy bombers or landing forces would get no assistance in locating their objective at night. Brownout provisions were introduced in streets across the nation and blackouts for buildings and homes. Street lights were hooded or turned off. In the low light, people fell over gutters or stumbled on uneven footpaths. Headlights on vehicles were fitted with a shield, limiting illumination to the road in front. Car bumper bars were painted white, to be better seen in the dim light; but, even with a speed limit of 20 mph (32 kph) during brownouts, road accidents increased.

Six soldiers were injured in Brisbane when their truck made a U-turn and crashed into a tram.[18] Following a serious collision between two trams at a Sydney intersection, tram drivers resolved to drive no faster than 8 mph (13 kph) during brownouts.[19]

The brownout regulations left the streets dark and gloomy at night. Eddie Leonski, a disturbed American soldier, used Melbourne's shadowy night-time to murder three young women. Dubbed 'the Brownout Strangler' by the press, Leonski was tried by US Army court martial and hanged at Pentridge Prison. For a while, the notoriety provided a disincentive for Melbourne women to be out after dark.

Retailers suffered, required to close at 6 p.m., except food and medical suppliers. Late-night shopping was cancelled and neon lighting prohibited at any time, as were night tennis and greyhound racing, external residential lighting, floodlit buildings and lighting matches after dark. Shop window lighting was allowed only from an hour after sunrise to an hour before sunset. In the lead-up to Melbourne's first Christmas with the dimmed lighting, the *Argus* noted 'the first real hint of the possibilities of war. Streets usually crowded with Friday night shoppers showed no neon signs, no brilliant illumination of Christmas goods.'[20]

Buildings visible from the sea had to be completely blacked out, so blackout curtains were hung in those suburbs. ARP wardens prowled the streets noting offenders. When rationing of certain supplies was introduced, the curtain material was not included and so it was sometimes used to make clothes. Trains were blacked out too. In summer months, long-distance night travel could be unpleasantly stifling, with no air-conditioning and shuttered windows.[21]

Australians were experiencing a strange unlit world. Mary Patterson was working in Sydney's CBD during a national blackout practice. 'I walked out onto the upstairs balcony,' she recalls, 'and looked over the city and there wasn't a light anywhere. It was just dark, dark, dark with no vestige of light. It was really quite eerie.'[22]

Not everyone complied with blackout regulations. In the early days of Melbourne's brownout, some motorists continued to drive with full headlights, but they could be identified by their number plates and chased up. Flinders Street railway station was reported to have stayed lit. Many of the offenders were part of the military. Windows weren't blacked out at Victoria Barracks, the RAAF offices or Southern Command HQ; and while Cairns was under blackout, military sites remained lit up.

Lighting wasn't the only factor that could guide air raiders to their target. Radio stations were required to cease broadcasting at night so enemy planes couldn't use the transmission as a direction-finder. Since daylight attacks were more likely, given that planes needed to return to aircraft carriers before dark, and blocking lighting and radio would not impede such aircraft, targets needed to be hard to discern from the air.

The Sydney Camouflage Group, made up of artists, photographers, architects and scientists, had been formed back in 1939 with a view to conducting camouflage experiments in consultation with the Army and RAAF. They tested such ideas as: colour matching to make objects blend into their surroundings; counter-shading, to hide the shadows that defined target structures; disruptive patterning with camouflage nets, to diffuse shadows visible from the air; 3D dummy objects and dummy installations. Having studied disguise in Australia's flora and fauna, zoologist Bill Dakin proposed a change from British methods of camouflage. In Australia, he noted, 'shadows are much darker and it is the shadows of objects which are the greatest guides to observers in aeroplanes'.[23]

Dakin, the Camouflage Group's leader, was seconded in 1941 to the Central Defence Camouflage Committee. This committee was within the non-military Department of Home Security and tasked with researching, advising and coordinating civilian and military camouflage. The military, however, where each service controlled its own camouflage operation, did not take kindly to advice that contradicted its camouflage practices. The artists had a working knowledge of the principles of abstraction and illusion—concealment and deception—but the military saw art merely as decoration.[24]

Dakin was appointed Technical Director of Camouflage within the Civil Construction Corps, an organised labour force under manpower controls, a form of industrial conscription. Some of the men drafted into the corps would become well known in post-war Australian art: William Dobell, Joshua Smith, Max Dupain. A labour gang of artists worked on camouflage projects at the RAAF's Sydney airfields at Bankstown and Richmond, painting structures or covering them with nets so they appeared from the air as fowl yards, farmhouses and fields of cabbage.[25]

Dobell painted papier-mâché cows so runways would look like pastures. 'The camouflage work was a waste of money,' he later said. 'The Japanese were not so stupid as to believe large aeroplane hangars were the farmers' cottages we had to make them look like. There was a lady who made white leghorn chickens and we dug up the grass around the place to look like ploughed fields. I even had to paint "R Fong" on the side of a farm cart. As if the pilot would come that low to be able to read it.'[26]

The name on the cart may have been unnecessary, but a warplane pilot has to make a snap decision on what he is seeing. Things that look fake on the ground can still mislead a pilot in the split second he has to process what he thinks he sees.

The artist Frank Hinder designed a 'dummy dam' using the shine of glass bottles to simulate a body of water, but he says when he showed his plan to the army, 'the boys in the field had hysterics'.[27] Hinder also designed dummy aircraft of hessian, timber and wire, able to be quickly erected. They looked more convincing from the air than the ground, and that was where it mattered.

Camouflage nets, to cover guns, vehicles and tents, were made at homes by volunteer knitting groups and by women in gaols and reformatories, using wooden needles coupled to a wooden frame. Elsewhere, buses in the cities were painted in camouflage colours, their glass replaced with sliding metal sheets in the same pattern. Military barracks in Dubbo were built with false chimneys to look like ordinary houses from the air.[28]

The *pièce de résistance* was a radio intercept station at Stuart Creek, out from Townsville. Housing a secret cryptographic unit, the square blockhouse of reinforced concrete had a sliding armour-plated door as its entrance and no windows. To ensure the anomalous structure in the middle of the scrub didn't attract unwanted attention from the air, its exterior was painted to resemble a Queenslander, the wooden house set up on timber or brick stumps that was widespread in the state. Paintwork included doors, windows, verandah, railings and trellis. The only features that weren't fake were a water tank and steps leading up to a false door. Photographs of the building at the time are remarkably convincing. From the air, the station would have looked like a typical Queensland farmhouse set among the gum trees, accessed by a rough dirt road.[29]

The effectiveness of the Sydney disguises would never be put to the test, but the Stuart Creek station with its *trompe l'oeil* paintwork was left untouched in Townsville's attacks.

Over 21 months from February 1942, Australia would endure 97 air raids, all in the north and 64 on Darwin alone. Measures taken against enemy air attacks have already been noted. Additional measures were put in place to frustrate an amphibious invasion force, were it to land in the populated south of the continent. Barbed wire was strung along the water's edge on many east coast beaches, leaving a small gap for swimmers. Lines of cement tetrahedrons, up to two metres high, were set up on beaches and roads—like giant jagged teeth—to block tanks and trucks.

Sydney journalist Jack Pollard recalls fear of invasion making the fabled beach at Bondi unrecognisable. 'Bondi had two marvellous promenade piers that stuck right out into the beach,' he says, 'and they blew those up because they felt in the event of a Japanese landing they'd provide good cover for the landing troops. So to get into the water you had to negotiate these little pieces of concrete that were the remains of the piers, and barbed wire all along—it was pretty difficult getting a swim.'[30]

Bridges were strengthened to carry home-force tanks and transporters; others were prepared for demolition. Roads under railway bridges were lowered to allow troops to be moved across Sydney in double-decker buses. Power lines were raised, trees lopped. Parks large enough to allow gliders to land were ploughed up or had slit trenches put across them.

All signs indicating place names and distances for 100 miles (161 kilometres) inland were removed, along with railway station names. Train travellers were forced to count stops and, especially at night, would sometimes get off at the wrong station. Without the signs, drivers—both army and civilian—would often get lost.[31] Eventually new signs were put up with the official number of the road, instead of its name.

How well Japanese soldiers could have read signs in Roman letters is debatable. Some officers could speak English, but probably not many. Then again, if the invaders were furnished with maps with relevant place names in English, no further knowledge of the language was required. Some Second World War veterans have noted that the maps they used were printed in Japan before the war. Like so many aspects of the feared invasion, defenders were dealing with a whole set of unknown and unknowable factors.

A government booklet gave advice about dealing with an invasion. Don't tell or give the enemy anything, it said. Widespread confusion and roads thronged with refugees assist the invader, so stay in your neighbourhood and carry on as normal, leaving the roads free for troop movement. Disable vehicles when told to by police or the military, or if they are about to be seized by the enemy. Destroy maps. Keep indoors if there is fighting nearby. Protect yourself and your family only if threatened. And so on.[32]

Women in country areas were told by emergency services to have ready a pack of basic items for each member of the family and a medical kit for a speedy evacuation. In northern New South Wales, Gladys Sneath put her personal trinkets in a box to be buried under a tree in the garden. 'It was a strange feeling going about your normal business thinking that maybe that same evening you would be on the road,' she says. 'If the call came, the women and children were to go ahead over the range. We were supposed to live off our cattle, milk them and kill them for meat.'[33]

'It was a very difficult route even for good bushmen,' says her husband, Jim, 'and we were supposed to take thousands of cattle and hundreds of people through. It would have been a futile effort, but we weren't offered any choice about it. Blind Freddie could see it wasn't going to be any good, but what else were we supposed to do?'[34]

A Sydney newspaper reported a poll that found 54 per cent of Australians expected a Japanese landing, and 93 per cent were prepared to fight the invaders even if they could expect no help. Another commented, 'There can surely be no Australian to whom the possibility of conquest by the Japanese would not seem incomparably worse than death in opposing them.'[35]

It was an oblique reference to the Rape of Nanking. Fear of Japanese atrocities had been fed into the moral climate of the time by a lurid account in the *Reader's Digest* of the behaviour of Japanese soldiers on capturing the Chinese city six years before.[36] As a result of that account and a 1942 Movietone newsreel with a British journalist who claimed to have been in Nanking at the time, many husbands gave their wives a revolver to use on themselves and their children, especially daughters, if capture was imminent.

In Sydney, pre-teen Yve Jeanneret was told by her mother: 'If the Japanese come and invade us, I'm going to kill you.'

'Why?' Yve asks rhetorically. 'Well, sexual reasons. Rape. That sort of thing. How I'd be treated. How girls were treated.' Her mother didn't elaborate and Yve had only the vaguest idea then what rape was.[37]

Barbara Doig of Perth was pregnant at the time. 'You heard stories of the Japs slitting open the pregnant women,' she says.[38]

In Rockhampton, Grace Dangerfield resolved to get a hand grenade, strip and pull the pin when the invaders arrived. 'I saw Veronica Lake do that in a movie,' she explains.[39]

Anne Boardman's family in the Darling Downs decided if the Japanese got close they would hold hands and jump into their dam. 'We weren't going to let the Japs get us or the children.'[40]

Children were the focus of family and government concerns. With war coming to the Pacific, New South Wales delayed the return from school holidays by two weeks so that proper trenches could be dug and covered. Queensland went one better and announced that schools near military targets would not open at all after the holidays, something New South Wales had earlier announced then quietly abandoned.

When schools resumed in mid-February, trenches had been dug and windows made shatterproof; pupils commenced daily air-raid drill. Schoolchildren carried a small home-made calico bag with ear plugs, bandages, barley sugar, ID disc and a piece of rubber hose or clothes peg to put between their teeth so they wouldn't be shattered by an explosion. Yve Jeanneret's mother made her a little cloth bag for her air-raid kit, including a tennis ball cut in half to cover her ears.[41]

Volunteer Cadet Corps at high schools did drill and route marches and learnt to signal with flags, lamps and Morse code. Kids could identify different enemy planes, Japanese and German, as well as Allied ones. Kellogg's had pictures and cutout models of army, navy and air force equipment on its cereal boxes.[42] The artefacts of war soaked into the imaginings of the young.

A week after Pearl Harbor, plans were announced to evacuate 100,000 New South Wales children to safe country areas, as had been done in Britain. Children's train fares would be reduced to a quarter the normal rate and escorts would be provided for children travelling alone. Registers were circulated, along with lists of food and clothing needed, but by February only 12 per cent of eligible children had been registered.[43]

In Melbourne, Eileen Beardsley's five-year-old son came home from school with a message to have a haversack with a spare set of clothes ready for an evacuation if the city was attacked.[44] Only half the forms sent to parents by Victoria's Education department were returned. Torn between the competing needs of children's safety and not needlessly disrupting their education, the department took no further action, leaving parents to make private arrangements.[45]

State governments backed away from their firm plans, with evacuation no longer compulsory until the military said so. In the confusion and inaction, mostly children of wealthy families were evacuated, moving to country boarding schools. In Melbourne, Brisbane and Townsville, some schools were re-established in country towns, not as a safety precaution, but so that their conveniently located school buildings could be taken over by the American military.

Queenslanders, closer to the teeth of war, were the first to observe war's dislocation. Unnerved and bedraggled, expatriates began arriving from New Guinea at airfields and ports along the state's coast, before heading south by rail. Relief agencies offered them meals, blankets, toys and clothes, their transient presence leaving a disturbing insight for locals into what might come.

At that time, Brisbane officials were encouraging residents to leave the city. Many went north to join friends and relatives, while officials in northern towns were urging women and children to leave as soon as they could. In one Ingham street, six of the eight houses were vacated.[46] Families moved in all directions around the state without much logic or consistency, eventually massing in the Queensland hinterland. Evacuation created ghost towns along the coast and overcrowded towns inland at places like Charleville, with makeshift accommodation and tent cities.

Moves were often on short notice, without much planning or forethought. Alice Clark and her two children were to evacuate from Rockhampton to Barcaldine, but her uncle asked them to wait until he dug a hole for a toilet.[47] Betty Purvey's family moved from Cairns to Brisbane to stay with her brother's family, but there were constant clashes and they came back after three months. 'That was virtually World War Three!' she says.[48]

State governments announced at the outset an intention to evacuate women and children from coastal cities to the country in the event of air raids or invasion, but provided no detailed plans. Thousands began evacuating on their own behalf, prompted by news stories of the blitz in Britain. Many left Sydney, for instance, for towns like Bowral, Katoomba and Bathurst. House prices and rents rose dramatically in those places.

By February, over 4000 women and children had left Sydney, but governments were becoming concerned that widespread evacuation might affect morale. Evacuation inland was becoming impractical too because of the limited accommodation there and the need to maintain a workforce near industry. Federal Home Security minister Bert Lazzarini insisted women should stay at home with their men.[49] They would soon be replacing their men. Limited evacuation, from high-risk suburbs close to munitions factories or military installations to other parts of the city, was the modified policy.

In one of the more remarkable stories of the war, 95 part-Aboriginal children were evacuated from Croker Island at the top of the Northern Territory. Transferred by lugger to Arnhem Land in April 1942, the children and their white carers began a six-week trek on a 90-kilometre unmarked track to the mission at Oenpelli. Two old lorries, one with no cabin or windscreen, shuttled some of the party to the mission over two days; those not on the shuttle kept walking until a lorry came back for them.

Sleeping in the open, they ate supplies cooked before they had left—74 loaves, 100 buns, 300 biscuits and five fruit cakes—along with what bush tucker they could find along the way.

Reaching Oenpelli, they waited for two weeks, living on depleting mission food and two slaughtered cattle, until they got word that government trucks were coming from Darwin to pick them up. After another two weeks, a policeman arrived on horseback to tell them the trucks were blocked by a river 100 kilometres away and the children would have to get there by foot, horse and mission lorry. That part of the journey involved looking for waterholes, cooking rice on enamel plates, river crossing by canoe, and carrying the lorry on a raft of petrol drums strapped together.

The five trucks waiting by the river were able to squeeze the whole party in with their luggage, and eventually arrived at a US Army base by the railway at Pine Creek. The children gave a concert on the base verandah, then went south by rail and military truck to Alice Springs, the military taking over feeding them. The remainder of the journey by train took the children to a hostel in Otford, south of Sydney.[50]

Aboriginal settlements nearer to Darwin were evacuated, before and after the bombing, to Delissaville across the harbour, then inland to new camps supplied and controlled by the Australian Army. A need was seen to move them away from areas where they might have contact with and provide assistance to the enemy, and to control frowned-on contact between soldiers and Aboriginal women.[51]

Some of the new homes became labour camps. At Mataranka, Aboriginal men worked in army workshops, where they were paid with tobacco and ten shillings a fortnight, one-sixth the amount then paid to army privates. They weren't enlisted, but received rations, army clothing and often a nominal rank.[52] Although there was an element of exploitation involved, these measures provided work and training opportunities that had not been available to Aboriginal people before the war.

Across the nation, valuables too were evacuated to safer areas. The Tasmanian government had plans afoot to move rare books and documents from its museum in Hobart and the Royal Society to the centre of the island.[53] In the Territory, as we have already seen, bank documents, notes and coins were moved inland to Alice Springs after the first Darwin bombing. About the same time, typists in External Affairs made copies of sensitive documents and stored them in steel trunks along with code books in case the government had to be moved out of Canberra.[54]

Most important of all was the nation's gold reserves, held by the Commonwealth Bank. In February 1942, gold was secretly transferred by rail under armed guard from Sydney and Adelaide to Broken Hill. The consignment included gold shipped from the Dutch East Indies before it was captured by Japan. While the bullion was held in the cells of a deserted jail until a special strongroom was built with a system of sirens, a rumour ran through Broken Hill that the jail was being reinforced to hold Rudolph Hess.[55]

In April, further gold was transferred from Melbourne. When the train stopped at Jerilderie, where identifying signs had been removed, a military guard asked the name of the station and was told, 'This is Jerilderie where Ned Kelly held up the bank.'[56]

At the other end of the scale, Betty Purvey's mother in Cairns withdrew all her money from the bank and carried it in her corset for the entire war.[57]

Having read reports of savagery in occupied Hong Kong, Australians were not prepared to let the Japanese land anywhere unopposed. Public meetings were hastily convened in January 1942 to form a local civil guard, inspired by the harassment of the German army by Russian men and women, and by guerrillas in the Spanish Civil War. Armed with shotguns, hunting rifles, picks and home-made pikes, like villagers in an old vampire movie, various groups began to train and drill.

By late January, they were being guided by veterans of the First World War and Spain's International Brigade. In Sydney, the *Daily Telegraph* campaigned vigorously for the formation of a People's Army of civilians, reporting that the War Cabinet had instructed the Army department to look into it. Civilians should be taught to use dynamite, the paper said, to make and use Molotov cocktails, to blow up bridges and impede the enemy, but they needed competent direction, which the government should organise.[58]

The *Telegraph* had useful support. Future NSW Governor Roden Cutler, at that time an AIF lieutenant with a Victoria Cross, said French guerrillas had hampered the Australian advance in Syria, where he had won his VC six months earlier.[59] He advocated a civilian army with skilled bushmen and riflemen operating in close liaison with the regular army. Bill Riordan, a Queensland politician, urged the Army minister to issue rifles and ammunition to north Queenslanders, his constituents, to fight enemy invaders. 'Well-armed civilians could put up a good show against paratroops,' he predicted.[60] Perhaps something better than 'a good show' would be needed.

The civilian units and their press champion drew heavily from the writings of Tom Wintringham. Drawing on his experience in the International Brigade, his book, *New Ways of War*, described making hand grenades and home-made mortars and making anti-tank mines from biscuit tins. The *Telegraph* produced diagrams showing these home-made devices, a forerunner of IEDs now shown on the Internet. 'If the Japanese come,' the paper proclaimed, 'they should find every street a death-trap, every house and factory a fortress, every tree and knoll a sniper's nest.'[61] Wintringham also wrote for the *Telegraph*, arguing that historically small forces fighting on their own ground had defeated greater forces of invaders.[62]

It was heady stuff! A 'tank busting' unit in Sydney's Redfern painted an old car like a tank and drove it through Centennial Park to test their marksmanship.[63] A People's Army unit in the city's well-heeled upper North Shore was particularly successful, its membership swelling to 1000 by the beginning of February, 300 of them women. With few arms, they trained as a 'broomstick' unit, using poles as rifles if they didn't own a shotgun and incongruously conducting exercises in the bush with a group of Cessnock miners.[64]

A photo in the *Sydney Morning Herald* of these guerrillas-in-training in the North Shore bush attracted the government's interest and concern about armed groups operating outside military control. Army minister Frank Forde, hesitant for a while, finally declared that the federal government wouldn't support a People's Army. The Volunteer Defence Corps (VDC), already in operation, was expanded and units of the People's Army incorporated into it.[65]

In 1940 the government had announced the formation of the Volunteer Defence Corps to 'preserve law and order, guard public utilities and prevent subversive activities by aliens and disaffected persons'.[66] Made up of First World War veterans and modelled on Britain's Home Guard, the VDC was initially run by the RSSAILA (now the RSL), before being incorporated into the army in May 1941. The government was not enthusiastic about a private army, capable of running its own agenda. It would be unenthusiastic again when the People's Army emerged nine months later.

A yawning gap separated what was expected of the VDC and what was provided to do it. Trained to build roadblocks, demolish bridges and piers, protect air bases and industrial sites and engage in guerrilla warfare, they often drilled with wooden rifles. A bridge across the Burdekin River in north Queensland was defended with a wooden machine gun.[67] Training equipment included rattles to make the sound of machine-gun fire and imitation hand grenades, socks filled with sand.[68] The organisation was in constant competition with the Citizen Military Force for scarce weapons, uniforms and equipment. The army's policy was to not service VDC needs until the CMF's were met.

The volunteers made do with what they could get, and carved a role. Three battalions were assigned to protect BHP's steelworks in Newcastle.[69] A demolition school in outer Sydney taught VDC how to blow up railway tracks and cut steel girders. Taken to the Hawkesbury River bridge, course participants were shown a plan to demolish it and impede a Japanese advance south.[70] Broome and Wyndham, considered indefensible in the remote northwest, were left in the hands of the local VDC and army engineers.

The VDC had Tom Wintringham for guidance and The Australian Guerrilla, a series of six handbooks explaining sniping and guerrilla tactics. One of them, *Trapping the Jap*, aimed at the expected invasion of Australia. Their author was Ion Idriess, who had been a sniper's spotter at Gallipoli and was already a celebrated writer of muscular non-fiction.[71]

Membership of the VDC had grown to 100,000 nationally by the end of 1942. Most were part-time participants, on duty only about six hours a week. Despite the constant battle for resources, they were ready to make last-ditch stands. Queenslander Judy Ballinger recalls long discussions about the invasion of Australia after Japan came into the war. 'My father was in the VDC,' she says, 'and he was quite prepared to fight to the end.'[72]

Other volunteer groups weren't armed, so they didn't require integration into the army. Civilians were expected to learn first aid and some volunteered as ambulance drivers, many of them women. 'There was quite a lot of public first aid training,' recalls Robert Brown. 'Particularly how to deal with wounds, how to deal with fractures. We teachers all had to have refresher first aid training.'[73]

In Adelaide, a volunteer civil defence group was set up in 1936 by Natalia Davies, a Welsh-born school teacher with a penchant for wearing blazer, collar and tie. Her Defence Society had grown to 130 members, mainly women, when war started in 1939. The society ran lectures in air-raid protections and classes in first aid, home nursing and aero engineering. After Japan entered the war, hundreds of women were taught how to use and look after a rifle. Classes were extended to pistol shooting, map reading and unarmed combat, preparing them for coming face to face with the Japanese.

Davies was a tireless experimenter, working on gas-proof garments and camouflage. The military took up a Camouflage Committee recommendation of her snipers' suits, made from hessian by Defence Society members. Tested in Adelaide's park-lands, they were surprisingly difficult to see.[74]

Women were replacing men in defence posts, in radar, cipher and signals operation and in administrative and clerical areas. Many of them left cities and towns to join the Australian Women's Land Army of volunteer farm workers, replacing men who had joined the armed forces. Plane-spotters in the Volunteer Air Observer Corps (VAOC) were mostly women, with older kids often rostered after school, especially in country towns. A course in aircraft recognition supplemented their knowledge from Kellogg's boxes.

The VAOC was linked to an early warning system called Air Flash. Spotters who saw something they thought worth report-ing just said 'Air Flash' to the telephonist, who was instructed to disconnect live calls and let the warning through. Observer posts were manned 24 hours a day, with volunteers doing shifts of six to eight hours.[75] Few of them ever saw an enemy plane and mostly reported American aircraft lost through poor navigation.

The European war hadn't prepared Australians very well for war in the Pacific. With limited press interest until Dunkirk, they had followed events in Europe half-heartedly. Public support in the First World War had been immediate and overwhelming, but alienation from the Depression, after promises of a better life following the Great War, had created caution and cynicism about another European war. Once people got over the shock of finding their country at war again, even a war in Asia and the Pacific seemed distant.

Retired US general Patrick Hurley arrived in Australia as an envoy in February 1942. Reporting back to Washington, he said, 'The people do not appear to be aware of the critical situation confronting them. The newspapers the day after the raid had much more news concerning the horse-racing than they did concerning the raid on Darwin. This is not a criticism of Australia. They give about as much space in their newspapers to racing, as we do to glamour, sex appeal and the figures of almost naked beautiful women. The point I'm trying to make is that the serious situation confronting the great continent of Australia has not fully aroused the populace.'[76]

Prime Minister Curtin expressed exasperation at the public mood, disturbed at the prospect of invasion one minute, wanting race meetings and a Christmas break the next. Politicians and the daily press agonised over people wishing each other 'a Jerry Christmas and a Jappy New Year', but to *The Bulletin* this indicated how little politicians understood their own people. 'The

Australian humour that talks sardonically about betting in yen at the races, working for Japanese or growing rice to feed the new population,' it said, 'they misjudge altogether.'[77]

There was a mix of bravado and apathy in the Australian attitude. The *Courier-Mail* boasted 'the prospect of being attacked does not affright Queenslanders'.[78] A letter to a Sydney paper saw it differently: 'The average Australian, be he in uniform or out of it, lives in a fool's paradise with a smug complacency born of censorship, propaganda and ineptitude.'[79]

In January 1942, Sydney debated whether *The Mikado* should be performed at the Theatre Royal. After protests, J.C. Williamson Ltd planned to exclude the Gilbert and Sullivan opera from its repertoire; but, after even more vehement protests, they reinstated it to packed houses and glowing reviews, 'in merry defiance of the Japanese menace', as the *Sydney Morning Herald* put it.[80]

Lurking behind the merry defiance, however, was a dread of an unfamiliar landscape. Sylvia Tate, a Victorian teenager, watched her parents read columns in *The Sun* of the 'dead', the 'missing presumed dead' and the 'missing': 'You'd go through them each day to see if anyone you knew was there.'[81]

Margaret Helm, married to a ship's pilot, thought each time he left home, 'Is this the last time I'll see you?'[82] That was in the seclusion of the home. Outside, people talked endlessly about high prices and shortages, but not the war.

By the middle of the year, the Japanese propaganda machine was broadcasting from Java the names of Australian prisoners of war, with letters to next of kin edited to emphasise good treatment and a longing for home. The aim of this was to generate public war weariness, and it created a dilemma for authorities in Australia. They couldn't stop the broadcasts and banning listening to them would cause more problems than it would solve. The best they could do was issue a press statement, stressing the propaganda nature of the broadcasts and assuring next of kin all essential information would be passed on to them as it became available. A ban was placed on press and radio from using content from the broadcasts.[83]

The threat of invasion seemed real to the Australian government and military, but the government had difficulty persuading the public to support the war effort whole-heartedly. A large propaganda bureaucracy, the Department of Information (DoI), was charged with informing and motivating the nation. A 'hate campaign' was launched in the press and on radio under the banner of 'Know Your Enemy', designed to harness a fear and loathing of Japanese people so as to increase the will for resistance.[84]

The enemy was demonised as vile and sub-human. 'Trained to hate from childhood', one poster ran, 'are they to ravage our homes? We've always despised them—NOW WE MUST SMASH THEM'.[85] Another asserted the 'Japanese Gestapo' even intimidated its own people with 'dangerous thoughts' using whips, rubber truncheons and itching powder.[86] More sedate posters warned against gossip and rumour-mongering.

Queensland premier Bill Forgan Smith objected to a poster showing a heavy-booted, ape-like Japanese soldier stepping on Australia with the slogan 'He's Coming South', not on grounds of taste but as defeatist. The slogan was replaced in Queensland with 'Go north and drive them into the sea'.[87]

'We are rapidly learning that in the Japanese we face a strange, unscrupulous and, in many ways, a reckless enemy,' said the *Sydney Morning Herald*, reporting on Japan's 'cult of death'. 'Fighting them is different from fighting any of the Occidental Powers, including the Germans. We have to fight fanaticism at its best and worst.'[88]

The deep-seated fear of sexual violence was widely played on. An *Argus* cartoon showed another ape-soldier, club in hand, holding a naked woman up by her hair.[89] Japanese were either goonish gorillas or buck-toothed, short-sighted weeds. It was an approach that had worked in the First World War, but times were changing and the Germans had been a different sort of enemy: arrogant bumpkins perhaps, but not a different race.

The campaign of hate provoked strong disapproval as crude, overstated racism and 'clumsy and unimaginative propaganda'. Writing for Sydney's *Daily Telegraph*, novelist Eleanor Dark claimed people wanted to know what to do, not how to feel. Those unmoved by the threat of bombs falling or invasion would 'not be moved by an abusive lecture or a scolding'.[90]

The government needed to build the nation's spirit to fight the war, cutting through people's inclination to irreverence, pursuit of leisure and the intractable belief that things turn out all right in the end. Ideas came flooding in from all directions. The Department of Information mostly borrowed from Britain. A publisher, K.D. Murray, proposed a Voluntary Publicity Panel of writers and journalists, devising slogans for the daily press, and fiction and feature stories for the weekly press. It wasn't taken up, probably because the DoI didn't want outside people intruding into its territory.[91]

Cynthia Skrine of Sydney proposed a small army of women as 'whisperers for victory' to combat defeatism, paying them ten shillings a day to talk loudly in trams of the strength of Australia's defences.[92] This idea wasn't taken up either. To a suggestion of inviting public opinion, Curtin responded tartly, 'The government is guided solely by war requirements and public opinion on such matters would not be of any assistance.'[93]

Anthropology professor A.P. Elkin bombarded the prime minister with proposals for a department of morale under Elkin's direction, and led a delegation to lobby Information minister Bill Ashley. Curtin passed the issue to former prime minister James Scullin, who asked a rising star of the bureaucracy, Alf Conlon, to prepare a report for the PM.[94]

Processing selection or exemption of students for the army as Sydney University's Manpower Officer, Conlon had caught the eye of Brigadier Victor Stantke, the army's Adjutant-General. Stantke was persuaded of the need for an army research section and put Conlon in charge, although what it might do was not clear. Conlon was handily placed to be assigned the morale report.[95]

The outcome was the advisory Prime Minister's Committee on National Morale, formed of 'distinguished and disinterested minds' hand-picked by Conlon from his allies, cronies and admirers.[96] Conlon and Elkin shared a mutual dislike of each other, so the professor was not among The Chosen. Appointed its chair, Conlon had branded the committee as the prime minister's to create the impression of close contact with Curtin, but it's more likely that the politician Curtin saw it as a means of sidelining a problem.

The Morale Committee first met for two days in Melbourne at the end of June 1942, meandering over a mish-mash of barely related topics reflecting the committee members' divergent interests and personal viewpoints.[97] Meeting again four weeks later, this time at the University of Sydney Law School, they considered various pre-existing reports, discussed what could and should be done and formed several sub-committees.[98] A pattern of periodic, unfocused meetings continued to the end of the year.

Central to this rambling, occasional talkfest was the low-key charisma of its chair. Softly spoken with pauses for dramatic effect, Conlon fidgeted constantly with his pipe, jabbing in the air with it for emphasis. On entering the army, he had been made a major. Tall and fleshy with a pallid face and steel-rimmed glasses, he looked quite unmilitary in uniform. To his admirers, Conlon was an intellectually stimulating visionary, a backroom operator with a direct line to the prime minister. To others he was an opportunist, an engaging talker, widely read but superficial.[99]

A delegation from the Morale Committee met briefly with Curtin in December to discuss creation of a national public relations body. But before discussion could go any further, Curtin wanted a report specifying the functions of the proposed service. The report, 'Plan for a National Public Relations Service', was delivered in January to the prime minister, proposing the Department of Information be disbanded and replaced with this new service, reporting directly to the prime minister.[100] A handwritten covering note by Conlon was addressed to 'Mr Curtain', raising doubts about his closeness to the PM.[101]

The report was considered by the War Cabinet on 2 March 1943 with critical notes by the Defence department attached. The argument for the service was dismissed as generalised, often vague and sometimes resorting to platitudes, more about what needed to be fixed than how to fix it. Curtin wrote to Conlon a week later, advising that the War Cabinet had decided no action was to be taken on the planned service.[102] By then Alf Conlon was in damage control, protecting his position in the army.

At the beginning of the year, Stantke had been succeeded by General Charles Lloyd, who disliked Conlon and thought his research unit was nonsense. He proposed to shut down the unit and return its head to civilian life, but Conlon was able to reach General Blamey through a mutual acquaintance and argue for the unit to be moved to come under Blamey's direct control. The military commander could see a potential use for a non-military conduit in post-war affairs. In February, Conlon's unit had been transferred to the Directorate of Military Intelligence.[103]

The PR proposal was the first report produced by the Morale Committee, which delivered only three more in the first nine months of 1943. Only one, on civilian morale in north

Queensland, involved original field research. There's no evidence the Committee had much effective influence; its reports were largely filed and ignored.

By the end of 1943, there was a new Information minister, Arthur Calwell, who told Curtin the committee's discontinuance 'would not mean any loss so far as my officers are concerned'.[104] The Morale Committee might have been part of the liberal intelligentsia 'debating the potential for a new order' in 'a new and better Australia', but it moved too slowly for wartime events. By the time it had convened and provided advice on pressing issues, the urgency had passed.

Australia's defence front line was its northern coastline, separated from the bulk of the nation's populace by inhospitable terrain, difficult to transport supplies across. Difficult also for invaders to advance across, but few in Australia seemed to comprehend that. However, if the assailants were to be stopped in the north, money and sweat had to be spent improving the access for military vehicles and supplies to the region. Major roadwork projects were carried out, first by a consortium of states, later by the federal government's wartime construction authority.

The Stuart Highway had originated as a dirt track known as the North–South Road, running over blacksoil plains alongside the Overland Telegraph Line. In the Wet it became a quagmire, in the Dry a corrugated dustbowl. In 1939, with war threatening to the north, Darwin's army commander, Colonel Horace Robinson, had put a convincing case for an all-weather road between Alice Springs and Birdum, the railhead from Darwin.[105]

The federal government funded construction of a lightly metalled road by the Main Roads departments of three states, New South Wales, Queensland and South Australia. Each worked on a one-third stretch of the 1000-kilometre upgraded track. Beginning September 1940, civilian road gangs were rushed from the three states to complete the project before the Wet set in. The Birdum railhead was moved to nearby Larrimah, to avoid Birdum's flooding in the Wet and the vulnerability of the Birdum Creek bridge to bombing. Men and machines pushed through virgin scrub and desert, finishing the job within 90 days.[106]

Convoys of three-ton trucks began taking men and supplies for Darwin on the four-day journey from Alice to Larrimah. In March 1941 the AIF 8th Division was brought up the road, en route to Malaya, at the peak of the Wet. The road soon became a watercourse, with trucks bogged and a concrete causeway washed out. Men were flown in to reinforce the road with sandbags and to cut timber to lay transversely, creating so-called corduroy sections.[107] Up to a hundred vehicles got bogged at any one time, and the road surface deteriorated to the point where maintenance gangs couldn't keep it serviceable.[108]

Drivers had to be stoic and resourceful in this unforgiving country. Ad hoc repairs were often called on; bush flies and red bulldust got in everything. There were kidney complaints from the constant jolting, irritated joints and muscles, dust-affected eyes and the accumulating strain of monotony. Where work was being carried out, drivers detoured on bulldozed tracks through spinifex and scrub.[109] Seven-ton Ford semi-trailers had been added to convoy fleets, churning up the sand so much that later trucks went wider on the harder undozed surface. On one occasion the Stewart brothers broke down on a wide detour and were not spotted or even missed for two days. They lived on tinned milk from their load and water from their radiator until a search party eventually found them.[110]

A road called the East–West Road had already been built from Mount Isa in 1941, joining the North–South Road north of Tennant Creek. It was later officially named the Barkly Highway. A major US Army transport unit set up camp at Mount Isa in mid-1942 with about 1500 vehicles, many of them ten-wheel GMC trucks, and 5000 American soldiers, mostly black drivers.[111]

With dramatically increased traffic, the East–West Road was tar-sealed in sections and needed constant maintenance and upgrading. The Americans carried supplies and men over 725 kilometres of rough road to Larrimah, ignoring the official limit of 25 mph (40 kmh) and digging up gravel at over 45 mph (72 kmh). Tyres burst in the 50°C heat, or the treads were thrown off from overheating, road corrugation or incorrect tyre pressure. There were often congestion problems, especially where it met the North-South Road. The Americans would skirt off-road to speed past stationary Australian convoys of Chevrolets, designed for the Indian Army.[112]

By mid-1942 the Wet had taken its toll on the North–South Road, the gravel surface worn away in many places and become corrugated or returned to bulldust. The federal government's Allied Works Council, formed early in the year, had raised a labour force, the Civil Construction Corps (CCC), responsible for roads, airfields and munitions factories. The CCC was a mix of volunteer labour and industrial conscripts supplied by the government's Orwellian Manpower Directorate. Re-gravelling and tar sealing the road that would become the Stuart Highway was one of its biggest projects.[113]

With a workforce that included conscientious objectors and 'enemy aliens', the highway upgrade from Alice Springs right through to Darwin took until early 1944 to complete. At the same time, a battalion of US Army Engineers was stationed in the Top End to build air bases. With new airfields and new aircraft and crew, the Allies began to dominate the skies to the north of

Australia. Medium and heavy bombers flew longer missions over occupied islands in the East Indies and southwest Pacific.

From 1942 the Australian Army established a network of hospitals in the north, mostly constructed through the Allied Works Council. Intended primarily for the battle-wounded, they also serviced local populations. After the bombing of Darwin and increasing air raids, Mount Isa in the middle of northern Queensland believed its rich copper mine made it a strategic target for Japanese air attack and invasion. With Japan having pursued rubber in Malaya and oil in Borneo and Sumatra, Mount Isa felt threatened and thinly defended. If there were to be casualties, Mount Isa District Hospital needed to be properly protected.

An underground hospital was built with equipment supplied by Mount Isa Mines, the town's biggest employer, and volunteer labour by off-duty miners. A tunnel with three parallel adits was excavated, forming an E-shaped shelter with a vertical shaft for ventilation. Timbered, furnished and fitted out as a hospital with male, female and maternity/children's wards and a surgical theatre, it was a hundred metres behind the main hospital and kept fully equipped with linen and medical supplies. Patients were wheeled up the steep gravel path to the underground hospital's entrance in weekly air-raid drills, but there were never any raids on Mount Isa. Eventually the drills ceased and the underground hospital became a nurses' dormitory and a storage facility.[114]

Like other construction in the north to meet the feared invasion—oil-storage tunnels built into Darwin's cliffs, for example—the underground hospital was never used for that purpose. Although the threat seemed real at the time, it never eventuated. However, it was a contingency that had an incidental benefit of helping discourage a widely held belief that the nation's leaders were prepared to abandon the north to the enemy if needs be.

———

Fear of invasion by the Japanese had brought another invader to Australia . . . the Americans. Their occupation of the country and its impact on the way of life changed Australia as profoundly as Japanese occupation would have, although in a quite different way. The seeds of social change may have been sown before the war, but if they were, Australia's wartime love affair with America consolidated it. A new generation was waiting in the wings.

Most Australians agreed with John Curtin that only American intervention could save the country from Japanese invasion. The build-up of US forces was incremental and unrelenting. By mid-1942, there were 80,000 American troops in Australia; by 1943, 250,000.[115] American uniforms could be seen everywhere, stylish and well-laundered. Soon hamburger and hot-dog stands sprung up. The American flag flew from public buildings, cinemas played 'The Star-Spangled Banner' after 'God Save the Queen', newspapers published home news and sports results from the United States and recipes for American tastes. Department stores put on window displays for the 4th of July, with no one seeming struck by the irony of celebrating the end of British rule over its American colony.

At the same time, despite the public adulation of the United States, Americans were ripe for exploitation. Roger Jones, a kid then in Mackay, recalls, 'The taxis would take them via the moon to go round the block if they could scrounge enough petrol, and the publicans were charging five quid [$10] for a 17s 6d [$1.75] bottle of Scotch and one reputable firm used to hire out push bikes to them with a quid [$2] deposit and five bob [50c] a day, and then they'd have the local kids going to pinch the bikes back.'[116]

Despite the apparent good relations between Curtin and MacArthur, there was less harmony between Americans and Australians within the machinery of the war effort. The Lend-Lease agreement, in which Australia received military equipment in return for providing food and other services to US forces, was a constant source of wrangling. Australian soldiers resented differences in rates of pay and canteen food quality between them and their comrades-in-arms, as well as taxis looking for American tips and pubs serving only Americans. Australian troops were denied admission to entertainers and movie stars brought out for the Americans.[117]

The US Hospitality Bureau organised dances and social events with local church and community groups, and with young Australian women as dance partners. Female company was much sought after by American soldiers and readily available, with many Australian men away on active service. The visitors were a novelty to the local women with their attractive uniforms, charming manners and access to scarce consumer items. They brought gifts of flowers and stockings to women who seldom saw either item once rationing began . . . or, indeed, before that.[118]

These soldiers displayed physical affection more publicly than Australian men. Their success with Australian women created animosity between the forces, and alcohol-fuelled brawls broke out from time to time, when exchanges of banter escalated. Even if women weren't mentioned they were often what lurked behind the punch-ups.

Bill Bentson, a US Army sergeant, recalls seeing Walt Disney's *Bambi* at a Brisbane cinema. When Bambi was lost and cried out 'Mother, Mother, I want my mother, where's my mother?' a male voice shouted out, 'She's out with a bloody Yank!' The cinema audience roared with laughter.[119]

By the end of 1942 the infatuation with GIs was waning, many beginning to see their showy charm as artificial and calculated, the preoccupation of their conversation with sex as an 'infantile pin-up type of obsession'.[120] The brutal Melbourne murders by Private Leonski didn't help. As the threat of invasion receded, public sentiment changed and the attitude towards Americans changed with it. Saviours and heroes were no longer needed. The growing change was most noticeable in the bigger cities, Sydney and Melbourne, while people in the outer suburbs and the country saw less of them and the novelty persisted.

Brisbane and Townsville were garrison towns, nearer to the war, with troops heading north and 3-ton trucks shuttling between the docks and camps. Brisbane had to accommodate 73,000 US service personnel on top of 300,000 people already living there.[121] Officers were put up in prestigious hotels, other ranks in camps on suburban racecourses.

Tensions built even more in Townsville, a small city swollen with transients, both Australian and American, to four or five times its normal population of 25,000.[122] American forces had arrived in Townsville in early 1942, sudden and unannounced. Meryl Stone remembers waking up one morning to a changed town: 'There were trucks and tents everywhere, alongside the railway lines leading to the wharf. They'd disembarked at the wharf during the night and had set up camp.'[123]

Townsville was transformed. The local military command encouraged evacuation of non-essential civilians. By the middle of the year, over 5000 had left. Private residences were requisitioned, as well as hotels and schools. Thirty houses were commandeered in Chapman Street for a US Navy hospital, residents given a week to vacate. The houses were linked by a walkway; one side of the street was converted to wards, the other to services like laundry, laboratories and kitchens.[124] Tank traps and barbed wire were set up along the seafront, searchlights installed in inner and outer circles around the town. Planes were everywhere at all hours, flying into and out of the expanded gravel runway of Garbutt Air Base. Radio stations were silent at night.

A Japanese ambush on a Malayan road, January 1942.

Australians operate an anti-tank gun near Bakri, Malaya, January 1942.

General Arthur Percival.

General Gordon Bennett.

Sailors evacuating from the doomed HMS *Prince of Wales*, off the Malayan coast, 10 December 1941.

The aftermath of Japanese bombing of the yards at Sembawang Naval Base, Singapore, in January 1942.

The surrender party being taken to General Yamashita's HQ at the Ford Motor Company building, Singapore. General Percival is at far right. The others from left are Major Wild, Brigadier Newbigging, Colonel Sugita and Brigadier Torrance.

British troops surrender to the Japanese in Singapore, 15 February 1942.

Repatriating POWs from AIF 8th Division arriving home at the end of the war, October 1945.

Darwin burning in background after the Japanese bombing on 19 February 1942.

The bombed out Darwin Post Office.

The L-shaped Darwin Wharf after the bombing. Note the gap at the rear with a temporary suspension bridge and *Neptuna* submerged to the right.

Returning from the Middle East, troops of AIF 7th Division pass through outer suburbs of Adelaide.

General Douglas MacArthur arrives at Melbourne's Spencer Street railway station on 21 March 1942.

From left to right: General Blamey, General MacArthur and Prime Minister Curtin.

An Australian propaganda poster.

An Air Raid Precautions advisory sign.

A public air raid shelter under construction on Ann Street in Brisbane's Fortitude Valley.

Barbed wire defences installed at Manly Beach, Sydney.

Digging school trenches, Ascot State School, Brisbane.

Members of Adelaide's Defence Society practice rifle shooting.

No 1 Wireless Unit RAAF, a radio signal intercept and decrypt station at Stuart Creek near Townsville. A concrete block, the station had a false roof and painted verandah, doors and windows. Only the water tanks and steps up to the fake verandah were real.

Native carriers with a coast watcher teleradio set, northern Papua.

Coast watchers, Paul Mason (left) and Jack Read (right), Bougainville.

Nackeroos on patrol in northern Australia.

Yolngu men instructed in guerrilla warfare by Donald Thomson.

The anti-submarine net in Sydney Harbour, looking towards Watsons Bay. Lieutenant Chuma's midget submarine struck the light pile, right of centre.

Kuttabul on the morning after Sydney's midget submarine attack on 1 June 1942.

Lieutenant Chuma's midget submarine being raised from the anti-submarine net and brought to Clark Island in Sydney Harbour.

Above: The aftermath of the Japanese submarine shelling of Sydney's eastern suburbs.

Left: Rear-Admiral Gerard Muirhead-Gould, Naval OIC, Sydney Harbour.

Australian soldiers make their way along the Kokoda Track.

General MacArthur's staged landing at Leyte in the Philippines, October 1944.

A map claiming to show the Japanese invasion plan for Australia obtained from Chinese Military Intelligence, October 1942.

Japanese 'invasion currency'.

Bruce Acland.

Robert Brown.

Yve Jeanneret with her brother, Bobbie.

On 25 July 1942, two Japanese flying-boat bombers flew over Townsville's jetty bathed in light. When they returned at midnight, the city was blacked out and searchlights were on. Their bombs fell on tidal flats near the jetty.[125] Two nights later, a lone bomber, caught in anti-aircraft fire, dropped its bombs on a ridge mistaken for a runway.[126] The following night another lone bomber, attacked by American Airacobras, dropped its payload in the bay and fled.[127] The only damage caused in the three raids was shattered racecourse windows and the splintering of a coconut tree, but it did remind the citizens of Townsville how close the war was.

In May, returning AIF troops had started passing through Townsville on the way to New Guinea. Soldiers constantly milled around in the city. There were traffic problems with crowded streets and Americans unsure which side of the road to drive on. Anti-military sentiment, sometimes mutating into anti-Americanism, simmered among the permanent residents, who felt pushed around while troops ran their town. Civilians stood in queues with ration cards while the US Army baked 5000 loaves a day for its GIs.

The Americans were unconcerned what they paid for food, and prices went up. Soldiers fell into two economies. Australian troops lined up at Townsville's wet canteen, exchanging tickets for beer served in old fruit tins. It was a far cry from the sophistication of the American canteens.[128]

The transients got drunk and joined queues outside brothels in Ford Street, known colloquially as Broadway. Cash-strapped Australian soldiers were known to stand in brothel queues and sell their place to an American when they were near the door. Demand in Ford Street far exceeded supply, and some prostitutes plied their trade in Townsville's parks.[129]

Through the latter part of 1942, complaints drifted into the various arms of government about the behaviour of troops and the poor treatment of Townsville's residents; there were claims of debauchery and waste, and of people being forced out of their homes. In January 1943, two members of Alf Conlon's National Morale Committee were assigned to investigate the complaints.

R.D. 'Panzee' Wright, a medical researcher, and Ian Hogbin, an anthropologist, met with officials and had casual conversations with civilians and soldiers from both armies over twenty days. In a 23-page report they discounted most of the principal complaints. On the claim of people being forced out of their homes, they found most requisitioning of houses had been by private arrangement, often on a lucrative lease. Complaints had been made about the military wasting petrol, but the two researchers found its use by civilians more inefficient.

Wastage of food by the military was mostly not verified. Townsville Council members had told of the US forces throwing 48 hams on the tip, knowing the story had already been investigated and found false. Civilian claims about brothels and debauched behaviour were mostly found to be exaggerated, notwithstanding the fact that brothels did exist.

Wright and Hogbin found that, despite the resentment, Townsville's residents were still committed to defeating Japan and had made strong contributions to war loans and local Red Cross work. People complaining about hardships they believed they suffered uniquely were generally unaware the southern cities were enduring the same restrictions and austerity. The report recommended grievances should be heeded, even if frivolous or ill-informed, and every effort should be made to meet reasonable demands. 'False notions are often as harmful as real grievances,' it said.[130]

The report was circulated to relevant ministers and departments, but by then the problem had mostly receded with the successes of the Allied counter-offensive and the consequent winding down of the military presence in north Queensland.

The particular experiences and concerns of the people of Townsville give an insight into northern Australia and its sense of vulnerability to the expected invasion. They would be the front line, but they had moments of doubt about the government and the military's commitment to keeping the Japanese juggernaut at bay in the north. Are we expendable, they asked themselves, something that could be sacrificed to the greater good of ultimately prevailing in the Pacific War?

Chapter 7

EXPENDABLE

A nation watched nervously in fear, uncertainty and inertia as the Japanese bludgeoned their way seemingly towards Australia. All the arrows on newspaper maps of the war pointed towards Australia. What do we do, people wondered, if an invasion force is landed on Australia's shores? What does the military and the government expect of us? What might the invaders look to seize and what might we do to stop them?

The campaign in Malaya had indicated what an invading force might seek for its own use. In its first two weeks, in December 1941, three airfields were captured along with seven planes, 157 motor vehicles and 33 goods train wagons, all intact and immediately useable.[1] The paved airstrip at Alor Setar was barely damaged, with bombs piled high alongside and hot soup left on the dining table.[2]

Landing unopposed at Penang, the Japanese captured weapons, boats and supplies left behind by European civilians and the evacuating army, as well as a working radio station from which they immediately began broadcasting anti-British propaganda. Further down the coast, the Malayan capital was taken. Withdrawing defenders had set fire to their fuel reserves, but the occupying force found trains loaded with military stores in Kuala Lumpur's marshalling yards. They nicknamed them 'Churchill supplies'.[3]

Japan's key target was the oilfields of the East Indies, a reason for it going to war. Paratroops were dropped on Palembang in South Sumatra on 14 February 1942. In the Dutch troops' hasty exit from there, huge oil tanks and a refinery remained undamaged. A fire in the boilers was easily put out by the invasion force, demolition charges disarmed and valves shut. Much of a second refinery was damaged by time-delayed charges and took six months to return to production.[4]

In seeking responses if the war came to them, Australians looked to the Russians. France had allowed Nazi Germany to take Paris and its factories without destroying anything, but in the blitzkrieg on an unprepared Red Army, Stalin determined that the invaders would get nothing useful. 'Partial' scorched earth was imposed on the Soviet Union. Troops burned crops, destroyed bridges and evacuated factories. Steel and munitions plants in western USSR were dismantled and railed east. Electrical generators were sabotaged and mineshafts were collapsed. Railway rolling stock was destroyed or removed. Soviet lines had a different gauge from those in Germany, so German rolling stock couldn't run on them.

Scorched earth was applied ruthlessly and efficiently in Ukraine, where factories were destroyed. The dam wall at Dnipropetrovsk was broken and Kiev's main street mined and blown up.[5] Across Russia, partisan units sabotaged bridges and roads, telephone and telegraph lines. They set fire to forests, stores and transport. Collective farmers were to drive off cattle and hand over their grain to be carried back with the retreating army.

Hitler had expected invasion to spur Russians' contempt for their government, but it rallied the people behind it instead. In the eyes of many Australians, Russians had ceased to be communists; they had become heroes, people willing to fight off the invader in defence of their land.

With the Pacific War only three weeks old and the Japanese advancing ominously, the *Sydney Morning Herald* urged, 'It is not too soon for the Australian Government to plan and prepare people for a "scorched earth" policy, guerrilla fighting, and all else that "total war" entails.'[6] By February 1942, the federal government had asked the states to draw up detailed scorched earth plans, with guidelines to be provided in due course by its Defence Committee, a cumbersome body made up of service chiefs, senior military strategists and departmental secretaries.

Newspapers picked up the idea with enthusiasm. The *Courier-Mail* urged north Queenslanders to be ready to destroy all sugar, dairy and timber mill equipment, empty stores and wreck all vehicles . . . but not until the enemy landed.[7] All invasion armies arrive short of transport, the *Sydney Morning Herald* said, so civilians should destroy their cars, boats and bicycles, and not repeat the mistakes of Malaya. The press encouraged Australians to emulate Russia's scorching of the land ahead of Napoleon's army and Hitler's.[8]

Others had their reservations. At a Hunter Valley council meeting, a farmer moved that scorched earth for primary producers be ruled as 'impracticable and inducive to a state of starvation'. It was impossible to scorch crops like potatoes and maize, he claimed; but his motion was defeated.[9]

In March, the press reported amendments to National Security Regulations, giving the military scorched earth powers.[10] The army could prohibit people leaving areas or evacuees returning, and could remove or destroy animals, buildings and anything else that might be useful to an occupation force. The promised scorched earth guidelines, however, had not been forthcoming.

The federal government had become wary of popular movements and concerned about the impact of scorched earth plans on morale. But it made no difference: the genie was out of the bottle. The states were setting up scorched earth plans, as instructed, with varying degrees of enthusiasm and efficiency. New South Wales was quick out of the blocks, thanks to a blustering bureaucrat called Harold Swain.

Head of the NSW Forestry Commission, Harold Swain was confident of his own opinion and impatient with those who disagreed with it. Nearing 60 and largely self-taught, he had a chip on his shoulder about politicians and academics. He was neither.[11] In January 1942, he wrote a booklet on his own initiative called 'Total War—and Total Civilian Collaboration'. It was submitted to then New South Wales premier, Bill McKell, as a call to arms and a plan for civil mobilisation in the event of invasion.[12]

The Japanese, Swain predicted, would make no distinction between soldiers and civilians, so the public needed to be properly informed, trained and organised. While the armed forces engaged in battle, civilian guerrillas should assist from the rear, withdrawing inland and leaving nothing useful behind. Twenty-one evacuation routes from the New South Wales coast were detailed in his treatise; but there was to be no retreat from the eastern state capitals, Canberra or the industrial hub of Newcastle–Sydney–Port Kembla. These would be the enemy's main objective, and had to be fortified and defended.

The document included the full range of ARP (Air Raid Precautions) requirements and specified in pedantic detail provisions to be packed for an emergency: '3x8 oz. tins beef; 2 lbs. rice;

1 large Bovril'[13] and so on. Livestock was to be removed, given to the military or slaughtered; publicans were to destroy beer and wine and transfer fortified wines and spirits to medical services; boats were to be removed, hidden or sunk, engines disabled. People were to remove or destroy maps, radios, tools, food, water and soap before leaving. Parts of his exposition were lifted from Wintringham's *New Ways of War*, with people required to learn how to scout at night, make and throw hand grenades and 'trip' tanks with a crowbar.[14]

Swain proposed a Civil Collaboration Column (CCC) be set up in each shire and community, something akin to the People's Army that was emerging at the same time. If a Japanese landing was imminent by sea or air, there should be a ringing of bells and blowing of car horns. Women, children and the infirm should be evacuated along his pre-planned routes. Members of the CCC were to remove goods by truck and fill water carts to take to the hinterland. 'Stragglers, aliens, spies and traitors' were to be rounded up, although he offered no advice on identifying these folk.[15] It smacked of the vigilante groups the federal government wanted to discourage.

Swain's writing is described by one commentator as having a 'dogged urgency more akin to a Biggles book than a government report'.[16] The paper provides invective on Japanese behaviour in occupation, not necessarily inaccurate, plus a rather idealised view of the citizens' campaigns in Russia and China, and a measure of Australiana. 'The Australian is a good axeman', he asserts, 'and has good axes to use as a bayonet at close quarters'.[17] The romance of the bush!

The paper takes for granted a high level of civilian morale. While its detail contains much useful advice on dealing with invasion, it required an extraordinary input from civil and military authorities for its implementation. What saved it was timing. Soon after receiving it, Premier McKell was looking for someone to head the New South Wales scorched earth subcommittee under the state's War Effort Co-ordination Committee. Harold Swain was an obvious choice: he was appointed to chair the subcommittee.

The scorched earth subcommittee met for the first time on 16 February 1942. It included a police inspector and an army officer. The group worked for the next six weeks on producing a 'Scorched Earth Code'.[18] With such a forceful personality at the helm, it was always going to be a reworking of Swain's earlier paper, but a code drawn up without that precedent would probably have been much the same anyway.

The code assumed civilians would be evacuated in stages: women, children and the aged and infirm first, with others to live and work in their home areas until the army issued an evacuation order. After that, key resources were to be disabled or destroyed in three stages: first, tactical demolition of bridges, roads and jetties; second, 'parched earth' destruction of water vessels, motor vehicles and foodstuffs; and finally, 'scorched earth' destruction of everything else.[19] The goals were to prevent enemy forces living off their conquered land and force them to use their own supplies, to obstruct and impede their movement, and to leave nothing to loot.

Actions specified in the code had to be calculated and selective. The list of resources to target was detailed and extensive, with few stones left unturned. Jetties, wharves, roads and bridges were to be disabled by explosive, fire and axe; boats by removing the engine, scuttling or burning; fuels by running off or firing; vehicles by smashing essential parts, running so the engine seized up, setting on fire or dumping in deep water. Valves of wireless receivers were to be smashed, raw materials and foodstuffs burned, buried or wasted, stock slaughtered and grain scattered or soaked. Against each item the code provided the name of a person required to prepare a plan of destruction.

A draft of the NSW Scorched Earth Code was released at the beginning of April. Scorched Earth Support Squads were formed comprising local residents, usually from the VDC or the fire brigade, and training in code provisions began within a couple of weeks. Priority was given to country areas on the coast outside the industrial hub of Newcastle–Sydney–Port Kembla.[20]

New South Wales and Victoria drafted tentative scorched earth provisions ahead of the federal Defence Committee's promised guidelines, although it's questionable whether Harold Swain would have regarded his provisions as tentative. The other states elected to wait for the directive from Canberra before embarking on their provisions, so they could use it as a framework.

The directive was completed by the end of March. Its provisions—to be selective, planned and applied thoroughly—were in two categories: total denial of resources where civilians had been evacuated and the military was withdrawing; and partial denial where civilians were still present. In the latter case, essential services were to be left intact and things likely to assist the enemy destroyed.[21] The local military commander was empowered to implement scorched earth provisions, their details to be proposed by civil authorities and managers for army approval.

Five days later, the War Cabinet determined the Defence Committee's guidelines should be 'referred for consideration' to the South West Pacific Area (SWPA) Command, in process of being set up under General MacArthur.[22] It was duly sent to SWPA and disappeared into a black hole in the new command structure. It's hard to discern its fate from that point. There are scattered references to it in the records, directly or indirectly, over the following months. By and large, different areas went in different directions in a fairly uncoordinated fashion . . . or chose to wait for further directions. While different people started actions towards a range of provisions in their code, others in authority were putting a halt to some over-enthusiastic actions.

The commonwealth government instructed its departments to draw up their own scorched earth provisions, in addition to the states' codes. Overlapping codes and the non-appearance of the federal directive led to confusion, inaction and second-guessing. By May, the federal Ministry of Munitions was advising its state bodies that the directive was not yet approved.[23] By the end of July, the prime minister was telling the Queensland premier that SWPA has endorsed it, but gives no further detail.[24] Curtin might have been covering for American tardiness, but a directive had evidently been released by the end of August as the Ministry of Munitions is able to quote from it.

The release was far from systematic. The NSW War Effort Committee, of which Harold Swain's group was a subcommittee, complained to the army's local area commander, General Albert Fewtrell, that it didn't have a copy. It took another month for it to arrive.[25]

There may have been a growing concern about the impact of scorched earth on public morale. Already 'scorched earth' had been replaced with the less vivid 'denial of resources to the enemy' in correspondence. Professor Elkin, the anthropologist ignored for the Committee on National Morale, had continued to sample the public mood, reporting his findings to the prime minister and to the *Sydney Morning Herald*. Talk of scorched earth and mass evacuation encouraged defeatism in people, he wrote.[26] In a letter to the *Herald*, he pointed to a problem in emulating Russians. 'The Russians could retreat hundreds of miles and still live off the earth and continue their industries. But once we scorch our coastal belt and retreat from two hundred to three hundred miles inland, we enter a zone of sparse pastoral country and spasmodic crops—we go to land which is only too frequently scorched by nature.'[27]

Without central guidelines for consistency, implementing scorched earth became scattered and uncoordinated. Different groups produced their own version, unrelated to what others were doing. Back in January, before it had drawn up its directive, the Defence Committee had endorsed laying mines under RAAF runways in northern Australia and coastal New South Wales. By August, MacArthur's chief engineer, General Pat Casey, had decided demolition by explosive was ineffective. It could be quickly repaired and mined runways were a danger to those using them in the meantime.[28] Lightning had set off explosives in airstrips on King and Bathurst Islands, fortunately without casualties.[29] Explosives were removed and shafts covered for aircraft safety. The War Cabinet had already ordered the removal of demolition charges placed under Sydney's Mascot (Kingsford Smith) runways.[30]

In response to the call for scorched earth actions, army engineers in Wyndham in northern Western Australia wired up the meatworks and planted explosives there. They wanted to demolish it immediately in case they were unable to do so when the Japanese invaded. The state premier, John Willcock, got wind of their plan and opposed the premature action. A hostile debate followed, but Willcock prevailed and the meatworks survived the war.[31]

Some targets were not so fortunate. As noted,[32] Bondi's two concrete piers were demolished, although they were more utilitarian than aesthetic. The Hawkesbury River Bridge survived, as did most scheduled structures in the absence of invasion. In Victoria, gelignite was put into drill holes in sections of a wooden bridge at Barwon Heads. Holes were drilled across runways on airfields at Malacoota and Wilsons Promontory with explosives inserted and wired to a central bunker. They weren't detonated, however, instead waiting for an invasion force to attack Victoria's shoreline. As with Bondi, it didn't.

One act of resource denial was carried out successfully without irreversible destruction. After the initial Darwin raid, a government plan was developed to relocate cattle away from areas the enemy might occupy. By the middle of the year a massive cattle trek was under way, with over 150,000 head of cattle driven from the Top End to southern Queensland, a journey of over 2500 kilometres that would take at least six months. Australia's top drovers were brought in, along with Aboriginal stockmen. Mobs of cattle were moved in supervised rotation, so there was only one mob at a time at any government water bore, its wind pump temporarily replaced by a more reliable portable motor pump, drawing water from 100 metres below the surface.[33] The stock drive was directed by the Northern Territory's administrator, Aubrey Abbott, who claimed the cattle arrived 'fatter than when they left their home grazing country'.[34] The drove was later immortalised in the 1946 movie *The Overlanders*.

It was not until November 1942, however, that a denial of resources scheme got under way in South Australia. A month later the Queensland scheme had barely begun. As the army was leaving supervision of code provisions to the discretion of its local commanders, the Ministry of Munitions gave up on a departmental plan. In mid-1943, Curtin advised state premiers that denial of resources planning was sufficient to meet the needs at that time and should be discontinued south of the Tropic of Capricorn.[35] The invasion of Australia had become a diminishing threat, but the strategic differentiation of northern Australia from the populated south was an ongoing thorn in the side of the people of the north.

On 20 October 1942, Eddie Ward, a fiery orator with a machine-gun delivery, told an ALP meeting in Hobart, 'The government found when it took office that there was a plan in existence which, if put into effect, would have meant abandoning the whole northern part of Australia without firing a shot. How many people are aware of that?'[36]

The statement went largely unnoticed but, campaigning in the Victorian state election a week later, Ward repeated his claim that the Menzies–Fadden governments had planned to abandon northern Australia to the Japanese. This time, journalists sought a response from Opposition leaders. Billy Hughes, the new UAP leader, called Ward's claim 'a wicked invention'[37] and Menzies dismissed it as 'a figment of Mr Ward's exuberant imagination'.[38] The Opposition threatened to withdraw from the fragile unity of the Advisory War Council.

Both Menzies and Fadden pointed out that the defence plans of their governments had been considered by the AWC, which included members of the Labor Party, among them Curtin and Forde. Any proposal to abandon the north would have been known to them at that time. Ward had never been on the council, so he was not in a position to know, but Menzies and Fadden neither confirmed nor denied it had been proposed.[39]

Ward continued to hammer the point on the campaign trail in Victoria, with increasing press coverage. By the middle of November, Opposition members of the Advisory War Council were pressing Curtin to rein in his Labour and National Service minister, whose claims could only be publicly challenged by compromising national security. Curtin agreed that Ward's statement should not have been made. He claimed he had sent him a telegram and said he would talk to him on the issue.[40]

Most probably no telegram was sent and Curtin didn't talk to Ward about it at that time. John Curtin didn't like or trust Eddie Ward, a pugnacious class warrior, but he had pressing reasons to tread softly with him. At General MacArthur's urging,

Curtin was trying to get Labor parliamentary support to allow the militia to serve outside Australia, in the islands to the north. The party had split over the issue of conscription in the First World War and Curtin didn't want the militia extension to cause another damaging split.

Cabinet had supported an amendment of the *Defence Act* to enable militia to serve overseas, but only after a long and hostile debate. Eddie Ward was vehemently anti-conscription and the Citizen Military Force (the militia) included conscripts. He had argued bitterly in Cabinet against the amendment, and Curtin was sure he would step up his opposition to it outside Cabinet if Curtin tried to silence him on abandonment of the north. That could lead to a rift in the ALP its leader didn't need.[41]

On 10 December, Ward again raised the northern defence line, this time in parliament. Shortly after Japan entered the war, he said, the Australian military formulated a plan to abandon northern Australia if an invasion force landed there. High Command had considered that defending large and important areas of north Australia was not feasible.[42] Ward's point was the unpreparedness of the previous government for war, but the predicament arguably continued under the Curtin government. For a while after that, he kept quiet on the subject.

So, did a plan exist to abandon the north to Japan (or any other attacker for that matter)? And, if so, how did Eddie Ward come across it?

As already noted, Australia has long been fixated on its supposed vulnerability to seizure by a foreign military force. In 1930, the Australian Army drew up plans for defence against invasion, unconvinced that construction of the Singapore base would ever be finished and, even if it was, whether it could hold off the Japanese until the British fleet arrived. The army assumed the attacking force's objective would be the areas 'necessary to the economic life of Australia', namely Sydney, the Hunter and Illawarra regions and Melbourne. While other capital cities were 'important to local state interest, their loss was not likely to disorganize economic life'.[43] This analysis may not have abandoned the north, but it certainly created a defence priority.

Strategic thinking from that point concentrated mostly on the significance of the Newcastle-to-Melbourne strip, not on what was expendable, although that was there to be inferred. The Defence Committee made it explicit in 1936. In February that year, it assessed Australia's defence capabilities including the strategic importance of northern Australia, 'taken as the area of Australia north of Brisbane's parallel of latitude'. A small force above that line, the report concluded, would offer little deterrent to an enemy.

It went on, 'The occupation of a portion of Northern Australia would not vitally affect the bulk of the Australian people who reside in the southern and eastern portions of the continent.'[44] If only the north was occupied, a defence force could be mobilised to drive the invader out. Among the signatories to this report was Colonel Vernon Sturdee, who had also contributed to the strategic plan of six years before and would go on to be chief of general staff by the time Japan entered the war.

By 1942, Australia was at war with Japan and General Iven Mackay was in command of Home Forces, the remnant left to defend Australia while the cream of the army was fighting in the Middle East. Japan's rapid advance south, the fall of Rabaul and the likely loss of Singapore laid Australia open to invasion. It was not possible to defend the whole coast of Australia with such limited numbers. The military needed to determine which areas were vital to defend and which had a lower priority.

On 4 February, Mackay wrote to Army minister Frank Forde for government approval of a strategic plan. He argued defence should be concentrated in the areas essential to carrying on the war effort and to providing a base for US operations against Japan. Mackay proposed the vital area to retain was the industrial hub of Newcastle–Sydney–Port Kembla, along with Melbourne. Earmarked as a base for the anticipated American forces, Brisbane was included.

Townsville and Tasmania could not be reinforced, because that would require moving forces from the vital southeast; but, for reasons of national morale more than military value, neither would their garrisons be reduced.[45] It was important to 'resist the creation of a false sense of security by the dispersion of the very limited number of troops available for the defence of Australia . . . It may be necessary to submit to the occupation of certain Australian areas by the enemy should local resistance be overcome.'[46]

It was a contingency plan, not a proposal for capitulation. Although northern Australia wasn't specified by General Mackay, it was clear that was an area—or *the* area—in mind. Frank Forde, whose electorate was Capricornia in north Queensland, certainly thought so. Sensing his seat under threat, Forde asked Vernon Sturdee, promoted to general and Mackay's superior officer, to consider an additional division in Queensland and more equipment allocated there. Sturdee's brisk reply was that this was not a matter to be dealt with 'on States' interests and boundaries alone', but on defence of the Commonwealth as a whole. In other words, 'No'.[47]

Forde lobbied the army against the priority for southeastern Australia; in this he was supported by Opposition Leader Arthur Fadden, whose electorate was in south Queensland. Mackay reiterated the lack of equipment for the Home Forces and their limited training, but Forde wouldn't budge. Two days later, Singapore fell.

The strategy of forward defence was now in limbo and events had given Forde a way out. Prime Minister Curtin broadcast from his sickbed, calling for 'resistance to an enemy threatening to invade our own shore'.[48] Military strategy was no longer a matter of contingency, but of dealing with the here and now.

At a meeting of the War Cabinet, Forde argued government had a duty 'to defend the whole of the populated areas of Australia to the utmost of our ability and to prevent the enemy by every means within our power from obtaining a foothold on our shores'.[49] The service chiefs should prepare a new analysis, he instructed, taking account of Australia as a base for the counter-offensive, of the AIF forces returning from the Middle East and of the coming concentration of American forces in Australia for the offensive against Japan.[50]

The next day Darwin was bombed, further undermining Mackay's analysis. By the end of the month the army had prepared a new analysis, based on the resources then available and not greatly different from the previous one, although increasing the Fremantle garrison and providing anti-aircraft defences for Townsville. It did note, however, that variations were possible once reinforcements had arrived from the Middle East and the United States. The importance of holding the industrial region was stressed, and a determination to defend Port Moresby, although not the wherewithal to do it.[51]

The disparity between the government's political need that all parts of Australia should be defended, and the military's shortage of men and materiel to do that, resolved itself within a few weeks during which no Japanese invasion was launched. The AIF 8th Division had been lost in its entirety at Singapore, but over March and April the 6th Division, most of the 7th Division and an American division arrived in Australia. The gaps in the north could start to be filled. Townsville, Darwin and Port Moresby were all reinforced. At the same time, Japan's unstoppable drive south struck speed humps. An amphibious invasion force heading for Port Moresby—and maybe north Queensland—was thwarted in the Coral Sea, and a successful landing at Milne Bay on the eastern end of New Guinea was driven off.

Fear of invasion hadn't gone, but it had lost some of its potency. John Curtin was still talking it up to enable public acceptance of the austerity measures necessary to fight a war in Australia's neighbourhood. Scorched earth planning was well advanced in the southeastern quarter, but largely fumbled in the more vulnerable north. Allied military leaders and strategists had been trying to second-guess Japanese intentions after Singapore and the East Indies. Was Australia next in their sights and, if so, where did they plan to strike?

After the devastating bombing of Broome in March, General George Brett, soon to be replaced by MacArthur as the senior American commander in Australia, had become convinced the main threat to Australia was from the northwest. However, the Australian general, Syd Rowell, didn't see Darwin as a stepping stone to the invasion of Australia. He thought the Japanese would want to prevent its use to launch an offensive against them, but their main attack would be on Australia's east coast. The Battle of the Coral Sea was still in the future.

At a meeting of military heads in Melbourne, Brett asked what the next defensive line would be if troops were withdrawn from Darwin through an attack on the northwest coast. What would the Australians do if the Japanese landed at Broome and headed for Alice Springs?

'Send out the Salvage Corps to pick up the bones of Japs who died in the desert,' replied Rowell.[52]

A Japanese landing in the north was still a long way from the conquest of Australia.

By the end of 1942, with the course of the war looking rosier than it had at the beginning of the year, the issue of abandoning the north to the enemy had lost momentum. It probably fed the National Morale Committee's research finding that north Queenslanders believed they had been singled out for restrictions and austerity measures, but elsewhere it was no longer important . . . until Douglas MacArthur revived it in a fit of self-aggrandisement.

On 17 March 1943, MacArthur released a press statement to selected journalists to mark the anniversary of his arrival in Australia. He also used the occasion to apply political pressure to Curtin, who wanted to bolster defences in the northwest against a perceived enemy intention to land there. These were men MacArthur wanted for a planned drive towards Rabaul.[53] The general claimed to have been horrified on his arrival to have found a High Command plan for the defence of Australia that involved withdrawing south of a line just above Brisbane and conceding the area north of it to the Japanese. The military called it the Brisbane Line, he said. He claimed to have overruled this 'defeatist attitude' and to have taken the Battle for Australia to the strategic islands to the north by pushing the bomber line forward and moving ground troops up 'to take up the slack from the so-called "Brisbane Line"'.[54]

MacArthur's allegation was widely reported in the Australian press, notably in an extensive article in the *Argus*. War correspondent George Johnston, who would later write *My Brother Jack*, reported MacArthur's claim that 'it was the intention of Australia to defend along a line somewhere near the Tropic of Capricorn, which would be known as the Brisbane Line'.[55]

The term Brisbane Line, coined in fact by MacArthur, gained currency. Australia's military leaders leapt to their own defence, pointing out that most of what MacArthur claimed to have done was already in train by the time he took command of South West Pacific Area. The garrison at Port Moresby had been increased by a brigade at the outbreak of war in the Pacific, indicating an intention to defend north of Australia. The 27 February assessment by the military had flagged increases to northern defences once reinforcements arrived. General Vasey had issued an operational order on 10 March that the Torres Strait Islands were to be defended 'to the limit of human endurance'. If Townsville could not hold off an assault force, defenders were to withdraw—not south, but inland to Charters Towers.

All of these were put in place before MacArthur came to Australia.[56] In addition, the Australian government had proposed a strategy for the south Pacific three weeks before MacArthur arrived and seven weeks before he took command of SWPA.[57]

MacArthur's first directive as Supreme Commander of SWPA was substantially the same as the Australian Army's plan two weeks earlier.[58] There's no record of the decision MacArthur asserts he made on arrival, apart from his claim a year later and repeated twenty years later in his book, *Reminiscences*. It may be that he had in mind his 'I shall return' speech at Terowie on the train journey from Alice Springs to Melbourne. If he did, he was drawing an extremely long bow.

MacArthur was never greatly interested in the defence of Australia, beyond preserving it as a base to reconquer the Philippines. If that end had necessitated conceding Australian territory to the enemy, he would have had no qualms about doing it. Indeed, he wasn't prepared to let his Rabaul mission be held up for the defence of northwest Australia.[59]

Notwithstanding MacArthur's claim to have moved the front line forward, no addition was made to the New Guinea force until May, and then it was ordered by the Australian, General Blamey. In fact, MacArthur's reluctance to reinforce Port Moresby's garrison created a problem when the Japanese started advancing along the Kokoda Track.

Even if the American's claim to have redirected the Allied initiative is an exaggeration or untrue, it still leaves open whether there was a Brisbane Line and who was responsible for it if there was.

Ward's original allegation in October 1942 had drawn on a speech a month earlier by Queensland politician Ned Hanlon, without knowing Hanlon was referring to the 1936 Defence Committee assessment.[60] Prompted by an insider in Forde's department, who thought he recalled it in a 1941 Sturdee proposal to the Menzies government, Ward had assumed this was the defence line to which Hanlon had referred.[61]

Around that time, Forde had passed on his staffer's unchecked recollection to Curtin, who used it in a press briefing before Ward had aired his allegation. Curtin had needed to head off criticism that his government wasn't ready for a renewed invasion threat with the Americans struggling in Guadalcanal at the time. 'We are now defending Australia two thousand miles north of where the past government planned,' he had claimed then.[62]

By the end of 1942 the issue had gone off the boil, the government undamaged by its risky management. The following May, ignited by MacArthur's posturing, Eddie Ward resumed his attack on the Menzies–Fadden government, storming an election campaign in Western Australia. He used the term Brisbane Line as if he'd always called it that. Confident it didn't exist, the now-Opposition demanded proof of Ward's claims.

For the next few weeks, the Army Ministry scoured its records for a Sturdee document proposing a Brisbane Line, but none could be found.[63] Fred Shedden advised his assistant that General

Mackay's 4 February 1942 memo was the only plausible analysis that might include a Brisbane Line.

He had good reason to narrow the search. As Secretary of the Defence Committee at the time, Shedden knew a line that could be described as a Brisbane Line was proposed in the 1936 Defence Committee plan.[64] Although that was well before the war with Japan, he was very aware it would be waved around mercilessly in the public arena by Ward and the Labor Party as they worked to skewer their political opponents. Shedden was politically astute enough to see this could come back and bite the committee's members, including himself.

Curtin, Forde and Ward were all unaware of the detailed content of the 1936 appraisal, if they even knew of its existence. Shedden did. It was in his departmental files and he ensured it stayed there . . . undisturbed.[65] Shedden advised Curtin that there was no reference to a Brisbane Line in the 1941 Cabinet records or a subsequent directive. Accepting that advice, Curtin told Fadden the Mackay proposal included a defence line rejected by the government. Steps were taken instead to reinforce Australia's defence.[66]

Ward continued to allege the Brisbane Line was conceived under the previous government. The *Daily Telegraph* accused Fadden of blaming Mackay for the Brisbane Line strategy[67] and Curtin leapt to Mackay's defence, refusing to allow him 'to be the scapegoat of any controversy about what is called the Brisbane Line'. He added that Mackay 'had the soundest of military reasons for avoiding a wide dispersal of an inadequate force', turning the heat back on previous governments.[68]

The *Sydney Morning Herald* blamed Curtin for bringing Mackay's name into the argument.[69] At that time, the Curtin government was dealing with the issue of denial of resources—scorched earth being its more eye-catching form. As that sat uncomfortably with the Ward allegations, Curtin was keen to bring an end to the Brisbane Line altercation.[70]

On 7 June 1943, Curtin and Shedden met with MacArthur, who advised Australia was no longer 'under the very great danger of invasion' that it had been when he arrived.[71] Curtin saw an opportunity to defuse the Brisbane Line controversy and told the Australian people that 'the holding war imposed on us in circumstances of great difficulty' was over and both limited and major offensives would be launched against Japan. There would be marauding raids, but invasion was no longer imminent.[72]

The move to an offensive war was a pressure release that made the defensive record of the government—or any past government—of passing interest only. The interest now became whether it heralded an early election.

In federal parliament on 22 June, the Opposition moved a vote of no confidence in the Curtin government. In the debate that followed, Eddie Ward 'revealed' that the Brisbane Line had been proposed not by General Mackay, who was in the Middle East at the time, but by General Sturdee, who was chief of general staff in 1941. 'But I am most reliably informed that one important report is now missing from the official files,' he said. Ward alleged the report was submitted to Percy Spender, who was Army minister at that time, an accusation Spender immediately denied.[73]

The 'no confidence' motion was narrowly lost, but in the course of claims and counter-claims, the government found itself backed into a political corner it could best escape by agreeing to a royal commission on the Brisbane Line, by suspending Ward as a minister until the commission had reported its findings and by a dissolution of parliament.

A royal commissioner was appointed: Justice Charles Lowe, who had held the enquiry into the first Darwin bombing. The terms of reference were deliberately narrow: whether a document was missing from official files, what its content was and how Ward had come by knowledge of its existence.[74] Much of the evidence was heard in camera. Ward elected not to appear, legitimately citing parliamentary privilege.

Lowe wrote his report the next day. Without Eddie Ward's evidence, he was unable to investigate his statement about the missing document. No witness admitted to being Ward's informant. Justice Lowe's sole finding was that no document existed that was missing from official files.[75]

After a sometimes rowdy election campaign, in which war preparedness and the Brisbane Line featured prominently, the Curtin government was swept back with a gain of thirteen seats. The Brisbane Line controversy appears to have had little impact on the result. The only seat lost by the ALP was Maranoa in rural south Queensland. The defeated MP was a Ward supporter, but the result was probably more a reflection of issues to do with the flood of American troops in the state.

The Brisbane Line didn't exist as a label until Douglas MacArthur used it, nor as an entity as generally understood. The nearest to the concept of a Brisbane Line was the Defence Committee's line in the sand separating the high priority industrial hub of southeast Australia from the lower priority of the thinly populated north. It didn't necessarily propose abandoning the north, but if the nation's limited home defences were overwhelmed and it was occupied by an enemy force, it was possible to continue the battle and drive the invader out. In 1936 Australia wasn't at war, so that appraisal related to a theoretical invader, albeit most probably Japan.

By the time General Mackay produced his strategy, Australia was at war with an unfaltering enemy and had understrength, undertrained and underarmed troops to resist an invasion force, if one were to appear on its home shores. The bulk of Australia's skilled forces were occupied in another war overseas. The need to defend the crucial area left the lower priority area with a limited capacity to repel an invader.

A contingency plan was developed in case that resistance was overwhelmed. It was not a case of conceding the north to the invader 'without firing a shot'. It was a scenario that was quite possible despite the military's best endeavours within its limited means, a contingency that had to be contemplated and for which a strategy had to be formulated.

Although the Mackay plan was politically problematic, the military continued to regard it as a contingency plan and the government turned a blind eye to that. At the time it was devised, in February 1942, the government had no alternative anyway until troops started arriving from the Middle East and the United States, a month or so later. The contingency plan presumably continued after that, although the likelihood of it coming into play was greatly reduced.

At least the Australian military had a contingency plan, unlike Britain in Singapore. There the British strategy had been only: what we'll do to stop the invader. There was no: what we'll do if we can't . . . unless it was to agree with the Americans that Singapore wasn't crucial after all.

That would have been very cold comfort for those in Japanese POW camps.

Chapter 8

WATCHERS OF THE NORTH

Conscious, after the First World War, of Australia's long, undefended shoreline, a naval officer in Western Australia, Captain James Clare, proposed a scheme for surveillance of the 25,000 kilometres of mostly isolated coast. The Naval Board established the Coast Watching Organisation in 1922, appointing unpaid civilians to report enemy activities and suspicious behaviour in wartime. Along the nation's northern and northeastern fringes, postmasters, teachers, police, missionaries and station managers were recruited as watchers, each given a printed sheet of instructions for passing on by telegraph or pedal radio anything significant they saw.[1]

Without a war there was little to report, but when war broke out in Europe the service was extended to New Guinea and the Solomon Islands. Coordinating it was the RAN's Lieutenant Commander Eric Feldt in Port Moresby.

The son of a Swedish-born north Queensland cane farmer, Feldt had served in both British and Australian navies. Rising to the rank of lieutenant, he retired at the ripe old age of 23 and went to New Guinea, where he worked as a district officer and, later, warden of the Wau goldfields.[2] Rejoining the Australian Navy in 1939, he was told to report to the Director of Naval Intelligence, Commander Rupert Long.

'Cocky' Long knew Feldt from their naval college days. He'd been trying to expand Coast Watching for some time, but found little support. Now that the country was at war, even though at a distance, his opportunity had come. He put Feldt in charge of naval intelligence in New Guinea and tasked him with extending Coast Watching into the surrounding region with volunteer civilians.[3]

Known as 'Islanders', the Europeans living there were a hard-bitten, self-sufficient lot. Feldt knew many of them personally and toured the islands to enlist as many as he could as coast watchers, especially those who already owned a radio telephone. Standoffish and correct with his naval colleagues, Feldt's dry, self-deprecating sense of humour appealed to the Islanders. He knew the islands and their people and they knew and trusted him, the sort of people who responded more to personal contact than to general orders.[4]

Most of the teleradios were cumbersome sets of transmitter, receiver and loudspeaker called Type 3B. Transported in three metal boxes along with a car battery charged by a 30-kilogram petrol engine, a set needed a dozen native carriers to move it from one location to another. Each transmitter was fitted with a crystal that operated on a rarely used frequency that receiving stations tuned to continuously. The 3B could send a signal up to 600 kilometres using voice and 1000 kilometres with Morse.[5]

By the end of 1940, there were more than a hundred teleradios in the network of coast watchers in the islands, feeding their messages in simple code to local hubs. When Feldt moved to Townsville with Area Combined Headquarters in early 1941, hubs at Port Moresby, Rabaul, Tulagi in the Solomon Islands and Port Vila in the New Hebrides (now Vanuatu) passed their watcher reports to the new command centre there.

Although they were in a paramilitary unit, the brief for coast watchers was to not engage with the enemy. Eric Feldt emphasised the point with the organisation's code name, 'Ferdinand', after the bull in the 1938 Walt Disney cartoon.[6] Ferdinand didn't fight but sat under a tree and smelt the roses. The watchers weren't to smell roses, but they were to sit under a tree watching the enemy and report what they saw. They were purely a surveillance unit.

The Pacific War was not then a reality, but there had been a Japanese presence around the waters of northern Australia for some time. By the twentieth century, pearling ships were operating around Broome and the Arafura Sea north of the Territory. Crews and divers on these Australian-owned luggers were mostly Japanese, using the Tiwi Islands and Arnhem Land for fresh water and ship repairs. Aboriginal men guided the luggers around shoals and reefs and offered their young women to the crews in exchange for tobacco, rice, flour and tinned food.

In more recent years, Japanese-owned vessels had joined the harvesting of pearl shell and the Japanese presence continued to grow. From 1936, the government launch *Larrakia* patrolled territorial waters to police poaching and intercept the 'lubra trade'.[7] There were up to 70 Japanese luggers off the Arafura coast at any one time by 1937, which meant there were as many Japanese men around there as the non-Aboriginal population of Darwin. The Yolngu people of Arnhem Land had more contact with Japanese than with white Australians.

As war approached, Japanese ships and aircraft were increasingly seen around New Guinea and its nearby islands. Merchant ships visited Rabaul, Moresby and other ports frequently with very little cargo. Something was of interest to them. There were concerns that some of the pearling luggers had been briefed by the Japanese military to gather intelligence and to influence Aboriginal communities, although nothing was done to counteract this.

Later, when the war had reached the Pacific and was heading in Australia's direction, the fear arose that an enemy landing force might bring crewmen from the luggers to collect native support. After the devastating attacks on Darwin and Broome, air raids continued across the north from Exmouth Gulf to Townsville. By the end of March there had been over twenty raids on the Australian mainland and it was feared they might be a prelude to landing an invasion force.

Assessing counter-espionage needs and security measures in the north, the deputy director of military intelligence claimed that the Northern Territory was 'a hotbed of Japanese espionage' and that it was likely that 'enemy agents are being landed at present by parachutes from aircraft coming in over the Gulf of Carpentaria'. The Japanese, he said, had won over the Aboriginal population 'for the purpose of: spreading terror amongst the whites; attacking whites if and when landings are attempted by the enemy; fifth column work generally'.[8]

Australia's second-ranked army intelligence officer didn't identify the source of this startling intelligence, but it was not at odds with the views of white Australians living in the harsh environment of the north. Unease was expressed by landowners and missionaries around Arnhem Land, the Gulf country and Cape York Peninsula that Japanese had been using gifts of tobacco to peddle influence with Yolngu people and recruit them as informers.

One Cooktown resident complained that 'mission natives would show little reluctance to the changing of masters'.[9] A Perth man wrote to the prime minister that the 'aborigines up North are wonderful bushmen—and unbeatable at finding water' and would willingly guide the Japanese for 'a plug of tobacco and gaudy clothes'. They should therefore be moved inland, far from any likely enemy landing places.[10]

Zeros were regularly seen around the Northern Territory's coastal islands after the Darwin attack and Japanese patrol vessels frequented the Gulf of Carpentaria. Len Harris, a Groote Eylandt missionary, had been a coast watcher since before the war. One day, men paddled across from Bickerton Island, between Groote Eylandt and the mainland, to tell Harris some Japanese had landed there. About 40 Aboriginal men waited with shovel-nosed spears to ambush the Japanese if they came over to Groote Eylandt, but they left Bickerton that night and never came back.[11]

On another occasion, an Aboriginal group camping at the Roper River mouth paddled out to nearby Maria Island in the Gulf of Carpenteria and saw a Japanese ship on the other side. A man they took to be the captain called out and tossed some things overboard in their direction. They paddled closer to the floating objects and found tobacco in them. The man shouted in English, 'Where's the Roper River Mission?'

'We don't know,' was the reply. 'We don't know about any mission!'

The 'captain' threw some more containers into the sea and, as the paddlers came closer, called out pointing to the Roper River mouth, 'This is the Roper River, isn't it?'

'You're too far south. That's the Limmen River.'

The ship turned to the north and headed off, away from the Roper River.[12] The Yolngu people of that part of Arnhem Land had a history of hostility to Japanese visitors that pre-dated the war, from disputes over barter arrangements that had escalated into bloodshed.

On 9 December 1941, two days after the attacks on Kota Bharu and Pearl Harbor, coast watcher Cornelius Page reported a reconnaissance plane heading towards Rabaul, the main town on New Britain, off the north coast of New Guinea. Mudgee-born, 30-year-old Page had come to New Guinea with his parents ten years earlier and was managing a coconut plantation on Tabar off nearby New Ireland, using its radio for coast watcher messages.[13] In early January, he signalled that bombers were approaching Rabaul, and its naval intelligence officer, Lieutenant Hugh Mackenzie, passed on the warning. Casualties were light as a result, but Rabaul's Wirraways were too slow to intercept the enemy aircraft.[14]

On 20 January, Con Page spotted twenty Japanese planes heading south. Rabaul was warned, its guns manned and its Wirraways scrambled, but to no avail. A force of more than a hundred dive-bombers and Zeros attacked the New Britain port, shot down the Wirraways and destroyed the coastal guns.[15] The small garrison force there moved to the western shore so its retreat wasn't cut off. The RAAF flew its last Hudson bomber out. Hugh Mackenzie burnt his confidential books and codes and went off air.

Two days later, a naval fleet was seen approaching New Britain, after which silence from Rabaul. It was assumed the Japanese had captured the town, but the fate of its garrison was unknown. Page and two planters on neighbouring New Ireland continued to send reports of enemy air movements, but they weren't in a position to know what had happened in Rabaul. During the attack, the Japanese had become aware of Page's radio signals. A warship shelled the Tabar plantation, but by then he had moved his teleradio to a hut in the jungle.[16]

Rabaul was lost. Reports of the enemy moving aircraft to its new base there were of limited use. From Townsville, Eric Feldt radioed Page, 'Your position is now dangerous if you continue reporting, and under present circumstances your reports are of little value. You are to bury your teleradio and take measures for safety.'[17] But Page was an Islander, typically headstrong. He ignored the instruction and continued to radio messages.

Supplied by air drops, sometimes weeks apart, Page reported sporadically and at great risk to himself for a few months. By May, the Japanese were enlisting native police to track him down. He suspected dogs were being used to find him.[18]

Con Page finally recognised the futility of continuing his campaign, its risk far outweighing it usefulness. He nominated a rendezvous point to be picked up by an American submarine, but it didn't appear three nights in a row. It had limped back to its base with a mechanical fault. By then the full moon was waning and the poorly charted reefs were too risky for a submarine to find its way in declining light. A Catalina flew from Cairns and circled low around Tabar's coast, but there was no sign of the Australian.[19]

Page had gone off air, as had the two New Ireland planters, Bill Kyle and Greg Benham. Page's fate was later revealed in a captured notebook. After hunting for the signaller for some time, the Japanese were told by natives a white man was in one of the bays. They found a radio and supplies and, following a shoe print, Page was found asleep in a hideout. He was taken to New Ireland and executed.[20]

Page was brave to the point of foolhardiness. His reports saved a few lives, but more importantly he set a pattern. Coast watchers continued to operate at great peril in battle zones on the islands. In doing so, they made a significant impact on the course of the war, blunting Japan's progression south and its intention to cut off supply lines between the United States and Australia.

Hugh Mackenzie was a planter who had joined the Royal Australian Navy when the Pacific War started. With an attack threatening, he had two men load his teleradio on a truck and take it down the road south out of Rabaul. They set up in the scrub by the road, but got no reply from Rabaul's abandoned AWA station. The Japanese had landed that night.

Mackenzie got out of town in time, joining the troops streaming out of Rabaul. He came to the coast watcher camp and found it surrounded by abandoned trucks and soldiers milling around. He figured they would attract enemy machine-gun fire from the air, and the radio would soon be spotted. There was nothing to report but disaster, and a lack of reports would indicate that anyway, so Mackenzie ordered the teleradio destroyed. The party packed essential items and followed a native track south through the jungle.[21]

Keith McCarthy, an assistant district officer at Talasea, was the watcher for the north coast of New Britain. A tall, unruly redhead of Irish descent, he'd heard continuing reports from Page and Kyle at New Ireland, but nothing from Mackenzie in Rabaul. McCarthy was helping to evacuate civilians by boat from the far end of New Britain when he got a signal from Eric Feldt in Townsville. There had been no word from the army or Mackenzie for two days, so McCarthy was to go to Rabaul and report on the state of play there.[22]

He returned to Talasea, picked up native police and a teleradio and headed by launch down the coast towards Rabaul, keeping radio silence for the next two weeks. The party heard that Japanese had landed at Pondo plantation on the north coast out of Rabaul, so McCarthy hid his boat up the Toriu River and the group trudged up a native hill track towards Rabaul. Refugees coming along the track told them of the town's fate. A scout was sent down to Pondo and reported back that the Japanese had left and Australians from the Rabaul garrison were camped there

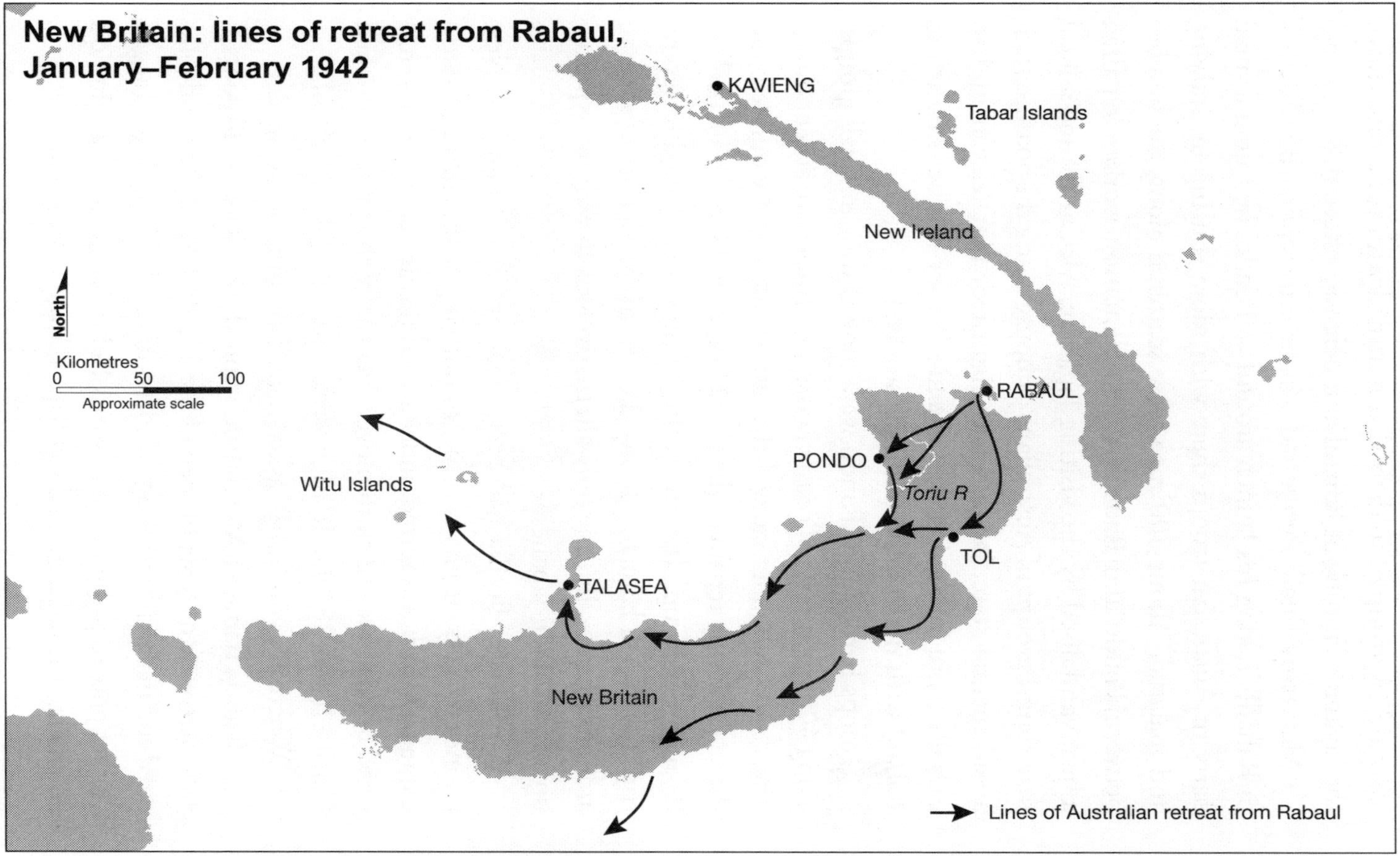
New Britain: lines of retreat from Rabaul, January–February 1942
KAVIENG
Tabar Islands
New Ireland
North
Kilometres
0
50
100
Approximate scale
RABAUL
PONDO
Toriu R
TOL
Witu Islands
TALASEA
New Britain
Lines of Australian retreat from Rabaul

instead.[23] A group of soldiers that returned with the scout told of the Japanese landing at Rabaul and defenders fleeing.

McCarthy finally broke radio silence to report the situation in Rabaul. Taking his launch around to Pondo, he found a small party of Australian troops there with more drifting in, starving and malarial. About 400 men were scattered along the beaches between Pondo and Rabaul. While plantation workers repaired a boat vandalised by the visiting Japanese, McCarthy and a local man found groups of Australians camping along the coast in such a bad mental state, languid and dispirited, that McCarthy had to bully them into going on to Pondo.[24] They had been posted to Rabaul with no training in jungle survival.

Troops herded into Pondo were moved west in small groups, along 400 kilometres of coast via staging camps with strict rations. The Pondo schooner carried the last 74 men, the wounded and the sick. Hastily repaired, the vessel limped as far as Talasea before its engine blew up. The rest of the journey was covered in several trips by a small launch.[25] Many died from the rigours of such an arduous journey, but the only alternative was to wait to be picked up by patrolling Japanese.

A volunteer flotilla had been organised from mainland New Guinea to ferry survivors across to outlying Witu Island, where a copra transport was seized under armed threat, its captain too terrified of Japanese attack to move. Eventually the refugees reached Cairns. It was 28 March, nine weeks after the fall of Rabaul.[26]

'Where are you from?' asked a garrison officer at Cairns.

'Victoria Barracks, Melbourne!' replied a soldier with no boots.[27]

There were only six fit men of the 212 on board, the rest debilitated and malarial, with tropical ulcers under dirty bandages, ragged clothes and stinking of stale sweat. Keith McCarthy, running on adrenaline for so long, finally collapsed from exhaustion.[28]

Aware by March 1942, if not before, that the Americans had set up a major command centre in Australia under General MacArthur, Japan's Imperial Command devised a strategy to thwart the counter-attack expected to come from there. The Japanese would capture the Papuan capital of Port Moresby so it couldn't be used as a staging post to attack the major base they had established at Rabaul. They would then use Moresby as a base themselves, to provide cover for their intended invasion of New Caledonia, Fiji and Samoa. With those islands under Japanese control, supply lines by sea and air between the United States and Australia—supplying MacArthur's counter-offensive—would be under constant threat. That would isolate Australia, perhaps as a prelude to invasion. The first step was to advance down the Solomon Islands.

The Solomons are a double chain of mountainous islands with an unobstructed channel between. Bougainville, at one time part of the German Solomon Islands, sits at the northern end of the chain, and now faced the advancing Japanese; Guadalcanal is towards the far end. Away from its coastal plantations, Bougainville was tangled vines, slippery mud on steep hills, mosquitoes and endless rain; it had no roads, only rough tracks. A handful of Europeans lived on the island among the Melanesian villages, as planters or missionaries or in administration.

Soon after war was declared in the Pacific in December 1941, the Australian government had ordered the evacuation of European women and children. Some planters elected to leave, some didn't. Sisters at the Marist mission stayed, as did three women on plantations, two of them widows, the third staying with her sick husband who refused to leave.[29] Two of the coast watchers who also stayed were Jack Read and Paul Mason. In time, they would move into a new phase of operation, working behind enemy lines.

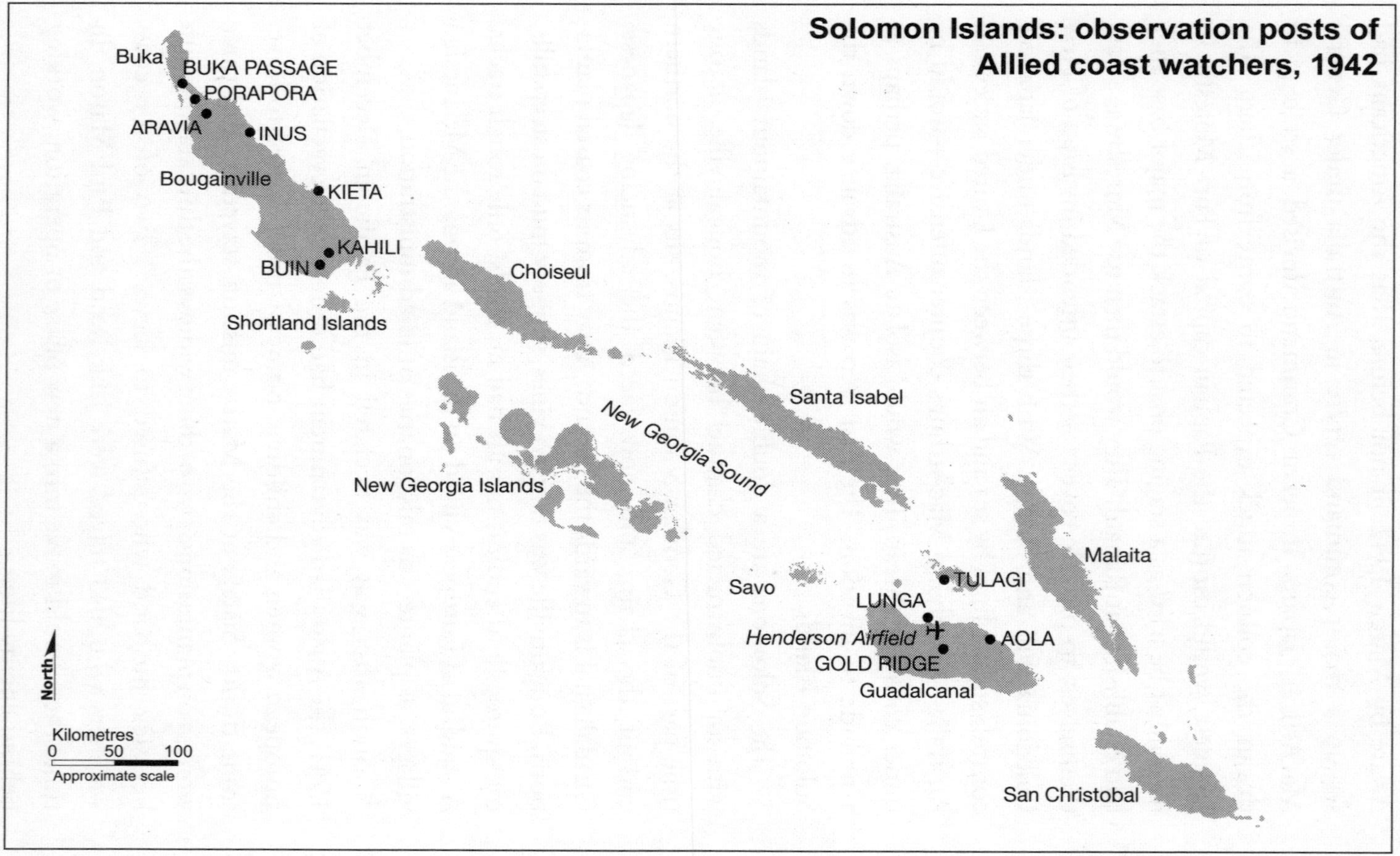
Solomon Islands: observation posts of
Allied coast watchers, 1942
Buka
BUKA PASSAGE
PORAPORA
ARAVIA
INUS
Bougainville
KIETA
KAHILI
BUIN
Shortland Islands
Choiseul
Santa Isabel
New Georgia Sound
New Georgia Islands
Malaita
TULAGI
Savo
LUNGA
Henderson Airfield
AOLA
GOLD RIDGE
Guadalcanal
San Christobal
North
Kilometres
0
50
100
Approximate scale

A Tasmanian, Jack Read was wiry in build and blunt in manner. After twelve years in New Guinea, he had begun duty a month before Pearl Harbor as assistant district officer on Buka Island, separated from the north end of Bougainville by a narrow strait.[30] His coast watcher reports were to go to Hugh Mackenzie in Rabaul, but none were sent until enemy reconnaissance planes first appeared in early January.

On 21 January 1942, things started heating up. Two RAAF Catalina flying boats, temporarily stationed at Buka, left hurriedly that morning. Later in the day, Read was instructed that Rabaul radio was off air and he was to report to Port Moresby instead. A few Japanese flying boats appeared, circled around Buka Passage and left.[31] Something was happening, but Read was unsure what.

An airfield was being built on Buka with fuel stored nearby. It was guarded by an Australian Army detachment of 26 men. A couple of days after the first visit, an enemy patrol plane returned and circled round the airstrip. On its second run, defenders fired shots at it. Having drawn attention to themselves and hearing Rabaul was likely in enemy hands, they moved temporarily across to neighbouring Bougainville, where they had set up ration dumps. A guard was left behind with explosives and ordered to destroy the airfield if need be.[32]

J.J. Merrylees, the district officer in Kieta, the main town on Bougainville, had heard that Rabaul was under threat of invasion. Seeing Japanese planes flying around, he advised the Europeans in Kieta—all ten of them—to sail with him the next afternoon to shelter on Woodlark Island off the tip of mainland New Guinea.

At midday, the AWA operator thought he saw an enemy plane landing. The Australians left immediately in a small overloaded launch for Toberoi plantation down the coast, telling the native police to 'go bush' and setting fire to the AWA building. When they got to Toberoi, they were told two enemy soldiers had landed at Kieta and raised the Japanese flag. Merrylees commandeered a Methodist mission schooner and got to Port Moresby two weeks later.[33]

Jack Read decided to abandon an observation post he'd set up on a small island between Buka and Bougainville. Moving his supplies and equipment by launch to the bigger island by night, he was strafed by a Japanese floatplane that was shot down by the airfield guard soon after. Later, five flying boats bombed the airfield and Read's abandoned post, but ignored his launch. Carriers hauled his supplies and teleradio up to a new inland post at Aravia on the northern end of Bougainville. Read set up camp there with a thatched hut and food dumps and in the morning reported his new post to Port Moresby.[34]

There had been no Japanese landing at Kieta. Instead nearby villagers had swarmed into the town and looted it until a German planter and a missionary took control and raised a white flag. A few days later, Read went to Kieta and found the white flag flying but no Japanese. He replaced it with an Australian flag.[35]

When Merrylees reached Port Moresby, he claimed—and this was reported by the ABC and *Pacific Islands Monthly*—that Kieta had been captured and the Japanese flag was flying there. It was said that he had burnt down the District Office to prevent records getting into enemy hands. In fact, the Japanese didn't land anywhere on Bougainville for another two months, and Kieta was not occupied until July.[36]

Meanwhile, Paul Mason had set up an observation post on a ridge overlooking Kieta Harbour. Short, with round, horn-rimmed glasses and fair, tousled hair, he looked more like a clerk than a plantation boss. Mason had come to the islands from Sydney as a teenager to join his trader half-brother. In 1925 he was hired to manage Inus plantation near Kieta, his predecessor having been hacked to death by plantation labourers.[37]

In recruiting workers from all over the island, Mason developed an intimate knowledge of Bougainville's terrain and its customs. He became fascinated with the wireless and taught himself Morse. Regarded locally as a scruffy eccentric, genial but gauche, to those who knew him he was quietly self-confident and dogged. Just the sort of personality that Eric Feldt looked out for. Paul Mason joined Coast Watching in 1939.

Following their capture of Rabaul in January, the Japanese used it as a base to attack Tulagi, a small island off Guadalcanal at the far end of the Solomons. Jack Read and Paul Mason, at the Rabaul end of the island chain, warned of the bombers' approach. Tulagi was the administrative and commercial centre of the British Solomon Islands Protectorate. The bombing was focused on the radio station with a conspicuous lattice-work mast, but its antiquated equipment was little used. Doing most of the work was the RAAF's unobtrusive new radio station on nearby Tanambogo Island, which escaped undamaged.[38]

An invasion force was expected sometime soon. On 11 February, the whole Solomon Islands administration moved to an inland location on neighbouring Malaita Island, while a Tulagi coast watcher, Lieutenant Don Macfarlan, took his teleradio across to the larger island of Guadalcanal and set up camp inland, above the grassy plains around Lunga plantation.[39] Stocky and cheerful, Macfarlan had been a dry goods buyer in Australia, and managed a rubber plantation in the Solomons before the war.[40]

Another coast watcher moved to the town of Aola on Guadalcanal, along the coast from Lunga. A 26-year-old Scotsman and Cambridge graduate, Martin Clemens had joined the British Colonial Service and was posted to the Solomons in 1938.[41] Observations by the relocated watchers were radioed to Malaita and passed on to the naval intelligence officer in the New Hebrides.

Only the RAAF remained at Tulagi, operating its small seaplane base until it was abandoned in May.

By the end of March, Japan was continuing its push south through the Solomons to stifle the Allied supply line. They occupied the Shortland Islands, south of Bougainville, then Buin across on the larger island and Buka at Bougainville's northern end. The enemy moved into Kieta, nine weeks after J.J. Merrylees had reported it taken, but left after a few days. The strategy to choke off supplies to Australia was progressing, but not yet completed.

With Eric Feldt's attention on coast watchers on the Pacific islands, those spread across northern Australia had slipped into the background. Air raids were frequent after Darwin, but nearly all were on coastal targets. Watchers on the mainland couldn't give advance warning and, in any case, radar was operating by then. Units were set up instead to patrol the remote northern shoreline for evidence of enemy landings, drawing on the bushcraft and intimate local knowledge of the region's long-time inhabitants. It was an opportunity for two anthropologists in particular, using their familiarity with Aboriginal communities in the north.

One of the anthropologists was Donald Thomson, the other Bill Stanner. Thomson was the first of the two to pull together a surveillance unit. Most of the men in his small Northern Territory Special Reconnaissance Unit (NTSRU) were Aboriginal, recruited from the Yolngu people of Arnhem Land to patrol their own patch at the Top End.

Trained as a zoologist, Thomson had moved into the new field of anthropology, and in 1928 carried out on horseback a field study of the Cape York Peninsula. Thomson was a lone wolf in academia. Quick to sense being wronged by others, he felt more at ease with Aboriginal people than white Australians; his support

Northern Australia: disposition of Australian surveillance groups, NTSRU and NAOU, 1942–43

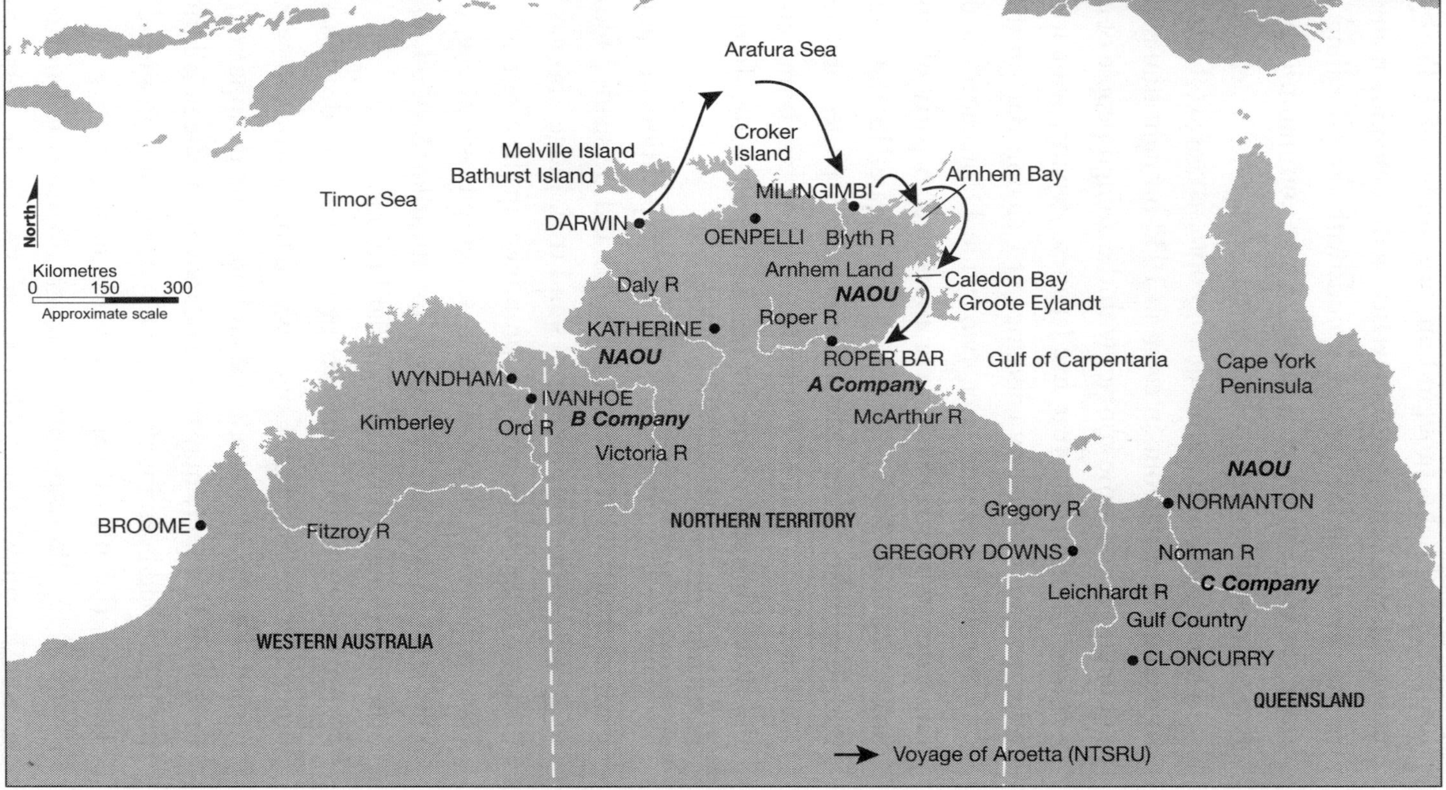

for Aboriginal rights brought him into conflict with Presbyterian missionaries at Aurukun. A maverick in the emerging mainstream of the new discipline, he was at odds with the prevailing enthusiasm for assimilation, advocating remote communities be left to live traditional lives.[42]

Donald Thomson's anthropology options closed off. He moved to medical research, but an event in 1932 brought him back into the fold and into close contact with the Yolngu people of eastern Arnhem Land. In that year, five Japanese trepang (sea-cucumber) fishermen were killed by tribesmen at Caledon Bay on the Gulf of Carpentaria. A year later, two white Depression-era drifters on nearby Woodah Island were also killed. A party of mounted police was sent from Darwin to investigate. In the course of that, Constable Albert McColl was fatally speared and Darwin went into panic that an Aboriginal uprising was imminent.[43] At the time, Europeans were far outnumbered in the Territory by Aboriginal people.

When police proposed a punitive expedition, a concerned mission group went to Arnhem Land and persuaded four men to go to Darwin with them and stand trial. Judge Thomas Wells, the same Judge Wells who was prominent in the aftermath of the Darwin bombing a decade later, sentenced one of the Yolngu, Dhakiyarr Wirrpanda, to death for spearing McColl, and the other three men to twenty years hard labour.[44]

An outcry in the southern press about the death sentence brought it to the High Court, where the conviction was overturned. Dhakiyarr was released and promptly disappeared, never to be seen again. He may have absconded, but the possibility that the police had been involved in a revenge killing simmered in the Territory. The other three remained in prison.[45]

In 1935, Thomson offered to go to Arnhem Land and try to ease hostilities there. After seven months, he persuaded the

Commonwealth government to release the three remaining prisoners and he brought them back to their country. For two and a half years Thomson lived with the Yolngu, familiarising himself with their culture and customs.[46] Returning to academia, he took up a research fellowship at Cambridge University. A year later, Australia was at war and Thomson enlisted in the RAAF.

In June 1941, Donald Thomson, now Dr Thomson, gave a lecture at Melbourne's Victoria Barracks to officers from the three services. He proposed a squad of tribesmen, Yolngu warriors, as guerrillas to defend Arnhem Land against future enemy incursions. Pearl Harbor was still six months away. Colonel Scott, the army's Director of Special Operations, was in the audience and approached Thomson after the talk with an idea for a radical unit: a guerrilla force of station workers and police with Aboriginal coast watchers.[47]

Thomson was seconded to the army three months later to raise and command a Territory force, the Special Reconnaissance Unit. He took up some of Colonel Scott's original idea—the force would have a surveillance role prior to any enemy landing and a guerrilla role after that—but its members would be mostly Aboriginal tribesmen, with only a few white men as officers. The recruits would not be trained in the use of modern firearms, but would use traditional war methods of scouting, ambush and spearing. They would, however, be trained in making and using Molotov cocktails to deal with machine-gun nests and aircraft on the ground.[48]

For his junior officers, Thomson sought men experienced in navigating through uncharted waters and working with native labour. He chose two men he'd known when briefly assigned to the Solomon Islands: Ambrose 'Ernie' Palmer, a Solomons planter, and Tom Elkington. Both had enlisted in the Australian Army in Brisbane. Palmer was sent to Townsville to oversee the refit of a 65-foot (20-metre) wooden ketch, *Aroetta*, as an armed patrol boat. Elkington was sent back to the Solomons to find six reliable and experienced seamen. Six were found, along with a Torres Strait Islander familiar with the Arnhem Land coast. He was engaged as bosun.[49]

By the time the new crew brought *Aroetta* to Darwin, the Pacific War was under way and the Japanese were advancing through Malaya and the Philippines. Thomson had meanwhile hired a Yolngu man to assist with recruiting. Raiwala had been his guide and interpreter when he had lived with the Yolngu a few years before. On 12 February 1942, the crewed-up *Aroetta* left Darwin to recruit men for the unit, heading along the Arafura coast towards eastern Arnhem Land.

Raiwala lined up fit young warriors from his own tribal groups around Blyth River as Section 1, which he would lead. Sections of the Special Reconnaissance Unit were organised on tribal lines, the second section with men from Arnhem Bay and the third from Caledon Bay. For these, too, Raiwala operated as contact man. Thomson had to persuade the head of the Caledon Bay mob, Wonggu, whose three sons had been jailed for killing the Japanese trepangers, that it was now okay to kill Japanese. It took some time to get warring tribes to agree to work together for a common cause, requiring a spearing ceremony before peaceful relations were possible.[50]

With 51 Yolngu tribesmen on board, the ketch proceeded to Roper River on the Gulf. Thomson had been surveying the Arnhem Land coast as they went and there seemed little reason for the Japanese to land there. Paratroop or amphibious landings to occupy Milingimbi or Groote Eylandt airfields were more likely, or commando detachments up rivers like the Alligator, Roper or McArthur.[51]

At Roper River, the recruits underwent training in camp. Taught the rudiments of reconnaissance, harassment and ambush, for the most part they were expected to use their own long-established methods. Historically, the warring tribes of Arnhem Land trekked with spears into enemy territory, sent out scouts and attacked with stealth just before dawn. Rushing in with war cries and bodies covered in white clay to create the impression of more attackers than there were, they made a quick kill and a speedy getaway. Surprise was the main ingredient.

Thomson proposed using the same element in attacking small groups of intruding Japanese.[52] Ironically, a somewhat similar disorientating pandemonium was often used by the Japanese in their jungle attacks at night.

The Yolngu men were not issued with uniforms or rifles, so they would not appear to the Japanese to be part of the military. They weren't anyway. Never formally enlisted, apart from Raiwala, they were paid with three tobacco sticks a week, and with rice, flour and tinned food when they couldn't hunt. They were issued with calico loin cloths and with fish hooks, knives and tomahawks to assist hunting.[53]

With the Darwin air raids still fresh in people's minds, a temporary observation post was set up at the mouth of the Roper, a pyre built on a high hill to warn of any enemy approaches by sea. Ernie Palmer meanwhile took *Aroetta* back to Darwin to be replenished with supplies sufficient for a planned six month patrol of the coast and nearby islands. That included a drum of bitumen and sacks of empty bottles from vacated hotels to make Molotov cocktails.[54]

General Ned Herring had replaced David Blake as commander of Northern Territory Force in the aftermath of the first Darwin bombing. Thomson was told by his new commander that the unit was to remain on Darwin's flanks and harass enemy landings and movement inland, but it was to prepare to hand over its Roper River post to a commando unit, the 4th Independent Company.

It was an early indication that the Special Reconnaissance Unit was seen by the army as a stopgap measure only.[55]

A permanent observation post was set up with a wireless on Gulnare Bluff, close to the Roper River mouth. Surrounded by salt pans and plains cut by mangroves, and without nearby water, Gulnare wasn't the best choice. Two filled 400-gallon water tanks had to be brought down the river. Balanced precariously on the deck of *Aroetta*, one slipped overboard. The tank was recovered, but had to be hand-filled from surrounding pools.[56]

As planned, the Gulnare post was taken over by the commando unit in July. The 4th Independent Company was one of two units brought into Arnhem Land for the same purpose as Thomson's force, but the enemy was never seen again in the vicinity of Roper River.

By March 1942, Japan's successes had so spooked the Australian military that it was feared they could invade anywhere they chose at any time. They could land on the undefended coastline and outflank and surround the Darwin garrison by speeding over uncrossable terrain to cut off the road south to Alice Springs and Mount Isa and isolate those troops. Alternatively, they could land and build airstrips to provide fighter cover for troopships landing an invasion force.

A meeting that month of Australia's military, the US Army and the Flying Doctor Service recommended forming an observer detachment to guard against Japanese incursions into northern Australia,[57] ignoring the fact that there were units already doing just that.

Anthropologist Bill Stanner, with civilian Territory experience, was advising Army minister Frank Forde when he was seconded to the army. He was to write a paper on surveillance, security and intelligence in the north and to design a dedicated body to provide it. Stanner flew to Darwin with an outline of what he had formulated and was grilled by General Herring's deputy, Brigadier Sutherland. Taken then to meet the commander, Stanner's proposal, which he called the 2/1st North Australia Observer Unit (NAOU), was well received. He was told he should raise and lead it himself.

'Surely this is a job for an experienced soldier,' said the civilian adviser.

Quietly but firmly, Herring replied, 'It is your duty to do what I've suggested.'[58]

There is some logic in Stanner's response. He was an anthropologist, not a military man, having studied the subject as a mature-age student at Sydney University after working as a journalist. On graduating, he had spent seven months in the Northern Territory documenting traditional life and cultural impacts on Daly River communities. After writing speeches for New South Wales premier Bertram Stevens, Stanner enrolled in a PhD at the London School of Economics, writing occasionally for *The Times* while he was there and gaining a grant for anthropological research in Kenya.

On the outbreak of war in Europe, Bill Stanner returned to Australia from East Africa, but was not required for immediate military service. Up to that point, he had worked in anthropology and economics with forays into journalism, but he'd had no involvement with the military. With contacts on the conservative side of politics, he stood unsuccessfully for the UAP in the 1940 federal election, and became an adviser to Percy Spender, Minister for the Army in the Menzies government. After the change of government in 1941, Stanner continued as adviser to new minister Frank Forde. Someone in the army liked what he wrote.[59]

The vision Stanner had for his North Australia Observer Unit was a highly mobile team, on horses rather than vehicles, men with a bush background and an adventurous spirit. They would live in open country for months, operating in small groups on their own initiative. Patrolling a wide spread of northern Australia from the Kimberley to Cape York Peninsula, they would look for signs of enemy incursions onto Australian soil.

His proposal drew on the exploits of South Africa's Boer commandos, as related by an army friend in Kenya, and stories of how a German officer in East Africa, Lieutenant Colonel Paul von Lettow-Vorbeck, with a handful of Europeans leading a few thousand Africans, had tied down the British Army during the First World War.[60]

The Australian Army considered the new surveillance unit to be 'urgent and important',[61] although it's not clear why. Stanner's proposal no doubt read well, but the Territory was already well served with groups carrying out its functions. A commando company, the 4th Independents, had arrived in the Territory to patrol rivers and the Gulf, and was instructed to liaise with Donald Thomson's team. Thomson was then surveying the Arnhem Land coast and recruiting for NTSRU, whose make-up had more in common with Lettow-Vorbeck's force than NAOU had.

There were already fourteen Coast Watching posts across northern Australia, as well as patrols and observation posts set up by all three military services. There were pedal radios on many cattle stations for Flying Doctor calls, and local VDC units made up of station stockmen. All were on the lookout for Japanese infiltration.

The formation of the North Australia Observer Unit was formally announced in May 1942 with Bill Stanner, about to be commissioned as a major, as commanding officer.[62] NAOU would have its headquarters in Katherine and three companies in the field, each with four small platoons mounted on a hundred horses and mules. There was to be a fleet of schooners and luggers, a hundred wireless sets and NAOU would take over three Flying Doctor base stations for its communications network. Patrols and forward posts were to live off the land indefinitely. If the Japanese occupied the north, they were to continue to do so behind enemy lines, passing back intelligence.

It was impressive on paper, a grand if unoriginal vision. But, unlike Feldt's navy-devised unit, it was an army initiative; and unlike Thomson's, it didn't have any Aboriginal people in key roles. Its main attraction to Ned Herring was probably what it wasn't. He had already commented to a senior Home Forces officer that coast watching was only efficient if it was under army control, and it depended on the willingness of civilians to stay put when a Japanese advance was imminent.[63] General Herring's view doesn't stand up well against the military's response to the first Darwin raid or the actions of coast watchers in New Britain and the Solomon Islands.

For nearly two months, all was relatively quiet in the Solomon Islands. Tulagi and other targets endured occasional bombing, but no invasion force was landed in the region. On 1 May, a raid damaged one of the RAAF's four Catalina flying boats at Tulagi and it limped to the coast near Aola. Asked to conceal it, Martin Clemens had it dragged up the beach and hidden under palm fronds. The next day, the three remaining Catalinas left with the last of the island's ground crew and garrison soldiers.[64]

At the same time, a coast watcher on Santa Isabel in the central Solomons reported a convoy, including a seaplane transport, heading south.[65] A formidable invasion fleet was on the way to Port Moresby, and these ships had been detached to capture Tulagi.

At 8 a.m. on 3 May, Japanese marines swarmed ashore from twelve ships and took Tulagi without resistance. As there were no defenders on the island and no Allied warships thought to be in the vicinity, the aircraft carrier *Shoho*, accompanying the landing, moved on and rejoined its strike force approaching the Coral Sea. Construction crew got to work building a seaplane base in the RAAF's abandoned facility.[66] Their undisturbed diligence would soon be shattered.

Next morning, from the other side of Guadalcanal, the American carrier *Yorktown* launched three strikes on Tulagi with 40 dive-bombers and fighters. Three mine-sweepers were sunk and a destroyer so badly damaged it had to be beached and abandoned. Unaware that Allied code breakers in Melbourne and Honolulu had penetrated their naval codes and were alert to the planned amphibious attack on Port Moresby, the Japanese were stunned.[67] In three days' time they would be confronted in the Coral Sea by an Allied fleet they hadn't anticipated. It would become a pivotal naval battle of the Pacific War.

As the Japanese resumed their work restoring the base on Tulagi after its pounding, observers on neighbouring Guadalcanal adjusted their positions—Martin Clemens to a village in the hills behind Aola and Don Macfarlan to Gold Ridge, high on the island. From there, Macfarlan could observe activity at both Lunga and Tulagi. Ashton 'Snowy' Rhoades, a local copra planter, was a third watcher on Guadalcanal, stationed on its western end.

On Savo Island, between Tulagi and Guadalcanal, Leif Schroeder, a Norwegian storekeeper, had been given a spare radio by Macfarlan. But his position had become too dangerous, so he moved across to Guadalcanal and joined Rhoades.[68]

Much was to be seen and reported. Ships and aircraft arrived as Tulagi's base moved towards completion. By July, the Japanese had occupied Guadalcanal. Tents were set up around Lunga, opposite Tulagi. A convoy unloaded garrison soldiers, along with more than 2000 indentured Korean labourers and equipment. Work commenced on an airfield there, a base to intercept Allied shipping and attack New Guinea.[69]

The watchers were able to report all this activity through the New Hebrides to Townsville and on to Allied GHQ, but now they could only escape from Guadalcanal by Allied re-conquest of the Solomons. Until that happened, they continued to operate their high-risk service behind enemy lines. Their day was about to come.

At the end of May 1942, a call had gone out to the AIF and CMF militia for bushmen and horsemen to volunteer for 'adventurous' duties requiring a high degree of personal resources and endurance. Many of the recruitment notices made no mention of northern Australia, so applicants thought they would be joining the fighting overseas.[70] Those who knew where they would be sent expected the north to be invaded by the Japanese anyway.

The response was double Bill Stanner's expectation of a North Australia Observer Unit of 400 recruits, although few were from the Northern Territory. Mostly they came from the southern states, looking for an alternative to the endless drills of army camp.[71] Many who joined lacked horsemanship or bush familiarity; they were enthusiastic but unskilled. An establishment with 465 personnel was issued, including fifteen Territory police to be sergeant-guides and, as local guides, 'native personnel may be employed as necessary'.[72] Stanner intended to use Aboriginal men as trackers, guides and horse-handlers, but not in any military capacity.

By mid-June, volunteers from all states had been set up in temporary headquarters at Ingleburn on the outskirts of Sydney. They spent the next eight weeks training for their mission:

learning skills in map reading, intelligence techniques, guerrilla tactics and weapons handling. They went on route marches, slept on straw mattresses and showered in cold water, much as they had in the camps they were escaping from. Potential signallers were taught Morse code and radio operation and maintenance at a wireless school in the middle of the city.[73]

Despite the amount of time given to training when invasion was thought imminent—much more than for reinforcements sent to Malaya—corners were still cut. Seventeen-year-old Keith Rogers had never driven a truck, but he was given a licence by the NAOU transport officer without having to take a driving test. Told to take the truck from Ingleburn into the city, the young man somehow survived the nerve-racking experience.[74]

Lieutenant Jack Travers, brought into the fledgling organisation to help set it up, coined the nickname 'Nackeroos' for the unit from its unpronounceable acronym. The name stuck.[75] Training helped polish some of the green edges on the men and to foster an esprit de corps, using the nickname as a badge of pride.

Stanner's second-in-command was Major Max White, a veteran of the First World War's Light Horse Regiment. He came from a prominent New South Wales pastoral family, but his rank had to be lowered to captain as Stanner was only a major. The laconic White, dedicated and unflappable, became something of a father figure to the young Nackeroos. Bill Stanner, on the other hand, was aloof. He spoke meticulously in a very English accent and dressed immaculately; yet somehow this incongruent pair, a battler and a silvertail, complemented each other in an uncharacteristically informal military outfit.[76]

In August, the whole contingent moved to the Northern Territory. Max White's advance party drove 3-ton Blitz truckwagons to Katherine to begin constructing NAOU headquarters. The day after the advance party left, the main body of Nackeroos left

Sydney, some driving trucks, most going by train on the first leg to Mount Isa. Spirits ran high. A three-day stopover in Brisbane resulted in several brawls with American soldiers. The trip from Brisbane to Mount Isa via Townsville took over three days, soldiers showering along the way while the train stopped for water, and farmers handing out pineapples to the travelling troops.[77]

To these boys from the southern states, Mount Isa was a Wild West town, full of black American army drivers, 'negroes' as they were then called. They took the Nackeroos in six-wheel trucks with no springs over a bulldozed track to the Territory railhead at Larrimah, bulldust rising in clouds behind them.

'The dust just poured in,' as one Australian recalls the experience. 'It was so difficult to see ahead that the negro drivers would stand out on the running board, with the door closed, and reach in to steer the truck through the window. They had their hand throttles pulled out to 40 miles an hour [65 kph] .'[78]

The last leg of their journey, by railway cattle truck to Katherine, was relatively tame, but the young Nackeroos had tasted the landscape they would soon be working in. They got to their destination fourteen days after leaving Sydney.[79]

NAOU had three companies in the field, located in areas Bill Stanner thought the most likely landing places for an invasion force. Within a few days of arriving at Katherine, the companies were trucked out to set up their bush headquarters, while the administration went about purchasing the horses essential to their patrols. 'A' Company covered the Arnhem Land and Roper River area, country already surveyed by Thomson's Special Reconnaissance Unit, his Yolngu warriors standing by and their observation post taken over by the 4th Independent commandos.

For its headquarters, 'A' Company occupied the police station at Roper Bar, a galvanised iron building beside the river. The outlying platoons built huts from bush timber and paperbark, with tents for stores. Until the promised horses arrived, six-man patrols on foot surveyed what coast they could reach and the meandering river, navigable by small landing craft for 140 kilometres.[80]

'B' Company was located at the top of Western Australia, around the Victoria and Ord rivers, its headquarters at Ivanhoe. Three of the four platoons were clustered around Wyndham to its east, and the fourth inland at Timber Creek. As Wyndham was a functioning river port, it was considered a key target for capture by the Japanese, and had already endured four air raids. Stanner's instructions for his unit included placing demolition charges on the town's wharves, water pipe and water tower, to be detonated on command if the enemy landed there.[81]

Wyndham, with its meatworks, was well primed with scorched earth provisions. If the Japanese came there, the Nackeroos were to take two post office staff to a 'shadow' post office, its location to be decided by Stanner, so the mail service to the adjacent Kimberley could continue, its pastoralists comfortable with evidence that the government was not abandoning them.[82]

'C' Company was assigned to the Gulf country in northern Queensland, its headquarters at Gregory Downs, up-river from Burketown. While waiting for horses to arrive, they too patrolled on foot after spreading as widely as their trucks could take them before the Wet made impassable slush of the roads. Early patrols were to familiarise themselves with the region. Army maps supplied were inaccurate; ironically, they had been printed in Japan before the war.[83]

Although the coast was flat and boggy, with a belt of impenetrable mangroves, behind that was firm red soil. An invasion force could conceivably land up one of the rivers at the bottom of the Gulf—the Flinders, Leichhardt or Albert—and drive 300 kilometres to the railway line at Cloncurry.[84] Nackeroo field units were to fall behind the invasion force as it advanced, hide behind Japanese lines in what bush they could find and report on the enemy's moves.

Each field section had a signaller attached, whose job was to report in enciphered Morse through platoon HQ or the existing outback pedal radio network to Katherine. Anything of importance was to be passed on to army headquarters in Darwin and RAAF bases in Darwin, Cairns or Townsville.

Unfortunately, Katherine HQ's powerful WS133 wireless transceiver was severely damaged along the way, rolled off the side of a truck by American drivers who thought it was an old refrigerator.[85] Reception from the FS6 field radio issued to each section was generally poor and unpredictable, often broken up by atmospheric interference or tropical storms. With a range of only about 10 kilometres, sets were powered by wet-cell batteries, their chargers vulnerable to tropical humidity, salt air and sand. A complete set required four pack horses to move it about.[86]

Signallers were not always well chosen. Despite the specialist training in Sydney, 'A' Company's 'Rod' Roddick admits he never mastered Morse key operation.[87] Until the horses arrived, patrols didn't take the heavy radio sets with them, so at that stage it didn't matter.

From April to July 1942, Donald Thomson had patrolled the estuaries and islands of the Gulf of Carpentaria. Nothing was reported apart from aircraft of little consequence. With the region surveyed and the Gulnare post handed over, it was pointless keeping the Yolngu men on board *Aroetta*.

After several months away, they returned with gifts to their communities. They would remain as a coastal watching nucleus, available if and when the enemy infiltrated the region.[88] It was hoped they would persuade others in their tribes to join any action against intruding Japanese.

In August, the Special Reconnaissance Unit set up a new observation post at Caledon Bay. A stringy-bark house and garden were built near a reliable water supply, but still no Japanese were spotted.[89] By 1943, the threat of invasion was diminishing and others had taken over much of NTSRU's role. The post was withdrawn from Caledon Bay; with the unit disbanded, Donald Thomson was transferred back to the RAAF. An expedition he led into Japanese-occupied Dutch New Guinea (Irian Jaya) was attacked by New Guineans sympathetic to Japan and he was badly wounded.[90]

The Northern Territory Special Reconnaissance Unit was a bold and innovative military venture, its efficacy never truly put to the test. Would a unit of primitive tribesmen, unerringly familiar with the inhospitable landscape, have frustrated a powerful modern war machine with traditional methods of fighting? We don't know, but perhaps the Vietnam War a few decades later indicates its possibility. Two incidents, however, reveal the vulnerability of the venture.

In May 1943, a station owner reported property stolen from his station to Roper Bar police, accusing Caledon Bay men in NTSRU of the theft. Thomson happened to be away when police visited *Aroetta*. The accused men slipped away soon after, back to home territory. It was subsequently found that station Aborigines had committed the theft, knowing the Caledon Bay mob would be blamed.[91]

In September, Thomson and Palmer took *Aroetta* to Townsville for a refit, leaving Tom Elkington in charge at Caledon Bay. Local men had been pilfering tobacco from a store Elkington had carelessly left unlocked. When he discovered the theft, the sergeant threatened the men with his Bren gun. Thomson returned to find most of the men gone.

The matter was eventually resolved under a traditional process of justice, with Elkington transferred to *Aroetta*.[92] Thomson grumbled about Elkington's unsuitability, ignoring the fact that he had hired him in the first place with glowing praise for his qualities.

Donald Thomson was in a unique position with the Yolngu, having a deep understanding of their customs and trusted by them. That was both NTSRU's strength and its weakness. He was able to keep traditionally warring communities united in a common cause, but that unity fell apart rapidly when he was not on hand to guide it.

In October 1942, while Thomson's unit was in standby mode, NAOU had 500 men. Of them, 137 were in HQ Company, a surprising number when field groups were intended to be largely self-sufficient.[93] By contrast, Eric Feldt had only one staff member at his Coast Watching headquarters overseeing some 800 watchers, delegating local administration to men at regional hubs like Don Macfarlan, and Hugh Mackenzie, rescued from New Britain.

For Nackeroos in the outposts, conditions were dispiriting. Within a few weeks of arriving, the men's clothing started to rot on them. Mosquitoes and sandflies, heat and mud preoccupied their days. At night they slept under cheesecloth netting, by day they gathered greenery to smoke out the insects. With no horses and no Japanese, nothing indeed to report, the men became restless and bored. Loneliness set in. The patrols they did on foot seemed pointless; the wireless set was their only link with civilisation.[94]

'A' Company was particularly unsettled. Bill Stanner was critical of their commanding officer and within a couple of months had replaced him. The men at Roper Bar were unhappy with that and felt ineffectual. One group decided to abscond to Brisbane, 4000 kilometres away, in order to transfer to a fighting unit.

After roll-call one November evening, a 3-ton Blitz truck was rolled quietly in neutral out of camp. Twelve men got on board down the track and drove off into the night. Although the truck had fuel for only a few hundred kilometres, a visiting driver had given them a petrol requisition book.

The absconders stayed ahead of military police by taking back roads across Queensland until, after fifteen days, a stump punched a hole in the truck's sump. By then they were near a railway line and able to get to Brisbane in two more days by train. They tried to give themselves up to provosts there, but their story wasn't believed. When it was verified, Northern Territory Force demanded they be returned to Katherine, where they were arrested and court-martialled, getting five to six months military detention. After serving half their sentences they were released, with most transferring to other units. Two of the deserters returned to NAOU.[95]

The Nackeroos didn't see much of their commanding officer. They tended to assume he was attending to other parts of his widespread command, but he was seldom with any of the field groups. In mid-1942, while he was setting up his organisation in camp at Ingleburn, Stanner was appointed to Alf Conlon's Committee on National Morale. While heading NAOU, Stanner continued to work on the committee and write radio broadcasts, travelling to the southern states probably more often than he visited his outposts.[96] He laid out principles for his company commanders to follow in his absence, leaving little room for the initiative touted as the unit's strength.

Bill Stanner's gift was writing. He could describe complex problems in simple and comprehensive terms, but he couldn't translate those ideas well into leadership. He was a perfectionist, agonising over whether what he was planning was the best way of doing it.[97] He became a ditherer. Recruiting for the force, Stanner wrote in his diary, 'I begin to realise what it means to be in command and to select a man from the thousands that offer and make him the instrument of plans involving lives, time and immense effort. Where does responsibility begin or end, and how can one find certainty or complete faith among the warring and inconstant elements of chance and life?'[98] He was a thoughtful man, but not a military man. Much that was intended didn't get done, and time slipped by as the threat of invasion fell away late in 1942.

Horses had been hard to locate for purchase. As they were slowly gathered, they were often discards local station owners were happy to sell to the army for an inflated price and were driven overland to Katherine in large mobs for breaking in. Wild brumbies and donkeys were also broken in to carry heavy gear. Pack animals had to be used when the Wet started in November and the soil got too boggy for trucks.[99]

Companies in the field started getting their horses late in December. Five Nackeroos drove 80 horses from Katherine across to the outpost in Western Australia, 700 kilometres away. Four of the animals were washed downstream crossing a river and were seized by crocodiles.[100] The men started training with the horses in the new year and, soon after, began regular patrols on horseback. Prior to that, only sporadic mounted patrols had been possible with a handful of horses.

Through 1943, the Nackeroos were able to conduct their patrols as intended, on horseback. These were missions with considerable hardship and risk. A patrol was typically made up of four men, one or two Aboriginal guides and some sixteen horses carrying fuel, rations and a field radio with associated equipment. They went out for days, sometimes weeks.

The men were to work with Aboriginal men from remote area communities and a position for an anthropologist was created in the unit, but no one was appointed to it. Instead, Bill Harney, an outback raconteur with strong connections to Aboriginal communities, worked with the men for a couple of months.[101]

These Aboriginal men were essential to patrol survival. Without them, some of the inexperienced bushmen would have perished in the parched terrain. They taught the Nackeroos how to supplement their army rations with 'bush tucker': goannas and snakes, witchetty grubs, berries and yams. Sometimes they caught barramundi or scrub cattle. They hunted bush turkeys by setting fire to small areas of dry grass and waiting for the birds to come and feast on grasshoppers moving ahead of the fire.

Most important of all, they knew where waterholes could be found. The horses needed regular watering and thirst was an issue for the men. The guides showed Nackeroos how to dig 'soaks' in dry creek beds and tap water from swellings on paperbark tree trunks.[102]

'I owe my life to a young Aboriginal named Oscar,' says Bill McAdam. 'He and I had been on patrol for over a fortnight when we ran out of water. My tongue swelled up and I'm sure I would have died if Oscar hadn't found water. He spotted a parrot in a tree and he reckoned that water must be nearby.'[103]

They were in danger when there was no water, and in danger where there was. Crocodiles were a constant threat on the coast and by rivers. Reg Oakley was at the rear of a patrol leading horses across flooded Gin Arm Creek in the Gulf country. In midstream he felt a thud and the water around him turned red. A crocodile had ripped open his horse's belly. It squealed, floundered and sank while Oakley swam desperately to the opposite bank and clambered out of the way, powered by his adrenaline. His horse and his equipment were never seen again.[104]

The men looked like frontiersmen, with rifles across their shoulders . . . or bushrangers, with beards grown long while out from base. Issued with leggings, bandoliers and corduroy breeches they found hot and uncomfortable, they patrolled instead in shirts and shorts, which rapidly became ragged and grubby, but not uncomfortable.

There was a lot of talk about spies. Suspicious footprints and light signals were reported, but no investigation produced any evidence of enemy presence. One patrol found a radio receiver, claimed to be Japanese, beside a smouldering fire not far out of Darwin. Nobody was found there.

By then, the Imperial Japanese Navy had lost the initiative in the Pacific Ocean through two major naval battles, in the Coral Sea and at Midway Island. Its army had lost its hold on Guadalcanal and pulled back off the Kokoda Track, its remnants being swept from the northern shoreline of Papua. The invasion, for which the Nackeroos were on the lookout, had become improbable.

The number of patrols was falling by July 1943. Three months later, Bill Stanner was transferred to Alf Conlon's army research group, but he was unhappy there and soon moved on.[105] His deputy, Max White, took over Stanner's role at NAOU. At the end of the year, the unit was dismounted and the field companies disbanded.

For the men of North Australia Observer Unit it had been an adventure and, in the harsh conditions they had to contend with, character building. But by the time it became operational, the force was of little military value.

Chapter 9

NIGHT OF THE MIDGETS

A nightwatchman for the NSW Maritime Services Board, Jimmy Cargill was a feisty, red-headed Scotsman. His beat, two pontoons near the western end of a boom net under construction as a submarine barrier inside the entrance to Sydney's harbour, Port Jackson. Steel mesh was stretched across the water from Watsons Bay to Georges Heights, with two large gaps where floating boom gates would eventually be installed.[1] Cargill had been in the merchant navy, but his role here was not a military one. Pilfering of building materials and tools stored overnight had become a problem as wartime austerity measures created shortages. He was there to put a stop to that.

A southerly chopped up the harbour surface, blowing spray about. Guy ropes had come free on a derrick and were swinging loosely, clattering annoyingly in the wind. Cargill rowed across in his skiff and secured the ropes, then paddled on to a nearby floating pile-driver to chat with his mate, another nightwatchman. A typical blowy winter's evening in late May in the harbour city, small craft scuttled around a variety of warships dotted about the water, at anchor or on buoys. A bit before eight, while the two were chatting, the brightly lit Manly ferry passed outbound through the boom's eastern opening. Five minutes later, another ferry came through on its way back to Circular Quay.

At 8.15 p.m., the pair noticed a shape about 50 metres away, between the net and the west channel pile light. It looked like it might be a fishing boat without lights. Cargill took his blunt-nosed boat over to investigate and found a metallic object with two protruding tubes and iron guards around them. Thinking it might be a mine, he stayed an oar's length away.[2]

Two channel patrol boats, converted pleasure launches, were keeping a watchful eye on the net at each gate. Jimmy Cargill paddled across to one of them to pass on what he'd seen. Looking down from *Yarroma*'s deck, the youthful skipper was sceptical, suggesting it was probably old naval junk caught in the netting.

The Scotsman would have none of it. 'I've been alongside,' he said. 'What I saw was shiny and new. It wasn't junk.'

Twenty-one years old, Harold Eyers had been a Melbourne shipping clerk before the war.[3] Now a sub-lieutenant in the RAN, he was in charge of a patrol boat and wasn't going to take any chances with what might be a magnetic mine if it wasn't naval wreckage. Cargill had suggested the patrol boat should investigate but, rowing back, found *Yarroma* had followed him only partway. It stopped and shone a searchlight from a distance. The object was thrashing in short jerky moves, back and forth. It looked like it had attached itself to the netting. It might even be a submarine.

The nightwatchman was getting irritated. He came back to *Yarroma* and shouted, 'Better hurry up or we won't have any navy left.' Eyers told him it was dangerous to go any closer. 'Give us one of your men then and I'll take him over,' Cargill said, his brogue getting more pronounced in his exasperation.

One of *Yarroma*'s men climbed down into the rowboat and was taken near the object, now higher out of the water. He shone his torch on it. A conning tower, bow cutting line and periscope were all clearly visible in the torchlight. The thrashing engine could be heard, trying to extricate itself from the steel mesh. A snared metal beast.

'It's a submarine, all right,' the *Yarroma* man shouted to his skipper.[4]

The discovery of a midget submarine in Sydney Harbour should have come as no surprise. There had been warning signs of various sorts for some time, for months in fact. Two-man submarines had been used at Pearl Harbor, without much success, but that should have alerted the Allies to their development and possible future use by the Japanese.

Imperial General Staff in Tokyo drew up a plan in February 1942 for simultaneous midget submarine attacks in the Indian and South Pacific oceans. First, reconnaissance flights were to be carried out over potential target ports to locate concentrations of naval shipping and assess their defences. When a decision was made on the most suitable target, midget submarines would be launched in the ocean nearby. Their mission, apart from destroying Allied warships, was to create fear and apprehension within the local civilian population.

The Japanese had developed a two-seater seaplane that could be carried on the deck of a large submarine and launched from it. With wood and fabric wings and cumbersome floats, the Yokosuka E14Y floatplane, called the 'Glen' by Americans, looked like a giant insect, but it was an effective patrol vehicle. Stowed with detached wings in a watertight compartment forward of the conning tower, it was catapulted from an inclined steel track on the submarine's forward deck. It was capable of five hours of aerial patrol.[5]

In a pre-dawn flight over Sydney on 17 February, Nobuo Fujita flew unnoticed near Mascot airport and the military airfield at Bankstown with its USAAF Kittyhawks, then followed the northern side of the harbour. His observer, Okuda, took photos of the dockyards at Cockatoo Island and Garden Island. The plane crossed North Head to rendezvous with the mother submarine, *I-25*, in the sea outside the heads. Landing on the water, the Glen was hauled onto *I-25* and stowed. Okuda had counted 23 ships in the harbour, including a three-funnel warship, two destroyers and five submarines.[6] Although it was prohibited to fly in the vicinity of Sydney's airports, there was no report of a small unmarked plane there that morning.

A week later, Warrant Officer Fujita flew his Glen over Point Lonsdale and across Melbourne's Port Phillip Bay above thick cloud. Dropping down over Laverton Air Force Base, the plane was spotted and the Japanese pilot climbed back into the cloud as two fighters scrambled. Coming down again and finding he was over the anti-aircraft battery at Williamstown, he quickly returned to cloud cover while permission was being sought to fire at him. Flying then over Melbourne's southeastern suburbs, with a clear view of the port with nineteen vessels, the floatplane was eventually picked up by *I-25* near Cape Wickham.[7] About a week apart, Fujita conducted further recce flights over Hobart, Wellington and Auckland, without ever being detected by observers on the ground . . . or if it was, it was never reported.

By April, Admiral Isoroku Yamamoto had ordered Captain Hankyu Sasaki of the 3rd Submarine Company to take six of his I-class submarines from the Solomon Islands and proceed to Australian and New Zealand waters, looking for the biggest concentration of naval vessels.[8] Four of the submarines were fitted to carry midget subs and two could carry floatplanes. The force was to assemble at the end of May near where the greatest number of enemy vessels had been found. The moon would be full at that time.

The two submarines with floatplanes were tasked with scouting harbours: Noumea, Suva and Auckland by one Glen, the Australian ports by the other. In Noumea, where they hoped to find the heavy cruiser USS *Chicago* and the destroyer USS *Perkins*, no warships could be located. A recce over Suva Harbour proved no more fruitful, nor was Auckland, which was cloaked in dense fog.

On 23 May, Fujita's floatplane was launched at dawn for a further recce over Sydney Harbour. This time two people spotted the plane. A signalman at the South Head signal station saw the Glen approach from the north and fly down the harbour. He reported his sighting by phone to Naval Headquarters at Garden Island and was told to let Richmond Air Force Base know so their Wirraways could investigate. The base decided inaction was the appropriate response.

'No use telling us,' said a voice on the other end of the phone. 'By the time we sent someone, he'd be gone.'[9]

A mobile radar station had been set up at Iron Cove and was being secretly tested on a Tiger Moth biplane flying around the city. Don Caldwell-Smith, the radar operator, found he was tracking a second plane. Without thinking it might be Japanese, he passed on the range and bearings of this aircraft along with his other readings. Regulations required the intruder be reported to Combined Defence Headquarters at Circular Quay. They phoned back a short time later that there were no RAAF aircraft in the air; the experimental radar must be malfunctioning.[10]

Having done its job, the Japanese floatplane headed out to sea over Bronte Beach, but was damaged on landing alongside its carrier submarine and sank. Pilot and observer were able to scramble to safety on the mother vessel and reported three battleships anchored in Port Jackson, along with four destroyers, patrol boats and merchant ships.[11] It was a tempting target.

With the other patrols revealing little, Captain Sasaki determined Sydney would be the target for the midget submarine attack, reduced to three after one of the mother vessels had been torpedoed two weeks before.[12] Two days prior to the planned strike, with his five remaining submarines 50 kilometres off Sydney Heads, Sasaki ordered a final reconnaissance of the harbour to confirm shipping there and locate the boom net, which had been spotted by the observer six days before.

Cloud hung low and thick in the pre-dawn of an overcast Friday, just before the full moon rose. The second Glen had been brought across from its unproductive flight over Auckland Harbour to take over patrol duties. Pilot Susumu Ito taxied across choppy sea and took off at 3.45 a.m., staying below the layer of cloud and crossing the coast just below Hornby Light at South Head. Ito descended to 200 metres so observer Iwasaki could sketch the position of the anti-submarine net and locate its openings. With clouds obscuring the moonlight, it wasn't easy to see.

The Glen was seen from the army artillery battery at Georges Heights and assumed to be from USS *Chicago*, in Sydney Harbour at that time. The sighting was reported by phone to Garden Island as an American Curtiss Falcon floatplane, prompting Lieutenant Percy Wilson, the security officer on duty, to check with *Chicago*, moored nearby. He took a launch out, circled around *Chicago* and saw all its planes were on deck and tied down. The Officer of the Deck on *Chicago*, himself an aviator, had seen the intruder plane and identified it as Japanese, but apparently didn't pass that on to shore defences. Returning to Garden Island, Wilson phoned RAAF Fighter Command, in its tunnel near Circular Quay, and reported an unidentified aircraft at low altitude over a prohibited area.[13]

Warrant Officer Ito continued his flight unimpeded over fully lit Garden Island and Darling Harbour, circling the naval dockyard at Cockatoo Island. Searchlight beams started to pick the plane out, but it slipped quickly into the clouds. Using his pre-war Admiralty chart, Ito turned back towards Garden Island and the adjacent anchorage with its cluster of warships. His observer noted the cruisers *Chicago* and *Canberra* at anchor, as well as destroyers, armed merchant ships and a submarine, sketching their positions in the harbour.[14]

Two Wirraways were dispatched a little before 5 a.m. from Richmond Air Force Base, fifteen minutes flying time from the harbour. The floatplane had disappeared into the thick cloud when searchlights started sweeping the sky again; it headed out to sea long before the Wirraways arrived.[15] The sea had become rougher from the freshening morning wind and the floatplane overturned when it touched down on the water. Ito and his observer swam across to their submarine, *I-21*. The plane's floats were punctured so it would sink.

The next day, RAAF Fighter Command was visited by an American officer to find out if Australian planes had been in the air during the night. Apart from the two Wirraways, they had not. None of that was passed to the army at Georges Heights, which officially identified the plane observed there as friendly. Although planes are prohibited from flying over Sydney Harbour, the naval officer-in-charge of the harbour chose not to raise the alarm or set up any precautionary defence.

Apart from the floatplane sightings, there were other indicators over the month of enemy submarine activity in the Tasman Sea. In mid-May, a submarine attacked the Russian ship *Wellen*, out from Newcastle. The ports of Sydney and Newcastle were closed to outward merchant ships while a search was conducted for the submarine. After 24 fruitless hours, it was assumed it had moved out of the region and ports were opened again.[16]

Over several nights before 31 May, USS *Chicago* reported Japanese radio chatter to Garden Island's Operations Room. Its radio direction finder placed the source in the Blue Mountains, but harbour surrounds are notorious for interference with radio signals.[17] More reliably, on 26 and 29 May, the New Zealand Navy intercepted Japanese radio transmission from somewhere east of Sydney. The Australian Naval Board was notified of the enemy presence, thought to be submarines, but no immediate action was taken. An anti-submarine patrol was considered after the second New Zealand report, but the patrol unit was tied up protecting a troop convoy.[18]

Sunday, 31 May 1942 was an overcast day in Sydney with heavy cloud and a biting sou'westerly blowing squally rain. Military uniforms were everywhere. The harbour was packed with warships. Newspapers reported horseracing form and daily progress of the war, including the names of Australians killed, wounded or missing. Rumours were circulating about the treatment of the 15,000 Australian soldiers and nurses captured in Singapore, by then in Changi POW camp.

With the influx of American servicemen, two cinemas were allowed to operate on Sundays. On this Sunday, the choice was between the Abbott and Costello service comedy *Keep 'Em Flying* (only one shilling for uniformed patrons), making the war more palatable at the State Theatre, or *The Corsican Brothers*, a swashbuckler with Douglas Fairbanks Jr playing Siamese twins at the Mayfair. Or you could brave the May weather on the afternoon showboat cruise on the *Kalang* with Miss Maggie Foster's

Orchestra.[19] By evening the rain had died down, but the sky remained overcast. The sun set over Sydney's western suburbs about five o'clock.

The harbour was protected by shore-based gun batteries, anti-aircraft posts on the headlands, searchlights and roaming patrol boats. Outside the harbour entrance, six indicator loops of insulated electrical cable lay along the ocean bed in a huge arc from Dover Heights to Dee Why. When any metal ship passed over them, it would register on stylographs in the loop station on South Head, but two of the loops had been damaged by a pilot ship's anchor. The outer loops had been giving faulty signals for nearly two years, so their readings were generally ignored.

Two further loops just inside the harbour were working, any signal deflection being checked visually. If no vessel was seen on the surface, the conclusion was that there must be a submarine below. The loop station had radio and phone contact with Garden Island, but the radio transmitter wasn't working, and phone lines were in demand and limited, so signal lights were generally more reliable over the 5-kilometre distance. On the anti-submarine boom net inside the harbour, the western shipping channel was kept closed and only opened for larger vessels. Ferries and other smaller traffic came constantly down the shallower eastern channel and through a gap in the net.[20]

There were over 40 warships in Port Jackson that day, including the heavy cruisers USS *Chicago* and HMAS *Canberra*, three light cruisers and the American destroyer *Perkins*. *Chicago* was moored off Garden Island after a minor refit at Cockatoo Island following the Coral Sea battle. Wharves and buoys were fully occupied, with more ships at anchor.

HMAS *Kuttabul* was permanently moored alongside a sea wall at Garden Island. A twenty-year-old passenger ferry made redundant by the opening of the Harbour Bridge, it had been a concert boat until requisitioned by the navy and converted into a barracks ship for sailors in transit. Hammocks were slung on its two decks, connected by an internal staircase. There were a few toilets and washbasins on board, but cooking and eating was done on shore, where showers were also provided.[21]

A party of New Zealanders had gone out for a taste of Sydney nightlife, even though it was Sunday. Leonard Howroyd had swapped duty times so he could meet his wife the next day. Howard Whittaker from Williamstown had swapped watch tickets with a fellow Melburnian and was on duty in his place. Lance Bullard secured his diving tender alongside *Kuttabul* by the sea wall and went home.

Rear Admiral Gerard Muirhead-Gould was an English officer posted for health reasons to the colonies as Naval Officer-in-Charge, Sydney. He and his wife lived at 'Tresco', a sandstone residence in Elizabeth Bay with a private wharf. A decorated veteran of the First World War, he was regarded by his staff officers and patrol boat personnel as pompous and dogmatic, and over-concerned with protocol. Behind his back he was known as 'Manurehead-Gould'.[22] That evening at Tresco, he was hosting Captain Howard Bode (pronounced 'Bowdy') and his senior officers from *Chicago* to an all-male dinner in black tie and full-dress naval uniform. It had been Muirhead-Gould's 53rd birthday two days before, but this occasion was to celebrate the Americans' safe return from the Coral Sea.[23] In the Royal Navy tradition, much pink gin would be consumed.

Just before sunset, Captain Sasaki's five submarines took up position 15 kilometres out from Sydney Harbour; they prepared to launch three midget submarines. Carried on the rear deck of large I-class submarines, the 27-metre-long midgets could remain

Sydney Harbour: key positions of Allied and Japanese vessels, 31 May–1 June, 1942

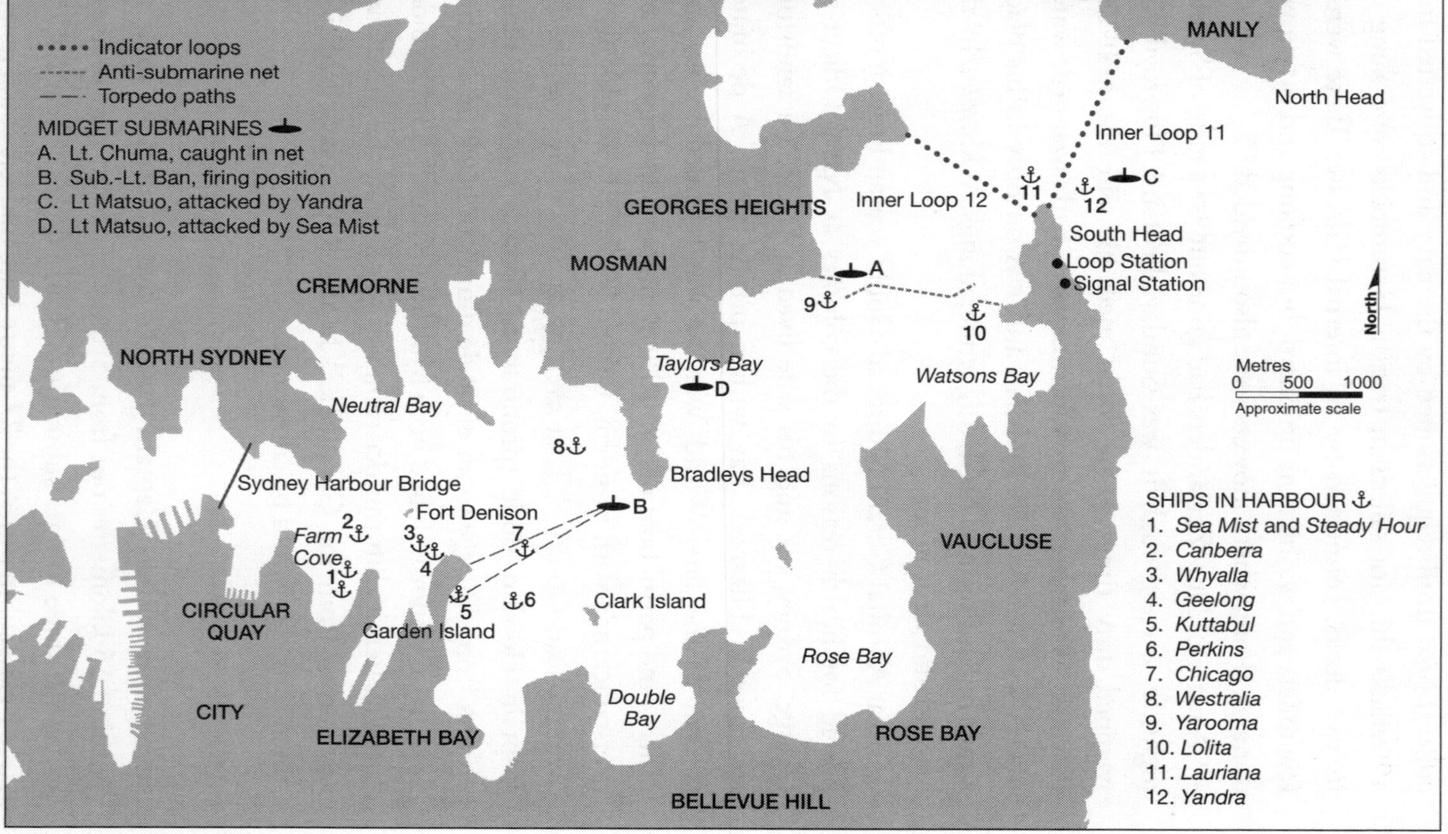

submerged for twelve hours, but they were difficult to steer and couldn't detect approaching vessels.[24] Their torpedoes, driven by a mix of kerosene, oxygen and sea water, moved at 44 knots, faster than any naval ship and leaving very little wake behind them.[25]

The sea that evening was rough with a fair swell. A full moon rose at 6.15, but was obscured by heavy cloud in the early part of the night. Hornby and Macquarie Lights on South Head were shining. Two submarines, the ones that had carried floatplanes, were positioned either side of the harbour entrance to observe shipping. They allowed the Dutch-Australian hospital ship *Oranje* to leave the harbour unmolested so no one was alerted to their presence.

The first midget, piloted by Lieutenant Kenshi Chuma, was launched from *I-27* just after sunset, reaching the heads as two Manly ferries passed by inside, one in each direction. Recorded on the inner loop at 7.55 p.m. and 7.59 p.m., these were the ferries the two nightwatchmen, Jimmy Cargill and his mate, had seen while they chatted. Chuma's midget followed close behind the second ferry across the loop, but its smaller signature went unnoticed. The midget then headed towards the western boom gate with the intention of sinking a ship to block the western channel.[26] Chuma slipped his vessel under the closed boom, undetected by four boats patrolling the entrance or *Yarroma,* guarding the western gate.

Just past the boom net, Chuma ran blindly into the pile light marking the entrance and, backing off, caught his propeller in the net ring. He swung his sub sideways and upwards to try to twist free, revving the engines as he did so, but all he could manage was to tangle his propeller more in the net.[27] It was on this thrashing midget submarine that *Yarroma* shone its searchlight, alerted by the Scottish watchman.

Yarroma tried to notify the South Head station with a signal lamp, but got no response. It was then about 9.30, an hour and a half after the *I-27* midget had entered Port Jackson. *Yarroma* had on board a radio, switchable between radio telephone and wireless telegraph, but the station's radio receiver was on the blink. After several frustrating attempts with the lamp, Harold Eyers tried his wireless telegraph and eventually, at 9.52, made contact with Garden Island.

Yarroma reported, 'Suspicious object in net.'

'Close and investigate,' was the response.

'Metal object with serrated edge on top, moving with swell,' signalled Eyers. No mention that it looked like a submarine.

'Give fuller description.'[28]

HMAS *Lolita*, the patrol boat at the eastern gate, was signalled by Aldis lamp to come over and ordered by Eyers to investigate. It was 10.20. *Lolita*'s skipper, 38-year-old Herbert 'Tubby' Anderson, was older but, as a warrant officer, junior in rank to the former shipping clerk. Lieutenant Eyers revelled in his new-found authority.

Anderson took *Lolita* to about 5 metres from the metal object, backing up to it so he had it covered with the boat's stern-mounted machine gun. The boat's lamp was shone on it.

'It's a baby submarine,' Anderson called out. 'About three feet out of the water. Periscope visible. Stern submerged. Struggling to free itself from the netting.' The periscope was rotating, the lamp's reflection flashing with its agitated turning. Whoever was in there must have been able to see them.

Tubby Anderson decided to attack the submarine before it broke free. Was he concerned the midget might fire a torpedo or was the vessel jammed in a position where *Lolita* was out of the line of fire? He may not have even considered the possibility of torpedoes. Whatever was in his thinking, the patrol boat skipper ordered his crew to 'Standby depth charge' and for one of the men to send a visual signal to South Head: 'Have sighted a submarine. Intend to attack.'

Lolita dropped two depth charges, but both failed to detonate in the shallowness of the water at that point, even with floats attached to the second charge. Anderson ordered another charge be prepared, set for even shallower detonation and creating some risk to his own vessel.[29]

While the third charge was being rigged, a sudden explosion, loud and forceful, pierced the tense calm, lifting *Lolita* out of the water and heeling it violently to its port side. An orange flash roared straight up in the air some 10 metres or more, carrying bits of metal that splashed back into the harbour, a couple clattering onto the patrol boat's deck.

A large oil patch appeared on the water's surface in the silence that followed, the shocked silence of incomprehension. It was a much greater explosion than anyone expected from a depth charge, which was yet to be dropped anyway. In fact, *I-27*'s midget submarine had been blown up by its captain. Nobody spoke for a while.

The time was 10.35 p.m. *Yarroma* reported to Garden Island that the midget submarine had exploded. The sound had carried through the harbourside suburbs in the stillness of the cloudy night. An anti-submarine vessel, HMAS *Yandra*, patrolling near the harbour entrance, sped across to investigate. Eyers had already made a note of the nightwatchman's name and told him he could return to his post.

Anderson returned his boat to the east gate, resuming its patrol there and awaiting instructions. Searchlights lit up along the harbour's edge, beams converging on the area from Georges Heights and Lady Bay. Patrol boats scurried along the boom net, but no instructions came from the South Head control room.[30]

Rear Admiral Muirhead-Gould, dining at his official residence with Captain Bode and his senior officers, was phoned from

Garden Island with a report that a suspicious object was caught in the boom net. He was unconcerned about that—seaweed and debris often clogged the net—but as a safeguard he issued a general alarm at 10.27 p.m. for all ships to take anti-submarine precautions.

The explosion 5 kilometres away at the net wasn't heard over the bonhomie of a navy dinner party, and the South Head station's communications lines became overloaded soon after. However, about eleven o'clock they were close enough to hear gunfire, naval artillery and pom-poms in the vicinity of nearby Garden Island. That stopped the conversation.

At 11.14 p.m., Muirhead-Gould issued an order by phone to darken all ships.[31] The English admiral and the American captain decided they should go and find out what was happening. Quite a lot was what was happening, although neither was ready to be persuaded!

The second midget submarine, launched from *I-24* and skippered by Sub-Lieutenant Katsuhisa Ban, had followed another Manly ferry over the inner loop at 9.48 p.m., the smaller deflection on the loop station's recording again going unnoticed. Travelling at periscope depth, the submarine kept bobbing to the surface, so Ban submerged and stayed out of sight for about an hour,[32] during which time Chuma's midget was investigated and had self-destructed.

At ten to eleven, Ban resurfaced, finding himself off the starboard bow of the American cruiser *Chicago*. An ensign on its deck saw the conning tower emerge close by and emptied his .45 pistol at it. Searchlights from the warship lit up the submarine, about 500 metres away, so that guns on *Chicago* and the Australian corvette *Whyalla* could train on it.

There was no order to fire by *Whyalla* for fear of hitting an approaching Manly ferry and small craft around at the time, but the Americans had no such qualms. The ship's gun crew had been on alert since the Japanese floatplane was spotted two days earlier. The senior officer on board, Lieutenant Commander Jimmy Mecklenberg, gave the order to fire.[33]

Rapid-fire pom-pom guns opened up with red tracer shells streaking across the harbour. At the same time, two 5-inch anti-aircraft guns began firing from the stern but they couldn't be tilted low enough and their shells ricocheted over the harbour towards North Sydney and Fort Denison's tower. Shell fragments were later found in Cremorne and Mosman.[34] The midget submerged, then resurfaced.

Air-raid sirens howled. Harbourside residents gathered in hastily pulled-on clothes, seemingly unconcerned for their own safety, as red tracer and searchlights swept the water around *Chicago*. Heavy smoke drifted through the beams.

Large-calibre bullets sent water spouts high in the air around the Manly ferry. The captain had to turn sharply to avoid hitting the midget's conning tower; the handful of passengers on board, who were lined along the railing while tracer hurled towards them, believed they were watching a naval exercise with blank shells. Remarkably, there were no casualties and no damage worse than chipped stone walls.[35]

Whyalla and *Geelong*, the corvette berthed alongside it, waited for the ferry to pass before opening up machine-gun fire, a quarter of an hour after the fusillade had started; but they were too late for much of the excitement.[36] Almost immediately the submarine submerged again, disappearing from sight for some time.

Knowing there was at least one submarine in the harbour and with the order to darken ships, Mecklenberg made the decision in the absence of the captain that *Chicago* should be prepared for leaving the harbour. He instructed *Perkins* to run a patrol around the cruiser and ordered the crew to fire up the ship's engines ready to depart.[37]

Intensely disliked by *Chicago*'s officers, Captain Bode returned to his ship about 11.30, more than a little the worse for wear. 'What's this rubbish I'm hearing? Where are the periscopes? Show me the subs?' he raged at Mecklenberg, ordering him to cease preparations for getting the ship under way, and to get the destroyer off its patrol and back on its mooring.

'I want a message sent to Garden Island HQ,' Bode ranted on, 'apologising for opening fire in their harbour. That's an order! Tell them it was done by junior officers without permission. They imagined an enemy sub in the water. I want all officers to assemble on the bridge. That's an order too!' He accused them of being drunk and incompetent, and said disciplinary action would follow in the morning. With his tirade running out of puff, Captain Bode slouched off to his quarters.[38]

From ground level, Sydney Harbour was bathed in light. In the brownout, street lamps were screened from the air but fully visible from below, the possibility of ground-level attack having not been considered. Navigation lights were operating; ferries and ships at anchor were fully lit; searchlights swept the harbour and waved across the sky. Construction of a graving dock behind Garden Island was a 24-hour operation, with banks of floodlights on tall poles beaming down on the work area. All these lights reflected on the harbour surface, making vessels difficult to discern through the sparkling silver shimmer.[39]

On Muirhead-Gould's 11.14 p.m. order ships turned their lights out, one by one, but the dockyard lights remained on. As there was no answer on the dockyard phone, the admiral sent his duty officer, Percy Wilson, to pass on the instruction in person.

Wilson set out on foot over a rough road and through work sheds, shouting, 'Get out fast! The port is under attack.'

It took some time to locate an engineer with authority to order the dockyard lights switched off and, when he did, the engineer argued the point. Hundreds of men were in the dock, he said, many of them below sea level. Wilson prevailed in the end and the engineer sent someone down to evacuate the dock and turn off the main switches.[40]

At Garden Island's Operations Room, the harbour commander was given a rundown of what had transpired, or appeared to have transpired, the signals from *Yarroma* and *Lolita* and, as best they could interpret it, the firestorm off Garden Island. Muirhead-Gould was sped in the admiral's barge across to the boom net to get a first-hand report on what was going on from 'officers on the spot'. He got to *Lolita* about midnight. As he was boarding, he said to its skipper, 'What are you fellows playing at? What's all this nonsense about a submarine?'

Truculent and jocular at the same time, creating a sort of sarcastic sneer, the admiral asked what made them think it was a submarine. Did they know what one looked like? Anderson replied that one of the men had been a submariner in the First World War.

'Did you see the Japanese captain of this submarine?' the harbour commander persisted. 'Did he have a black beard?'[41]

At 12.25 a.m, Garden Island's lights went out, moments before Ban's midget submarine resurfaced off Bradleys Head on the harbour's north side. The priority target *Chicago* was no longer silhouetted against the floodlit dockyard, but nor was it lost in the shimmering surface. The full moon finally broke through the cloud, providing a reasonable view of the American cruiser.

Torpedoes are ideally fired from a point side-on to a ship, giving the widest possible target. Still on its mooring, *Chicago* was pointing up harbour, but the armed merchant cruiser *Westralia* was anchored off Taronga Zoo, directly out from *Chicago*'s starboard side. Rather than risk interference from the Australian ship, Ban compromised his firing line. He took up a position off Bradleys Point, astern of *Chicago*, lined up his torpedoes at this narrower target . . . and fired. The torpedo would take 30 seconds to cover the 500 metres to the American ship.

Ban waited. After 30 seconds, there was no explosion. The torpedo had missed, it seemed. Ban quickly adjusted his firing line, levelled his vessel and fired the other torpedo. On *Chicago*'s bridge, Bode had come up to give the officers there another going over. A couple of them, catching a glimpse of the second torpedo's wake crossing their bow, interrupted their captain's tirade.

'It's just a motor launch going by,' he said, his irritation rising.

Bode's next words were buried under an explosion 600 metres away at Garden Island.[42] The first torpedo had passed in front of *Chicago*, travelled on and under a Dutch submarine and the barracks ship moored alongside it. Slamming into a retaining wall immediately behind *Kuttabul*, it detonated.

A ball of orange flame from 350 kilograms of high explosive billowed from below the old ferry, shooting a massive column of water into the air. The explosion blasted a hole in the steel hull of *Kuttabul* and ripped through the wooden vessel, breaking it in two. Lifted up from the water, it crashed back with the rear section sliding rapidly down to the harbour bed. For a while the rest of the ferry stayed afloat.

Wooden pylons were uprooted and tossed on the road, empty drums on the wharf thrown about, the diving tender splintered. Garden Island's power supply was disabled, its phones and remaining lights went off. The Dutch submarine berthed alongside *Kuttabul* was severely damaged.[43]

On *Chicago*, after hesitating a moment, Bode continued, 'There you are. You've got the shore batteries opening up now!' Then he turned to Mecklenberg.

'Commander Mecklenberg, I want you to take my gig and go over to Garden Island. Present my compliments to Rear Admiral Muirhead-Gould and say there's been an explosion reported. Say I request the nature of the explosion.'[44]

Rear Admiral Muirhead-Gould wasn't at Garden Island, however. He was on *Lolita* and, as he was leaving, remarked to Warrant Officer Anderson, 'If you see another sub, see if the captain has a black beard. I'd like to meet him.'

Just then the echo of an explosion rolled down the harbour, followed shortly after with pom-pom fire.

'What the hell was that?'

'If you proceed up harbour, sir,' said Tubby Anderson, 'you might find your Japanese captain with a black beard.'[45]

At Garden Island, pandemonium reigned. Klaxon horns and sirens screamed. Men leapt out of hammocks and raced to gun turrets, firing indiscriminately at imagined submarines. Searchlights swept the harbour waters. Small craft scurried about, looking for an invisible enemy. A group of men stripped off their clothes and dived inside the shattered *Kuttabul*, oblivious to the cold water, looking for survivors.

Boats came across from USS *Perkins* with men to help put out the fire on the wharf and to join others looking after the injured. The forward section of *Kuttabul* stayed afloat for about fifteen minutes, slowly sinking until only its funnel and roof deck were visible.

Bandsman M.N. Cumming had returned to *Kuttabul* five minutes before the explosion. Escaping with minor cuts, he stripped and dived through the splintered timber and broken glass, pulling to safety three critically injured men trapped inside.[46] Petty Officer Littleby should have been sleeping on board, but was asleep instead on a nearby launch. Manoeuvring the launch alongside the wrecked barracks ship, he was able to rescue several men.[47] Captain Doyle, tending to survivors on the wharf, was badgered to turn off his torches by jittery personnel, concerned the enemy might see them.[48]

Gerard Muirhead-Gould arrived back to the bedlam around Garden Island as Mecklenberg motored up in the *Chicago* captain's tender. The admiral suggested to the American that US naval forces should be taken out to sea to avoid further attacks from other submarines that might be in the harbour. He was now persuaded there were enemy submarines about and possibly more than one. At ten past one, 40 minutes after *Kuttabul* was blown up and nearly five hours since Jimmy Cargill noticed Chuma's snagged midget, the admiral notified all ships, 'Enemy submarine is present in the harbour. *Kuttabul* has been torpedoed.'[49]

The explosion had been heard for miles and shook houses and apartments along the waterfront. Windows rattled in Potts Point and Elizabeth Bay flats. Pictures fell from walls, books from shelves. Some put on dressing gowns and watched from balconies, or rushed out onto lawns to see what was happening. Others thought it was an earthquake, although they'd never experienced one.

Radio stations broadcast urgent appeals for sailors to return to their ships. Rumours spread through the city that the Japanese invasion had started. An air-raid warden knocked on doors in his street, shouting, 'The Japs are coming. They've flattened Brisbane, now over Gosford. Get children under the table with a mattress on top.'

In Manly, Yve Jeanneret was woken by her parents and sent scurrying with her brother across the neighbours' tennis court below them to a games room where they sheltered under the billiards table.[50] Donald Dunkley, a twelve-year-old in Chatswood, heard sirens about midnight. The entire family, his mother and her three kids, got under his parents' double bed. 'We couldn't hear any guns, no bombs and we thought this was very strange,' he later recounted. 'We were waiting for the bombs. We were listening and thinking it'll come soon, it'll come soon, it'll come soon. And nothing happened.' After the all clear, they turned on ABC radio, but there was no mention of it.[51]

There were estimated to have been 35–40 sailors on board *Kuttabul* when the torpedo struck the sea wall. Ernie Higgins had been woken earlier by gunfire and was told Japanese subs were in the harbour. He didn't believe that—the boom net was there to prevent it—and went back to his hammock, waking two days later in Sydney Hospital. His body had been fished out of the water and placed with other bodies on the wharf, but a passing American doctor had seen him move. Higgins spent three months in hospital with spinal, head and facial injuries.[52]

Charlie Brown had been on *Kuttabul* for six weeks, waiting for a posting to HMAS *Hobart*. He saw a big orange ball of fire, then was thrown headfirst between the wash basins on the lower deck and through the ship's side. Wooden debris piled on top of him, but his hand was seen flailing through it. He was pulled out and onto the wharf.[53]

The New Zealand sailors came back to Garden Island to find their accommodation sunk to the harbour floor, their money, dog tags, paybooks and papers down with it.[54] Howard Whittaker returned to find himself on a list of those missing, having swapped watch tickets with his mate, Jack Gardner. Assisting on divers' pump handles and watching as bodies came up from the wreck, he had the gut-wrenching experience of seeing Gardner's body, the last to be brought up.[55] Leonard Howroyd was also unlucky:

the meeting with his wife never took place.[56] In the final count, nineteen Australian and two British sailors were killed. Their bodies were taken for burial at Rookwood Cemetery.

When the second midget submarine had entered the harbour, a third midget, skippered by Lieutenant Keiu Matsuo, remained at the harbour entrance, biding his time while Chuma's vessel got caught in netting and Ban's remained submerged and undiscovered inside the harbour. At 10.52 p.m., someone on *Lauriana*, a requisitioned timber yacht belonging to the Arnott's biscuit family, noticed a 'flurry' in the water. It was thought it might be a paravane towed from a minesweeper nearby; but when the ship's light was beamed on it, it was clearly a conning tower, about 25 metres away as *Lauriana* motored past it.

The ship's light was swung towards the South Head signal station and flashed an alarm signal, but there was no reply. By the time *Lauriana* turned around, the submarine had submerged. The patrol boat had no other means of warning of or dealing with the enemy presence. It had been promised rockets, Very pistol flares and depth charges, but these were still to be delivered.[57]

A couple of minutes later, a Danish-built coastal steamer, fitted for minesweeping and anti-submarine patrol work, sighted the midget turning, 400 metres away, just outside the harbour mouth. HMAS *Yandra* had depth charges on board, but the skipper, Lieutenant Taplin, decided there were too many boats around to use them.

Taplin, a veteran of fourteen years in the navy, attempted to ram the diving midget with his 990-ton vessel. A glancing impact could be felt on the bridge. The intruder broke the surface on *Yandra*'s rear starboard side, and listed before turning away. By then about 100 metres astern of *Yandra*, it disappeared from sight to be spotted again shortly after, further away.

Yandra's gun crew tried to train the ship's weapon on it as they turned towards the target, but the gun couldn't tilt down enough to fire. Once again, the submarine slipped below the surface, but not to safety. It was located underwater with ASDIC, an early form of sonar.

Having exhausted other means of dealing with this particular enemy, and with less shipping around by then, James Taplin decided to use his depth charges. A pattern of six charges set to 100 feet (30 metres) was fired from *Yandra*. The force of the explosions caused temporary failure of the ship's steering gear, as well as its ASDIC, degaussing and phone equipment. Fifty-three tons of *Lauriana* was briefly lifted clear of the water, before landing with a thud. The midget submarine was not seen after the explosion.

When steering and ASDIC were restored, *Yandra* conducted an anti-submarine sweep, but found nothing. Matsuo must have waited on the seabed until 3 a.m., when a crossing registered on the harbour's indicator loop. Once more, it went unnoticed at the loop station on South Head.[58]

Meanwhile, in the aftermath of the explosion that sank *Kuttabul*, rescuers were desperately retrieving the injured from the stricken vessel and launches were buzzing randomly around the harbour out from Garden Island. On instruction from Sydney's Naval Officer-in-Charge, warships in the harbour were preparing to leave. The three American ships, Australian cruisers and corvettes and an Indian corvette were all aiming to get under way as soon as possible.

The Dutch submarine, damaged in the explosion, was towed further up the harbour. Within a quarter of an hour of the explosion, *Perkins* was under way and circling *Chicago*. If the warships had departed earlier in the night, they would have steamed between the two Japanese I-class submarines lying outside the heads, but by now the pair of enemy subs had moved south to rendezvous off Port Hacking with the returning midgets.

Having fired two torpedoes and unable to assess the result, Sub-Lieutenant Ban submerged his vessel and moved away. The loop indicators show that the midget left the harbour at 2 a.m. For two days, five submarines waited in the rendezvous area, but Ban never appeared. The mystery was resolved in 2006 by divers who found the remains of the midget on the sea floor, 5 kilometres out from Newport, one of the city's northern beaches.[59] It's speculated Ban elected not to rendezvous in case he was being followed.

By 2.14 a.m. on the night of the raid, *Chicago* was ready to leave the harbour, departing so hurriedly that disconnection of the phone line to Garden Island was overlooked and it snapped as the cruiser pulled away. As well, a crew member was left stranded on the buoy after the line had been released. Mecklenberg had to race back in the captain's gig and pick him up.[60]

Muirhead-Gould issued an order for patrol boats moored in Farm Cove to patrol Bradleys Head and the boom net areas, but signal lights from Garden Island were not visible at Farm Cove, tucked around Mrs Macquaries Point. With Garden Island's phones disabled by the torpedo, the only way to pass on the instruction was for the duty staff officer to scurry around by boat, shouting out the order to each launch in turn. Some vessels were unaware of the alarm until the next morning.[61]

Reg Andrew had taken command of the patrol boat *Sea Mist* that afternoon with minimal handover. Coming directly from six weeks training at Flinders Naval College in Victoria, he had been instructed in disassembling and assembling a battleship gun, about torpedoes and the history of pistols, but little about signals and nothing about the Vickers sub-machine gun or depth charges. Woefully under-prepared for armed harbour patrol, he was told by his flotilla leader, Lieutenant Townley, to hold *Sea Mist* off Bradleys Head and set depth charges at 50 feet (15 metres). That would give the boat little time to get clear.[62]

As *Chicago* headed out of the harbour entrance at about 3 a.m., a periscope was spotted slicing through the water in the opposite direction. Alongside the warship, too close for its guns, the third Japanese midget submarine was coming in. Matsuo's intention might have been to crash into *Chicago* so his torpedoes would be detonated by the collision. If so, the attempt failed and the midget continued into the harbour. Captain Bode ordered a signal to Garden Island, 'Submarine entering harbour.'[63]

Twenty minutes later, an armed merchant cruiser, HMAS *Kanimbla*, having sighted the periscope in Neutral Bay, near the Harbour Bridge, pointed its searchlight at it and opened fire. The periscope disappeared before any other boat could get there. Soon after, the heavy cruiser *Canberra*, moored out from Farm Cove, reported torpedo tracks from the direction of Bradleys Head, and the minesweeper HMAS *Doomba* reported an ASDIC contact off Cremorne Point.[64]

In fact, no torpedo was fired by the Japanese raider. The two torpedoes were later found to have jammed in their tubes, so the 'torpedo tracks' were either streaks of compressed air bubbles released from behind the jammed torpedoes or the product of an overactive imagination aware of midget subs infesting the harbour.

Either way, Matsuo was moving his vessel eastwards down the harbour. A young accountant, Robert Dulhunty, spotted the conning tower in Little Sirius Cove from his Mosman balcony. He and his father fired a couple of shots each from .22 rifles before the target disappeared.[65] Further east, the minesweeper HMAS *Goonambee* saw a suspicious object in Taylors Bay; Reg Andrew's *Sea Mist* was sent to investigate, but found nothing more than an old buoy.

At five in the morning, still well before the winter sunrise, Matsuo had retreated to a secluded part of Taylors Bay to try to fix his jammed torpedo tubes. When the patrolling *Sea Mist* came back into the bay, Andrew saw a dark object in the full moon's glow. Approaching without needing a spotlight, the crew of four was close enough to see a conning tower poking a metre out of the water.

A store manager from nearby Mosman in civilian life, Reg Andrew had never before been anywhere near a Japanese naval vessel of any kind. The experience unnerved him, but he circled the midget in his requisitioned Halvorsen launch, calling for red flares as the sub started to dive. He ordered a depth charge dropped over the *Sea Mist* stern. With the charge set to detonate at 50 feet (15 metres), Andrew had four or five seconds to get clear at the boat's maximum speed of 10 knots.

The charge was dropped and the launch throttled clear. The detonation was followed by a wall of water. *Sea Mist* rode it like a surf boat and a column of water shot up behind it.

When *Sea Mist* was turned around to assess the outcome, Andrew could hear propellers whirring. Then the midget slowly rose from the sea, its contra-revolving propellers first, and lay upside down on the surface for a short while before sinking into the embrace of the bay.

While he was overseeing a second depth charge and another Very flare, Reg Andrew was distracted by the impression that two more subs had surfaced behind him. The second charge was released. But as his boat tried to get clear, it was hit with the force of the explosion, putting one of *Sea Mist*'s engines out of action.

Andrew signalled Athol Townley, on board *Steady Hour* nearby, but got no response. After that, he limped at half speed over to the flotilla leader's vessel and explained through a megaphone what had taken place. He was told to return to Farm Cove.[66]

A swarm of small naval vessels gathered around Taylors Bay, hyenas coming in for the kill. Townley on *Steady Hour* dropped two depth charges in a spot where someone imagined they'd seen a periscope or ASDIC had produced an apparent contact. *Yarroma* came over from guarding the western channel gate, perhaps to atone for its captain's caution earlier in the night, and dropped a charge on its ASDIC contact.

This was followed soon after by another attack, from which an oily smear was reported to have arisen. *Steady Hour* continued its attack with a 'definite' ASDIC contact, its depth charges producing oil and air bubbles.

During the turkey shoot, Townley reported *Steady Hour*'s anchor was caught in the submarine with light oil and large bubbles seen. Oil and air bubbles had become the *sine qua non* of depth charging wherever in Taylors Bay the attack was carried out. At another point, a ferry appeared at the mouth of the bay. The ferry skipper ignored a patrol boat instruction to move out of the way until threatened with machine-gun fire. Ferry masters would later complain about patrol boats running around the harbour indiscriminately dropping depth charges.

The sun had risen on a new day when, at 8.30 a.m., *Yarroma* mounted the last attack, with oil and air bubbles once again reported. Over the previous three and a half hours, it had been a free-for-all without one verifiable sighting of even a periscope.[67]

The ferry masters may have had a point. In the course of the night, seventeen depth charges were dropped. But the ferry skipper's attitude in refusing to change course also illustrates something about the public's response to the Japanese threat. For a while, Australians were so paralysed by it that they virtually gave up hope of stopping it, yet at the same time they refused to take it seriously enough to change the things they did habitually. Perhaps these are two sides of the same coin: simultaneously defeatist and fatalist.

Lance Bullard came to work on the morning of 1 June to find his diving tender in splinters and *Kuttabul* on the harbour bed. With a replacement dive boat and gear, the four-man navy team worked through the sunken barracks vessel. Many of the men lost on *Kuttabul* had been caught by hammock ropes twisting around their bodies. When the divers cut the ropes, bodies emerged from their cocoons, floating to the surface in boiler suits and pyjamas.[68]

The second torpedo had run aground on Garden Island and failed to detonate. It was discovered in the morning at low tide, its warhead broken off and spilling yellow explosive onto the rocks.[69]

In the afternoon, the dive team moved to Taylors Bay, where patrol boats had reported a contact. People had been wading barefoot in the shallows all morning, looking for souvenirs. Kicking up mud as he clomped over the bay floor, Bullard could hear the dull throb of an engine still slowly turning, but the murky water prevented him spotting its source. Eventually he found the midget, lying on its keel in 25 metres of water, two torpedoes protruding from its nose and probably live. Its stern section was buried in the muddy bottom, partly detached from the main body.[70]

Risking detonation of either the torpedo warheads or a suicide charge in the tail, the minesweeper *Samuel Benbow* tried to tow the submerged vessel to shallower water with torpedoes pointing away. Stuck in the mud, it couldn't be budged and the wire straps broke. It took another two days of trial and error before a barge and a tug towed the damaged midget to shallow water, where it was shackled to a block on a floating crane.

The crane lifted the block and its shackles and slings the next morning, but no submarine followed. Its serrated net cutter had sliced through the slings. Finally, on the afternoon of 5 June, Matsuo's midget sub was raised. Crowds and reporters watched excitedly from the shore and naval ratings raised their caps in salute to the Japanese sailors presumed to be dead inside the vessel.[71]

While Matsuo's midget was carried by the harbour crane to Clark Island, off Double Bay, the divers moved on to the western boom gate. The midget caught in the net there was cut clear with an oxy-burner and lifted out of the water without the difficulties of the earlier recovery. Chuma's vessel too was taken to Clark Island.[72]

The bodies of the four men from the salvaged submarines were taken to the city mortuary. Post-mortems revealed all had died of self-inflicted gunshot wounds. Matsuo's crewman was found with his boots off, thought to indicate he was planning to leave the vessel, but the explanation could just as well be a mundane one—perhaps the boots weren't comfortable and he preferred working without them.[73]

The morning after the attack, knowing an internal report would be required and perhaps concerned he mightn't look good in it, Gerard Muirhead-Gould called for accounts of the night from ships and others involved. The secretary of the Maritime Services Board wrote back, purporting to quote the board's employee, James Cargill. When compared with the watchman's later account to the press, it reads like a selective and convenient version of his story.[74] The letter has handwritten comments by the *Yarroma* skipper, correcting trivial details, but asserting Cargill first noticed the intruder an hour later than the actual time.

Norman Makin, Minister for the Navy, wanted no negative repercussions from the incident. He assured federal parliament the submarines were 'instantly detected' and counter measures were 'so prompt and so effective'.[75] In the New South Wales parliament, Premier McKell was asked if there would be an inquiry and if there had been 'culpable negligence'. McKell replied that there must be evidence of negligence before an inquiry could be set up. 'My own view at the moment,' he said, 'is that the men entrusted with our naval defence have given very fine service to Australia.'[76]

'It's a fact that they got through,' countered one MP. 'We want to know why they were not discovered before they got through.'[77]

The Americans too had not been impressed. The captain of *Perkins* observed there was no net at the entrance and ferries were always coming through there, making it easy for submarines to enter. He pointed out that the torpedoes had barely missed both US warships. Admiral F.X. McInerney of SWPA's naval arm complained he'd seen ships enter without showing their identifying signal. An 'enemy flying false colours and making false signals' could enter, he concluded.[78]

After the attack on Darwin in February, the federal government had brought in legislation forbidding war reports unless they were approved by the prime minister. At 3.30 a.m., while patrol boats were busy depth-charging Taylors Bay, the federal censor in Canberra sent an urgent telegram to all newspapers, radio stations, magazines and wire services: 'Pending official statement no reference whatsoever to incident in Sydney Harbour last night.'[79]

A former *Daily Telegraph* reporter was working on a navy switchboard, where she heard what was happening as events unfolded on the night of the attack. She rang the newspaper, in time for the early edition and before the censor's embargo, but the editor didn't believe a story about Japanese subs in the harbour—word of mouth clearly hadn't reached him—and the story was spiked.[80]

The official statement came from MacArthur's GHQ in Melbourne in the early afternoon. It was brief. 'In an attempted submarine raid on Sydney three enemy submarines are believed to have been destroyed, one by gunfire, two by depth charges. The enemy's attack was completely unsuccessful. Damage was confined to one small harbour vessel of no military value.'[81]

No military value? Families of the 21 sailors killed by the explosion might have felt put out by that. Certainly *Kuttabul* was not a vessel of great military value, but one would like to think the RAN's men were. And while the attack could not therefore be described as completely unsuccessful, nor was it a howling success. At least two of the midget submarines and their crews had been lost and no warship had been taken out. The attack reinforced briefly the Australian public's fears of invasion, particularly in more sceptical Sydney where it was waning after the Coral Sea battle. However, 'she'll be right' complacency soon returned.

Newspapers dutifully quoted the GHQ assertion of an unsuccessful attack with no military damage, then described what people saw as if it were a sporting fixture. Thousands had been wakened and treated to a 'grandstand view'.[82] 'Harbour-side residents had an exciting experience,' enthused the *Sydney Morning Herald*, 'when they saw searchlights try to pick up the raiders and heard guns fired when the periscope of one of the submarines was spotted.'[83]

Patrol vessels 'dashed around the harbour like mosquitoes'. A seaman on watch on a steamer saw 'machine-gun bullets spitting all around us, tracer streaking like shooting stars'.[84] Ferry passengers described shells throwing spouts of water hundreds of feet in the air. Within a few days, submarine fever had taken hold of Sydney. Every fisherman had seen a sub. Ferry passengers had seen periscopes and conning towers.

For some time Sydneysiders, like other Australians, had lived in dread of Japanese invasion with Rape of Nanking brutality, but now that it might conceivably be happening, it was all too exciting to be bothered about that. The *Daily Mirror* did the government's bidding, warning that the attempted raid brought the war closer to the industrial heart of Australia,[85] but the time for dread had passed. When the attack happened, it was assumed to be an exercise. Now people knew better; but no invasion force had landed, thanks to 'prompt and effective' harbour defences. There would be no rape of anyone's daughters. Not yet, anyway.

On 6 June, *Smith's Weekly* pricked the balloon, publicly questioning the harbour's defences. Headlining 'Battle of Port Jackson—Whose Responsibility?', the weekly fulminated: 'How submarines entered Sydney harbour calls for inquiry and sackings. If it's the navy or the coastal defences that neglected safeguarding the great port of Sydney, the responsibility should be sheeted home.'[86]

Outraged at the weekly's lack of patriotism, the RAN's director of intelligence, 'Cocky' Long, presented a charge sheet and draft letter to the Navy Board. He wanted the Attorney-General's department to prosecute the publisher under National Security regulations for prejudicing public opinion against defence, and for revealing specific defences. Long claimed *Smith's Weekly* had 'deliberately attempted to foster public disquiet by discrediting and belittling counter-submarine measures taken by the RAN, by drawing odious comparisons between the efficiency of Allied ships [that is, American ships] and ships of the RAN.' The Navy minister noted on the draft letter that there was little chance of a conviction and the letter was duly filed.[87]

But *Smith's Weekly* had the bit between its teeth. The next issue had a front-page headline, 'With War at the Door—Our Navy Must Never be Caught Napping'. The article highlighted conflicting statements about the raid, relying on a considerably more detailed version of events from Jimmy Cargill—probably second-hand—than the MSB secretary had supplied. The article reported that an enemy patrol plane had flown unchallenged over Sydney two or three days before the attack. The paper called for a public inquiry, a week later reporting the Navy minister had rejected this demand.[88]

By this time, Gerard Muirhead-Gould's first report had been submitted to the Navy Board, but not released to the public. It was brief, running for only two pages and providing an account of the action with five midget submarines. Four of them, he claimed, had been destroyed inside the harbour, and the fifth outside.[89]

Instructed to produce a fuller account, the harbour's naval commander came back with one five days later. This time he focused on lessons learnt, allocating blame to several participants. He wasn't one of them, but he was astute enough to lay no blame either on the cavalier Americans.

'There was a regrettable failure of the loop watchkeepers to identify the unusual crossings,' he wrote. The loops worked, humans failed. Cargill saw the submarine but 'took some time' to inform the patrol boat. Lack of action by *Yarroma*—by implication its callow skipper, Harold Eyers—was 'deplorable and inexplicable'.

He revised his earlier assessment that *Steady Hand* alone had sunk the midget in Taylors Bay, to a view that *Sea Mist* and *Yarroma* 'equally contributed', whatever that might mean.[90] Subsequent analysis suggests *Sea Mist* actually knocked out Matsuo's vessel with its initial depth charge and the other two patrol boats were repeatedly dropping explosives on a destroyed midget.

Unfortunately for Reg Andrew he lacked the political skills of Athol Townley, who later became a minister in the Menzies government. Townley's smooth advocacy in his own cause and

Andrew's resentful intractability ensured the *Sea Mist* skipper got little credit for an achievement that was undoubtedly his alone.

RAN chief Admiral Guy Royle wrote, in response to a Muirhead-Gould proposition, 'I don't like the idea of trying the Commanding Officer of *Yarroma* for failing to engage the enemy. I feel his chief fault was foolishness and that an admonition by you would meet the case.' At the end of the letter, Royle added in a handwritten PS that he wanted to use the salvaged submarines to raise funds for marine charities.[91]

Captain Sasaki's 3rd Submarine Company waited at the rendezvous off Port Hacking for two nights, but no midget submarines returned. RAN intercepts had picked up wireless traffic between the submarines, and patrol aircraft were sent to find the source. By then, Sasaki had abandoned the wait and the submarines had dispersed.[92]

After the drama of the harbour raid, Sydneysiders settled back to their normal routines, hampered by increased rationing and distracted by reports of submarine attacks on merchant ships along Australia's east coast. On the evening of 3 June, the BHP-owned freighter *Iron Chieftain*, laden with coke, was sunk off Newcastle with twelve lives lost.[93] The next night, *Iron Crown*, with a cargo of manganese bound for Newcastle, was torpedoed off Gabo Island to the south.[94]

Then, shortly after midnight, eight days after the Sydney raid, *I-24* surfaced in open sea 16 kilometres off the city's Eastern Suburbs. Ten high-explosive shells were fired from its deck gun in the direction of well-to-do Bellevue Hill and Rose Bay. Windows were shattered. Woken by the roar of guns and scream of shells, people switched on bedroom lights and rushed out onto the street.

Air-raid sirens didn't sound, with city lights blacked out, until twenty minutes after the last enemy shot. Searchlights beamed onto the source of the gunfire, but *I-24* submerged before any coastal battery could return fire.

The attack lasted no more than four minutes, with six of the ten shells failing to explode.[95] One smashed through a bedroom wall in the Rose Bay home of Ernest Hirsch, showering debris on his elderly mother. An electrical engineer and escapee from Nazi Germany, Hirsch had his ankle broken by a heavy metal lamp-stand, knocked onto his foot while he slept in the sitting room. The shell came to rest on the staircase without exploding, a wall separating it from Hirsch's wife and eighteen-month-old baby in the next room.[96]

Another shell exploded near a Bellevue Hill home, shattering every window in the house, demolishing the kitchen and damaging the house next door. Woken by the explosion, Mrs McEachern rushed to her verandah to hear a shell whistling past and a second explosion nearby. Back inside, dust was settling in the remnants of her kitchen. Refusing to go to a neighbour's house, she asserted, 'My house is still standing and I don't see why I should go elsewhere.'[97]

Two hours after *I-24* shelled Sydney's suburbs, another of the Japanese flotilla, *I-21*, surfaced 9 kilometres off Newcastle and sent up white flares followed by a salvo of 26 shells. Walter Watson, the battery commander at Fort Scratchley, overlooking Newcastle's city beaches, saw the gun flash out at sea and phoned Fire Command for permission to return fire. He got no reply, but fired anyway. Four rounds were shot late in the sixteen-minute attack, but all fell short of *I-21*.

One of his men passed on a message. 'Fire Command says engage when ready, sir.'

'Tell them I bloody well have!' snorted Watson.[98]

A second round from Fort Scratchley overshot. Vision for a third round was obscured by thick black smoke from a steamer running for safety. By the time it had cleared, the submarine was gone.

The Japanese attack might have been aimed at Newcastle's shipyards or the BHP steelworks or just sent randomly to unsettle the city's residents. All but three of the high-explosive shells failed to detonate. One fell in Stewarts & Lloyds' yard by the steelworks, one near the seawall of the swimming baths, and one on the road at Parnell Place behind the fort. The unexploded shells were examined later in the day and found to be manufactured in England in 1914.[99]

When she heard shells screaming over her Parnell Place home, Mrs Wilson scooped up her two small children from their bed and carried them downstairs. The next day, she found that shrapnel from the explosion outside had torn through the children's wire mattress base. There was a gaping hole in the wall.[100] Running across Parnell Place towards the fort, Stan Newton was less lucky, wounded by a piece of flying shrapnel. The blast knocked Bruce Williams to the ground, giving him gravel rash from the road's new blue metal surface.[101]

Air-raid sirens had sounded in Newcastle shortly after midnight on news of the Sydney shelling and this was followed soon with the 'All Clear'. They remained silent when Newcastle itself was attacked.

In Sydney, ten-year-old Barbara Woodward told the *Sydney Morning Herald*, 'I heard a bang on the road and grabbed my kitten, Mr Churchill, and went with the other children to a room at the back of the flat. Mr Churchill wasn't frightened.'[102] But the *Daily Mirror* perhaps best captured the change of public attitude to the possibility of invasion with its story about a battling granny, Mrs J. Reed, headlined: 'Blow the Japs! Says Woman Sleeper of 91'.[103]

So Australian! One moment the Japanese are a nightmare about to overwhelm us, the next a nuisance the authorities should be dealing with.

Gerard Muirhead-Gould ordered the enemy sailor's bodies be cremated with full military honours, reasoning that showing respect for the Japanese dead might help improve conditions for Australians in Japanese POW camps. The admiral later claimed he'd been heavily criticised for his gesture.

'It must take courage of the very highest order to go out in a thing like that steel coffin,' he argued. 'Theirs was a courage which is not the property or the tradition or the heritage of any one nation.'[104] In fact, there had been no press criticism apart from the *Telegraph* and the *Sydney Morning Herald* roping in the general secretary of the ultra-patriotic Australian Natives' Association for predictable comment.[105]

The sailors were cremated at Sydney's Eastern Suburbs crematorium on 9 July. Four coffins were draped in Japanese flags, three volleys were fired in the air by a naval guard and a bugler sounded 'The Last Post'. Ashes of the four were returned to Japan through the Swiss Consul General. The gesture was made public in Japan at the time and well received there, although there's no evidence it had any impact on the treatment of prisoners of war.[106]

The remains of the two salvaged submarines were used to reconstruct a single composite vessel. First, it was on public display by the tram depot at Bennelong Point,[107] raising money for the RAN Relief Trust Fund and the King George Fund for Merchant Sailors.[108] When public interest faded there, the midget was loaded on an army transport and taken on a 4000-kilometre journey from Sydney to Melbourne and on to Adelaide. Stopping at bush towns along the way, gatherings of curious countryfolk around this artefact of the feared enemy were invited to make donations to the charities. £28,000 was raised.[109]

The tour ended in Canberra, where the composite vessel was put on open-air display at the Australian War Memorial. Lieutenant Matsuo's conning tower remained at Garden Island. Leftover material from the composite assembly was made up for sales as souvenirs. Bits of brass pipe and pieces of electric cable were sold with Admiral Muirhead-Gould's printed signature as a certificate of authenticity. Metal from the subs was converted into ashtrays with appropriate inscriptions, and the navy produced tiny lead submarines and commemorative postcards. Proceeds from these enterprises were added to the charities' coffers. The wind was going out of the sails of fear and the war had sunk to a rush for tacky souvenirs.[110]

The Pacific War had finally reached a more populated part of Australia and had been greeted with apprehension and excitement, but there appeared to be no follow-up invasion in store. Although submarines had been a recent concern for coastal shipping, they weren't perceived as vehicles of invasion. In any case, the mood of the nation was already slowly turning after the battle in the Coral Sea, thought by many to have been the repelling of an invasion fleet heading for Australia. It wasn't, and the fleet was withdrawn rather than repelled, but it was the end of a string of Japanese successes. A few days after the midget submarine raid, a major Allied naval victory at Midway Island, far away but decisive, would consolidate the turning tide of the Pacific War.

Chapter 10

THE TURNING TIDE

In the first three months of the Pacific War, Japan had extinguished the French, British and Dutch empires in southeast Asia and driven the Americans out of most of the Philippines. Four hundred years of European colonisation had been ended by an Asian power in less than 90 days. With such stunning success, the Japanese were beset with a new and unanticipated problem they called 'victory disease', the hubris and complacency that comes with a swift outcome, swifter even than their more optimistic expectations. Having got this far with such ease, where should they go next? Consolidate or push on?

On the other side, the Allies grappled with a similar conundrum. In which direction would the enemy drive the next phase of its campaign? North, south, east or west? North was unlikely. Although Japan had troops stationed defensively to resist a Soviet attack, it had poked the Russian bear at Nomonhan in 1939 and was still paying the price, with Japanese soldiers in POW camps somewhere in Siberia.[1] The Japanese navy had conducted a damaging raid west into the Indian Ocean against Allied shipping and naval bases around Ceylon in April 1942, but then turned for home.[2] No consideration of a major assault across the Pacific was detected at that time to follow Pearl Harbor. The only option left, it seemed, was standing still or continuing south.

The Australian government, its military and the Australian people stared anxiously north, looking for a sign of the next move. After the bombing raids in the north began, the Australian military determined that Port Moresby was key to the defence of the north, but units were not available to reinforce Moresby until the AIF started returning from the Middle East late in March and the American division arrived the following month.

Meanwhile, a Japanese invasion force had landed at Lae and Salamaua on the northern coast of New Guinea. Despite sustaining losses from air attacks by the US carriers *Lexington* and *Yorktown* and B-17 bombers from Townsville, the Japanese began building a base and airfield there.[3]

The commander of Home Forces, General Mackay, had visited Darwin in March in the aftermath of repeated air attacks and reported serious personnel and supply problems. General Herring, just returned from the Middle East, was ordered to Darwin with the core of his 6th Division HQ staff to take command of Northern Territory Force. He found morale low, supplies unreliable and troops scattered thinly along the coast, not unlike General Percival's ill-considered disposition of Singapore's defences. The new Territory commander replaced several officers and stationed his forces in depth down the Stuart Highway to counter-attack any enemy landings more effectively.[4]

Japanese aircraft were detected at one time when Herring was addressing his officers. He continued speaking as the officers got up to head for shelter and clearly he had no intention of stopping. They sat down, bombs fell 12 kilometres away and morale improved sharply.[5] Ned Herring was a leader.

In April, with Douglas MacArthur about to take command of South West Pacific Area, the new Allied Land Forces commander, General Blamey, provided the Australian government with a current assessment of the Pacific War. A major attack on Australia was unlikely, he said, but the Japanese could aim to capture Port Moresby, then work south after landing on Australia's northeast coast.[6] MacArthur offered similar advice: predatory raids were far more likely than a large-scale attack. Nonetheless, Curtin told the House of Representatives that invasion was a 'constant and undiminished danger'.[7] The nation's commitment to the war needed firing up.

Although MacArthur presented a public image of the supremely confident commander, in private he was in despair, bitterly disappointed with the resources he had been given.[8] Having had his request for aircraft carriers rejected by US Army Chief of Staff General Marshall, MacArthur asked Curtin to push for additional troops and a carrier from Churchill. When the British turned that request down, Churchill asked Roosevelt if MacArthur had authority to pursue resources by that path, earning the SWPA commander a rebuke from his superiors.[9] Douglas MacArthur was in a chain of command, even if he was God in Australia.

In relying on MacArthur for advice, Curtin was unaware of where support for the Pacific theatre was strongest in Washington. There for six weeks to argue for more resources, Bert Evatt noted the influence of Admiral Ernest King, Commander in Chief of the US Fleet. King loathed the British and paid no more than lip-service to 'beat Hitler first'. To him, the Pacific was an equally important theatre,[10] to be waged through his Hawaii-based commander of South Pacific Area, Admiral Chester Nimitz, with whom MacArthur would forge an operational partnership seasoned with personal and inter-service rivalry.

Unbeknown to the Japanese, the Americans were making significant progress in penetrating their main naval operational code, called JN-25. Radio intercepts during April, at Moorabbin in suburban Melbourne and at Pearl Harbor, had been decoded to reveal references to a task force for a coming campaign, inferred to be around the Coral Sea, north of Australia. Aircraft carriers returning from the Indian Ocean were not returning to Japan, but going to Truk, a naval base on the Caroline Islands in the northwest Pacific. Decrypts indicated that three carriers were to provide protection in early May for an assault force, with Port Moresby and Tulagi the apparent objectives. Nimitz ordered his carriers *Yorktown*, provisioning in Tonga, and *Lexington*, refitting at Pearl Harbor, to the Coral Sea.[11]

On 30 April 1942, a Japanese fleet left Rabaul, bound for Tulagi in the southern Solomon Islands. A few days later, a larger force left Rabaul for Port Moresby, and three carriers left Truk to rendezvous with it in the Coral Sea. The Japanese assumed the Allies knew nothing of their planned operation.

The Tulagi force was spotted by SWPA air patrols from New Guinea and coast watchers in the Solomons, but the Tulagi base had already been abandoned by the RAAF. The attackers were able to land on the island unopposed and seemingly well away from Allied warships.

Next morning, the Tulagi occupation force was surprised by air strikes from *Yorktown*. Unaware that the American ship was already in the Coral Sea, Admiral Shigoyoshi Inouye sent patrols out to look for an enemy carrier approaching from the central Pacific, but they returned without seeing one. Realising the Americans were possibly already in the vicinity, Inouye had to rapidly recalibrate his plans.[12] For the next two days, the

American and Japanese fleets manoeuvred around the Coral Sea without sighting each other.

At dawn on 7 May, patrols sent out from aircraft carriers on both sides produced a day of misidentified sightings and attacks on lesser craft. The only significant damage was the sinking of the Japanese light carrier *Shoho*. The following dawn, patrols from both sides this time found major opposing carriers. Japan's *Shokaku* was badly damaged and withdrew, but under cloud cover *Zuikaku* was not sighted. On the American side, *Yorktown* was badly damaged and an attack on *Lexington* left it burning out of control.

Unaware that the Americans had lost *Lexington* and withdrawn *Yorktown*, Inouye recalled the invasion force back to Rabaul. Despite high aircraft losses, *Zuikaku* was still operational and, as the only remaining carrier, may well have won the day had Inouye pressed on. A warship force under command of the Australian admiral, John Crace, was the main remaining Allied defence, and it no longer had air cover. Allied losses were greater, but the Japanese had failed in their mission to land an invasion force at Port Moresby, their first major setback of the war. It was the first naval battle in history where participating ships never sighted or fired at each other.

On the morning of the second day of the battle, John Curtin announced to the House of Representatives that a Washington press release had good news of a sea battle, but offered no detail. It was actually the *Yorktown* attack on Tulagi, where the Japanese had lost ships.[13] In the afternoon, however, furnished with a MacArthur communiqué, the prime minister told an almost empty parliament that 'a great naval battle is proceeding' with an outcome 'of crucial importance to the conduct of the war'.[14]

Newspapers the next morning were full of cautious hope, with an article headlined 'GRIM NAVAL BATTLE IN CORAL

SEA' reporting ten Japanese ships lost, including at least one carrier, but no mention of Allied losses, recall of the Japanese invasion fleet or Port Moresby as the invaders' target. 'If it should go advantageously, we shall have great cause for gratitude and our position will be clearer,' Curtin was quoted. 'If not, we shall have a stern ordeal and a greater and graver responsibility.'[15]

Ray Adams was with the VDC, who were standing by in New South Wales with trains to take them north if the Japanese won the sea battle. It was thought Japan's intention would be to land in northern Queensland, where Adams and the other volunteers would have been 'gun fodder for the first Japs that came in'.[16]

The nation had become so apprehensive that the failure of Japan's mission was greeted with relief rather than elation. Ralph Doig recalls, 'There was no immediate feeling when the Coral Sea battle was over, "Oh, well, that's the end of it, there's no more danger from the Japanese", because they still had this powerful navy, almost on the foreshores of Australia. This was only one encounter.'[17]

As time passed, this battle was increasingly seen by Australians as a critical turning point of the war. Douglas MacArthur assured John Curtin that the Japanese had suffered a significant reversal and had probably abandoned for the time being any attempt to occupy Port Moresby or get a foothold on the Australian mainland.[18]

The bipartisan Advisory War Council took a different view. Briefed by RAN chief Admiral Guy Royle on the outcome at the Coral Sea, it expressed disappointment that the Allies hadn't taken greater advantage of the 'ample warning of the enemy's intentions' and failed to achieve complete victory.[19] Stung by this criticism, having puffed up SWPA's role in these events, MacArthur countered that the battle 'undoubtedly saved Australia from a definite and immediate threat'.[20]

Curtin continued his requests to the US and Britain for military equipment and reinforcements after Australia had 'sacrificed 60,000 of its men on overseas battlefields in the last war' and sent forces to fight overseas in this one. Cables in response offered only limited support: British aid if Australia was attacked in force, but not otherwise. MacArthur commented that this was 'an extremely weak reed on which to rely', unlikely to be in sufficient strength or early enough to assist. Along with General Blamey, he urged Curtin to press for a return of the AIF's 9th Division, still in the Middle East.[21] That was postponed when Rommel started gaining the upper hand in North Africa.

Notwithstanding his assurances to Curtin, MacArthur had argued to his superiors that, after Coral Sea, Australia would be Japan's next target. It fell on deaf ears. America's Joint Chiefs of Staff knew from signals intelligence, analysed in Melbourne and Pearl Harbor, that the Imperial Japanese Navy (IJN) planned to seize Midway Island in the north Pacific and draw the US Pacific Fleet into a decisive naval battle.[22]

Combined Fleet commander Admiral Isoroku Yamamoto's complex battle plan required coordination of several fleets over a vast expanse of open sea. Japanese intelligence advised that USS *Enterprise* and USS *Hornet* were the only carriers available to the Pacific Fleet and they were thought to be in the Coral Sea still. *Yorktown* was believed to have been so badly damaged that it was either out of action or had sunk. Yamamoto would disperse his forces widely so their full extent would not be apparent to the Allies until too late, but widespread forces aren't well placed to come to each other's aid if the going gets tough.

Yamamoto's plan was for a strike force of aircraft carriers to attack Midway Island, along with an occupation force with battleship escort. The American fleet would rush to the island's defence and, weakened by that encounter, would be ambushed by Yamamoto's powerful battleship force lurking further to the west. The intention was for the US fleet to be crushed in a triple pincer, thus completing the strategy launched six months before at Pearl Harbor.[23]

At least, that was the plan. After ensuring they had been spotted by a patrol from Tulagi, the American carriers in the south Pacific slipped away to Hawaii under cover of night. Meanwhile, IJN radio signals had been intercepted and decoded by Allied cryptanalysts, revealing components of Yamamoto's Midway offensive assigned to his various fleet commanders. They prescribed routes and positioning of the fleets with timings, coordination of air attacks and a diversionary raid on the Aleutian Islands.[24]

The Americans had the advantage of surprise, an advantage the enemy imagined itself to have. Nimitz had the US carriers standing by northeast of Midway by 2 June to ambush the ambush. He had land-based aircraft on Midway and Hawaii and submarines as back-up.

In the pre-dawn of 4 June and with poor visibility from bad weather, dive-bombers from the four Japanese aircraft carriers launched a strike against Midway Island's air base, causing some initial damage. While they re-armed for a second attack soon after sunrise, a flotilla of American ships was sighted, followed by the arrival of carrier-launched torpedo bombers. Their attack on the Japanese carrier fleet was disorganised and fairly ineffectual, but it left the Japanese fleet commander, Admiral Chuichi Nagumo, bewildered. Now dealing with unanticipated ships at sea, instead of an air base on land, he ordered the bombs unloaded and replaced with torpedos as he switched from attack to defence.

In the confusion, mistakes were made by both sides, but luck favoured the Americans and within twenty minutes three of the Japanese carriers were ablaze. The fourth, *Hiryu*, moved away to launch a successful onslaught on *Yorktown* with dive-bombers and torpedo-bombers. The American carrier was abandoned in the afternoon. Later that afternoon, *Hiryu* was finally spotted, attacked and left burning.

By nine o'clock the next morning, all four Japanese aircraft carriers had sunk. It had all happened so quickly that Yamamoto with his battleship force was too distant to be able to intervene in time. When he got to the battle scene the American fleet had retreated, its job done.

The Australian press was still absorbed with Sydney's midget submarine attack a few days earlier when first reports of the Midway Island battle came in on 6 June. The *Courier-Mail*'s 'JAPS SUFFER IN MIDWAY IS. RAID' told of the enemy losing many planes and suffering damage to battleships and carriers in a heavy raid on the Pacific island two days earlier. The raid was thought to be linked somehow to raids in the Aleutians and perhaps to the midget submarines.[25]

Two days later, a naval victory was proclaimed, although the enemy was reported as losing only two carriers with a possible third destroyed. The US had suffered a carrier hit and 'some planes lost'. The victory was seen as primarily America's revenge for Pearl Harbor, but there was a note from 'an authoritative SWPA source'—for which, read General MacArthur—that it temporarily lifted the invasion threat to Australia and paved the way for a second front in the west Pacific.[26]

In Washington, Admiral King was keen to discourage any suspicion that Allied code-breaking might have been instrumental in the American success. The US Navy guessed there would be an assault on Midway Island and Alaska after Coral Sea, he said without elaborating. 'If we'd known exactly when, where, and with what force the enemy intended to strike,' he added disingenuously, 'we might have diverted some forces from our other vital areas of protection.'[27]

They did know . . . and they did divert forces. Midway was arguably the turning point of the Pacific War. Newspapers at the time expressed cautious optimism, but no more than that. The *Sydney Morning Herald* editorialised that the battle 'might determine the outcome of the war in the Pacific, but we are still without sufficient details . . . to judge how far this guarded opinion has been borne out by events'.[28]

The Battle of Midway Island had changed the ascendancy in the naval war. Coral Sea had been a setback; Midway was a disaster for the Japanese. SWPA had been only peripherally involved in the first and MacArthur had not participated at Midway. He would have been under Nimitz's command there.

Douglas MacArthur needed to get on the front foot. He told Curtin that Australia's security was assured and persistent demands for assistance in its defence would be seen as 'a timid cry for help'. They should now argue for forces for an offensive to retake Rabaul and New Guinea.[29] MacArthur repeated the self-serving message a week later to the Advisory War Council. 'We should take the initiative and strike at Japanese bases in the islands to the north and throw the enemy bomber line back 700 miles,' he declared.[30] Later on, in the Brisbane Line debate, this was a position he'd claim to have taken three months before.

The US Joint Chiefs of Staff (JCS) issued a directive on 2 July, ordering an offensive to take the New Britain–New Ireland–New Guinea area. General Marshall supported MacArthur's grandiose proposal for an amphibious force to capture Rabaul with aircraft carrier support, but Admiral King objected that the carriers would be exposed to Japanese land-based aircraft, too far away from backup Allied air protection. The JCS compromise was for Nimitz's South Pacific Area Command to push up the

Solomon Islands chain and for MacArthur's South West Pacific Area to leapfrog along the New Guinea coast, with the two forces positioning to attack Rabaul from two directions.[31]

After occupying Tulagi, the Japanese had crossed to Guadalcanal and started building an airstrip there. The two-pronged offensive ordered by JCS would start with US Marines seizing these two enemy air bases in the southern Solomons. MacArthur would meanwhile occupy Buna on the north coast of New Guinea, build airfields there and begin moving west along the coast. He took little notice of naval intelligence that Japan planned to use Buna as an air base itself and to carry out an overland assault on Port Moresby.[32]

Port Moresby's garrison, New Guinea Force, had consisted of three militia battalions from Australia and two local volunteer units, one of native Papuans, the Papuan Infantry Battalion (PIB), the other of white expatriates. At the end of May 1942, three more militia units had arrived; but they were considered poorly trained and were used mostly to unload ships. The defenders were there to resist any further amphibious assaults on Port Moresby, considered a low probability. An overland offensive from the north, crossing the towering Owen Stanley Range, seemed even more fanciful. The AIF 7th Division was by then in Townsville after being brought back from the Middle East, but it was held back by MacArthur, consumed with his planned advance towards Rabaul.

In June, the PIB was ordered to conduct reconnaissance patrols around the north coast. The following month, militia units set out along the Kokoda Track to patrol the Buna area in readiness for its construction as a base for MacArthur's offensive. A muddy, precipitous jungle pathway over the Owen Stanley Range, the Kokoda Track crossed a succession of razorback ridges along the spine of New Guinea, the only overland route from north to south.

In preparation for the planned offensive, SWPA moved its headquarters from Melbourne to Brisbane in July, setting up in the AMP Building while MacArthur's family moved into Lennons Hotel. Blamey installed a forward operational base at St Lucia, a few kilometres from the city centre, but he remained at Land Forces Headquarters in Melbourne. The Prime Minister's War Conference met less frequently after these moves and the military priorities of Australia and the United States began slowly and subtly moving apart. Curtin's primary concern was the security of Australia; MacArthur's the recovery of the Philippines. Their joint concern was the defeat of Japan.

All of these were thrown into reverse on 21 July, when a Japanese force of 900 landed near Buna, forestalling MacArthur's plan to set up there. It wasn't clear whether the enemy intended to build a base at Buna, to advance across the Owen Stanleys, or both. Notwithstanding the intelligence available, Allied strategists believed an overland assault was too difficult and gave it little credence. Japanese army engineers had been landed and began constructing the base. Following skirmishes with small PIB units, a Japanese advance force of 230 overran the airfield at Kokoda on 29 July.[33] It was retaken briefly ten days later, but by 13 August the defenders had been driven back up the Kokoda Track to Isurava in the northern foothills of the Owen Stanleys. By then, a problem was looming for the Japanese in the more strategically important Solomon Islands.

The Japanese had consolidated on Guadalcanal by July 1942, building an airfield there at Lunga in its north, in addition to its seaplane base across the water on Tulagi Island. Australian coast watchers on Bougainville were now told to move inland and keep radio silence until further notice. Something was brewing. Jack Read set up an observation post at Porapora overlooking Buka Passage at the north end of Bougainville; Paul Mason moved to a position above Buin on its south end.

On 5 August they were told to start reporting enemy activity in full: fighters at Buka airfield, shipping in Buin harbour and air movements heading south over them. They were to report air movements in plain language, not code, so that the Americans could be ready to repel any attack without the delay of decoding the message. The bomber route to Guadalcanal from Japan's base at Kavieng passed over Buka, where Read was watching, and from Rabaul over Mason near Buin. Read would see an attack formation some two hours before it got to Guadalcanal, Mason about an hour and a half before.[34]

Two days later, the reason for going on the alert became clear. At sunrise on 7 August, 75 American warships launched an operation to retake Guadalcanal. Carrier-borne bombers attacked Japan's seaplane base and 16,000 Marines began landing on Tulagi and at Lunga, taking defenders by surprise. After eight months of desperate defence, Allied forces were embarking on a major offensive in the Pacific for the first time. Outnumbered, Japanese garrison troops and indentured Korean construction workers at Lunga scattered into the rainforest. The small garrison at Tulagi resisted fiercely, but after three days it was virtually wiped out.

As soon as Admiral Sadayoshi Yamada in Rabaul got word of the onslaught, he ordered torpedo-bombers to attack the Allied vessels unloading supplies. Perched above Buin in the mid-morning, Paul Mason heard the growl of approaching aircraft, then saw an array of escorted bombers heading south, migratory birds of prey roaring overhead. His observation was picked up 500 kilometres away, a clear voice repeating, 'Twenty-four bombers heading yours.'[35]

This gave Grumman Wildcat fighters on three carriers 90 minutes to get into position to take on the enemy's fighter escort. They needed sufficient time to refuel, take off and climb above the approaching attackers before they arrived. The Zero was a superior fighter to the Grumman, whose best chance lay in diving from above.[36]

Assault aircraft came in low, east of Guadalacanal, but found they hadn't caught their quarry by surprise. The ships had suspended unloading and dispersed; their anti-aircraft guns were ready and firing. Grumman fighters pounced from above. Only one of the bombers would return to Rabaul. It was a surprising outcome, but the Japanese were not discouraged.

Early the next day, Jack Read was listening to a radio report that the Marines had taken Tulagi when 27 Japanese dive-bombers passed over his post, followed a few minutes later by a second formation of eighteen. Read quickly turned his radio to transmit mode, reporting in uncoded voice, 'Forty-five dive-bombers going south-east.'[37]

Admiral Fletcher had moved his carrier force back, so Read's warning couldn't be acted on productively. Only three of the carrier planes arrived before the Japanese attacked. Enemy losses were light, but an American destroyer was sunk and Wildcat losses were mounting. Concerned about aircraft attrition and likely further air attacks, Fletcher withdrew the carrier task force completely on the night of 8 August. Commanding a landing force that had lost its air cover, a furious Admiral Kelly Turner decided to withdraw his ships as well by morning, even though they had not finished unloading.[38]

While the transports readied to depart, the outer fleet guarding them was attacked by a Japanese naval force led by Admiral

Gunichi Mikawa that had come down the channel through the Solomon Islands chain, undetected by coast watchers or reconnaissance patrols. In the overnight Battle of Savo Island, HMAS *Canberra* and three American cruisers were sunk.

Unaware the American carriers had already left and having no air cover himself, Admiral Mikawa withdrew before daylight, rather than risk attacking the Allied transports without air protection. Had he done so, as at Coral Sea the war might have taken a different turn. Instead, Turner was able to withdraw his force with equipment, provisions and troops still on board.

Among the casualties in the Battle of Savo Island was Howard Bode, captain of USS *Chicago,* which had been in Sydney on the night of the midget submarine raid. Facing court martial after the Savo Island debacle, because his ship failed to go to the aid of *Canberra,* Bode committed suicide.

The 11,000 Marines who had been abandoned on Guadalcanal formed a defensive perimeter around Lunga and the half-built airfield. With landed supplies and captured equipment, they completed construction of the air base. By 18 August, it was ready for operation as Henderson Field. Two days later, two squadrons of Marine aircraft were delivered by carrier and went into action the next day.

Japan's 17th Army was ordered by Imperial General Command in Tokyo to retake Guadalcanal. All the resources that could be mustered were to be thrown at the task, now that this had clearly been a major Allied operation. Ichiki Detachment, standing by to reinforce Buna, was sent by the 17th Army's General Harukichi Hyakutake to the Solomons instead, landing near Lunga on 20 August.

An ambitious frontal assault the next day left Ichiki Detachment wiped out.[39] In response, a large Japanese expeditionary force was despatched from Truk and Rabaul with more reinforcements. Before landing troops, three aircraft carriers approached Guadalcanal, one of them sent in to attack Henderson Field and draw its pilots into retaliation. As the other two carriers moved in, a US carrier force arrived. Both fleets suffered heavy damage in the ensuing battle and both withdrew, but none of the Japanese reinforcements had been landed. Although neither side had prevailed, it provided a respite for the Americans, giving them time to consolidate their new air base on Guadalcanal.

Meanwhile, Japanese soldiers driven from Lunga in the initial American landing had fled west towards the coast watcher post of Snowy Rhoades and Leif Schroeder. As they neared, the watchers moved back until they found themselves hemmed in by a Japanese outpost; they hid in a cave.[40] Martin Clemens was more fortunate, able to get down to Henderson by mid-August.[41] Hugh Mackenzie arrived there by supply ship soon after, having eventually got away from New Britain early in the war, and he and the two coast watchers set up a receiving station at the base. Air battles between Allied aircraft from Henderson Field and Japanese fighters and bombers from Rabaul continued almost daily around Guadalacanal through August and into September, with the coast watchers to the north on Bougainville, Jack Read and Paul Mason, often providing advance warning of coming Japanese air strikes. It wasn't going well for the Japanese. They were slowly losing a war of attrition.

The two regiments of *Nankai Shitai* (South Seas Force) were well established at Buna by mid-August. Their commander, General Tomitaro Horii, set about planning a full-scale attack on the Australian militia dug in at Isurava, up on the Kokoda Track. Now concerned that the enemy might push on further, Allied command strengthened New Guinea Force, putting General Syd

Rowell in command. With the AIF 7th Division finally brought to New Guinea, two of its battalions were soon moving along the mountain path to bolster Isurava's defence. Douglas MacArthur meanwhile assured John Curtin that the Japanese 'could not attack Port Moresby with any strength of land forces over the mountain range'.[42]

After a hiatus, General Horii launched a frontal attack on Isurava on 26 August with flanking movements on both sides. Joined by soldiers from the AIF battalion, who arrived on foot in batches and were thrown straight into the battle in conditions radically different from their Middle East experience, the defenders held on grimly for four days. Finally, they were withdrawn to a new defensive position further back along the track.

A pattern of strategic withdrawals by the Australians followed, with little notification to the Australian public of the deteriorating position there, beyond general newspaper references to 'increased enemy activity in the Kokoda area'. The press had turned its attention to a new Japanese attack in the region.

On the morning of 24 August, a RAAF Hudson had spotted an invasion force off the Trobriand Islands, east of New Guinea. As bad weather closed in, the fleet slipped out of sight, but a coast watcher the next day reported that it was approaching the eastern tip of New Guinea. Overnight, a Japanese force of 800 naval troops came ashore in pouring rain at Milne Bay, and drove back militia defenders that initially opposed them. This was the same day that General Horii had resumed his offensive on the Kokoda Track.

The Japanese had discovered the Allies were building airfields at Milne Bay, despite the torrential rain, oppressive humidity and rampant malaria there. Part of MacArthur's preparation for the Rabaul offensive, these airfields were a threat to a new Japanese seaborne attack planned to coincide with its overland assault on

Port Moresby.[43] Poor Japanese intelligence had concluded only a small garrison was stationed at Milne Bay, but Australian decryption of Japanese submarine messages indicated an attack was imminent.

General MacArthur rushed the AIF 18th Brigade there and ordered strikes against Japanese airfields around Buna. By the time the small Japanese force landed on 25 August, the Allied garrison had been increased to 7500 Australian and 1500 American personnel, many of them engineers to build the airfields but half of them infantry.

In the morning, the Japanese moved down a track along the edge of Milne Bay, behind two light tanks that had been landed with the troops. Attacked by RAAF Kittyhawks, and with little air protection after the earlier strike on Buna's airfields, the beachhead support base lost landing barges, supplies and men. In 2-feet-deep mud, the Japanese troops meanwhile progressed slowly along the shore, managing to reach the first of the airfields. By then, both of their tanks had become irretrievably bogged in the mud and abandoned.[44]

A two-day lull in fighting followed, with the downpour continuing. The Australians consolidated their defences, moving an AIF battalion forward, while the Japanese landed 800 more troops with supplies. In Brisbane, with little knowledge of conditions at Milne Bay, Douglas MacArthur began to worry that his superior numbers were failing to drive the invaders out.[45]

The seed of doubt had been lodged in the SWPA commander's mind before dawn on 31 August, when a succession of Japanese attacks launched at the airfield were driven back by machine-gun and mortar fire. It wasn't sufficient to ease MacArthur's concern; but, with heavy casualties, it dawned on the invaders that their intelligence had been faulty. They were facing a much larger force than they had expected.

After two failed attempts to land further reinforcements, Japan's high command ordered a withdrawal. By then, the Japanese force was reduced to only 50 fully fit soldiers. None of their company commanders and only three platoon leaders had survived. This was the first major battle of the Pacific War that was a decisive defeat of Japanese land forces. Milne Bay's impact on morale was profound, dispelling Allied notions of the invincibility of Japanese soldiers, even as far afield as British troops fighting in Burma.[46]

The strategic picture was changing on both sides of the conflict in the islands to Australia's north, neither side aware of the other's evolving assessments. Initially, Japanese intelligence had concluded that the strong American force inferred from radio communications was to reinforce Australia and stop Japan's Moresby offensive. The Guadalcanal attack was assumed to be primarily a disruptive raid. It was realised too late that it was actually the major offensive.[47]

General Hyakutake, responsible for Imperial Japanese Army (IJA) operations in both New Guinea and the Solomons, told General Horii on 28 August that the Port Moresby offensive was postponed for six weeks or more, 'until the situation in Guadalcanal stabilises'. Horii was ordered to secure the north side of the Owen Stanleys with the main component of *Nankai Shitai,* their South Seas Force. A lesser force was to advance short of Moresby and await further instructions.[48] Only 3500 troops moved beyond Isurava—too few to even consider taking Moresby with its 22,000-strong garrison, but sufficient to patrol and block any movement along the precipitous Kokoda Track.

On the Allied side, by the end of August General MacArthur was advising General Marshall in Washington that the situation in Papua might get critical without naval support. He laid the blame on

Australian troops for a possible 'disastrous outcome' in the Pacific. MacArthur was conscious of his need for something positive in the Pacific to erase the stain of his retreat from the Philippines.

'The Australians have proven themselves unable to match the enemy in jungle fighting,' he complained to Marshall. 'Aggressive leadership is lacking.'[49]

'Make the best of what you have,' was the response.[50]

At a secret session of parliament on 3 September, John Curtin reviewed the war situation, citing MacArthur that the Japanese intended to attack supply lines from the United States and then the Australian mainland. 'We are in for a long war,' the PM said. 'Public morale must be strong, resolute and determined. The capacity to "stick it" better than the enemy may be the deciding factor.'[51]

That evening Curtin kept up his public trepidation about a battle on Australian soil. 'Today Port Moresby and Darwin are the Singapores of Australia,' he said in a national broadcast. 'If those two places fall, then inevitably we are faced with a bloody struggle on our soil, a struggle in which we would be forced to fight grimly, city by city, village by village, until our fair land might become a blackened ruin.'[52]

Blamey was more sanguine, putting the view to the prime minister that, although the Australian troops were being pushed back on the Kokoda Track, it was mainly due to the greater difficulty of keeping them supplied over that distance and that terrain. As the Japanese advanced, the Australian problem became their problem. A week later, he emphasised the point at a press conference. 'The Japs will be beaten by their own advance with its attendant problems of supply,' Blamey said. 'It will be a Japanese advance to disaster, an Australian retreat to victory.'[53]

The Australian press had been vague for several days about action 'in the Kokoda area'. The battleground became more specific on 10 September. Fighting was now 'in mist and rain-soaked jungle' near the pass across the Owen Stanleys. This advance was a disturbing development for the Australian public and it got worse. The next day the enemy was reported as having crossed The Gap and moved 16 kilometres further south.

In fact, newspapers trailed a couple of days behind events. By then, the Australians had been pushed back to Ioribaiwa Ridge, just 42 kilometres from Port Moresby. The *Sydney Morning Herald* noted the remarkable Japanese progress during the days of silence. 'The news,' it editorialised, 'cannot fail to raise certain anxiety.'[54] The *Herald* wasn't the only party anxious about the enemy's approaching front line.

In May, four months before the Battle of Ioribaiwa, General Marshall had sent General Robert Richardson to Australia to investigate command weaknesses. Richardson was appalled to find General George Brett had integrated the RAAF and USAAF so that some American units were commanded by Australians, and that US ground troops in Australia were under General Blamey's command. On his return to the United States, he told Marshall, 'The present organisation is an affront to national pride and to the dignity of the American Army.'[55] As a result, Marshall quietly shelved a plan to transfer Richardson to SWPA. The US War department nonetheless advised MacArthur to form a task force under an American commander as soon as they were likely to be sent into battle. US corps should be assigned to that task force, he was told.[56]

The instruction suited MacArthur. Brett had questioned his order for a bombing mission when MacArthur was still in the Philippines. He hadn't forgotten that and General Brett was replaced in July by General George Kenney.

Short and stocky, Kenney was dynamic and generally competent. He set about his reforms vigorously, replacing several of his air force generals and separating command of the Australian and American air units. Soon Allied air forces were inflicting significant damage on the Japanese. Kenney clashed with Richard Sutherland and flattered Douglas MacArthur, who increasingly relied on Kenney's advice over that of his comrades from his Bataan days.[57]

Kenney made a brief visit to New Guinea, talking to his air commanders and reporting back to MacArthur that Moresby was lost and that General Rowell was defeatist and planning to abandon the airfields. He hadn't actually spoken to Rowell, and what his commanders had told him was both rumour and incorrect. Kenney wanted American troops to defend Moresby's airfields, but MacArthur was reluctant to have them under Australian command in the field.[58] Kenney muttered to others that if the Japanese got to Goldie River, between Ioribaiwa and Moresby, he'd pull his aircraft out of New Guinea.[59]

A sense of crisis had crept into Allied command and on to the Australian government, exacerbated by a new field commander on the Kokoda Track. Brigadier Ken Eather had immediately withdrawn the Australian defenders from Ioribaiwa Ridge to the ridge before it.[60]

At the urging of his minister, Frank Forde, Blamey visited Port Moresby, conferring with senior officers there. He returned optimistic that Moresby could be held, reporting the troops' confidence in their leaders and that Rowell had the situation under control. The Japanese couldn't bring sufficient men and artillery over the mountains to attack Port Moresby, he told the Advisory War Council, but General Kenney was in his commander-in-chief's office every day convinced that Moresby would fall.[61]

Strategists on both sides of the conflict knew the Japanese force on the Kokoda Track couldn't take Port Moresby unaided, but Douglas MacArthur feared his career was at stake. His earlier confidence that the Japanese couldn't get to Papua's capital had vanished. His reputation couldn't survive the loss of such a key location and anything that might flow from that. MacArthur phoned Curtin and told him Australian troops were inefficient and he was sending US troops to stem the tide. Blamey should go to New Guinea, he insisted, take personal command and 'energise the situation'.[62] It was a move to ensure Australia would take the blame for any disaster that might eventuate.

Told by Curtin he should go to New Guinea and take command, Blamey procrastinated, knowing his arrival in Port Moresby would create a flap. He notified Rowell of the instruction, saying it was not a reflection on his performance, but 'we have very inexperienced politicians who are inclined to panic on every possible occasion'.[63] He might well have included MacArthur in that group.

In Washington, General Marshall sent USAAF chief, General Henry 'Hap' Arnold, to visit the Pacific and assess the mood there. Arnold met with MacArthur on 25 September and was told the Australians 'were not good in the field, they were not good in the jungle, and they came from the slums of the cities of Australia'. Arnold's diary notes a MacArthur 'obsessed by a plan he can't carry out [his assault on Rabaul]—frustrated—dramatic to the extreme—much more nervous than when I formerly knew him. Hands twitch & tremble—shell shocked.'[64]

After five days, Blamey was still in Australia. Curtin had a good working relationship with his army chief, but here he put his foot down. 'If you value your position,' he said, 'you'll not remain in Brisbane another day.'[65]

Blamey left the next day, arriving in Port Moresby to find the Japanese had not advanced for two weeks and the Australians were patrolling forward. A series of discussions took place between the commander-in-chief and his New Guinea Force commander.

Tom Blamey was capable but blunt; Syd Rowell tended to see a slight whenever the opportunity arose, and it arose here. Despite his commander's reassuring letter, Rowell thought Blamey's presence did indicate lack of confidence in him and that Blamey lacked 'moral courage' in not challenging the order.

The two had a past. Rowell had clashed with Blamey in the ill-fated campaign in Greece in 1941, where they had faced overwhelming German forces with minimal air support; Rowell had been very critical of Blamey's judgement at that time. In a series of acrimonious exchanges in Port Moresby, Rowell made clear his personal dislike of Blamey. As a result, Blamey felt they couldn't work constructively together and that he had no choice but to relieve Rowell of his command.[66] Syd Rowell left for Brisbane the next day.

On 26 September, with Australian patrols having probed the enemy lines at Ioribaiwa without drawing a strong response, Brigadier Eather ordered a full-scale advance on the Japanese positions, with artillery support. Two days later they reached the ridge to find the enemy had vanished; they had been bombarding empty trenches. It was the day before General Rowell left New Guinea. The Australians now advanced cautiously along the Kokoda Track, wary of ambushes. They didn't catch up with *Nankai Shitai* for another two weeks.[67]

An order for a radical change of direction had been received by General Horii on 23 September. 'The commander of the South Seas Force will assemble his main strength in the Isurava and Kokoda areas and secure these as a base for future offensives,' General Hyakutake's instruction said. 'In addition, the defences in the Buna area will be strengthened.'[68]

Events in Guadalcanal and Milne Bay had triggered the withdrawal, particularly a 13 September attack on Henderson Field, where the Japanese assault force had been badly defeated. With

Japanese forces struggling to take control of the Solomons, the Kokoda Track had been abandoned. It had always been only an option, never supremely important. A fighting withdrawal would allow Japan to dig in on swamplands on the northern coast.

The main body of the force had left Ioribaiwa later that day, four days before the Australians arrived to find them gone. Horii's force withdrew to defensive positions on the Kokoda Track, prepared in advance to slow the Australian pursuit and provide time for the Japanese to build substantial defences around Buna. Japan was never able to recover the initiative, but the invasion of Port Moresby had only ever been planned as a defensive operation, to protect its base at Rabaul and to maintain control of the Coral Sea, in conjunction with air bases in the Solomons.

The two coast watchers on Bougainville, Jack Read and Paul Mason, were experiencing increasing difficulties as villagers switched allegiance to the Japanese. A day after supplies had been air-dropped for the small Australian Army detachment still on the island, locals had stumbled on some packages the soldiers had missed and kept them. The platoon commander there held an enquiry and ordered native police to burn the house of a suspect who had disappeared; he imposed fines and twenty strokes of a cane on those found guilty of the theft.

This turned Bougainvillians against the Australians.[69] With the Japanese present in greater numbers and promising gifts, the locals became pro-Japanese and flew Japan's flag in their villages.

Read reported to Guadalcanal in late August that the airfield at Buka Passage had been extended by the Japanese and fighters were operating from it. Soon after, Mason detailed ship movements at Buin anchorage in the south of Bougainville, with transports unloading tractors, lorries, guns and equipment at nearby Kahili. An airfield was under construction there.

With the Japanese occupying Buin, Mason had had to move inland with his teleradio, but he still had some loyal villagers with him. They got jobs at Kahili airfield, reporting back on construction progress, fuel and food storage under tarpaulins and gun sites. They told him some missionaries had been interned.[70]

Two armies were struggling for ascendancy in the Solomons. Down the island chain at Guadalcanal, the Americans landed reinforcements at Henderson Field, while the Japanese brought more fighters and bombers to Rabaul for an all-out effort to wrest control of that island. In late September, the IJN shuttled additional troops down New Georgia Sound to reinforce those scattered around Guadalcanal. A series of US Marine patrols and raids on Japanese positions yielded mixed results, with both sides enduring heavy casualties in the confrontations. However, the Japanese were ultimately forced back as tropical disease and hunger added to their problems.

Two fresh coast watchers arrived at Guadalcanal, but illness was preying on those concealed in the hinterland. Don Macfarlan came down to Henderson from his ridge with severe malaria and was shipped back to Australia, while Snowy Rhoades and Leif Schroeder, in equally bad shape, were rescued from their hideout by boat.[71]

On Bougainville, the Japanese were told Paul Mason was in the area around Buin and a patrol brought dogs to track him down. Warned, Mason moved far into the interior and the patrol lost his trail. It lost the dogs as well to a Catalina bombing raid and returned without finding either their quarry or his observation post. Read was also warned and moved inland. By the beginning of November, both Bougainville watchers were back at their post.[72]

The Japanese cause on Guadalcanal was getting desperate. A new task force to recover the airfield brought 7000 troops with ammunition, food and equipment from Rabaul, along with a protective naval force to bombard Henderson Field. The planned operation was picked up by Allied intelligence and a large force assembled to land troops and engage the enemy before it could attack the American base. On 10 November, Mason reported over 60 enemy warships in the vicinity of Buin, and Read noted a dozen troop transports coming down the coast.[73] Although attacked from the air, most of the American men and supplies were landed by 12 November.

The Japanese fleet was confronted, short of its target, in a night battle at close quarters off nearby Savo Island. Most of the American warships in this engagement were sunk. The Japanese also suffered losses, although not to the same extent, but they withdrew without bombarding the airfield or landing troops.

The following morning a fresh naval force did manage to bombard Henderson Field, causing limited damage. A Japanese transport convoy following behind was attacked with heavy losses before turning back. Yet another Japanese attack retired after losses on both sides, with less than half the transported troops landing on Guadalcanal. Further attacks over the next month resulted in serious losses of men and materiel on both sides. The Americans, unequalled masters of mass production, were readily able to bring in new aircraft while Japan, with less capacity to replace its losses, could make no headway.

On 26 December, Japan's Imperial General Headquarters gave up the struggle and ordered a withdrawal from Guadalcanal; it began evacuating its remaining forces on the island. A shift of priorities and resources to the campaign on hold in New Guinea came all too late: holding the northern coastline was already a lost cause for the Japanese after a long, grim defence and it was abandoned a month later.

The Coast Watching Organisation, its operators working at great personal risk, had played a significant role in neutralising Japan's initiative in the southwest Pacific. Admiral William 'Bull' Halsey, assigned by Chester Nimitz to work with MacArthur on the twin advance towards Rabaul, commented to Jack Read and Paul Mason, 'The coast watchers saved Guadalcanal and Guadalcanal saved the south Pacific.'[74]

As 1942 rolled into 1943, Australian land victories at Milne Bay and on the Kokoda Track, and in late stages on the coast around Buna, had turned the conflict around in New Guinea. US naval victories at Coral Sea and Midway had gained control of the sea and the air in the Pacific, and Japan's retreat from Guadalcanal had preserved the US–Australia supply line. The tide of the Pacific War had turned. It never turned back and the threat of invasion of Australia disappeared with it.

It's easier to see in hindsight that the turning point was either the Midway or Guadalcanal victories—or both of them. On the face of it, neither Australia nor MacArthur played a significant role in either, but only if you ignore the contribution of cryptographers in Melbourne and coast watchers on Bougainville. Nonetheless, to this day Australians regard Coral Sea and Kokoda with greater reverence because both are still seen by many as having halted the invasion of Australia.

That was the cautious perception at the time too. The prime minister tried to balance hope with continuing austerity, in a war that was receding but was still far from over. 'We can see the first glimmer of the turning point in the struggle but nothing that has happened would justify any relaxing or slackening off,' John Curtin told the nation in the lead-up to Christmas 1942.[75]

The *Sydney Morning Herald* greeted the new year with this summation: 'We may fairly feel that the worst of the danger is past, and that nothing the future can hold is likely to approach in menace what has gone before. The end may be far off, but at least it is an end.' At the same time the newspaper warned that, even with Germany on the brink of defeat in north Africa and the Soviet Union, 'it would be foolish not to recognise Japan's capacity to carry on the war long after her Axis partners may have been brought down'.[76] One of the cornerstones of 'beat Hitler first' had been that it couldn't.

Nonetheless, there was a discernible change in the public mood, the sort of change Curtin constantly worried about in trying to keep the nation vigilant. Civilian morale improved, civil defence drills were eased. Air Raid Precautions (ARP) languished as the danger from the sky diminished. Brownout requirements were relaxed and air-raid trenches filled with water.

There was no obvious point at which the threat of invasion was seen by Australians to have gone, no universal road-to-Damascus moment. There was a growing optimism through the latter part of 1942 that it might be receding and by 1943 it was becoming more certain. A significant milestone along that path had been the retaking of Kokoda on 2 November 1942 by the advancing AIF.

This had symbolic rather than strategic value, given that the Japanese had left there several days before. The *Sydney Morning Herald* nonetheless used it to sound an early note of optimism. 'Australia can never be sufficiently grateful to the brave men who have relieved the threat to Port Moresby and the mainland beyond,' it told its readers. 'Japan's southward drive has been definitely checked. She will be forced to look to the safety of her present holdings rather than plan any further advance.'[77]

The *Herald*'s headline, 'THE TURNING TIDE IN SOUTH PACIFIC', reflects how some still interpret that event. In fact, the tide had been turning since Midway, but that was seen as repelling the invasion of the United States, too far away to have immediacy for Australians. But it was the same enemy.

The Kokoda Track was in Allied hands and Douglas MacArthur could resume his campaign for redemption, the return to the Philippines. In November, MacArthur set up an Advanced HQ for SWPA in Port Moresby, indicating he no longer saw the Papuan capital under threat. Seemingly in contradiction, MacArthur told Curtin in March 1943, after yet another air raid on Darwin, that Japan could launch a major attack in the following months. Wanting Australia to continue providing troops and supplies, he was unwilling to admit Australia was safe.

Blamey, on the other hand, said he was not worried about possible Japanese attacks in the immediate future.[78] In the military sphere, Australia and the United States were moving in different directions.

General Robert Eichelberger had arrived in Australia in August 1942 to take command of the two US Army divisions then in training camps in Brisbane and Rockhampton. In combat at Buna by November, the American soldiers, for the most part militia, struggled with the task of digging the entrenched enemy out of Papua's northern coastal wetlands. Their inadequate training, poor leadership and lack of spirit were badly exposed by stubborn Japanese resistance. To a MacArthur proposal to send American troops into one section of the fray, Blamey archly replied, 'I would rather send in more Australians. At least I know they'll fight!'[79]

MacArthur sacked the American field commander and ordered Eichelberger to take command of the battle and 'remove all officers who won't fight'. 'Bob, I want you to take Buna, or not come back alive,' he said.[80]

Papua was cleared of the tenacious Japanese by February 1943, and MacArthur reorganised his command structure, removing US forces from Blamey's supervision as he had been instructed. He created the Alamo task force, directly under his own command rather than within Blamey's Allied Land Forces, and moved SWPA's growing number of American divisions into it. General Walter Krueger, already over 60, was sent out from the United States to lead Alamo Force.

Courteous and competent, Eichelberger was the only American commander who had cordial relations with Australian Army officers. Soon after arrival, he sensed the Australian field commanders regarded their American counterparts as inexperienced theoreticians, but were too polite to say so. His opinion of Blamey is particularly telling. 'I found General Blamey a very fair commander,' he wrote in his memoirs, 'and I would have taken his judgment at any time far above the three characters who were behind me in the command chain—I refer to MacArthur, Krueger and Sutherland.'[81]

The war was moving slowly away from Australia and national pride and differing priorities prevailed. While MacArthur's forces leapfrogged along the northern coast of New Guinea into Dutch New Guinea, Nimitz's South Pacific commander, Admiral Halsey, island-hopped up the Solomon chain. The giant Rabaul base was bypassed altogether in the end, leaving it blockaded and isolated.

On 20 October 1944, MacArthur's army, with token Filipino units and no Australians other than a radio intercept unit, landed on the Philippine island of Leyte and fulfilled his promise to return, made 32 months before at a South Australian railway junction. In the afternoon, when the cameras were ready, General MacArthur strode ashore.

By then, John Curtin had long conceded that Australia was no longer threatened with invasion. On 10 June 1943 he announced,

'As in the case of Britain, we had a close call at one stage. The Battle of the Coral Sea was a deliverance and the return of the AIF enabled us to stop the Japanese advance in New Guinea just in time. I do not think the enemy can now invade this country.'[82]

It's widely assumed Curtin delayed this acknowledgement in order to keep Australians focused on seeing the war through to Japan's capitulation. That was no doubt part of his thinking at the time, but he had to contend also with mixed reports from MacArthur, depending on the general's changing needs. Three days before Curtin's announcement, MacArthur had told him that 'the days of the holding war were over and it was time to commence the offensive against Japan'.[83] This sounds suspiciously like what he claimed to have been advocating since March 1942, when he says he ditched the Brisbane Line.

With the war receding north, the Australian government began planning post-war construction, rebuilding the nation's family and domestic life, and anticipating demobilisation of its military, when women would move from the workforce back into the home. That was, in effect, still two years away, but it reflected a new purpose in a nation that had been, not long before, uncertain of its own security. People started thinking about what they too might expect of post-war Australia.

A confident government's planning for that future encouraged a new focus. Only the military was stuck in the present, fully occupied with driving the Japanese back to their homeland and ending the war. For government and people, a future of many possibilities lay in front of them, uncertain but hopeful. The initial assumption was that the nation would return to 1941 and pick up from there, but it didn't happen like that.

As well as the progressive notions his government pursued, John Curtin advocated Britain's return to Singapore and expected the Western colonial powers—the Dutch, the French, the Portuguese and especially the English—to resume their pre-war territories, so Australia could not be threatened again by the 'teeming millions of coloured races' to the north. He didn't live long enough to see that Japan's biggest achievement, by waging a war in which it gained little, was putting an end to colonialism in Asia.[84]

Attitudes were changing, not universally but incrementally. A softer approach emerged, even towards the barbaric enemy. In rural New South Wales, Edith Lugsdin watched a convoy of Japanese prisoners driving past. 'The locals stood by the roadside watching and several began to shout at the prisoners,' she recalls. 'Then one of the women, a mother who had a son and daughter away with the forces, said, "We have sons and daughters who are prisoners of war. I hope no one shouts at them." There was silence after that.'[85]

There was a war that everyone had to live with, but it was now somewhere else, not on the doorstep, and an end to it could be seen. Robert Brown, the Brisbane school teacher, had joined the army in 1942. Starting in a medical unit, he was told to report for an interview with 'Army Education', which turned out to be Central Bureau, MacArthur's cryptographic unit that had moved up to Brisbane with SWPA. Robert spent the remainder of the war decoding enemy weather reports from recce patrols by air. They had their own code and their messages provided timely intelligence about coming air raids.[86]

The DCA operator Bruce Acland stayed working in Darwin through a succession of raids after its first devastating attack, developing a psychological condition known there as 'bomb happiness'. It was time to get out and in October 1942 he was repatriated to Sydney. He continued working with the Department of Civil Aviation through the rest of the war and beyond.[87]

Yve Jeanneret spent the remainder of the war growing into a teenager and learning about adult life without luxuries. Rationing continued and her mother would often put her ration book on the shop counter and distract the shopkeeper with chatter. As she paid, she'd take back the ration book before the coupons were taken. 'She used to come home with a great sense of pride about that, which was wrong,' says Yve in retrospect, 'almost shop-lifting.' Her only thought at the time was that her mother was 'a bit naughty', but that was a different time, a different world. After the war, Yve found the Australia she was in was not the Australia of her childhood and the war years. The adult Yve Close, married with a family, developed her talent for painting, working closely with one of the wartime camouflage artists, Joshua Smith.[88]

Like many, Dorothy Singe, a farmer's daughter from Orange, New South Wales, had no idea what her world would be like after the war. 'You knew it was coming to an end. You knew it had to finish somehow and after the Coral Sea we started to feel that we were on top,' she says. 'We thought we'd go back to how we were, but there was no way Australia was going to go back to how it was. It had to change and it did.'[89]

It would be a new and different world. That's another story.

Chapter 11

THE INVASION OF AUSTRALIA

On Anzac Day in 1992, the Prime Minister of Australia, Paul Keating, kissed the ground of the Kokoda Track and declared it sacred to Australians. 'There can be no deeper spiritual basis to the meaning of the Australian nation than the blood that was spilled on this very knoll,' he intoned, 'in defence of the liberty of Australia.'[1]

The Labor government of the time was pursuing the replacement of Gallipoli—a military disaster in faraway defence of Britain—with Kokoda as Australia's principal military icon. Unlike Gallipoli, Kokoda was in defence of the nation, its outcome a measure of the quality of Australian soldiers . . . or so it's asserted.

There's no question that the Australians fought bravely at Kokoda against a formidable enemy under dreadful conditions, but were they holding back the invasion and occupation of Australia as contended? Certainly much of the Australian public at the time thought so. Many still do, under the rubric of the 'Battle for Australia'.

The phrase 'Battle for Australia' was used by John Curtin following the fall of Singapore. It was resurrected in the 1990s by a group of military enthusiasts, with support from RSL office-holders, concerned that the sacrifices of the Second World War were being forgotten. In 2008 Veterans' Affairs minister Alan Griffin announced 'Battle for Australia Day', commemorated on the first Wednesday in September to mark the 1942 victory at Milne Bay. A view put from several quarters that the Japanese never mounted an invasion of Australia drew a peevish response, particularly towards Australian War Memorial historian Peter Stanley.

The case for Japan's High Command planning to invade Australia is largely built on anecdotal evidence that isn't always coherent and doesn't bear close examination. Evidence of spying, for instance, is often said to indicate that intention. There's no doubt Japanese were gathering information about Australia long before the Pacific War, but for what purpose is not as clear-cut as some believe. Was it for military use, or for trade, immigration, cultural exchange or some other benefit? At different times, any or all of those possibilities. Japan has long had a sense of kinship with *Nan'yo*, the South Seas, meaning the Micronesian islands to its immediate south. This promoted a fascination with Australia beyond that, well before any military interest arose.[2]

Japanese tourists armed with cameras, merchant ships steaming close to the Newcastle shore and pearling fleet crew members wearing 'officer' clothing were all thought by Australian authorities to be associated with espionage activities between the wars and earlier, without anyone being able to nominate what nefarious information these people might be collecting. All had benign alternative explanations: the Japanese, like Americans, were camera-mad; British Admiralty recommended steaming inside the strong southward current; Australia had no surveys of its northern coastal reefs.

Major Sei Hashida of the Imperial Japanese Army visited Australia in early 1941, eleven months before Pearl Harbor, ostensibly to investigate purchase of wool and other materials for Japan's military. He visited and made notes at coastal areas and harbours, then left for the East Indies, where he was detained and his notebook confiscated. Australian authorities discussed with the Dutch the possibility of extraditing Hashida, but abandoned it when it was realised that the information he had gathered was generally available to the public and visitors anyway.[3]

It has been claimed Hashida's intelligence was used in Sydney's midget submarine raid, but the floatplanes at the time would have gathered far more relevant information—warships in the harbour, position of the boom net—than he did. Hashida's activities do indicate, however, a different approach to intelligence gathering from that of Britain, America and Australia. Like the Germans, on whose army Japan modelled its own, the Japanese collected information widely, even in countries they were unlikely to be fighting. The rationale was that you can't foresee where a war might spread. Hashida and other visitors to Australia at the time were part of that low-level, broad-sweep approach to intelligence gathering, not necessarily part of any plan to invade, but who knew where it might prove useful?

Incidents of espionage are part of a grab-bag of purported evidence. Often raised is the discovery of 'Japanese invasion banknotes' in denominations of pounds and shillings, the currency imprinted 'Japanese Government'. Reported as captured by Allied forces, presumably in New Guinea, it was touted at the time, September 1942, as 'proof of Japan's intention to invade Australia and could have been printed for distribution only here or in New Zealand'.[4] For some that argument still holds, but there is no reference to either Australia or New Zealand on the notes. They could just as well have been printed for distribution in New Britain or New Guinea.

Japanese-printed currency was used in both those occupied areas. Soldiers returning from active service in New Guinea, with 'invasion banknotes' souvenired from dead Japanese, kept the myth alive, but it's hard to see why banknotes intended for occupied Australia would be in soldiers' pockets before Australia was invaded. When you have a gun, you don't need money.

Also cited in support of the invasion plan is a map claimed to have been captured from Japanese troops in China. In October 1942, it was passed to Canberra by China's director of military intelligence, Admiral H.C. Yang, through the Australian Legation in Chungking, China's wartime capital. The map, headed 'Sketch of Japanese General Headquarters Plan of Attack', shows Australia and its adjacent region with attack and defence lines. An occupation force was to land at Fremantle and Perth, then advance across the Nullarbor. At the same time, a diversionary force was to be landed at Darwin to engage American and Australian forces in the Northern Territory. The map is dated late May, presumably 1942. Its cartography is sloppy; place names and annotations are in 'Japanese' with English translations alongside.[5]

Some still insist the map shows a formal plan to invade Australia, although Australian military intelligence at the time believed it was a forgery. It's unlikely the Japanese military would put English translations on their plans, or that a soldier fighting in China would carry a top-secret strategic document. More to the point, the 'Japanese' text is not Japanese at all, but Mandarin.[6] It is clearly a Chinese document. The first character in the title is an old Chinese term for Japan with a condescending tone. More literally translated, the title is 'Jap (or Nip) General Headquarters . . .'. The map is most likely Chinese speculation on what Japan might have in mind.

Some months later, John Curtin showed the map to Australian journalists to demonstrate Japan's intention to invade.[7] That's held out as evidence he thought it genuine. It may, however, be no more than he thought it useful. He was a politician, after all, in constant pursuit of public support for Australia's war effort. Would he have displayed intelligence publicly if he thought it genuine?

A Japanese journalist has described a different invasion force tasked with landing on mainland Australia. Interviewed for the Melbourne *Herald* by Denis Warner in 1946, Ken Sato claimed a convoy was heading for the beaches between Townsville and Brisbane in early 1942. After it established a foothold in Queensland, the force was to advance down the coast and attack Sydney, then Melbourne. Covered in the Japanese press, Australia's complaint of being deserted by Britain and the switch of its allegiance to America were seen to indicate low morale, fostering the belief that Australia would be prepared to sign a peace treaty without Britain's agreement. The invasion force didn't get to Queensland, Sato told Warner. Halted at Rabaul by Imperial Headquarters, the invasion was shelved when orders were issued to take Milne Bay and Port Moresby. The hierarchy wasn't willing to risk a third operation at the same time.[8]

Sato had a particular interest here, claiming he was to be the civil administrator of occupied Australia. Fluent in English from an education in the United States, he had spent five months in Australia in 1934 as part of a goodwill mission. In 1942, he joined the Australia section of Japanese Naval Intelligence. Ken Sato had a reputation as a bon vivant who tended to big-note himself.[9] It's hard to see why a journalist so recently recruited to the military would be earmarked as a military governor. In any case, his story, for which there's no evidence in Japan's military records, looks suspiciously like a rehash of the invasion force turned back at the Coral Sea. It had been the force that captured Rabaul and later fought on the Kokoda Track, the ill-fated *Nankai Shitai*.

The internet and libraries abound with stories of Japanese invasion plans and landings on the Australian mainland. Ozatwar.com, a treasure trove of military bric-a-brac, lists 27 of them, with a German plan thrown in for good measure. As the website's curator notes, 'the majority are unsubstantiated and more than likely not true'.[10] There are reports of: Japanese parachutists landing, but not of any parachutists caught; of attaché cases and radio transmitters found with 'Japanese markings'; of footprints identified as made by Japanese army boots; and of headlights turned on to guide enemy bombers.

The 'Gulf Scare' of April 1943 illustrates how these stories develop a momentum of their own. On 11 April, Galbraith station in Queensland's Gulf country reported Japanese marines landing by barge and heading towards the town of Normanton, supposedly confirmed by the local VDC. Two days later, residents were fleeing from nearby towns and stations, although no evacuation had been ordered. The NAOU (Nackeroo) platoon at Normanton was ordered to investigate and drove by truck to Vanrook station, where they met the VDC. A joint party on horses and in trucks trekked 100 kilometres to Inkerman and set up camp. Two men and a guide rode on to the landing site and found nothing: no landing barges, no footprints, no Japanese. Local Aborigines reported seeing nothing.[11]

Later, it was found that an Aboriginal boy had reported to the Inkerman manager he'd seen a ship and soldiers on the beach. It had been radioed to the RAAF base at Cloncurry. Three Wirraways were sent out and, seeing nothing, shot up a shed at Galbraith station just for the hell of it. Station people hiding nearby thought they had been attacked by Japanese aircraft.

Most of the reports of landings are equally dubious; a few are plausible, but not confirmed. One of the latter is that noted earlier,[12] reported by Groote Eylandt missionary Len Harris. Another is by coast watcher Alan Samuels, stationed 100 kilometres north of Broome. He reported seeing some 30 Japanese marines busy on a nearby beach. They left in small boats at the end of the day. Two days later, Army intelligence officers arrived and were shown where the soldiers were seen. A cache of supplies and equipment with Japanese markings was uncovered and taken away by the officers, who warned Samuels of his 'obligations under the Official Secrets Act'. He told his son the story in his seventies, but to date no official record of the investigation has been unearthed.[13]

The one verified landing took place in 1944. Members of the landing party and the officer who ordered the landing spoke to an Australian journalist in 1985. His story was published in *Australasian Post*, which might raise suspicions about its authenticity, but it has been corroborated by Japanese military records.

Four Japanese soldiers steamed from Koepang in Timor to northwestern Australia in a native fishing boat. Their brief was to investigate intelligence reports that the Americans were building a huge naval base at Admiralty Gulf and to check the terrain for the possibility of setting up beachheads on the Australian coast. Led by Lieutenant Suzuhiko Mizuno, the group from *Matsu Kikan* (Pine Tree intelligence agency) was expecting to return later with a guerrilla force made up of prisoners released from Japanese gaols.

The party arrived at York Sound, Mizuno says, on a misty January morning. Camouflaging their boat, they went ashore for two days, noting red rocks, small trees, heat and humidity. Remnants of old campfires were found, but no signs of human habitation. Having recorded it all on an 8 mm movie camera, they returned to Koepang.[14] Although there are some discrepancies between the stories—there always are when memory is involved—they might well be the soldiers observed by the coast watcher Alan Samuels. The guerrilla offensive against isolated homesteads and towns, penetrating through to the east coast, was never pursued. It was a plan devised out of sheer desperation.

Reports of enemy landings on the Australian mainland were infrequent. Mostly they were unsubstantiated, but some were plausible and there is the possibility that some went unobserved. They were reconnaissance patrols, however, never anything remotely resembling an invasion force or even an advance party of one.

That doesn't necessarily mean there wasn't a plan to capture Australia that was either not put into action or was thwarted before its purpose became manifestly clear. The Battle for Australia lobby argues for both.

In the early days in particular, the Imperial Japanese Army saw the war against the United States in the Pacific as a navy war. The IJA had planned operations in Malaya and southeast Asia—New Guinea and Australia weren't considered—and left the Pacific and the Dutch East Indies to the IJN. There was no formal agreement to that effect, just a tacit understanding of the division of responsibilities.[15] The army continued its obligations in the uneasy occupation of China and towards meeting any renewed incursion from the Soviet Union.

It soon became evident, as the Allies were forced back in Asia, that Australia would become the American base for a counter-offensive. Strategic planners within Japan's Navy General Staff felt Australia had to be knocked out quickly or cut off from the United States. To be brought to the negotiating table, the Allies had to be kept constantly on the defensive.

In early January 1942, middle-ranking naval officers in Tokyo were proposing an invasion of parts of Australia to forestall its use as a major base. Led by Captain Sadatoshi Tomioka, the planning head in Naval Operations, the faction argued that Australia had to be neutralised, its supply route from the United States blockaded and key parts of northern and northeast Australia occupied. There was no plan to subjugate Australia or to occupy the whole country, only to capture strategic locations. Apart from cutting off supplies, that could be expected to demoralise Australians, who would then pressure their government to find a way out of the war.[16]

The proposal was discussed with the head of Military Operations, General Shinichi Tanaka. Tanaka regarded the plan as 'risky and fanciful', likely to lengthen the war, not end it.[17] The proposal's advocates insisted three divisions would be sufficient to secure key footholds, but IJA chief of staff General Hajime Sugiyama told his naval counterpart Admiral Osami Nagano that any campaign to seize parts of Australia would inevitably spread over the whole country. Unlike Malaya, where much of the population was happy to see the last of its colonial rulers, Australians could be expected to fight ferociously for their homeland.[18]

The army estimated at least ten divisions would be necessary to occupy Australia. They would have to be withdrawn from China, where the occupation was far from settled, and Manchuria, where they were the first line of defence against Soviet attack. The invasion would need the support of 1.5 million tonnes of shipping, more than Japan had available, to transport supplies over the vast distance involved. Merchant shipping that would otherwise be bringing vital resources from occupied areas would be tied up.[19]

By February the dispute between army and navy had become more heated. The question of the invasion of Australia was argued at Imperial General Headquarters, Navy General Staff proposing an assault on the northeast coast. The army countered that this would dispose of neither Britain nor America. It didn't want to get bogged down in another war of attrition, when they were still dealing with one in China. At a conference on 7 March 1942, IGHQ made its decision. The invasion of Australia was postponed indefinitely and the country would instead be isolated by blockading its supply lines.[20]

The proposal to invade always had high-ranking opponents. Prime Minister Hideki Tojo, an army general, was one. After the war, he denied it was seriously contemplated. 'We never had enough troops to do so,' he said. 'We expected to occupy all New Guinea, to maintain Rabaul as a holding base, and to raid northern Australia by air. But actual physical invasion? No. At no time.'[21]

Admiral Isoroku Yamamoto, Japan's Combined Fleet commander, was also unpersuaded. His view was that the prime objective should be to destroy the American fleet in the Pacific and the British fleet in the Indian Ocean. Invading Australia would be an expensive distraction, leaving those fleets intact.

An American air raid on Tokyo in April 1942 known as the Doolittle raid, while causing only limited damage, had spooked the Japanese by its ability to reach the capital. Yamamoto was arguing for the capture of Midway Island and destruction of the US Pacific Fleet to protect Japan from future such raids. To negotiate approval for his Midway operation, he supported the isolation of Australia, but not its invasion.[22]

The IJN proposal to invade Australia was shelved in March 1942. Whether it would have been revived is anyone's guess. Japan's fortunes steadily declined after Midway and it was never in a position to seriously reconsider it. However, an argument is put in the Battle for Australia debate that the subsequent advance along the Kokoda Track, primarily an army manoeuvre, was the first stage of the invasion of Australia, thwarted by Australian troops driving that force back. It's a supposition that, viewed from Australia, looked plausible at the time. Allied strategists, however, came to the view after Midway that the threat of invasion was remote, despite MacArthur's see-sawing advice to Curtin.

No evidence has been found in searching Japanese government archives of a strategic plan or intention before the Pacific War to invade Australia.[23] Post-war access to Japan's military communications, and commentary by its senior officers, provide insight into Japanese strategic thinking during the war. 'Southern operations' were conceived to seize key resource-rich locations in Malaya and the East Indies and build a defensive perimeter around them. The IJA saw its prime responsibility to be in China and Burma, and to guard against the USSR. Army Chief of Staff General Sugiyama determined that once the southern operations were completed, his forces would be redeployed to Manchuria. From late January, however, increased attacks on Rabaul by aircraft coming from Port Moresby alerted the Japanese to the vulnerability of their new base.

Japan's expectation was that the Allied counter-offensive would come from Australia through the Coral Sea. To counteract that and to protect Rabaul, it was resolved to build air bases around Buna and in the Solomon Islands. Capturing Port Moresby as further protection was only to be pursued if the opportunity presented itself. A small force of only 900 crossed the Owen Stanley Range. That wasn't many for an assault force, but it was a lot to cram onto a narrow goat track through dense, rain-soaked jungle across a succession of razorback ridges. It was certainly not enough to capture Moresby unaided, let alone push on to the Australian continent. From his own intelligence, General Horii knew his strength on the Kokoda Track couldn't possibly overcome a garrison the size of Port Moresby's, even if General Sugiyama thought the intelligence was an exaggeration (it wasn't!).[24]

The joint assault on Port Moresby was put on hold after the failure to capture the airfields at Milne Bay. As prospects in the Solomons deteriorated, the Moresby operation, only ever a secondary consideration, was abandoned by the Japanese altogether. Far from driving the Japanese back, it took two weeks to chase them down.

There had been neither the intention nor the wherewithal for *Nankai Shitai* to advance on Australia. The Japanese were sufficiently aware of the terrain past Darwin to know it would be an ill-chosen location to commence an invasion of the Australian continent. Had it been intended, it would have followed the February 1942 bombing of Darwin, as the people of Darwin expected at the time. That would have required only 'a hundred Japs armed with frying pans'.[25]

America had been caught by surprise at Pearl Harbor, not because the attack by Japan was unexpected, but because the Japanese naval forces were known to be advancing off southeast Asia and it was thought Japan didn't have the capacity to launch a war on two fronts. The Japanese made a similar miscalculation in the south Pacific. Expecting only one counter-offensive and aware of the press adulation in the United States of the insatiable self-publicist, Douglas MacArthur, they believed the 'Lion of Luzon' would be its architect.

It didn't occur to Japan's high command that there might be two counter-offensives. So, when their intelligence detected a major operation brewing, they assumed it was to add to Allied muscle in New Guinea and Australia. It took too long for them to realise the assault on Guadalcanal was a major offensive, not a distraction. Japan never regained the upper hand there.

Japanese strategists took some time to comprehend that the island-hopping of Admirals Nimitz and Halsey, in the Solomons and beyond, was not a sideshow. By the time they did, the American naval force was in the Micronesian islands. The major north Pacific base of Truk in the Caroline Islands was captured, then the Marianas, within bomber range of Japan itself. From there the enemy's cities could be subjected first to incendiary carpet bombing, and then to the atomic bomb.

The war had been lost long before that and the Japanese knew it, but in the closing stages they tried to broker through Russia the least onerous surrender conditions. When the Soviet Union came into the Pacific War the night before the Nagasaki bomb, Japan recognised it no longer had the luxury of time. The surrender process started the next day.[26]

There is no evidence that Japan's strategic planners ever seriously contemplated invading and occupying Australia, even if a handful of individuals thought it was a good idea. Taking an objective view, as the Japanese presumably did and the Allies could have—and some did—it was not a good idea. It would have been an expensive campaign, likely to draw out into the millstone of attrition, with very little return for the investment.

Australia didn't have the resources Japan desperately needed at the time. What it had could be obtained more cheaply through trade once hostilities ceased, and that is how the post-war relationship between the two nations developed. Japan hasn't been to war since.

There was no invasion by Japan, and none planned; but there was perhaps an invasion of sorts. Not by Japan and not military, but cultural and political. The United States of America, the anticipated saviour of Australia in the event of an invasion attempt, brought its troops home after the war but stayed in occupation. The global spread of American popular culture had started before the war and continued apace after it, boosted by the wartime American presence in Europe and the Pacific.

It continues to this day across most nations, not just Australia, but decreasingly dictated by America. It is constantly redefining itself with offshoots, inputs and new directions from around the world. Cultures evolve and American popular culture has internationalised.

In the political sphere, however, Australia's invasion is more singular. Since its successful participation in the Second World War, America has embarked on a number of military adventures—Korea, Vietnam, Iraq, Afghanistan—none turning out particularly well for it, and all judged poorly—or will be—by history with the possible exception of Afghanistan. Australia has been a willing participant in every one of America's incursions.

Invasion and occupation can take different forms. Japan may have had no intention of either for Australia, but has Australia been occupied anyway by the United States, geopolitically, and become a vassal state?

'Without inhibitions of any kind,' John Curtin said in 1941, 'Australia looks to America, free of any pangs as to our traditional links.' The Pacific War had come. It ran its course and went, with America as Australia's insurance policy against foreign invasion. In that regard, little has changed.

ACKNOWLEDGEMENTS

This book began life as the story of the 97 air attacks on the Australian mainland in the Pacific War, and has evolved into the story of a nation in fear of invasion. I'm grateful to Allen & Unwin for their faith in me to fashion the initial idea into a finished book, and particularly to Rebecca Kaiser and Richard Walsh for their support, guidance and critical assessment. We are now in our fifth book together. The team at Allen & Unwin is a great team to work with.

As always with books of this nature, there are people who give willing assistance along the way. In no particular order, Geoff Barnes, Caroline and Graham Gould, Helen Kershaw, Walter Burroughs, Helen Ellerker, Richard Walker, Paddy Conroy, Velta Whyte, Ian Fretwell, Peter and Sheila Forrest, Tom Lewis, Françoise Barr and the staff at the Northern Territory Archives Centre have all assisted in various ways as this book was brought into existence. Yang and David Clark, Rebecca Suter and the Japan Foundation were instrumental in identifying the text in the Chungking map, and Robert Brown (for the second time), Yve Close and Josie Clements all shared their wartime experience with me.

I'm grateful to the gang of three—Jan Stretton, Sue Murray and Tony Biddle—for going through drafts of the manuscript as proxy for the eventual reader, drawing attention to clumsy or ambiguous expression and making suggestions that might bring the story more to life. They've saved the reader from ploughing through some fairly wooden prose. These word police have all combined to produce a far more readable work than the one I wrote. It's now up to the reader to enjoy it.

NOTES

CHAPTER 1 Grazing gazelles

1 Lloyd & Hall, *Backroom Briefings*, p. 18.
2 Robson, *A History of Tasmania*, p. 35.
3 Spratt, 'The Tasmanian Royal Engineers Building'.
4 Boyce, 'Defending colonial Sydney'.
5 Clements, 'The sea forts of Victoria—Forts that never were!'
6 Parks Victoria—*Point Nepean Forts, Conservation Management Plan.*
7 Boyce.
8 Burke, *Fear of Security*, p. 28.
9 Burke, p. 29.
10 Burke, pp. 39–40.
11 Burke, p. 41.
12 Zakaria, 'Sembawang Naval Base'.
13 Burke, p. 58.
14 Horner, *Crisis of Command*, p. 1.
15 Horner, *Crisis of Command*, p. 2.
16 Piesse, *Japan and the Defence of Australia*, pp. 17–18.
17 *Argus*, 'News received calmly', 4 September 1939, p. 7.
18 *Age*, 'How Melbourne heard news', 4 September 1939, p. 10.
19 McKernan, *All In!*, p. 5.
20 *Argus*, 'Deserted German club', 4 September 1939, p. 7.
21 *Sydney Morning Herald*, 'Ports closed at night', 4 September 1939, p. 13.
22 *Sydney Morning Herald*, 'Amateurs off the air', 4 September 1939, p. 10.
23 *Sun*, 'In the war news', 4 September 1939, p. 9.
24 Penglase & Horner, *When the War Came to Australia*, p. 16.
25 Penglase & Horner, p. 16.
26 O'Hara-Close, oral history.
27 *Sun*, 'Guard fires shot at 2 a.m.', 4 September 1939, p. 3.

28 *Argus*, 'War stories blamed', 5 September 1939, p. 7.
29 *Sydney Morning Herald*, 'Stone thrown through window', 4 September 1939, p. 10.
30 *Sun*, 'Italian & Greek citizens', 4 September 1939, p. 8.
31 Martin & Hardy, *Dark and Hurrying Days*, p. 14.
32 McKernan, *All In!*, p. 23.
33 Horner, *Crisis of Command*, p. 11; Lodge, 'Bennett, Henry Gordon'.
34 *Argus*, 'Duty of women in crisis', 5 September 1939, p. 5.
35 McKernan, *All In!*, p. 17.
36 McKernan, *All In!*, p. 19.
37 Penglase & Horner, p. 16.
38 McKernan, *All In!*, p. 36.
39 McKernan, *All In!*, p. 25.
40 Brown, oral history.
41 O'Hara-Close, oral history.
42 Penglase & Horner, p. 61.
43 O'Hara-Close, oral history.
44 Chew, *Of Hearts and Minds*, pp. 41–2; Cavendish, 'Singapore Naval Base Opened'; Thompson, *The Battle for Singapore*, pp. 5–6.
45 Moreman, *The Jungle, The Japanese and the British Commonwealth*, pp. 20–2.
46 Horner, *Crisis of Command*, pp. 18–19; Robertson, *Australia Goes to War*, p. 68.
47 Horner, *Inside the War Cabinet*, p. 24.
48 Horner, *Crisis of Command*, p. 19.
49 Martin & Hardy, p. 64.
50 Martin & Hardy, p. 71.
51 Martin & Hardy, p. 84.
52 Day, *John Curtin*, pp. 399–400.
53 *Age*, 'Critical but not alarming', 18 February 1941, p. 8.
54 McKernan, *All In!*, p. 93.
55 Spender, *Politics and a Man*, p. 146.
56 McKernan, *All In!*, p. vi.
57 McKernan, *All In!*, p. 95.

CHAPTER 2 Unstoppable

1 Warren, *Singapore 1942*, p. 9.
2 Chant, 'Operation Matador'; Percival, 'Opening of hostilities'.
3 Chant.
4 Kennard, 'Jap fifth column in Malaya was small'.
5 Kossen et al., 'Seventy minutes before Pearl Harbor'; Hackett et al., 'IJN Seaplane Tender KAMIKAWA MARU'; Wilcock, 'Archive Report'; Burton, *Fortnight of Infamy*, p. 88; Wurth, *The Battle for Australia*, p. 45.
6 Chant; Percival; Hudson & Stokes, *Documents on Australian Foreign Policy, 1937–49*, nos. 139 & 162.
7 Hackett et al.; Percival.
8 Kossen et al.; Shores et al., *Bloody Shambles*, pp. 80–4; Warren, p. 56; Tsuji, *Japan's Greatest Victory*, p. 75.

9 Wilcock; Wigmore, *The Japanese Thrust*, pp. 137–8; Kossen et al.
10 Kossen et al.
11 Wilcock.
12 Percival.
13 Wigmore, p. 137.
14 Thompson, *The Battle for Singapore*, pp. 135–7; Wigmore, p. 138; Elphick, *Singapore*, pp. 223–4.
15 Rahil, 'Remembering the war's first battle'.
16 Horner, *Inside the War Cabinet*, p. 76.
17 Ross, *John Curtin*, p. 240.
18 Day, *John Curtin*, p. 430; Horner, *Inside the War Cabinet*, p. 77; *Sunday Telegraph*, 'Political Roundabout', 6 December 1942, p. 8.
19 Curtin, 'National Broadcast by Prime Minister'.
20 NAA A5954, 555/10; NAA A5954, 768/12.
21 *Sydney Morning Herald*, 'Japan's significant move southward', 6 December 1941, p. 13.
22 *Age*, 'News spreads quickly', 9 December 1941, p. 6.
23 Acland, oral history, tape 1 p. 4.
24 Brown, oral history, 2017.
25 *Daily Mirror*, 'Japs rounded up by police', 8 December 1941, p. 1; *Sydney Morning Herald*, 'Japanese detained in Sydney', 9 December 1941, p. 6; *Age*, 'Enemy aliens interned', 9 December 1941, p. 9.
26 NAA A5954, 807/1.
27 *Daily Mirror*, 'Japanese attack on Malaya and Hawaii', 8 December 1941, p. 1.
28 Percival; Wigmore, pp. 139–40.
29 *Sydney Morning Herald*, 'Japan brings war to the Pacific', 9 December 1941, p. 1.
30 *Sydney Morning Herald*, 'Failure of first attacks on Malaya', 9 December 1941, p. 7.
31 *Daily Mirror*, 'American air raid on Japan claimed', 10 December 1941, p. 1.
32 Penglase & Horner, *When the War Came to Australia*, p. 60.
33 Wigmore, pp. 142–3.
34 Wigmore, p. 143; Matthews, 'The Sinking of Prince of Wales and Repulse'.
35 Wigmore, p. 143; Matthews.
36 Wigmore; p. 144; Matthews.
37 Wigmore, p. 144.
38 Owen, *The Fall of Singapore*, p. 63.
39 *Daily Mirror*, 'Grim battle for Malaya as Japanese beaten back', 11 December 1941, p. 1.
40 *Sydney Morning Herald*, 'Very heavy Japanese losses at Kota Bharu', 12 December 1941, p. 1.
41 McMullin, *The Light on the Hill*, p. 215.
42 NAA A5954, 768/12.
43 Horner, *High Command*, p. 142.
44 NAA A5954, 555/10.
45 NAA A5954, 571/4.
46 Day, p. 442.

47 Trueman, 'The Attack on Malaya by Japan'.
48 Thompson, p. 45.
49 Thompson, p. 86; Lodge, 'Bennett, Henry Gordon'; Bell, 'Gordon Bennett'.
50 Thompson, pp. 88–91; Moremon, *A Bitter Fate*, p. 12; Smith, *Singapore Burning*, p. 52.
51 Moremon, pp. 14–16.
52 Moremon, p. 17.
53 Moremon, p. 21.
54 Moremon, pp. 22–4.
55 Horner, *Crisis of Command*, p. 38.
56 Thompson, p. 41.
57 Thompson, pp. 39–41; Elphick, p. 39.
58 NAA A5954, 571/4.
59 NAA A5954, 571/4.
60 Horner, *Crisis of Command*, p. 37.
61 Curtin, 'The Task Ahead'.
62 Day, p. 438.
63 Long, *The Six Years War*, p. 137; Lloyd & Hall, *Backroom Briefings*, p. 38.
64 Moremon, p. 57.
65 Moremon, pp. 60–5; Warren, pp. 155–6.
66 Moremon, p. 57.
67 Wigmore, pp. 222–36; Moremon, pp. 67–70.
68 Wigmore, pp. 236–40; Warren, pp. 172–4; Moremon, p. 71.
69 Wigmore, pp. 241–4; Moremon, pp. 72–4; Warren, p. 177.
70 *Daily Telegraph*, 'Ambulance tries to dash through Japs', 26 January 1942, p. 1; Smith, pp. 381–2; Wigmore, pp. 243–4.
71 Smith, pp. 390–3; Moremon, pp. 74–6; Wigmore, pp. 244–9; Warren, p. 177.
72 Brown, oral history, 2017.
73 McKernan, *All In!*, p. 108.
74 Thompson, pp. 250–1.
75 Moremon, p. 90; *Sydney Morning Herald*, 'No big attack in first 30 hours', 2 February 1942, p. 5.

CHAPTER 3 Gibraltar of the East

1 Farrell & Pratten, *Malaya 1942*, p. 18.
2 Thompson, *The Battle for Singapore*, p. 27.
3 Thompson, pp. 29–30.
4 Farrell & Pratten, p. 19.
5 Farrel & Pratten, p. 21.
6 Farrel & Pratten, pp. 23–4.
7 Thompson, p. 40.
8 Elphick, *Singapore*, p. 156.
9 Elphick, p. 157.
10 Thompson, pp. 42–3.
11 Thompson, p. 69.
12 Smith, *Singapore Burning*, p. 23.

13 Thompson, pp. 72–3.
14 Thompson, pp. 93–4.
15 Thompson, p. 97.
16 Elphick, pp. 59–60.
17 Thompson, p. 79.
18 Legg, *The Gordon Bennett Story*, p. 192.
19 Thompson, p. 267.
20 Warren, *Singapore 1942*, p. 212; Thompson, p. 256.
21 Moremon, *A Bitter Fate*, p. 94.
22 Warren, p. 214.
23 Felton, *The Coolie Generals*, p. 33.
24 Smith, p. 444.
25 Smith, p. 445.
26 Thompson, p. 262.
27 Warren, p. 223; Thompson, pp. 269–70.
28 Smith, p. 447.
29 Thompson, p. 271; Moremon, p. 95.
30 Warren, p. 210.
31 Warren, p. 218.
32 Elphick, p. 284.
33 Warren, p. 223.
34 Thompson, p. 285.
35 Thompson, p. 284.
36 Smith, p. 453; Thompson, p. 286.
37 Warren, p. 216.
38 Elphick, p. 286.
39 Thompson, p. 287.
40 Thompson, p. 7.
41 Freudenberg, *Churchill and Australia*, pp. 364–5; Robertson, *Australia Goes to War*, p. 83.
42 Edwards, *John Curtin's War vol. 1*, p. 394.
43 Robertson, p. 83; Day, *John Curtin*, p. 444.
44 Thompson, pp. 291–4; Smith, pp. 460–2.
45 Thompson, pp. 295–6; Warren, p. 230.
46 Warren, pp. 229–30.
47 Thompson, p. 297.
48 Elphick, pp. 324–5; Smith, p. 472; Warren, p. 233.
49 Elphick, p. 324; Smith, p. 449.
50 Thompson, p. 308.
51 Thompson, p. 307.
52 Elphick, p. 293; Warren, pp. 234, 237.
53 Thompson, p. 310.
54 Thompson, p. 312.
55 Elphick, p. 299; Warren, p. 242.
56 Leasor, *Singapore*, p. 246.
57 Warren, p. 243.

58 Elphick, p. 300.
59 Warren, p. 249.
60 AWM52, 18/2/21.
61 Smith, pp. 520–1.
62 Elphick, pp. 306–10; Smith, p. 523.
63 Warren, p. 251; Elphick, p. 310; Smith, p. 523.
64 Thompson, pp. 315–16.
65 Thompson, p. 316; Legg, p. 252.
66 Smith, pp. 493–4.
67 Shores et al., *Bloody Shambles*, p. 383.
68 Thompson, p. 318.
69 Warren, p. 260; Elphick, p. 354; Moremon, p. 113; Wigmore, *The Japanese Thrust*, p. 369.
70 Elphick, p. 354.
71 Thompson, p. 326; Warren, p. 255.
72 Thompson, p. 326.
73 Thompson, pp. 329–30.
74 Thompson, p. 330; Smith, p. 509.
75 Thompson, pp. 333–4.
76 Thompson, p. 339.
77 Thompson, pp. 339–40; Maynard, *Hero or Deserter?*, pp. 190–1.
78 Thompson, p. 340; Wigmore, p. 377; Maynard, p. 192.
79 Thompson, p. 341; Smith, p. 546.
80 Thompson, p. 342.
81 Thompson, pp. 343–4.
82 Thompson, p. 345.
83 *Sydney Morning Herald*, 'Amazing escape in fighters', 18 February 1942, p. 10.
84 Thompson, p. 48.
85 Thompson, p. 349.
86 Thompson, p. 326; Legg, p. 253.
87 Thompson, p. 347.
88 Maynard, pp. 196–7.
89 Maynard, p. 198; Legg, p. 254.
90 Maynard, p. 199.
91 Thompson, p. 348; Legg, p. 255.
92 Thompson, p. 13.
93 Maynard, pp. 202–3; Elphick, pp. 369–70; Thompson, pp. 348–9; *Sydney Morning Herald*, 'Singapore escape', 27 February 1942, p. 5.
94 Elphick, p. 370.
95 Cargo riverboat.
96 Thompson, pp. 348–9; Elphick, p. 370; Maynard, pp. 204–5: *Daily Telegraph*, 'Bennett escapes in sampan', 27 February 1942, p. 1.
97 Elphick, pp. 369–70; *Courier-Mail*, 'Major-General Bennett reveals', 28 February 1942, p. 1.
98 Thompson, p. 351; Lodge, 'Bennett, Henry Gordon'.
99 Lodge.

100 Lodge, *The Fall of General Gordon Bennett*, pp. 165–7; Lodge, 'Bennett, Henry Gordon'.
101 Legg, p. 276.
102 Elphick, p. 177.
103 Robertson, p. 90.
104 Morgan, 'A Burning Legacy', p. 13.
105 Thompson, p. 353; Smith, p. 529.
106 *Sydney Morning Herald*, 'The fallen bastion',17 February 1942, p. 4.
107 *Sydney Morning Herald*, 'The fallen bastion', 17 February 1942, p. 4.
108 *Sydney Morning Herald*, 'The fallen bastion', 17 February 1942, p. 4.
109 *Sydney Morning Herald*, 'Failure at Singapore', 26 February 1942, p. 4.
110 *Sydney Morning Herald*, 'Singapore defeat analysed', 19 February 1942, p. 5.
111 Clements, oral history.
112 Acland, oral history, tape 1, p. 4.

CHAPTER 4 Frontier town

1 Alcorta, *Australia's Frontline*, p. 16.
2 Powell, *The Shadow's Edge*, pp. 38–42.
3 Alcorta, p. 18.
4 Acland, oral history, tape 1, p. 4.
5 Lockwood, *Australia Under Attack*, p. 17; Connaughton, *Shrouded Secrets*, p. 39.
6 Lockwood, pp. 38–9; Connaughton, p. 41.
7 Hall, *Darwin 1942*, p. 174.
8 Hall, pp. 174–6; Powell, p. 49.
9 Lockwood, pp. 60–2; Hall, p. 176.
10 Powell, pp. 46–8.
11 Powell, p. 51; Connaughton, p. 42.
12 Lockwood, pp. 12–13.
13 Lockwood, pp. 11, 13–14; Forrest & Forrest, *Battling*, p. 64; Connaughton, pp. 42–3.
14 Forrest & Forrest, *Federation Frontline*, pp. 74–5; Forrest & Forrest, *Battling*, pp. 66–7; Wells & Mulholland, 'The Japanese bombing of Darwin'.
15 Lockwood, p. 15.
16 Lockwood, p. 16.
17 Connaughton, p. 43; Powell, p. 52; NAA A816, 37/301/293, p. 383.
18 Weston, oral history.
19 Lockwood, p. 17; Connaughton, p. 44.
20 Penglase & Horner, *When the War Came to Australia*, p. 77.
21 Connaughton, p. 49.
22 Bleakley, *The Eavesdroppers*, p. 27; Collie, *Code Breakers*, p. 54.
23 Lewis & Ingman, *Carrier Attack*, pp. 62–8; Lewis, *The Empire Strikes South*, pp. 133–6; Lockwood, p. 28.
24 Lockwood, pp. 22–3; Powell, p. 42; Connaughton, p. 48.
25 NAA A431, 1949/687, pp. 14, 27.
26 NAA A816, 37/301/293, p. 181.
27 Lockwood, p. 27; Brown & Studdy-Clift, *Darwin Dilemmas*, p. 88.

28 Alcorta, p. 21.
29 Grose, *An Awkward Truth*, pp. 6–8, 81; Lewis, p. 15.
30 Forrest & Forrest, *Federation Frontline*, p. 44.
31 Lewis, p. 15; Lockwood, p. 24.
32 Grose, p. 85; Forrest & Forrest, *Federation Frontline*, p. 45.
33 Lockwood, p. 21; Forrest & Forrest, *Battling*, p. 9; Grose, p. 86; Powell, p. 75; Wilkinson, 'Australia's Pearl Harbor'.
34 Connaughton, p. 48; Grose, p. 84.
35 NAA A816, 37/301/293, pp. 337–8; Lockwood, pp. 21–2; Grose, p. 86.
36 Collie, *Code Breakers*, pp. 61–2; Bleakley, p. 27.
37 NTRS 226, TS677, Acland; Hall, p. 27.
38 Connaughton, p. 56; Lockwood, p. 24, Hall, p. 61.
39 Lockwood, p. 24.
40 Forrest & Forrest, *Battling*, p. 43; Powell, p. 78.
41 Chan, *War on Our Doorstep*, p. 128.
42 Forrest & Forrest, *Battling*, p. 54; Lockwood, p. 65.
43 Lockwood, pp. 29–32; Powell, pp. 814.
44 Alcorta, pp. 24–5.
45 Lockwood, pp. 99–100.
46 Lockwood, p. 91.
47 Brown & Studdy-Clift, p. 104.
48 Acland, oral history, tape 1, p. 7.
49 Acland, oral history, tape 1, p. 8; NTRS 226, TS677, Acland.
50 Vose, oral history; Grose, pp. 50, 134; Hall, p. 90; Forrest & Forrest, *Federation Frontline*, p. 29.
51 Lockwood, p. 45.
52 Reid, *Australia Under Attack*, p. 2; Lockwood, pp. 44–5; Brown & Studdy-Clift, p. 90; Alcorta, p. 23.
53 Lockwood, pp. 47–9.
54 Lockwood, pp. 52–4.
55 NAA A816, 37/301/293, pp. 207–9; Grose, pp. 110–11; Connaughton, p. 65.
56 Alcorta, p. 21.
57 Lockwood, pp. 57, 71; Forrest & Forrest, *Battling*, p. 44; NAA A816, 37/301/293, p. 146.
58 Lockwood, pp. 49–50; Powell, p. 80; Hall, p. 48; Penglase & Horner, p. 85.
59 NAA A816, 37/301/293, p. 209; Grose, p. 121; Lockwood, p. 128; Connaughton, p. 67.
60 Forrest & Forrest, *Battling*, p. 1.
61 Luke, diary; Lockwood, p. 150.
62 Acland, oral history, tape 1, p. 8; NTRS 226, TS677, Acland.
63 Grose, p. 132; Lockwood, p. 129.
64 The Dutch East Indies is now Indonesia; Celebes is now Sulawesi.
65 Grose, pp. 132–3.
66 Grose, pp. 132–4; Lockwood, pp. 129–30; Collie, p. 62.
67 Vanovac & La Canna, *ABC News*, 20 February 2017.
68 Forrest & Forrest, *Battling*, p. 46; Lockwood, pp. 57, 119.

69 NAA A816, 37/301/293, pp. 27, 300, 327, M249; Day, 'Darwin's finger of shame points at military'.
70 NAA A816, 37/301/293, pp. 209–10; Grose, p. 121.
71 Acland, oral history, tape 1, p. 10; NTRS 226, TS677, Acland; NTRS 226, TS677, Shepherd; Hall, p. 29.
72 Alcorta, p. 33; Powell, p. 85.
73 Alcorta, p. 26.
74 Lockwood, p. 132; NAA A431, 1949/687, p. 22.
75 NAA A816, 37/301/293, pp. 220–6; Hall, pp. 96–100; Lockwood, pp. 133–5; Grose, p. 165.
76 Connaughton, p. 99.
77 NAA A431, 1949/687, p. 11; NAA A816, 37/301/293, pp. M28, M160.
78 Weston, oral history.
79 Lockwood, pp. 1, 149; Grose, pp. 143–5; Alcorta, pp. 2, 31; Brown & Studdy-Clift, p. 98; Powell, p. 89; Hall, p. 132.
80 Forrest & Forrest, *Battling*, p. 90; Lockwood, p. 110; NAA A816, 37/301/293, p. M251.
81 Lockwood, pp. 103–4; NAA A816, 37/301/293, p. 274.
82 Lockwood, p. 105; Hall, p. 119.
83 NAA A816, 37/301/293, p. 273.
84 NAA A816, 37/301/293, p. 353; Hall, p. 118.
85 Lockwood, p. 163.
86 NAA A816, 37/301/293, p. 392.
87 Connell, *The War at Home*, p. 47; NAA A816, 37/301/293, p. 393.
88 Lockwood, pp. 158–9; Hall, pp. 161, 216; Forrest & Forrest, *Battling*, p. 51; Powell, p. 86; Brown & Studdy-Clift, p. 100.
89 Forrest & Forrest, *Battling*, p. 72; Lockwood, p. 101; NAA A816, 37/301/293, pp. M210–2.
90 NAA A816, 37/301/293, pp. 268, M19–20, M25.
91 Hall, pp. 139–40; Grose, p. 142; Powell, p. 88; NAA A816, 37/301/293, pp. 391, M206–9, M236.
92 Lockwood, pp. 154–7.
93 Lockwood, pp. 120–2, 132; Forrest & Forrest, *Battling*, p. 46.
94 Lockwood, pp. 54–5, 126.
95 Hall, p. 132; Lockwood, p. 152; NAA A816, 37/301/293, p. M250; Burton, diary; Frost, diary.
96 Lockwood, p. 149.
97 NTRS 226, TS677, Acland; NTRS 226, TS677, Shepherd; Acland, oral history, tape 2, p. 2.
98 Acland, oral history, tape 2, p. 2.
99 NAA A816, 37/301/293, p. M123; Hall, p. 142.
100 Forrest & Forrest, *Battling*, p. 51.
101 Forrest & Forrest, *Battling*, p. 71.
102 Lockwood, pp. 151–2; NAA A816, 37/301/293, p. 11.
103 Lockwood, p. 163.

104 Horner, *Inside the War Cabinet*, p. 103; McKernan, *The Strength of a Nation*, p. 225.
105 Grose, p. 177; *Sydney Morning Herald*, 'Two big air raids on Darwin', 20 February 1942, p. 4.
106 Grose, pp. 177–9.
107 Grose, p. 180.
108 *Courier-Mail*, 'Darwin bombed heavily in two day raids', 20 February 1942, p. 1.
109 *Courier-Mail*, 'Dramatic stages of Darwin raids', 21 February 1942, p. 1.
110 Lockwood, oral history; Grose, p. 179.
111 *Sydney Morning Herald*, 'No particulars of Darwin damage', 24 February 1942, p. 5.
112 *Sydney Morning Herald*, 'The war comes to Australia', 20 February 1942, p. 4.
113 *Age*, 'Two air raids on Darwin', 20 February 1942, p. 1.
114 Stephens, 'The bombing of Darwin, 75 years on'.
115 *Advertiser*, 'It has happened here', 20 February 1942, p. 6.
116 *Courier-Mail*, 'Harrying of sea traffic is Jap aim at Darwin', 21 February 1942, p. 4.
117 Grose, p. 182; NAA A816, 37/301/293, p. M255; Hall, p. 161.
118 Grose, p. 196.
119 Penglase & Horner, p. 90.
120 O'Hara-Close, oral history.
121 Brown, oral history, 2017.
122 Alcorta, pp. 33, 49; Lockwood, p. 36.
123 Alcorta, p. 47; Lewis, p. 58.
124 Forrest & Forrest, *Federation Frontline*, p. 62.
125 Connaughton, pp. 87–93; Powell, p. 95; Wells & Mulholland, 'The Japanese bombing of Darwin, Broome and northern Australia'.
126 Powell, pp. 95–6; Saunders & Finch, 'Northern Australians' Fear of Invasion', p. 108; Connaughton, p. 95.
127 Grose, p. 182.
128 Grose, p. 185; Australian War Memorial, *Soldiering On*, pp. 155–81.
129 Lockwood, p. 5.
130 Hall, p. 7.
131 NAA A431, 1949/687; Grose, pp. 197–8; Lockwood, pp. 179–80.
132 *Herald*, '240 killed on first raid on Darwin', 30 March 1942, p. 3.
133 Frame, 'The Bombing of Darwin'.
134 Powell, p. 56.

CHAPTER 5 Great and powerful friends

1 Edwards, *Curtin's Gift*, pp. 1–2, 5–7; Green, *Servant of the House*, p. 128; Ross, *John Curtin*, p. 261.
2 Day, *John Curtin*, pp. 3–4, 24–6.
3 Freudenberg, *Churchill and Australia*, pp. 293–6.
4 Freudenberg, pp. 298–9.
5 Edwards, pp. 29–30.

6 NAA A5954, 571/4.
7 Plowman, *Across the Sea to War*, p. 326; Edwards, *John Curtin's War vol. 1*, pp. 372–4; Edwards, *Curtin's Gift*, pp. 38–9; Gill, *Royal Australian Navy*, p. 562.
8 Ross, p. 254.
9 Plowman, pp. 327–8.
10 Horner, *High Command*, p. 152.
11 Edwards, *Curtin's Gift*, p. 36.
12 Plowman, pp. 328–9.
13 Edwards, *Curtin's Gift*, pp. 7–8, 40; Plowman, p. 348.
14 Freudenberg, p. 375; NAA A5954, 807/2.
15 Horner, *Inside the War Cabinet*, p. 98; Edwards, *Curtin's Gift*, p. 40.
16 Plowman, pp. 331–2.
17 Horner, *Inside the War Cabinet*, p. 107; Robertson, *Australia Goes to War*, p. 94; NAA A5954, 571/4; NAA A5954, 813/2.
18 Horner, *Inside the War Cabinet*, p. 99; Long, *The Six Years War*, p. 161; Plowman, p. 343.
19 Horner, *Inside the War Cabinet*, pp. 99–100; Day, p. 446.
20 Gill, p. 600.
21 Horner, *Inside the War Cabinet*, pp. 102, 105; Edwards, *Curtin's Gift*, p. 43; Freudenberg, p. 377.
22 Edwards, *John Curtin's War vol. 1*, p. 418; Freudenberg, p. 377; Ross, p. 260.
23 Freudenberg, p. 380.
24 Edwards, *John Curtin's War vol. 1*, p. 419.
25 Edwards, *John Curtin's War vol. 1*, pp. 418–20; Edwards, *Curtin's Gift*, pp. 44–5; Day p. 452.
26 Freudenberg, p. 379.
27 Horner, *Inside the War Cabinet*, p. 104.
28 Edwards, *Curtin's Gift*, p. 47.
29 Horner, *Inside the War Cabinet*, p. 105.
30 Freudenberg, pp. 380–2; Ross, p. 259; Edwards, *John Curtin's War vol. 1*, p. 422.
31 Plowman, p. 346.
32 Horner, *Inside the War Cabinet*, p. 106; Edwards, *Curtin's Gift*, p. 49.
33 Edwards, *John Curtin's War vol. 1*, p. 422.
34 Ross, p. 261.
35 Edwards, *John Curtin's War vol. 1*, p. 422.
36 Ross, p. 262.
37 Horner, *Inside the War Cabinet*, p. 107.
38 Edwards, *John Curtin's War vol. 1*, p. 424.
39 McKinlay, *Australia 1942*, p. 128.
40 McKinlay, p. 107; Palazzo, 'The Overlooked Mission', pp. 59–60.
41 Edwards, *Curtin's Gift*, p. 381.
42 McKinlay, p. 107; Penglase & Horner, *When the War Came to Australia*, p. 101.
43 Day, p. 462; Ross, p. 244.
44 Horner, *Crisis of Command*, p. 37.
45 McKernan, *All In!*, p. 229.
46 Schaller, *Douglas MacArthur*, p. 65.

47 Horner, *Inside the War Cabinet*, p. 110 (quoting *True* magazine, 1947).
48 Horner, *Crisis of Command*, p. 63.
49 Manchester, *American Caesar*, p. 145.
50 Schaller, p. vii.
51 Horner, 'MacArthur, Douglas'.
52 James, *The Years of MacArthur*, pp. 494–5, 513.
53 Schaller, pp. 55–6.
54 Long, *MacArthur as Military Commander*, p. 63; Schaller, p. 56.
55 Long, pp. 67–70; Schaller, p. 56.
56 Falk, 'Douglas MacArthur and the War Against Japan', pp. 4–5.
57 Schaller, p. 58.
58 Schaller, pp. 56–8, 61; Falk, pp. 1–2.
59 Schaller, p. 61.
60 Schaller, p. 61.
61 Falk, p. 7; Bowen, 'The Battle for Australia'.
62 Dunn, 'General Douglas MacArthur in Australia During WWII'.
63 Dunn, 'General Douglas MacArthur in Australia During WWII'.
64 Bowen.
65 Dunn, 'General Douglas MacArthur in Australia During WWII'.
66 Dunn, 'General Douglas MacArthur in Australia During WWII'.
67 McCarthy, *South West Pacific Area*, p. 17.
68 McCarthy, p. 18.
69 McKernan, p. 230.
70 Dunn, 'General Douglas MacArthur in Australia During WWII'.
71 Dunn, 'General Douglas MacArthur in Australia During WWII'.
72 McKernan, p. 231; Dunn, 'General Douglas MacArthur in Australia During WWII'.
73 Manchester, p. 271; Schaller, p. 62.
74 Long, p. 85; Dunn, 'General Douglas MacArthur in Australia During WWII'.
75 *Argus*, 'Great welcome to Gen. MacArthur', 23 March 1942, p. 3; Dunn; Black, 'The General and the Prime Minister'; Darian-Smith, 'The Home Front and the American Presence in 1942', p. 76.
76 Darian-Smith, p. 76; McKernan, p. 232, Dunn, 'General Douglas MacArthur in Australia During WWII'.
77 *Sydney Morning Herald*, 'The ANZAC leader', 19 March 1942, p. 4.
78 Horner, *Inside the War Cabinet*, p. 111.
79 Day, p. 464.
80 Robertson, p. 111.
81 Long, p. 86.
82 Edwards, *Curtin's Gift*, p. 58; Long, p. 87.
83 Chester, *John Curtin*, p. 136.
84 McKernan, p. 133.
85 Bell, *Unequal Allies*, pp. 100–1.
86 Long, pp. 91–2; Horner, *Inside the War Cabinet*, p. 113.
87 Thorpe, *East Wind, Rain*, p. 91.
88 Horner, *Inside the War Cabinet*, p. 114.

89 Horner, *Inside the War Cabinet*, pp. 109, 115–6.
90 Lloyd & Hall, *Backroom Briefings*, p. 32.
91 Penglase & Horner, p. 105.
92 O'Hara-Close, oral history.

CHAPTER 6 Home fires burning

1 *Sydney Morning Herald*, 'Letters', 21 January 1942, p. 6 ; McKernan, *All In!*, p. 118.
2 Connors et al., *Australia's Frontline*, p. 33.
3 Hall, 'Were public bomb shelters ever constructed . . .'.
4 *Sydney Morning Herald*, 'Shortage of materials for shelters', 16 December 1941, p. 9.
5 *Sydney Morning Herald*, 'State's war plans', 9 December 1941, p. 6.
6 Hall.
7 Connell, *The War at Home*, p. 35.
8 Darian-Smith, *On the Home Front*, p. 20.
9 *The Australian Women's Weekly*, 'What to do in an air raid', 27 December 1941, p. 25; McKinlay, *Australia 1942*, p. 49.
10 Pennay, *On the Home Front*, p. 15.
11 *Sydney Morning Herald*, 'The war comes to Australia', 20 February 1942, p. 4.
12 *Sydney Morning Herald*, 'Air-raid alarm in Darwin', 13 December 1941, p. 13.
13 *Sydney Morning Herald*, 'First daylight N.E.S. trial', 20 February 1942, p. 6.
14 Pennay, p. 15.
15 *Age*, 'Daylight air-raid test', 11 March 1942, p. 2 & 1 April 1942, p. 3.
16 Connell, p. 35.
17 D.H. Foard, *Argus*, 'Our trench', 30 May 1942, 'Weekend Magazine', p. 8.
18 *Courier-Mail*, '10 injured on roads in brown-out', 6 June 1942, p. 3.
19 *Sydney Morning Herald*, 'Trams to go slow in brown-out', 26 February 1942, p. 5.
20 *Argus*, 'City in partial blackout', 13 December 1941, p. 1.
21 Connell, p. 34.
22 Connell, p. 33.
23 Elias, 'The organisation of camouflage in Australia . . .'.
24 Elias, 'The organisation of camouflage in Australia . . .'.
25 Donaldson & Donaldson, *William Dobell*, p. 28: Close, *Joshua Smith Artist*, p. 27; Moore, *Over-Sexed, Over-Paid & Over Here*, p. 30.
26 Donaldson & Donaldson, p. 28.
27 AWM PR88/133; Elias.
28 Connell, p. 35.
29 Collie, *Code Breakers*, p. 186.
30 Penglase & Horner, *When the War Came to Australia*, p. 96.
31 Connell, p. 34; Penglase & Horner, p. 66.
32 Dept of Home Security, 'Advising the Public'; McKernan, p. 120; *Sydney Morning Herald*, 'If invaders come', 2 March 1942, p. 4.
33 Connell, p. 28.
34 Connell, p. 29.
35 McKinlay, p. 90.

36 Stanley, *Invading Australia*, pp. 116, 127.
37 O'Hara-Close, oral history.
38 Penglase & Horner, p. 92.
39 Connors et al., p. 63.
40 Connors et al., p. 64.
41 Connell, pp. 35–6; O'Hara-Close, oral history.
42 Connell, p. 81.
43 Chan, *War on Our Doorstep*, p. 2; McKernan, p. 129.
44 Dinan, *Between the Dances*, p. 47.
45 McKernan, pp. 127–8; Darian-Smith, p. 23.
46 McKinlay, p. 53.
47 Connors, p. 60.
48 Connors, p. 61.
49 McKernan, p. 129.
50 Somerville, *They Crossed a Continent*, pp. 5–83; McKinlay, p. 82.
51 Forrest & Forrest, *Battling*, pp. 109–10.
52 Darian-Smith, 'War and Australian society', p. 60.
53 McKernan, p. 104.
54 Hasluck, *Diplomatic Witness*, p. 44.
55 Eagles, *HMAS Sydney and Operation Fish*, pp. 29–33, 93–4.
56 Eagles, p. 94.
57 Connors, p. 64.
58 *Daily Telegraph*, 'Learn how to fight in the streets', 26 January 1942, p. 4; 27 January 1942, 'Govt. plans People's Army, orders report', p. 2; McKernan, p. 122.
59 *Daily Telegraph*, 'V.C.'s experience, guerrillas needed', 29 January 1942, p. 5.
60 *Daily Telegraph*, 'V.C.'s experience, guerrillas needed', 29 January 1942, p. 5.
61 Norman Bartlett, *Sunday Telegraph*, 'Let's have a real people's army!', 1 February 1942, p. 18.
62 Tom Wintringham, *Daily Telegraph*, 'How to train citizens for a People's Army', 2 February 1942, p. 4.
63 *Daily Telegraph*, 'Move to launch People's Army', 2 February 1942, p. 2.
64 McKernan, p. 123; *Sydney Morning Herald*, 'People's Army plan', 2 February 1942, p. 6; *Daily Telegraph*, 'Govt. plans People's Army, orders report', 27 January 1942, p. 2.
65 Connell, p. 38; *Daily Telegraph*, 'Public votes strongly for a People's Army', 5 February 1942, p. 4.
66 McKernan, p. 48; Harris, 'Volunteer Defence Corps (WW2)'.
67 Connell, p. 38.
68 Connell, p. 39.
69 Harris.
70 Connell, p. 39.
71 McKernan, p. 120; Croft, 'Idriess, Ion Llewellyn 1889–1879'.
72 Connors et al., p. 36.
73 Brown, oral history.
74 Jones, 'Davies, Natalia (Nat)'; Davies, 'The Defence Society'.
75 Connors et al., p. 40; Dinan, p. 36.

76 McKinlay, p. 111.
77 Connell, p. 27; *The Bulletin*, 'Are they "perturbed"?', 18 March 1942, p. 6.
78 *Courier-Mail*, 'Are we learning Darwin lesson?', 23 February 1942, p. 4.
79 Moore, p. 229.
80 *Sydney Morning Herald*, 'Music and drama', 17 January 1942, p. 10; McKinlay, p. 51.
81 Connell, p. 77.
82 Connell, p. 77.
83 NAA A5954, 358/1.
84 McKinlay, pp. 515–18; Pomeroy, 'Morale on the homefront in Australia', pp. 138, 143; Stanley, p. 117.
85 McBride & Taylor, *Brisbane Remembers*, p. 26.
86 Stanley, p. 118; NAA SP109/6, 6.
87 Stanley, p. 115.
88 Stephen Kelen, *Sydney Morning Herald*, 'Japan's cult of death', 3 January 1942, p. 9.
89 Stanley, p. 116.
90 Dark, 'Australians don't want pep talks'.
91 Pomeroy, pp. 132–6.
92 Pomeroy, p. 137.
93 NAA A1608, W57/1/1.
94 Pomeroy, pp. 178–9; Pybus, *The Devil and James McAuley*, p. 29.
95 Charlton, 'Shadowy organisation had undue influence'.
96 Pomeroy, p. 202; Pybus, p. 29.
97 Pomeroy pp. 204–6.
98 Pomeroy, p. 208; NAA A5954, 328/21.
99 Pybus, 'Conlon's Remarkable Circus', pp. 55–6; Ryan, 'Conlon, Alfred Austin'; Pomeroy, p. 194.
100 Pomeroy, pp. 216–19.
101 Pomeroy, p. 223.
102 NAA A5954, 328/21.
103 Charlton; Pybus, 'Conlon's Remarkable Circus', p. 60.
104 Pomeroy, p. 227.
105 Forrest & Forrest, p. 98.
106 Tanner, *The Long Road North*, pp. 1–17; Michael Terry, 'Engineers Show the World', *Sydney Morning Herald*, 15 February 1941, p. 9; Powell, p. 27; Forrest & Forrest, pp. 98–9.
107 Timber poles laid side by side across a boggy road to enable vehicles to drive along that section.
108 Tanner, pp. 23–9, 162; Forrest & Forrest, p. 99.
109 Tanner, p. 153.
110 Tanner, p. 153.
111 Tanner, p. 117; Powell, p. 101.
112 Tanner, pp. 117–30; Moore, p. 125.
113 Tanner, pp. 147–51.
114 Wikipedia, 'Underground Hospital, Mount Isa'.

115 McKernan, p. 186.
116 Penglase & Horner, p. 109.
117 McKernan, pp. 191–2, 195–6.
118 Penglase & Horner, p. 169.
119 Penglase & Horner, p. 172.
120 More, p. 96.
121 McBride & Taylor, p. 1.
122 McIntyre, *Townsville at War*, p. 54.
123 McIntyre, p. 28.
124 McIntyre, p. 61.
125 McIntyre, p. 68; Copeman, pp. 7–10; Collie, pp. 187–8.
126 McIntyre, p. 69; Collie, p. 188.
127 McIntyre, p. 68; Collie, pp. 188–9.
128 Moore, pp. 190–3.
129 Moore, p. 191.
130 NAA A816, 37/301/199; Pomeroy, pp. 219–21.

CHAPTER 7 Expendable

1 Tsuji, *Japan's Greatest Victory*, p. 75.
2 Tsuji, p. 105.
3 Tourism Malaysia, 'The Fight for Malaya'.
4 De Vries, 'The battle for oil in the Dutch East Indies'.
5 Wheeler, 'Between Hitler & Stalin'.
6 *Sydney Morning Herald*, '"Co-prosperity" on the march', 2 January 1942, p. 4.
7 *Courier-Mail*, 'North must be ready for scorched earth', 21 February 1942, p. 6.
8 *Sydney Morning Herald*, 'Civilians' tasks in an invasion', 26 February 1942, p. 5.
9 *Sydney Morning Herald*, 'Scorched earth', 25 February 1942, p. 6.
10 *Sydney Morning Herald*, 'Scorched earth', 10 March 1942, p. 5.
11 Rosen, *Scorched Earth*, p. 1; Holzworth, *A Tribute to Edward Harold Fulcher Swain,* pp. 104-5.
12 Rosen, pp. 1–85.
13 Rosen, pp. 25–7.
14 Rosen, p. 37.
15 Rosen, p. 53.
16 Day, 'Australia prepared a secret plan to repel a Japanese invasion', *The Australian*, 18 May 2017.
17 Rosen, p. 39.
18 Rosen, pp. 87–119.
19 Rosen, p. xix.
20 Rosen, pp. 273–9.
21 NAA A5954, 357/1.
22 NAA A5954, 808/1.
23 NAA J2808, 400/2/8.
24 NAA BP262/2, 9352.
25 NAA SP1048/7, S10/1/700.
26 McKernan, *All In!*, p. 129; Abbott, 'Scorched earth flames are fanned again?'.

27 A.P. Elkin, *Sydney Morning Herald*, 'Australia at war', 14 March, 1942, p. 8.
28 NAA BP262/2, 9352.
29 NAA A5954, 357/1.
30 NAA A5954, 357/1.
31 Penglase & Horner, *When the War Came to Australia*, pp. 94–5.
32 In Chapter 6.
33 Forrest & Forrest, *Battling*, p. 92; McKinlay, *Australia 1942*, p. 89; *Courier-Mail*, 'Australia's biggest stock drive goes on', 16 July 1942, p. 3.
34 *Sydney Morning Herald*, 'Huge cattle trek', 16 July 1942, p. 6.
35 NAA BP262/2, 9352.
36 Burns, *The Brisbane Line Controversy*, p. 120.
37 Burns, 'The Brisbane Line' (thesis), p. 144.
38 Burns, thesis, p. 145.
39 Burns, *The Brisbane Line Controversy*, p. 121.
40 Burns, thesis, pp. 146–7.
41 Burns, *The Brisbane Line Controversy*, pp. 123–4.
42 Burns, *The Brisbane Line Controversy*, p. 124; Burns, thesis, p. 149.
43 Burns, thesis, p. 9.
44 Burns, *The Brisbane Line Controversy*, p. 14.
45 Burns, *The Brisbane Line Controversy*, pp. 66–7, 71-2; NAA A5954, 568/4; Johnston, *Australia's Home Defence*, pp. 5–6.
46 Burns, *The Brisbane Line Controversy*, p. 72.
47 Burns, *The Brisbane Line Controversy*, pp. 72–4.
48 Burns, *The Brisbane Line Controversy*, p. 75.
49 Burns, *The Brisbane Line Controversy*, p. 75; Dedman, 'The "Brisbane" Line', p. 147.
50 NAA A5954, 568/4.
51 Burns, *The Brisbane Line Controversy*, pp. 78–80, 83; Dedman, pp. 148–9; NAA A5954, 568/4,
52 Burns, *The Brisbane Line Controversy*, pp. 98–9.
53 Burns, thesis, pp. v, 153.
54 Burns, *The Brisbane Line Controversy*, p. 128; Burns, thesis, pp. ii, 153.
55 Johnston, 'Eventful Year in S.W. Pacific'; Dedman, p. 143.
56 NAA A5954, 1300/1; Dunn, 'The Brisbane Line'; Horner, 'Australia Under Threat of Invasion', p. 263; Dedman, p. 151.
57 Dedman, p. 148.
58 Long, *MacArthur as Military Commander*, pp. 94–5.
59 Burns, thesis, pp. v, 153.
60 Burns, *The Brisbane Line Controversy*, pp. 117–18, Burns, thesis, p. 140.
61 Burns, thesis, p. 182.
62 Burns, thesis, p. 141.
63 Burns, thesis, pp. 166–7.
64 Burns, *The Brisbane Line Controversy*, pp. 138–40.
65 Burns, *The Brisbane Line Controversy*, p. 137.
66 Burns, *The Brisbane Line Controversy*, p. 140.

67 *Daily Telegraph*, 'Hard facts dictated the Brisbane Line', 28 May 1943, p. 6; Burns, *The Brisbane Line Controversy*, p. 142.
68 Dedman, p. 147; *Canberra Times*, 'No military scapegoat of Brisbane Line', 27 May 1943, p. 2; Burns, *The Brisbane Line Controversy*, pp. 142–3.
69 Burns, *The Brisbane Line Controversy*, p. 144.
70 Burns, thesis, p. 175.
71 Burns, *The Brisbane Line Controversy*, p. 149; Burns, thesis, p. 178.
72 Burns, thesis, p. 180.
73 Burns, thesis, pp. 188–9; Burns, *The Brisbane Line Controversy*, p. 158; Hasluck, 'The "Brisbane" Line', p. 714.
74 Hasluck, p. 714; Burns, thesis, p. 208.
75 Hasluck, p. 715.

CHAPTER 8 Watchers of the north

1 Feldt, *The Coast Watchers*, pp. 16–17; Brown, 'Coast Watchers in the Solomons'.
2 Gill, 'Feldt, Eric Augustas'.
3 Feldt, pp. 18–19.
4 Lord, *Lonely Vigil*, p. 7.
5 Feldt, pp. 21–7; Dept of Veterans Affairs, 'The Coastwatchers'.
6 Wikipedia, 'Eric Feldt'.
7 Wilcox, 'Archive Report: Allied Forces'.
8 Walker & Walker, *Curtin's Cowboys*, p. 3; NAA MP729/6, 29/401/618.
9 NAA MP729/6, 29/401/626.
10 NAA MP508/1, 82/712/1773.
11 Harris, 'Simply a Question of Duty'.
12 Harris, 'Simply a Question of Duty'.
13 Feldt, pp. 69–71.
14 Feldt, p. 72.
15 Feldt, pp. 41–2; Lindsay, *The Coast Watchers*, p. 63.
16 Feldt, p. 73.
17 Feldt, p. 73.
18 AWM54, 629/1/11.
19 Feldt, pp. 76–7; AWM54, 629/1/11.
20 Lindsay, pp. 97–9; AWM54, 629/2/1.
21 Feldt, pp. 54–6.
22 Feldt, p. 48; McCarthy, *Patrol Into Yesterday*, p. 194.
23 McCarthy, pp. 195–7; Feldt, pp. 57–9.
24 McCarthy, pp. 199, 201; Feldt, pp. 59–60.
25 McCarthy, pp. 204–5; Feldt, pp. 60–1.
26 McCarthy, pp. 206–11; Feldt, pp. 62–5.
27 McCarthy, p. 212.
28 Feldt, p. 65.
29 Feuer, *Coast Watching in the Solomon Islands*, p. 1.
30 Feldt, p. 119; Lindsay, p. 149.
31 Feuer, pp. 3–5.
32 Feldt, pp. 120–1; Feuer, pp. 3–6; Nelson, 'Bougainville in World War II'.

33 Nelson, pp. 180–1.
34 Feuer, pp. 6–8; Feldt, pp. 121–2.
35 Lindsay, pp. 157–8.
36 Lindsay, pp. 154, 158.
37 Griffin, 'Mason, Paul Edward'; Lindsay, pp. 146–8; Feldt, p. 124.
38 Feldt, p. 104; Moore, *Solomon Islands Historical Encyclopaedia.*
39 Feldt, pp. 104–6; Moore.
40 Lord, p. 10.
41 Lindsay, p. 193.
42 Morphy, 'Thomson, Donald Finlay Fergusson'; Djokovic, 'Northern Territory Special Reconnaissance Unit'; Gray, 'A deep-seated aversion or a prudish disapproval', pp. 84–6.
43 Riseman, 'Defending Whose Country?', p. 83; Burroughs, 'AK 121 *Aroetta*'; Wikipedia, 'Caledon Bay crisis'.
44 Riseman, p. 83.
45 Riseman, p. 83; Dewar, 'Dhakiyarr Wirrpanda (1900–1934)'.
46 Morphy; Riseman, pp. 83–4.
47 Riseman, p. 84; Hall, *The Black Diggers*, p. 90; Djokovic.
48 Djokovic; Riseman, p. 84.
49 Burroughs.
50 Thomson, pp. 7–8, 12, 38; Djokovic; Burroughs; Long, 'Raiwala, Ray (1907–1965)'.
51 Thomson, p. 12.
52 Thomson, p. 36; Djokovic; Long.
53 Thomson, p. 44; Djokovic; Burroughs.
54 Thomson, p. 28.
55 Burroughs.
56 Thomson, pp. 24, 28; Vane, *North Australian Observer Unit*, pp. 43–4; McLay & McLay, 'History of Pearling in Australia'.
57 Gray, 'W.E.H. Stanner', p. 98; Walker & Walker, p. 3.
58 Walker & Walker, p. 3.
59 Mulvaney, 'Stanner, William Edward (Bill)'; Gray, pp. 95–7; Vane, pp. 5–6.
60 Walker & Walker, p. 6; NT Government, 'The "Nackeroos"'.
61 Walker & Walker, p. 4.
62 Gray, p. 98; Vane, pp. 9–10.
63 Walker & Walker, p. 5.
64 Lindsay, pp. 194–5; Lord, p. 12.
65 Feldt, p. 109; Lord, p. 12.
66 Feldt, pp. 109–10; Lord, p. 15.
67 Lord, p. 16.
68 Lord, pp. 10, 12, 21.
69 Moore; Lord, p. 21; Feldt, p. 111; Lindsay, p. 186.
70 Boyd, *The 'Nackeroos'*; Walker & Walker, pp. 6, 8.
71 Walker & Walker, pp. 9, 49.
72 Walker & Walker, p. 12.
73 Walker & Walker, pp. 10–11.

74 Walker & Walker, pp. 13–14.
75 Walker & Walker, p. 10.
76 Walker & Walker, pp. 15–16.
77 Walker & Walker, pp. 17–21; Vane, pp. 21–2.
78 Powell, *The Shadow's Edge*, p. 100.
79 Walker & Walker, pp. 22–4.
80 Vane, pp. 31–3, 41; Walker & Walker, p. 30.
81 Vane, pp. 57, 59, 62–3.
82 Vane, p. 12.
83 Vane, p. 75.
84 AWM54, 831/3/70; Walker & Walker, p. 63.
85 Walker & Walker, p. 35.
86 Walker & Walker, pp. 35–8, 74–5.
87 Boyd.
88 Thomson, pp. 32–4.
89 Thomson, p. 34.
90 Seekee, 'One ilan man'.
91 Riseman, pp. 85–6; Thomson, pp. 46–7.
92 Thomson, pp. 50–1.
93 Vane, p. 28.
94 Walker & Walker, pp. 76–9, 128–30; Boyd.
95 Walker & Walker, pp. 93–107; Vane, pp. 46–7; AWM52, 18/2/45.
96 Gray, 'A chance to be of some use to my country', p. 30; Gray, 'W.E.H. Stanner', p. 87.
97 Gray, 'W.E.H. Stanner', pp. 96–7.
98 Vane, p. 57.
99 Walker & Walker, pp. 40, 44; Boyd.
100 AWM52, 25/1/2; Harrison, '2/1st North Australia Observer Unit'.
101 Gray, 'A chance . . .', pp. 31–2.
102 Walker & Walker, pp. 51, 143–5.
103 Walker & Walker, p. 138.
104 Walker & Walker, p. 47.
105 Gray, 'A chance . . .', pp. 28–9; Gray, 'W.E.H. Stanner', p. 99.

CHAPTER 9 Night of the midgets

1 Grose, *A Very Rude Awakening*, pp. 7–8; Carruthers, *Japanese Submarine Raiders 1942*, p. 109.
2 Grose, pp. 8–9; Carruthers, p. 17.
3 Jenkins, *Battle Surface!*, p. 208.
4 Grose, pp. 10–11, 106–7; Carruthers, p. 121.
5 Jenkins, p. 127.
6 Carruthers, pp. 59, 173; Grose, pp. 50–1.
7 Grose, pp. 51–3.
8 Carruthers, pp. 59–60.
9 Grose, p. 63.
10 Grose, pp. 63–4.

11 Carruthers, p. 87.
12 Carruthers, pp. 32, 88.
13 Grose, pp. 72–5.
14 Grose, pp. 72–6; Carruthers, pp. 29–30.
15 Grose, p. 76; Carruthers, p. 30.
16 Carruthers, p. 87.
17 Carruthers, pp. 31, 89.
18 Carruthers, pp. 31, 89; Stevens, *A Critical Vulnerability*, p. 192.
19 *Sydney Morning Herald*, 'Showboat tourist harbour cruise', 30 May 1942, p. 2.
20 Fullford, *We Stood and Waited*, pp. 5, 190; Jenkins, p. 222; Grose, p. 7; NAA SP338/1, 201/37.
21 Grose, pp. 144–5.
22 Grose, pp. 85–6; Carruthers, p. 107.
23 Grose, p. 87.
24 Carruthers, pp. 47, 58–9.
25 Grose, pp. 54–5.
26 Carruthers, p. 117.
27 Grose, pp. 105–6; Carruthers, p. 119.
28 Grose, pp. 108, 113; Carruthers, pp. 119, 121.
29 Carruthers, pp. 121–3; Grose p. 113.
30 Carruthers, p. 123.
31 Grose, pp. 130–1; Jenkins, p. 213.
32 Jenkins, p. 210; Carruthers, p. 129.
33 Carruthers, pp. 134–5; Fullford, pp. 186–7; Grose, p. 125; Jenkins, p. 211.
34 Grose, p. 125; Fullford, p. 187; Carruthers, p. 135.
35 Grose, pp. 125–6, 151–2; Carruthers, p. 135.
36 Carruthers, pp. 134, 136; Jenkins, pp. 212–3; Grose, p. 126; NAA SP338/1, 201/37.
37 Grose, pp. 127, 133; NAA MP1049/5, 2026/21/79.
38 Grose, pp. 133–4; Carruthers, p. 137.
39 Fullford, pp. 186–7.
40 Carruthers p. 139.
41 Carruthers, p. 136; Grose, p. 135.
42 Grose, pp. 138–42; NAA MP1049/5, 2026/21/79.
43 Carruthers, pp. 136, 143; Grose, pp. 142, 145; NAA MP1049/5, 2026/21/79.
44 Grose, p. 142.
45 Carruthers, p. 136.
46 *Sydney Morning Herald*, 'Wounded Men Interviewed', 3 June 1942, p. 9.
47 Carruthers, 'Remembering the *Kuttabul*. Attack on Sydney–31 May 1942'.
48 Carruthers, 'Remembering the *Kuttabul*'.
49 Carruthers, *Japanese Submarine Raiders*, pp. 137, 155; Grose, pp. 152–3.
50 O'Hara-Close, oral history.
51 Grose, p. 204.
52 Carruthers, *Japanese Submarine Raiders*, p. 145.
53 Carruthers, *Japanese Submarine Raiders*, p. 147.
54 Warner & Seno, *The Coffin Boats*, p. 122.

55 Warner & Seno, pp. 122–3.
56 Carruthers, 'Remembering the *Kuttabul*'.
57 Carruthers, *Japanese Submarine Raiders*, pp. 129–31; Jenkins, p. 212.
58 Carruthers, *Japanese Submarine Raiders*, pp. 131–3; NAA SP338/1, 201/37.
59 Grose, p. 192; Carruthers, *Japanese Submarine Raiders*, p. 155.
60 Grose, p. 156; NAA MP1049/5, 2026/21/79.
61 Carruthers, *Japanese Submarine Raiders*, pp. 124, 157.
62 Grose, p. 46.
63 Carruthers, *Japanese Submarine Raiders*, p. 157; Warner & Seno, p. 118; NAA MP 1049/5, 2026/21/79.
64 Carruthers, *Japanese Submarine Raiders*, p. 159.
65 Carruthers, *Japanese Submarine Raiders*, p. 164.
66 Carruthers, *Japanese Submarine Raiders*, pp. 159–62; Jenkins, p. 218; Fulford, p. 188.
67 Carruthers, *Japanese Submarine Raiders*, pp. 162–4; NAA SP338/1, 201/37.
68 Grose, pp. 176–8.
69 Carruthers, *Japanese Submarine Raiders*, p. 137.
70 Grose, pp. 178–9; Carruthers, *Japanese Submarine Raiders*, p. 211; NAA SP338/1, 201/37.
71 NAA SP338/1, 201/37; Grose, pp. 208–9; Warner & Seno, p. 125.
72 Grose, p. 179; NAA SP338/1, 201/37.
73 Carruthers, *Japanese Submarine Raiders*, pp. 211–12; NAA SP338/1, 201/37.
74 NAA SP338/1, 201/37.
75 Grose, pp. 201–2.
76 NAA SP338/1, 201/37.
77 NAA SP338/1, 201/37.
78 NAA MP1049/5, 2026/21/79.
79 Grose, pp. 187, 201.
80 Grose, p. 188.
81 Grose, p. 188; *Sydney Morning Herald*, 'Enemy Submarines Enter Sydney Harbour', 2 June 1942, p. 5.
82 *Daily Mirror*, '3 Jap. subs. sunk: tried to raid Sydney', 1 June 1942.
83 *Sydney Morning Herald*, 2 June 1942, p. 5.
84 *Sydney Morning Herald*, 'Residents see guns blaze on harbour', 2 June 1942, p. 5.
85 *Daily Mirror*, '6 dead, 13 missing in sub. attack', 2 June 1942, p. 1.
86 Grose, p. 213.
87 Grose, pp. 226–7.
88 NAA SP338/1, 201/37; Grose, pp. 223–6, 228.
89 NAA SP338/1, 201/37; Grose, p. 230.
90 Grose, pp. 232–5; Carruthers, *Japanese Submarine Raiders*, pp. 176–9; NAA SP338/1, 201/37.
91 NAA SP338/1, 201/37.
92 Carruthers, *Japanese Submarine Raiders*, p. 189.
93 Grose, p. 206.
94 Carruthers, *Japanese Submarine Raiders*, p. 195; Warner & Seno, p. 159.

95 Grose, pp. 215–16; Carruthers, *Japanese Submarine Raiders*, p. 195; *Sydney Morning Herald*, 'Sea raiders shell Sydney and Newcastle', 8 June 1942, p. 5.
96 *Sydney Morning Herald*, 8 June 1942, p. 5: Grose, p. 217.
97 *Sydney Morning Herald*, 8 June 1942, p. 5; Grose, p. 217.
98 Carruthers, *Japanese Submarine Raiders*, p. 197.
99 Carruthers, *Japanese Submarine Raiders*, pp. 197–8; Grose, pp. 218–19; Fort Scratchley Historical Society, 'The Shelling of Newcastle, 8th June 1942'.
100 Carruthers, *Japanese Submarine Raiders*, pp. 198–9.
101 Fort Scratchley Historical Society.
102 *Sydney Morning Herald*, 8 June 1942, p. 5.
103 *Daily Mirror*, 'Blow the Japs! Says woman sleeper of 91', 8 June 1942, p. 2.
104 Carruthers, *Japanese Submarine Raiders*, p. 215.
105 Grose, p. 221; *Sydney Morning Herald*, 'Cremation of Japanese', 9 June 1942, p. 5.
106 Carruthers, *Japanese Submarine Raiders*, p. 215; Warner & Seno, p. 125; Dept of Veterans Affairs, 'Sydney Harbour'; NAA MP1049/5, 2026/21/79.
107 The Sydney Opera House now stands there.
108 Carruthers, *Japanese Submarine Raiders*, pp. 221–4; Dept of Veterans Affairs.
109 Grose, pp. 250–1; Dept of Veterans Affairs.
110 Carruthers, *Japanese Submarine Raiders*, p. 224; Grose, p. 253.

CHAPTER 10 The turning tide

1 Coox, *Nomonhan*, p. 1176.
2 Horner, *The Second World War*, p. 22.
3 Horner, 'Australia in 1942', p. 23.
4 Horner, *Crisis of Command*, pp. 70–2; Johnston, *Australia's Home Defence 1939–1945*, p. 13.
5 Horner, *Crisis of Command*, p. 73.
6 Horner, *Crisis of Command*, p. 75.
7 Horner, 'Australia Under Threat of Invasion', p. 266.
8 Horner, *High Command*, p. 188.
9 Long, *MacArthur as Military Commander*, p. 98.
10 Edwards, *John Curtin's War vol. 2*, p. 58; Freudenberg, *Churchill and Australia*, p. 391.
11 Collie, *Code Breakers*, pp. 121–3; Edwards, p. 62; Long, p. 98.
12 Collie, p. 128; Bullard, *Japanese Army Operations in the South Pacific Area*, p. 70.
13 Edwards, p. 66.
14 Day, *John Curtin*, p. 470; Edwards, p. 67.
15 *Sydney Morning Herald*, 'Great naval battle in Coral Sea', 9 May 1942, p. 9.
16 Penglase & Horner, *When the War Came to Australia*, p. 125.
17 Penglase & Horner, p. 126.
18 Edwards, p. 70; Day, p. 472.
19 Robertson, *Australia Goes to War*, p. 127; Edwards, p. 71.
20 Horner, *Inside the War Cabinet*, p. 119.
21 Day, p. 474; Horner, *Inside the War Cabinet*, p. 119.
22 Schaller, *Douglas MacArthur*, p. 70.

23 Collie, p. 144.
24 Collie, pp. 147–8.
25 *Courier-Mail*, 'Japs suffer in Midway Is. Raid', 6 June 1942, p. 2.
26 *Courier-Mail*, 'Big Jap fleet smashed off Midway Island', 8 June 1942, p. 1; 'Invasion threat lifted', p. 2.
27 *Courier-Mail*, 'Japs out-guessed', 9 June 1942, p. 1.
28 *Sydney Morning Herald*, 'The Pacific naval battles', 10 June 1942, p. 6.
29 Day, p. 475; Horner, *Inside the War Cabinet*, p. 120, Edwards, p. 84.
30 Horner, *Crisis of Command*, p. 95; Edwards, p. 85.
31 Long, pp. 100–1; Horner, *Inside the War Cabinet*, p. 121.
32 Horner, 'Defending Australia in 1942', p. 9; Schaller, p. 70; James, 'On Australia's Doorstep', p. 202.
33 Williams, *The Kokoda Campaign 1942*, pp. 18, 47–9; Horner, *Inside the War Cabinet*, p. 133; Day, p. 476.
34 Feldt, *The Coast Watchers*, pp. 133, 140–2; Moore, *Solomon Islands Historical Encyclopaedia 1892–1978*.
35 Lindsay, *The Coast Watchers*, p. 196; Feldt, p. 144.
36 Feldt, 'The Coast Watchers'; Lundstrom, *The First Team and the Guadalcanal Campaign*, p. 45.
37 Feldt, *The Coast Watchers*, p. 144; Lindsay, p. 196; Feuer, *Coast Watching in the Solomon Islands*, p. 51.
38 Lundstrom, pp. 80–1.
39 Williams, pp. 84, 90.
40 Feldt, *The Coast Watchers*, p. 149.
41 Lord, *Lonely Vigil*, p. 53.
42 Horner, *Inside the War Cabinet*, p. 137.
43 Bullard, pp. 141, 180; Edwards, p. 73; Horner, 'Defending Australia in 1942', p. 11.
44 Horner, *Crisis of Command*, pp. 141–4.
45 Horner, *Crisis of Command*, p. 141; Long, p. 103.
46 Stanley, *Invading Australia*, p. 189.
47 Bullard, p. 141.
48 Williams, pp. 4, 84–5.
49 James, p. 207; Horner, *Crisis of Command*, p. 149.
50 Long, p. 108.
51 NAA A5954, 611/4.
52 McKernan, *The Strength of a Nation*, p. 301; *Argus*, 'Stirring call to nation for austerity', 4 September 1942, p. 1; *Sydney Morning Herald*, 'Mr. Curtin's call to nation', 4 September 1942, p. 5.
53 Horner, *Crisis of Command*, p. 157.
54 *Sydney Morning Herald*, 'Bitter fighting in New Guinea', 10 September 1942, p. 5.
55 Horner, *Crisis of Command*, pp. 113–14.
56 Horner, *Crisis of Command*, p. 114.
57 Horner, *Crisis of Command*, pp. 116–17; Robertson, p. 129.
58 Horner, *Crisis of Command*, p. 159; Long, p. 109.

59 Horner, *Crisis of Command*, p. 161.
60 Horner, *Crisis of Command*, p. 160.
61 Horner, *Inside the War Cabinet*, pp. 141–2, 161, 163; *Sydney Morning Herald*, 'Troops in Papua restive for initiative', 16 September 1942, p. 7.
62 Horner, *Crisis of Command*, pp. 162, 164–5.
63 Horner, *Crisis of Command*, p. 170.
64 Horner, *Crisis of Command*, p. 162; Schaller, p. 71.
65 Day, p. 486.
66 Horner, *Crisis of Command*, pp. 172–84.
67 Williams, p. 188; *Sydney Morning Herald*, 'Further successes likely in New Guinea', 1 October 1942, p. 5 & 'Australians advance in Owen Stanleys', 2 October 1942, p. 5.
68 Williams, p. 185.
69 Nelson, 'Bougainville in World War II', p. 183.
70 Dunn, 'Coast Watcher Paul Edward Mason'; Feldt, *The Coast Watchers*, p. 168.
71 Feldt, *The Coast Watchers*, pp. 156–7.
72 Feldt, *The Coast Watchers*, pp. 170–1; Dunn, 'Coast Watcher Paul Edward Mason'.
73 Dunn, 'Coast Watcher Paul Edward Mason'; Feldt, *The Coast Watchers*, p. 171.
74 Robertson, p. 138.
75 Chan, *War on Our Doorstep*, p. 270.
76 *Sydney Morning Herald*, 'The year ahead', 1 January 1943, p. 4.
77 *Sydney Morning Herald*, 'The turning tide in south Pacific', 4 November 1942, p. 6.
78 Horner, 'Australia Under Threat of Invasion', p. 268.
79 Penglase & Horner, p. 168.
80 Schaller, p. 71.
81 Horner, *Crisis of Command*, p. 75, n6.
82 Horner, 'Australia Under Threat of Invasion', p. 269; Day, p. 505.
83 Black, 'The General and the Prime Minister'.
84 Edwards, *The Weekend Australian*, 'Period of greatest national peril was Curtin's finest hour', 3–4 November 2018, pp. 20–1.
85 Connell, *The War at Home*, p. 78.
86 Brown, oral history.
87 Acland, oral history, tape 2, pp. 2–3.
88 O'Hara-Close, oral history.
89 Dorothy Singe, *Australians at War Film Archive*, #563.

CHAPTER 11 The invasion of Australia

1 Curran, *The Power of Speech*, p. 220.
2 Peattie, *Nan'yo*, p. 244; Oliver, 'Interpreting "Japanese activities" in Australia 1888–1945'; Bullard, 'Japanese Strategy and Intent Towards Australia', p. 124.
3 NAA A367, C65663; NAA A816, 25/301/176; Oliver.
4 *Courier-Mail*, '"Invasion" notes', 25 September 1942, p. 1.
5 Stanley, *Invading Australia*, p. 195; AWM123, 189.
6 Clarke, personal communication; Suter, personal communication.

7 Burns, *The Brisbane Line Controversy*, pp. 119, 126; Jacobs, 'Australia's WWII Japanese Invasion Paranoia'.
8 Warner, 'Jap Invasion Plan For Australia'; Dunn, 'Japanese Landings in Australia During World War 2'.
9 Stanley, p. 201.
10 Dunn, 'Japanese Landings in Australia During World War 2'.
11 AWM54, 622/1/1; Walker & Walker, *Curtin's Cowboys*, pp. 64–7.
12 In Chapter 8.
13 Dunn, 'Japanese Landings in Australia During World War 2'.
14 McArthur, 'The Rising Sun Over Australia', pp. 2–5; Piper, *The Hidden Chapters*, pp. 145–8.
15 Shindo, 'The Japanese Army's "Unplanned" South Pacific Campaign', pp. 108–9.
16 Bullard, p. 129; Frei, *Japan's Southward Advance and Australia*, p. 162; Stanley, pp. 154–5.
17 Stanley, p. 155.
18 Bullard, *Japanese Army Operations in the South Pacific Area*, p. 82; Bullard, 'Japanese Strategy and Intent Towards Australia', p. 135.
19 Alcorta, *Australia's Frontline*, p. 9; Brown & Anderson, 'Invasion 1942?', p. 7; Frei, pp. 162–3.
20 Brown & Anderson, p. 8; Robertson, *Australia Goes to War*, p. 104; Bullard, *Japanese Army Operations in the South Pacific Area*, p. 80.
21 Brown & Anderson, pp. 7–8.
22 Frei, p. 168.
23 Oliver.
24 Bullard, *Japanese Army Operations in the South Pacific Area*, p. 131.
25 See Chapter 4, n130.
26 See Collie, *Nagasaki.*

BIBLIOGRAPHY

NATIONAL ARCHIVES OF AUSTRALIA

A367, C65663 HASHIDA Sei (Major)
A431, 1949/687 Bombing of Darwin—Report by Mr Justice Lowe
A571, 1944/4124 Enlistment of Canadian Nisei interpreters in AIF
A816, 25/301/176 Major Hashida—Visit to Australia
A816, 37/301/199 Report on Civilian Morale in North Queensland
A816, 37/301/254 Dr Cunningham's Report on Evacuation
A816, 37/301/293 Commission of Inquiry on the Air Raid on Darwin 19th Feb 1942
A981, Jap 31 Japan: Activities of Hirosi Ono
A981, JAP 55 Japan Espionage—General
A1196, 37/501/263 Civilian Morale in North Queensland—Report on—1943
A1608, W57/1/1 War Section Public Morale—General
A2684, 881 Scorched Earth Policy
A2684, 905 Appreciations on defence of Australia & ANZAC area
A5954, 328/19 Building up the Morale of the People—Suggested Press Statement
A5954, 328/21 Prime Minister's Committee on National Morale
A5954, 357/1 Defence Committee Agenda & Minutes. 1942. December 1941 to October 1942
A5954, 358/1 Defence Committee Agenda & Minutes. 1942. May 1942 to January 1943
A5954, 555/10 War in the Pacific. Defence of Australia and adjacent areas—Chiefs of Staff appreciation. December 1941
A5954, 568/4 Criticism by Minister for Labour & National Service (Mr Ward) of Defence Policy of Previous Government. 'Brisbane Line' Controversy
A5954, 571/4 The Fall of Singapore and Strategical Position in Far East and Pacific
A5954, 611/4 Notes for Prime Minister's Speech, Secret Session, 3rd September 1942
A5954, 768/12 Book, Part 2 Chapter 7—Initial Defence Measures for War with Japan.

A5954, 770/5 Book 4 (Original) Chapter 34—The 'Brisbane Line' Controversy
A5954, 807/1 War Cabinet Minutes, volume 9, Meetings 30 Oct 1941 to 30 Dec 1941
A5954, 807/2 War Cabinet Minutes, volume 10, Meetings 31 Dec 1941 to 24 Feb 1942
A5954, 808/1 War Cabinet Minutes, volume 11, Meetings 28 Feb 1942 to 29 Jul 1942
A5954, 813/1 Advisory War Council Minutes, volume 3, Meetings 6 Aug 1941 to 12 Dec 1941
A5954, 813/2 Advisory War Council Minutes, volume 4, Meetings 16 Dec 1941 to 26 Mar 1942
A5954, 1300/1 Strategic plans for defence of Australia following arrival of General MacArthur, March 1942
A7941, 46 Japanese Plan for Invasion of Australia
A8681, 1942/1247 Public relations bulletin—man offers himself as human bomb
A9186, 208 RAAF Unit History sheets, Station Darwin Jun 40–Jun 52
C123, 12630 Stanner, William
CP80/1, BUNDLE 2/S227 Scorched Earth Policy. Denial of Resources to the Enemy
J2808, 400/2/8 Scorched Earth—as applied to Queensland
M431, 2 B Acland—Diary & Personal Papers. Diary Expanded
MP508/1, 82/712/1773 Mr S.S. McClintock suggested relocation of Northern Aborigines
MP729/6, 29/401/618 North Australia Observer Organisation—Provision of Funds (NAOU)
MP729/6, 29/401/626 Japanese activities among the Aborigines
MP981/1, 448/201/1547 Awards to Coast Watchers
MP1049/5, 1855/6/20 Sydney—Attack by Midget Submarines from Study of Japanese Charts
MP1049/5, 2026/21/79 Midget Submarine Attack on Sydney Harbour
SP109/6, 6 Department of Information—Anti-Japanese master copies
SP338/1, 201/37 Midget Submarine Attack on Sydney Harbour, May 31st June 1st, 1942

AUSTRALIAN WAR MEMORIAL

AWM52, 18/2/21 8 Division Provost Company
AWM52, 18/2/45 Northern Territory L of C Provost Company—September 1942 to April 1943
AWM52, 25/1/2 North Aust Observer Unit—May 1942 to March 1943
AWM54, 511/2/1 North Australia Observation Unit (NAOU)—Movement, supply and maintenance 1942
AWM54, 622/1/1 Reports on the 'Gulf Scare', April 1943
AWM54, 629/1/11 The Stubborn Coast Watcher Cornelius Lyon Page
AWM54, 629/2/1 Captured Documents—Notebook describing search & capture of Coastwatcher Page
AWM54, 831/3/70 Report on the possibility of travel in all weathers from the shores of the Gulf of Carpentaria southwards to the Cloncurry Railway
AWM123, 189 Japanese Plan for Invasion of Australia
PR88/133 Hinder, Frank C. (Lieutenant, Camouflage Research, Dept of Home Security)

NATIONAL LIBRARY OF AUSTRALIA

MS4744 Papers of Charles Lydiard Aubrey (1886–1975) and Hilda Abbott

NORTHERN TERRITORY ARCHIVES SERVICE

NTRS226, TS677 Acland, Bruce—'Darwin—the big raid', *D.C.A. News*, November 1968

NTRS226, TS677 Shepherd, Ray—'Bombing of Darwin' (1993), unpublished manuscript

MITCHELL LIBRARY, SYDNEY

MLMSS 9393 John Pomeroy papers

BOOKS

Akashi, Yoji and Yoshimura, Mako (eds) (2008), *New Perspectives on the Japanese Occupation in Malaya and Singapore, 1941–1945*, NUS Press, Singapore

Alcorta, Frank (1991), *Australia's Frontline: The Northern Territory's War*, Allen & Unwin, Sydney

Alford, Bob (2017), *Darwin 1942: The Japanese Attack on Australia*, Osprey, Oxford

Australian War Memorial (1942), *Soldiering On: The Australian Army at Home and Overseas*, Australian War Memorial, Canberra

Beazley, Kim E. (1972), *John Curtin: An Atypical Labor Leader*, Australian National University Press, Canberra

Bell, Roger J. (1977), *Unequal Allies: Australian-American Relations and the Pacific War*, Melbourne University Press, Melbourne

Black, David (ed.) (1995), *In His Own Words: John Curtin's Speeches and Writings*, Paradigm Books, Perth

Bleakley, Jack (1992), *The Eavesdroppers*, AGPS Press, Canberra

Boyd, Betty (1999), *The 'Nackeroos'*, F.E. Boyd, Melbourne

Brown, Ron and Studdy-Clift, Pat (1992), *Darwin Dilemmas*, Hesperian Press, Perth

Bullard, Steven (tr. & ed.) (2007), *Japanese Army Operations in the South Pacific Area: New Britain and Papua Campaigns, 1942–43*, Australian War Memorial, Canberra

——(2013), 'Japanese Strategy and Intent Towards Australia' in (Dean, Peter J., ed.) *Australia 1942: In the Shadow of War*, Cambridge University Press, Melbourne

Burke, Anthony (2008), *Fear of Security: Australia's Invasion Anxiety*, Cambridge University Press, Melbourne

Burns, Paul (1998), *The Brisbane Line Controversy: Political Opportunism Versus National Security, 1942–45*, Allen & Unwin, Sydney

Burton, John (2006), *Fortnight of Infamy: The Collapse of Allied Airpower West of Pearl Harbor*, Naval Institute Press, Annapolis MD

Byrnes, Matthew (ed.) (1995), *Wartime Recollections*, Moreton Commemorative Committee, Brisbane

Carruthers, Steven L. (2006), *Japanese Submarine Raiders, 1942: A Maritime Mystery*, Casper Publications, Sydney

Chan, Gabrielle (ed.) (2003), *War on Our Doorstep: Diaries of Australians at the Frontline in 1942*, Hardie Grant, Melbourne

Chester, Alan (1943), *John Curtin*, Angus & Robertson, Sydney

Chew, Melanie (1998), *Of Hearts and Minds: The Story of Sembawang Shipyard*, Sembawang Shipyard, Singapore

Churchill, Winston (1950), *The Grand Alliance, Volume 3 of The Second World War*, Houghton Mifflin, Boston

Close, Yve (1998), *Joshua Smith Artist, 1905–1995*, self-published, Sydney

Collie, Craig (2011), *Nagasaki: The Massacre of the Innocent and Unknowing*, Allen & Unwin, Sydney

——(2017), *Code Breakers: Inside the Shadow World of Signals Intelligence in Australia's Two Bletchley Parks*, Allen & Unwin, Sydney

Collie, Craig and Marutani, Hajime (2009), *The Path of Infinite Sorrow: The Japanese on the Kokoda Track*, Allen & Unwin, Sydney

Connaughton, Richard (1994), *Shrouded Secrets: Japan's War on Mainland Australia 1942–1944*, Brassey's, London

Connell, Daniel (1988), *The War at Home, Australia 1939–1949*, Australian Broadcasting Corporation, Sydney

Connors, Libby, Finch, Lynette, Saunders, Kay and Taylor, Helen (1992), *Australia's Frontline: Remembering the 1939–45 War*, University of Queensland Press, Brisbane

Coox, Alvin D. (1985), *Nomonhan: Japan Against Russia, 1939*, Stanford University Press, San Francisco

Cox, Jeffrey (2014), *Rising Sun, Falling Skies: The Disastrous Java Sea Campaign of World War II*, Osprey Publishing, Oxford

Curran, James (2004), *The Power of Speech: Australian Prime Ministers Defining the National Image*, Melbourne University Press, Melbourne

Darian-Smith, Kate (1996), 'War and Australian society' in (Beaumont, Joan, ed.) *Australia's War 1939–45*, Allen & Unwin, Sydney

——(2009), *On the Home Front: Melbourne in Wartime, 1939–1945*, Melbourne University Press, Melbourne

——(2013), 'The Home Front and the American Presence in 1942' in (Dean, Peter J., ed.) *Australia 1942: In the Shadow of War*, Cambridge University Press, Melbourne

Day, David (1999), *John Curtin: A Life*, HarperCollins, Sydney

Dean, Peter J. (ed.) (2013), *Australia 1942: In the Shadow of War*, Cambridge University Press, Melbourne

Dennis, Peter et al. (2008), *The Oxford Companion to Australian Military History*, Oxford University Press, Melbourne

Dinan, Jacqueline (2015), *Between the Dances*, Jane Curry, Sydney

Donaldson, Elizabeth and Donaldson, Robert (2011), *William Dobell: His Life, Art and Home*, self-published, Wangi Wangi, New South Wales

Eagles, James H. (2003), *HMAS Sydney and Operation Fish, 1941*, James & Anne Eagles, Townsville

Edwards, John (2005), *Curtin's Gift: Reinterpreting Australia's Greatest Prime Minister*, Allen & Unwin, Sydney

——(2017), *John Curtin's War, volume 1*, Viking, Melbourne

——(2018), *John Curtin's War, volume 2*, Viking, Melbourne

Elphick, Peter (1995), *Singapore: The Pregnable Fortress*, Hodder & Stoughton, London

Fahey, John (2018), *Australia's First Spies*, Allen & Unwin, Sydney

Falk, Stanley L. (1988), 'Douglas MacArthur and the War against Japan' in (Leary, William M., ed.) *We Shall Return! MacArthur's Commanders and the Defeat of Japan 1942–1945*, University Press of Kentucky, Lexington, Kentucky

Farrell, Brian and Hunter, Sandy (eds) (2010), *A Great Betrayal?: The Fall of Singapore Revisited*, Marshall Cavendish, Singapore

Farrell, Brian and Pratten, Garth (2009), *Malaya 1942*, Army History Unit, Canberra

Feldt, Eric (1946), *The Coast Watchers*, Penguin, Melbourne

Felton, Mark (2008), *The Coolie Generals: Britain's Far Eastern Military Leaders in Japanese Captivity*, Pen & Sword Military, Barnsley, UK

Ferrell, Robert H. (ed.) (1981), *The Eisenhower Diaries*, Norton, New York

Feuer, A.B. (ed.) (1992), *Coast Watching in the Solomon Islands: The Bougainville Reports, December 1941–July 1943*, Praeger, New York

Forrest, Peter & Forrest, Sheila (2001), *Federation Frontline: A People's History of World War II in the Northern Territory*, Centenary of Federation Northern Territory, Darwin

——(2012), *Battling: Territorians and Their War*, Shady Tree, Darwin

Frei, Henry P. (1991), *Japan's Southward Advance and Australia: From the Sixteenth Century to World War II*, Melbourne University Press, Melbourne

Freudenberg, Graham (2008), *Churchill and Australia*, Macmillan, Sydney

Fullford, R.K. (1994), *We Stood and Waited: Sydney's Anti-Ship Defences,1939–1945*, Royal Australian Artillery Historical Society Inc., Sydney

Gallagher, Ron (2000), *The Long Island Massacre*, Epic Publications, Yeppoon, QLD

Gill, G. Hermon (1957), *Royal Australian Navy, 1939–1942*, Australian War Memorial, Canberra

Gray, Geoffrey (2005), 'A deep-seated aversion or a prudish disapproval: relations with Elkin' in (Rigsby, Bruce and Peterson, Nicolas, eds) *Donald Thomson, the Man and Scholar*, The Academy of Social Sciences in Australia, Canberra

——(2008), '"A chance to be of some use to my country": Stanner during World War II' in (Hinkson, Melinda and Beckett, Jeremy, eds) *An Appreciation of Difference: W.E.H. Stanner and Aboriginal Australia*, Aboriginal Studies Press, Canberra

——(2012), 'W.E.H. Stanner: Wasted War Years' in (Gray, Geoffrey, Munro, Doug and Winter, Christine, eds) *Scholars at War: Australasian Social Scientists, 1939–1945*, ANU E Press, Canberra, pp. 95–118

Green, Frank (1969), *Servant of the House*, Heinemann, Melbourne

Grose, Peter (2007), *A Very Rude Awakening: The Night the Japanese Midget Subs Came to Sydney Harbour*, Allen & Unwin, Sydney

——(2009), *An Awkward Truth: The Bombing of Darwin, February 1942*, Allen & Unwin, Sydney

Hall, Robert A. (1997), *The Black Diggers: Aborigines and Torres Strait Islanders in the Second World War*, Aboriginal Studies Press, Canberra

Hall, Timothy (1980), *Darwin 1942: Australia's Darkest Hour*, Methuen Australia, Sydney

Hasluck, Paul (1970), 'The "Brisbane Line"—A Study in Wartime Politics', Appendix 4 of *The Government and the People, 1942–1945*, Australian War Memorial, Canberra

——(1980), *Diplomatic Witness: Australian Foreign Affairs, 1941–1947*, Melbourne University Press, Melbourne

Haultain, C.T.G. (1971), *Watch Off Arnhem Land*, Roebuck Society, Canberra

Hilvert, John (1984), *Blue Pencil Warriors: Censorship and Propaganda in World War II*, University of Queensland Press, Brisbane

Holzworth, Peter (2014), *A Tribute to Edward Harold Fulcher Swain*, self-published, Brisbane

Horner, D.M. (1978), *Crisis of Command: Australian Generalship and the Japanese Threat, 1941–1943*, Australian National University Press, Canberra

——(1982), *High Command: Australia and Allied Strategy 1939–1945*, George Allen & Unwin, Sydney

——(1988), 'Australia Under Threat of Invasion' in (McKernan, M. and Browne, M., eds) *Australia, Two Centuries of War & Peace*, Australian War Memorial, Canberra

——(1996), *Inside the War Cabinet: Directing Australia's War Effort, 1939–45*, Allen & Unwin, Sydney

——(2002), *The Second World War (1): The Pacific*, Osprey, Botley, UK

——(2013), 'Australia in 1942: A Pivotal Year' in (Dean, Peter J., ed.) *Australia 1942: In the Shadow of War*, Cambridge University Press, Melbourne

Hudson, W.J. and Stokes, H.J.W. (eds) (1982), *Documents on Australian Foreign Policy, 1937–49. Volume V: July 1941–June 1942*, Australian Government Publishing Service, Canberra

Idriess, Ion (1942), *Trapping the Jap*, Book 4 of The Australian Guerrilla series, Angus & Robertson, Sydney

Ienaga, Saburo (1978), *The Pacific War, 1931–1945: A Critical Perspective on Japan's Role in World War II*, Pantheon, New York

James, D. Clayton (1970), *The Years of MacArthur, Volume 1, 1880–1941*, Houghton Miffen, Boston

James, Karl (2013), 'On Australia's Doorstep: Kokoda and Milne Bay' in (Dean, Peter J., ed.) *Australia 1942: In the Shadow of War*, Cambridge University Press, Melbourne

Jenkins, David (1992), *Battle Surface!: Japan's Submarine War Against Australia 1942–44*, Random House, Sydney

Johnston, George (1984), *War Diary 1942*, Collins, Sydney

Johnston, Mark (2006), *Australia's Home Defence 1939–1945*, Department of Veterans' Affairs, Canberra

Kerr, Sir John (1978), *Matters for Judgment: An Autobiography*, Macmillan, London

Knox, Ralph M. (1999), *The Emperor's Angry Guest: A World War II Prisoner of the Japanese Speaks Out*, Southfarm Press, Middletown, Connecticut

Leary, William M. (ed.) (1988), *We Shall Return! MacArthur's Commanders and the Defeat of Japan 1942–1945*, University Press of Kentucky, Lexington, Kentucky

Leasor, James (1968), *Singapore: The Battle that Changed the World*, Hodder & Stoughton, London

Lee, Norman E. (1983), *John Curtin: Saviour of Australia*, Longman Cheshire, Melbourne

Legg, Frank (1965), *The Gordon Bennett Story*, Angus & Robertson, Sydney

Lewis, Tom (2017), *The Empire Strikes South: Japan's Air War Against Northern Australia 1942–45*, Avonmore Books, Adelaide

Lewis, Dr Tom and Ingman, Peter (2013), *Carrier Attack—Darwin 1942: The Complete Guide to Australia's Own Pearl Harbor*, Avonmore Books, Adelaide
Lindsay, Patrick (2010), *The Coast Watchers*, William Heinemann, Sydney
Lloyd, Clem and Hall, Richard (eds) (1997), *Backroom Briefings: John Curtin's War*, National Library of Australia, Canberra
Lockwood, Douglas (2005), *Australia Under Attack: The Bombing of Darwin—1942*, New Holland, Sydney
Lodge, A.B. (1980), *The Fall of General Gordon Bennett*, Allen & Unwin, Sydney
——(1984), 'Lieutenant-General Henry Gordon Bennett: A Model Major-General?' in (Horner, D.M., ed.) *The Commanders: Australian Military Leadership in the Twentieth Century*, George Allen & Unwin, Sydney
Long, Gavin (1969), *MacArthur as Military Commander*, Angus & Robertson, Sydney
——(1973), *The Six Years War: A Concise History of Australia in the 1939–45 War*, Australian War Memorial, Canberra
Lord, Walter (1977), *Lonely Vigil: Coastwatchers of the Solomons*, Viking Press, New York
Loxton, Bruce and Coulthard-Clark, Chris (1994), *The Shame of Savo: Anatomy of a Naval Disaster*, Allen & Unwin, Sydney
Lundstrom, John B. (1994), *The First Team and the Guadalcanal Campaign: Naval Fighter Combat from August to November 1942*, Naval Institute Press, Annapolis, Maryland
MacArthur, Douglas (1964), *Reminiscences*, Heinemann, London
Manchester, William (1978), *American Caesar*, Little Brown, Boston
Martin, A.W. and Hardy, Patsy (eds) (1993), *Dark and Hurrying Days: Menzies' 1941 Diary*, National Library of Australia, Canberra
Maynard, Roger (2017), *Hero or Deserter?: Gordon Bennett and the Tragic Defeat of the 8th Division*, Penguin Random House, Sydney
McBride, Frank and Helen Taylor (1995), *Brisbane Remembers: The Home Front 1939–1945*, Brisbane City Council, Brisbane
McCarthy, Dudley (1959), *South West Pacific Area—First Year: Kokoda to Wau*, Volume 5 in Second World War Official History: Series 1, The Army, Australian War Memorial, Canberra
McCarthy, J.K. (1963), *Patrol Into Yesterday: My New Guinea Years*, F.W. Cheshire, Melbourne
McIntyre, Darryl (1992), *Townsville at War 1942: Life in a Garrison City*, Townsville City Council, Townsville
McKernan, Michael (1995), *All In!: Fighting the War at Home*, Allen & Unwin, Sydney
——(2006), *The Strength of a Nation*, Allen & Unwin, Sydney
McKinlay, Brian (1985), *Australia 1942: End of Innocence*, Collins, Sydney
McMullin, Ross (1991), *The Light on the Hill: The Australian Labor Party, 1891–1991*, Oxford University Press, Melbourne
——(2013), 'Dangers and Problems: Unprecedented and Unpredictable: The Curtin Government's Response to the Threat' in (Dean, Peter J., ed.) *Australia 1942: In the Shadow of War*, Cambridge University Press, Melbourne
McNab, Alexander 'Sandy' (1998), *We Were the First: The Unit History of No 1 Independent Company*, Australian Military History Publications, Sydney

Meaney, Neville (1985), *Australia and the World: A Documentary History from the 1870s to the 1970s*, Longman Cheshire, Melbourne

Moore, John Hammond (1981), *Over-Sexed, Over-Paid & Over Here: Americans in Australia 1941–1945*, University of Queensland Press, Brisbane

Moreman, T.R. (2005), *The Jungle, the Japanese and the British Commonwealth Armies at War 1941–45: Fighting Methods, Doctrine and Training for Jungle Warfare*, Frank Cass, Oxford

Moremon, Dr John, with Reid, Dr Richard (2002), *A Bitter Fate: Australians in Malaya & Singapore, December 1941–February 1942*, Department of Veterans' Affairs, Canberra

Naoto, Sudo (2010), *Nanyo-Orientalism: Japanese Representations in the Pacific*, Cambria Press, Amherst, New York

Nelson, Hank (2015), 'Bougainville in World War II' in (Regan, Anthony J. and Griffin, Helga M., eds) *Bougainville Before the Conflict*, ANU eView, Canberra

Oliver, Pam (2010), *Raids on Australia: 1942 and Japan's Plans for Australia*, Australian Scholarly Publishing, Melbourne

——(2013), 'World Wars and the Anticipation of Conflict: The Impact on Long-Established Australia-Japanese Relations, 1905–43' in (Dean, Peter J., ed.) *Australia 1942: In the Shadow of War*, Cambridge University Press, Melbourne

Owen, Frank (1960), *The Fall of Singapore*, Michael Joseph, London

Palazzo, Albert (2013), 'The Overlooked Mission: Australia and Home Defence' in (Dean, Peter J., ed.) *Australia 1942: In the Shadow of War*, Cambridge University Press, Melbourne

Peattie, Mark R. (1988), *Nan'yo: The Rise and Fall of the Japanese in Micronesia, 1885–1945*, University of Hawaii Press, Honolulu

Penglase, Joanna and Horner, David (1992), *When the War Came to Australia: Memories of the Second World War*, Allen & Unwin, Sydney

Pennay, Bruce John (1992), O*n the Home Front: Albury During the Second World War*, Albury and District Historical Society, Albury, NSW

Perry, Roland (2012), *Pacific 360°*, Hachette, Sydney

Piper, Robert (1995), *The Hidden Chapters: Untold Stories of Australians at War in the Pacific*, Pagemasters, Melbourne

Plowman, Peter (2003), *Across the Sea to War*, Rosenberg Publishing, Sydney

Pogue, Forrest C. (1966), *George C. Marshall: Ordeal and Hope 1939–1942*, Viking Press, New York

Powell, Alan (1996), *War by Stealth: Australians and the Allied Intelligence Bureau 1942–1945*, Melbourne University Press, Melbourne

——(2007), *The Shadow's Edge: Australia's Northern War*, Charles Darwin University Press, Darwin

Pratten, Garth (2009), *Australian Battalion Commanders in the Second World War*, Cambridge University Press, Melbourne

Pybus, Cassandra (1999), *The Devil and James McAuley*, University of Queensland Press, Brisbane

——(2012), 'Conlon's Remarkable Circus' in (Gray, Geoffrey, Munro, Doug and Winter, Christine, eds) *Scholars at War: Australasian Social Scientists, 1939—1945*, ANU E Press, Canberra, pp. 55–72

Reid, Richard (2007), *Australia Under Attack: Darwin and the Northern Territory 1942–1945*, Department of Veterans' Affairs, Canberra

Robertson, John (1984), *Australia Goes to War*, Doubleday, Sydney

Robson, Lloyd (1983), *A History of Tasmania, Volume 1, 'Van Diemen's Land from the Earliest Times to 1855'*, Oxford University Press, Melbourne

Rosa, S.A. (1920), *The Invasion of Australia*, Judd Publishing, Sydney

Rosen, Sue (ed.) (2017), *Scorched Earth: Australia's Secret Plan for Total War Under Japanese Invasion in World War II*, Allen & Unwin, Sydney

Ross, Lloyd (1977), *John Curtin: A Biography*, Macmillan, Melbourne

Russell, David Lee (2019), *Early U.S. Navy Carrier Raids, February–April 1942: Five Operations that Tested a New Dimension of American Air Power*, McFarland & Co, Jefferson, North Carolina

Ruwoldt, Rex (2005), *Darwin's Battle for Australia,* Darwin Defenders 1942–45 Inc, Geelong, Victoria

Saunders, Kay (1993), *War on the Homefront: State Intervention in Queensland 1938–1948*, University of Queensland Press, Brisbane

Saunders, Kay and Lynette Finch (1993), 'Northern Australians' Fear of Invasion' in (Fry, Gavin, ed.) *The Battle of the Coral Sea 1942: Conference Proceedings 1992*, Australian National Maritime Museum, Sydney

Schaller, Michael (1989), *Douglas MacArthur: The Far Eastern General*, Oxford University Press, New York

Shindo, Hiroyuki (2013), 'The Japanese Army's "Unplanned" South Pacific Campaign' in (Dean, Peter J., ed.) *Australia 1942: In the Shadow of War*, Cambridge University Press, Melbourne

Shores, Christopher, Cull, Brian and Izawa, Yasuho (1992), *Bloody Shambles, volume 1, 'The Drift to War to the Fall of Singapore'*, Grub Street, London

Smith, Colin (2005), *Singapore Burning: Heroism and Surrender in World War II*, Viking, London

Somerville, Margaret (2011), *They Crossed a Continent*, Shady Tree, Darwin

Spender, Percy (1972), *Politics and a Man,* Collins, Sydney

Stanley, Peter (2008), *Invading Australia: Japan and the Battle for Australia, 1942*, Viking, Melbourne

Stevens, David (2006), *A Critical Vulnerability: The Impact of the Submarine Threat on Australia's Maritime Defence, 1915–1954*, Sea Power Centre, Canberra

Tanner, Alex (1995), *The Long Road North*, Alex Tanner, Adelaide

Terry, Michael (1945), *Bulldozer: The War Role of the Department of Main Roads, New South Wales*, Frank Johnson, Sydney

Thompson, John (1962), *On Lips of Living Men: Six Great Australians*, Lansdowne Press, Melbourne

Thompson, Peter (2005), *The Battle for Singapore: The True Story of the Greatest Catastrophe of World War II*, Portrait, London

Thorpe, Elliott R. (1969), *East Wind, Rain*, Gambit, Boston

Tsuji, Colonel Masanobu (1997), *Japan's Greatest Victory, Britain's Worst Defeat*, Spellmount, Staplehurst, Kent

Ugaki, Matome (1991), *Fading Victory: The Diary of Admiral Matome Ugaki 1941–1945* (Chihaya Masataka, tr.; Goldstein, Donald M. and V. Dillon, Katherine V., eds), University of Pittsburgh Press, London

Vane, Dr Amoury (2000), *North Australian Observer Unit: The History of a Surveillance Regiment*, Australian Military History Publications, Sydney

Walker, Richard and Walker, Helen (1986), *Curtin's Cowboys: Australia's Secret Bush Commandos*, Allen & Unwin, Sydney

Warner, Peggy and Seno, Sadao (1986), *The Coffin Boats: Japanese Midget Submarine Operations in the Second World War*, Leo Cooper/Secker & Warburg, London

Warren, Alan (2002), *Singapore 1942: Britain's Greatest Defeat*, Hambledon & London, London

Wigmore, Lionel (1957), *The Japanese Thrust, Volume IV of Australia in the War of 1939–1945* in (Long, Gavin, ed.) Series 1—Army, Australian War Memorial, Canberra

Wilkes U.S.N., Charles (1845), *Narrative of the United States Exploring Expedition: During the Years 1838, 1839, 1840, 1841, 1842, Volume 1*, Lea & Blanchard, Philadelphia, Pennsylvania

Williams, Peter (2012), *The Kokoda Campaign 1942: Myth and Reality*, Cambridge University Press, Melbourne

Wintringham, Tom (1940), *New Ways of War*, Penguin, London

Wurth, Bob (2008), *1942: Australia's Greatest Peril*, Pan Macmillan, Sydney

——(2013), *The Battle for Australia: A Nation and its Leader Under Siege*, Pan Macmillan, Sydney

PAPERS, ARTICLES, LETTERS, WEBFILES

Abbott, Derek (2017), 'Scorched earth flames are fanned again', *Honest History*, Canberra, www.honesthistory.net.au/wp/scorched-earth-flames-are-fanned-again-review-of-rosen

ABC Radio National (2005), 'WWII and Home', in *Saturday Extra*, 13 August 2005, Australian Broadcasting Corporation, Sydney, www.abc.net.au/radionational/programs/saturdayextra/wwii-and-home/3367542

'Albatross' (E.L. Piesse) (1935), *Japan and the Defence of Australia*, Robertson & Mullens, Melbourne

Alsleben, Allan, Hackett, Bob and Kingsepp, Sander (2011), 'IJN Seaplane Tender KAMIKAWA MARU: Tabular Record of Movement', in *Imperial Japanese Navy Page* (Parshall, Jonathan and Tully, Anthony, eds), available at www.combinedfleet.com/Kamikawa_t

Ammentorp, Steen (2000), *The Generals of WWII*, www.generals.dk

Anon. (1942), *They Shall Not Pass: A Preliminary Plan for a People's Defence*, Current Book Distributors, Sydney, www.nla.gov.au/nla.obj-52801124/view?partId=nla.obj-95269244#page/n7/mode/1up

Ayers, Lucy Lockett (1945), 'A.R.P. diaries of Lucy Lockett Ayers', in *South Australians at War*, State Library, Adelaide, www.samemory.sa.gov.au/site/page.cfm?c=4959

Bartlett, Norman (1942), 'Let's have a real people's army!', *Sunday Telegraph*, Sydney, 1 February

Bayne, Mollie (ed.) (1943), *Australian Women at War*, Research Group of the Left Book Club of Victoria, Melbourne [pamphlet]

Beazley, K.E. (1966), 'John Curtin Labor's most effective leader', *Canberra Times*, 1 March 1966, p. 8 and 2 March 1966, p. 11

Bell, Morgan (2008a), 'John Curtin', in *World War II Database*, Lava Development LLC, https://ww2db.com/person_bio.php?person_id=96

——(2008b), 'Gordon Bennett', in *World War II Database*, Lava Development LLC, https://ww2db.com/person_bio.php?person_id=470

Black, David, (2014), 'The General and the Prime Minister: Douglas MacArthur and John Curtin', John Curtin Prime Ministerial Library, Perth, available at www.john.curtin.edu.au/macarthur/essay1

Bowen, James (2018), *The Battle for Australia 1942–43*, Pacific War Historical Society, Melbourne, available at http://www.battleforaustralia.org/

Boyce, Dean (2008), 'Defending colonial Sydney', in *Dictionary of Sydney*, City of Sydney, available at www.dictionaryofsydney/defending_colonial_sydney

Bramston, Troy (2016), 'John Curtin argued case of putting Australia's defence first', *The Australian*, available at: https://www.theaustralian.com.au/nation/inquirer/john-curtin-argued-case-of-putting-australias-defence-first/news-story/fb775755bf16862f3a9ff8f69d0519c5

Brown, Gary and Anderson, David (1992), 'Invasion 1942? Australia and the Japanese Threat', *Parliamentary Research Service: Background Paper*, number 6, Department of the Parliamentary Library, Canberra

Brown, John (2018), 'Coast Watchers in the Solomons', in *Warfare History Network*, available at www.warfarehistorynetwork.com/daily/wwii/coast-watchers-in-the-solomons

Brown, Malcolm (2012), 'The day that changed Australia', *Sydney Morning Herald*, available at https://www.smh.com.au/national/the-day-that-changed-australia-20120217-1teiu.html

Burns, Paul (1986), 'The Brisbane Line 1909–1963', MA (hons) thesis, University of New England, Armidale

Burroughs, Walter (2017), 'AK 121 *Aroetta*', *Naval Historical Review*, vol. 38, no. 3, pp. 4–9, Naval Historical Society of Australia, Sydney

Burrowes, James (2016), 'How the Coastwatchers turned the tide of the Pacific War', *The Australian*, available at https://www.theaustralian.com.au/commentary/opinion/how-the-coastwatchers-turned-the-tide-of-the-pacific-war/news-story/9970844d373306941faa45748e9217a1

Carment, David (1993), 'Abbott, Charles Lydiard (1886–1975)', in *Australian Dictionary of Biography*, vol. 13, Melbourne University Press, Melbourne

Carruthers, Steven (2013), 'Remembering the *Kuttabul*. Attack on Sydney—31 May 1942', in *Inside History Magazine*, available at www.insidehistory.com.au/2013/05/remembering-the-kuttabul-attack-on-sydney-31-may-1942

Casey, Dr Steven (2010), *The Prime Minister and the President: John Curtin and Franklin D. Roosevelt in World War II*, John Curtin Prime Ministerial Library, Perth, available at www.john.curtin.edu.au/roosevelt/index

Caulfield, Michael (project dir.), *Australians at War Film Archive*, Department of Veterans' Affairs (Australia) & Mullion Creek Productions, in UNSW Canberra website, http://www.australiansatwarfilmarchive.unsw.edu.au/

Cavendish, Richard (2013), 'Singapore Naval Base Opened', *History Today*, vol. 63 issue 2, available at www.historytoday.com/archive/Singapore-naval-base-opened

Chant, Christopher (2016) 'Operation Matador', in *Codenames: Operations of World War 2*, available at https://codenames.info/operation/matador-i/

——(2018), 'Operation Stepsister', in *Codenames: Operations of World War 2*, available at https://codenames.info/operation/stepsister

Charlton, Peter (2005a), 'General's scheme to erase Australians', in *The Peace Generation, Courier-Mail*, Brisbane, available at www.couriermail.com.au/extras/ww2/generalsscheme.htm

——(2005b), 'Shadowy organisation had undue influence', in *The Peace Generation, Courier-Mail*, Brisbane, www.couriermail.com.au/extras/ww2/shadowyorganisation.htm

Clements, Bill (2011), 'The sea forts of Victoria—Forts that never were!', Military History and Heritage Victoria Inc., www.mhhv.org.au/?p=1741, 28 December

Copeman, Gai and Vance, Diane (1992), '"It Was a Different Town" being some memories of Townsville and District 1942–1945', Thuringowa City Council, Townsville

Coulthard-Clark, Chris (2002), 'Remembering 1942: The Fall of Singapore', Australian War Memorial, https://www.awm.gov.au/articles/blog/1942-fall-of-singapore

Croft, Julian (1983), 'Idriess, Ion Llewellyn (1889–1879)', in *Australian Dictionary of Biography*, vol. 9, Melbourne University Press, Melbourne

Curtin, John (1941), 'National Broadcast by Prime Minister', John Curtin Prime Ministerial Library, Perth, available at http://john.curtin.edu.au/diary/primeminister/fulltext/fulltext%20prime%20minister_1941_4.html

——(1941), 'The Task Ahead', *The Herald*, Melbourne, available at www.john.curtin.edu.au/pmportal/text/00468

Dark, Eleanor (1942), 'Australians don't want pep talks', *Daily Telegraph*, Sydney, p. 4

Davies, Natalia (1946), 'The Defence Society', in *South Australians At War*, State Library of South Australia, Adelaide, available at www.samemory.sa.gov.au/site/page.cfm?c=5323

Day, Mark (2012), 'Darwin's finger of shame points at military', *The Australian*, available at www.theaustralian.com.au/news/inquirer/darwins-finger-of-shame-points-at-military/news-story/c30933e17bfd9a29f7a1b059c39997f6

——(2017), 'Australia prepared a secret plan to repel a Japanese invasion', *The Australian*, 18 May 2017

Dedman, John J. (1968), 'The "Brisbane" Line', *Australian Outlook*, 22:2, pp. 141–161, www.doi.org/10.1080/10357716808444311

Department of Home Security (Australia) (1942), 'Advising the Public in the Event of an Invasion: Notes for the Guidance of Police and Air Raid Wardens', Canberra

Department of Veterans' Affairs (Australia), 'Australia Under Attack 1940–45', in *Australia and the Second World War*, The Anzac Portal, https://anzacportal.dva.gov.au/wars-and-missions/world-war-ii-1939-1945/events/australia-under-attack-1940-1945

——'The Coastwatchers 1941–1945', in *Australia and the Second World War* in The Anzac Portal, https://anzacportal.dva.gov.au/wars-and-missions/world-war-ii-1939-1945/resources/coastwatchers-1941-1945

De Vries, Ben (2018), 'The battle for oil in the Dutch East Indies: Pladjoe, the pearl in the crown of the Bataafsche Petroleum Maatschappij (Shell), in the turmoil of the 1940s', https://journals.open.tudelft.nl/iphs/article/view/2676/2885

Dewar, Mickey (2005), 'Dhakiyarr Wirrpanda (1900–1934)', in *Australian Dictionary of Biography*, supplementary volume, Melbourne University Press, Melbourne

Djokovic, Peter (2009), 'Northern Territory Special Reconnaissance Unit', *Pathfinder*, vol. 74, in *Pathfinder Collection*, vol. 3, pp. 89–92, Air Power Development Centre, Canberra

Donovan, Peter (1989), 'The Northern Territory in the Defence of Australia: Historical Overview', Working Paper No. 176, Strategic & Defence Studies Centre, ANU, Canberra

Dunn, Peter, 'General Douglas MacArthur in Australia During WWII', in *Australia @ War*, Brisbane, https://www.ozatwar.com/macarthur.htm

——'Coast Watcher Paul Edward Mason', in *Australia @ War*, Brisbane, www.ozatwar.com/sigint/pemason

——'2/1 North Australia Observer Unit (2/1 NAOU), the "Nackeroos"', in *Australia @ War*, www.ozatwar.com/ausarmy/naou

——'"The Brisbane Line": Was It Fact or Was It a Myth?', in *Australia @ War*, https://www.ozatwar.com/ozatwar/brisbaneline.htm

——'The Japanese bomb Townsville, Qld during WW2', in *Australia @ War*, www.ozatwar.com/thejaps

____'Japanese Landings in Australia During World War 2', in *Australia @ War*, www.ozatwar.com/japsland/japsland

Edwards, John (2018), 'Period of greatest national peril was Curtin's finest hour', *The Weekend Australian*, pp. 20–1

Edwards, Peter (2002), 'Another look at Curtin and MacArthur', in *Remembering 1942*, Australian War Memorial, Canberra, available at https://www.awm.gov.au/visit/events/conference/remembering-1942/edwards

Egan, Ted (1994), 'Makarrta: The Caledon Bay and Woodah Island Killings 1932/33', MA thesis, Department of History, University of Adelaide

Elder, Peter (2002), 'Wells, Thomas Alexander (1888–954)', in *Australian Dictionary of Biography*, vol. 16, Melbourne University Press, Melbourne

Elias, Dr Ann (2003), 'The organisation of camouflage in Australia in the Second World War', *Journal of the Australian War Museum*, no. 38, https://www.awm.gov.au/articles/journal/j38/camouflage

Ellen, Rosa and Garrick, Matt (2018), 'Bombing of Darwin war hero may have actually "bugged out" under fire, historian says', ABC News Online, available at https://www.abc.net.au/news/2018-11-16/bombing-of-darwin-war-hero-may-have-actually-bugged-out/10500108

Feldt, Commander E.A. (1962), 'The Coast Watchers', *Journal of the Royal Historical Society of Queensland*, pp. 762–78, available at https://www.textqueensland.com.au/item/article/228ac847b3c5f47ed0383039d7e5199c

Fisk, Robert (2010), 'Robert Fisk: Churchill reckoned the Japanese preferred war-war to jaw-jaw', *Independent*, available at https://www.fepow-community.org.uk/arthur_lane/Percivals_Report/html/opening_of_hostilities.htm

Fort Scratchley Historical Society Inc., 'The Shelling of Newcastle, 8th June 1942', in *Fort Scratchley Historical Society Inc.*, available at www. fortschrachley.org.au

Frame, Tom (2009), 'The Bombing of Darwin', *Quadrant*, available at https://quadrant.org.au/magazine/2009/05/the-bombing-of-darwin/

Harper, Glynn (1992), 'Threat perception and politics: the deployment of Australian and New Zealand ground forces in the second world war', *Journal of the Australian War Memorial*, vol. 20, pp. 36–43

Gill, J.C.H. (1996), 'Feldt, Eric Augustas (1899–1968)', in *Australian Dictionary of Biography*, vol. 14, Melbourne University Press, Melbourne

Griffin, James (2000), 'Mason, Paul Edward (1901–1972)', in *Australian Dictionary of Biography*, vol. 15, Melbourne University Press, Melbourne

Hackett, Bob, Kingsepp, Sander and Tully, Anthony (2012–13), 'Assault on Hainan Island, China—1939', in *Rising Sun: The Imperial Japanese Navy and China 1939–1941*, www.combinedfleet.com/HainanRS_t

Hall, Louise (2017), 'Were public bomb shelters ever constructed in Sydney during World War II?', in *Curious Sydney*, ABC News Online, Sydney, available at www.abc.net.au/news/2017-10-12/curious-sydney-air-raid-shelters-wwii/9013568

Harris, John (2016), 'Simply a Question of Duty: A coastwatcher in north Australia', Part 2: 'Coastwatching on Groote Eylandt during WWII', *Naval Historical Review*, Naval Historical Society of Australia, Sydney, www.navyhistory-org.au/simply-a-question-of-duty-a-coastwatcher-in-north-australia-part-2-coastwatching-on-groote-eylandt-during-wwii

Harris, Ted (ed.) (2013), 'Volunteer Defence Corps (WW2)', in *Digger History*, available at www.diggerhistory.info/pages-conflicts-periods/ww2/vol-def-corps.htm

Harrison, Lieutenant-Colonel Des, '2/1st North Australia Observer Unit', The Australian Light Horse Association, Brisbane, available at http://www.lighthorse.org.au/2-1st-north-australia-observer-unit/

Henderson, Margaret (2015), 'Constant fear of living next to the Brisbane Line in WWII', *The Northern Star*, Lismore, 28 September 2015, https://www.northernstar.com.au/news/the-infamous-brisbane-line-plan/2788066/

Hill, A.J. (2002), 'Rowell, Sir Sydney Fairbairn (1894–1975)', in *Australian Dictionary of Biography*, vol. 16, Melbourne University Press, Melbourne

Holman, Brett (2012), 'Commemorating the Adelaide River Stakes', in *Airminded*, Melbourne, available at www.airminded.org/2012/03/03/commemorating-the-adelaide-river-stakes

Horner, David (1993a), 'Defending Australia in 1942', *War and Society*, vol. 11, p. 1–20, University of New South Wales, Sydney

——(1993b), 'Blamey, Sir Thomas Albert (1884–1956)', in *Australian Dictionary of Biography*, vol. 13, Melbourne University Press, Melbourne

——(2000), 'MacArthur, Douglas (1880–1964)', in *Australian Dictionary of Biography*, vol. 15, Melbourne University Press, Melbourne

——(2002), 'Shedden, Sir Frederick Geoffrey (1893–1871)', in *Australian Dictionary of Biography*, vol. 16, Melbourne University Press, Melbourne

Jacobs, Frank (2015), 'Australia's WWII Japanese Invasion Paranoia, in Three Maps', in *The Big Think*, Big Think Inc, New York, https://bigthink.com/strange-maps/australias-invasion-paranoia

Jenkins, David (1992), 'Kokoda blunder cost thousands of lives: Invasion warnings were ignored', *Sydney Morning Herald*, 14 August 1992

Johnston, George (1943), 'Eventful Year in S W Pacific: Island Moves By Japs Countered', *Argus*, Melbourne, 18 March 1943

Jones, Helen (1993), 'Davies, Natalia (Nat) (1907–1951)', in *Australian Dictionary of Biography*, vol. 13, Melbourne University Press, Melbourne

Joyce, R.B. (1976), 'Scratchley, Sir Peter Henry (1835–1885)', in *Australian Dictionary of Biography*, vol. 6, Melbourne University Press, Melbourne

Kelantin Times (2011), 'December 8, 1941: The Battle of Kuala Pak Amat', Kota Bharu, available atwww.muhammadismailibrahim.wordpress.com/2011/12/08/December-8-1941-the-battle-of-kuala-pak-amat

Kennard, Allington (1947), 'Jap fifth column in Malaya was small', *The Straits Times*, p. 6

Kennedy, David (2003), 'The Midget Submarine Attack against Sydney: May 1942', in 'Mysteries/Untold Sagas of the Imperial Japanese Navy' (Tully, Anthony, ed.), *Imperial Japanese Navy Page*, http://www.combinedfleet.com/atully00.htm

Kossen, Bert, Bernaudin, Pierre-Emmanuel, Niehorster, Dr Leo, Takizawa, Akira, Carr, Sean, Broshot, Jim, Leulliot, Nowfel and Klemen L., '"Seventy minutes before Pearl Harbor": The landing at Kota Bharu, Malaya on December 7th 1941', in *Axis History Forum*, 1999–2000, http://web.archive.org/web/20150701195128/http://www.dutcheastindies.webs.com/kota_bharu.html

Lockwood, Rupert (1941), *Scorched Earth*, NSW Aid Russia Committee, Sydney

Lodge, A.B. (1993), 'Bennett, Henry Gordon (1887–1962)', in *Australian Dictionary of Biography*, vol. 13, Melbourne University Press, Melbourne

Long, Jeremy (2002), 'Raiwala, Ray (1907–1965)', in *Australian Dictionary of Biography*, vol. 16, Melbourne University Press, Melbourne

Macinnis, Peter (2001), 'Charles Wilkes and the US Exploring Expedition', in *Ockham's Razor*, ABC Radio National, www.members.ozemail.com.au/~macinnes/ockhams/wilkes

Matchett, Stephen (2008), 'Get over it, we weren't at the heart of World War II', *The Australian*, Canberra, p. 21

Matthews, Alan (1999), 'S.S. Automedon. The Ship That Doomed A Colony', in *Force 'Z' Survivors*, POWRSA, www.forcez-survivors.org.uk

——(2006), 'The Sinking of Prince of Wales and Repulse', in *Force 'Z' Survivors*, POWRSA, www.forcez-survivors.org.uk

McArthur, Ian (1985), 'The Rising Sun over Australia', *Australasian Post*, pp. 2–5

McLay, Dan and McLay, Wendy (2015), 'History of Pearling in Australia', Pearl Lugger Cruises, Nungurner VIC, www.pearlluggercruises.com.au/history-of-pearling-in-australia.php

McMullin, Ross (2002), 'Ward, Edward John (Eddie) (1899–1963)', in *Australian Dictionary of Biography*, vol. 16, Melbourne University Press, Melbourne

Meaher IV, Augustine (2008), 'The Road to Singapore: Australian defence and foreign policies 1919–1941', PhD thesis, Department of History, University of Melbourne

Menzies, Trevor (2004), 'Mapping to defend Australia's north in the Second World War', *Journal of Northern Territory History*, vol. 15, pp. 91–106

Meyer, Roger, 'DCA's Role in the Second World War', Civil Aviation Historical Society & Airways Museum, available at www.airwaysmuseum.com/DCA%20in%20WWII%20pt%201

Moles, Ian Newton (1974), 'Townsville During World War II', in *Lectures on North Queensland History* (Dalton, B.J., ed.), pp. 213–39, James Cook University, Townsville QLD, available at www.textqueensland.com.au/item/chapter/5b892bfbfa8235cb9f258731f67f56c8

Moore, Clive (ed.) (2013), *Solomon Islands Historical Encyclopaedia 1893–1978*, www.solomonencyclopaedia.net/index

Morgan, Joseph (2013), 'A Burning Legacy: The "Broken" 8th Division', *Sabretache: The Journal of the Military Collectors Society of Australia*, vol. 54, pp. 4–14

Morphy, Howard (2002), 'Thomson, Donald Finlay Fergusson (1901–1970)', in *Australian Dictionary of Biography*, vol. 16, Melbourne University Press, Melbourne

Mulvaney, D.J. (2012), 'Stanner, William Edward (Bill) (1905–1981)', in *Australian Dictionary of Biography*, vol. 18, Melbourne University Press, Melbourne

Murdoch, Lindsay (2012), 'The day the empire died in shame', *Sydney Morning Herald*, available at www.smh.com.au/national/the-day-the-empire-died-in-shame-20120214-1t462

Museums Victoria (2017), 'Air Raid Precautions (ARP) badges', in *Victorian Collections*, available at www.victoriancollections.net.au/items/566423ab2162f1258417a745

Nelson, Hank (2009), 'Tracking Kokoda', *Inside Story*, Swinburne University of Technology, Melbourne, available at https://insidestory.org.au/tracking-kokoda/

New South Wales Office of Environment & Heritage (2012), 'Sydney on 31 May 1941', in *Heritage of NSW*, available at www.environment.nsw.gov.au/M24/raid/index

Northern Territory Government (2017), 'The "Nackeroos"—North Australia Observer Unit', in *The Territory Remembers 75 Years*, Northern Territory Government

Northern Territory Library, 'The Track: 1000 Miles to War', available at www.ntlexhibit.nt.gov.au/exhibits/show/track

Oliver, Dr Pam (2002), 'Interpreting "Japanese activities" in Australia, 1888–1945', *Journal of the Australian War Memorial*, vol. 36, available at www.awm.gov.au/articles/journal/j36/oliver

Parfitt, Allen (2013), 'Bicycle Blitzkreig—the Japanese Conquest of Malaya and Singapore 1941–1942', in *The War in Malaya*, available at www.thewarinmalaya.wordpress.com/2013/08/25/bicycle-blitzkreig-the-japanese-conquest-of-malaya-and-singapore-1941-1942

Percival, Lt General A.E. (1947), 'Opening of hostilities', in *The War in Malaya, in FEPOW Community*, available at https://www.fepow-community.org.uk/arthur_lane/Percivals_Report/html/opening_of_hostilities.htm

Perry, Warren (2002), 'Wynter, Henry Douglas (1886–1945)', in *Australian Dictionary of Biography*, vol. 16, Melbourne University Press, Melbourne

Perryman, John, 'Japanese Midget Submarine Attack on Sydney Harbour', in Navy website, Royal Australian Navy, available at www.navy.gov.au/history/feature-histories/japanese-midget-submarine-attack-sydney-harbour

Pike, John (ed.), 'The Brisbane Line', in *GlobalSecurity.org*, available at https://www.globalsecurity.org/military/world/australia/brisbane-line.htm

Pomeroy, John (1995), 'Morale on the homefront in Australia during the Second World War', PhD thesis, Department of History, University of Sydney

Queensland Heritage Register (2016), 'Former Underground Hospital, Mount Isa', in Queensland Government website, available at https://apps.des.qld.gov.au/heritage-register/detail/?id=601102

Rahil, Siti (2009), 'Remembering the war's first battle', *Japan Times*, Tokyo, available at https://www.japantimes.co.jp/news/2009/12/10/national/remembering-the-wars-first-battle/#.XnbMK5MzbNA

Rechniewski, Elizabeth (2010), 'Remembering the Battle for Australia', *PORTAL*, vol. 7, May 2010, pp. 1–18

Riddell, Elizabeth (1946), 'These "medicine men" counted Australia's heart beat', *Sunday Telegraph*, Sydney, 23 June 1946, p. 11

Riseman, Noah Jed (2007), 'Defending Whose Country? Yolngu and the Northern Territory Special Reconnaissance Unit in the Second World War', *Limina*, vol. 13, pp. 80–91

Robertson, Scott, Boyd, Noni and Kass, Terry (2006), *The War at Home: Identification of War Sites in NSW,* Robertson & Hindmarsh, Sydney www.aicomos.com/wp-content/uploads/2009_UnlovedModern_Robertson_Scott_War_at_Home_Slides.pdf

Ryan, Peter (1993), 'Conlon, Alfred Austin (Alf) (1908–1961)', in *Australian Dictionary of Biography*, vol. 13, Melbourne University Press, Melbourne

Schubert, Steven (2017), 'World War II attacks outside of Darwin need more recognition, historians say', ABC News Online, available at https://www.abc.net.au/news/2017-02-16/call-for-more-recognition-of-wwii-attacks-outside-of-darwin/8275498

Seekee, Vanessa (2017), '"One ilan man": the Torres Strait Light Infantry', *Wartime*, vol. 12, pp. 32–7, Australian War Memorial, Canberra, available at https://www.awm.gov.au/about/our-work/publications/wartime/12/ilan-man

Serle, Geoffrey (1993), 'Curtin, John (1885–1945)', in *Australian Dictionary of Biography*, vol. 13, Melbourne University Press, Melbourne

Sharkey, Neil, 'Fall of Singapore', in *Kokoda Historical*, available at http://kokodahistorical.com.au/history/fall-of-singapore

Shindo, Hiroyuki (2001), 'Japanese air operations over New Guinea during the Second World War', *Journal of the Australian War Memorial*, vol. 34, available at www.awm.gov.au/articles/journal/j34/shindo

Singapore Government (2014), 'King George VI Dock Opens: 14 Feb 1938', in *HistorySG*, available at http://eresources.nlb.gov.sg/history/events/16e4cb2c-7e75-4d33-b1cf-b11cf2da4104

Spratt, P.E. (1992), 'The Tasmanian Royal Engineers Building', available at www.consuleng.com.au/Tas%20Royal%20Engineers%20Building%20(Spratt)%2001.pdf

Stanley, Peter (2002), 'He's (not) coming south: the invasion that wasn't', 'Remembering 1942' Conference, Australian War Memorial, Canberra, www.ajrp.awm.gov.au/ajrp/ajrp2.nsf/WebI/Chapters/$file/Chapter2.pdf?OpenElement

——(2007) 'What is the Battle for Australia?', *Australian Army Journal*, vol. iv, issue 2, pp. 17–34

Stanner, W.E.H. (1942), 'Criticism by Major W.E.H. Stanner of the draft Interim Report to the Prime Minister', Mitchell Library, MLMSS 9393, Box 6

Stephens, David (2017), 'The bombing of Darwin, 75 years on: some alternative views', in *Honest History*, Honest History Inc, Canberra, available at www.honesthistory.net.au/wp/the-bombing-of-darwin-75-years-on-some-alternative-views

Tanaka, Hiromi (1997), 'The Japanese Navy's operations against Australia in the Second World War, with a commentary on Japanese sources', *Journal of the Australian War Memorial*, vol. 30, available at www.awm.gov.au/articles/journal/j30/tanaka

Tebbutt, Geoffrey (1942), 'Major-General Bennett Reveals—A.I.F. Had Ample Food & Arms When Singapore Surrendered', *Courier-Mail*, 28 February 1942, p. 1

Thomson, Donald (1992), 'Report on the Northern Territory Coastal Patrol and the Special Reconnaissance Unit, 1941–43' (Mulvaney, John, ed.), *Aboriginal History*, vol. 16, nos 1–2, pp. 1–57, available at www.press-files.anu.edu.au/downloads/press/ p72311/pdf/article0110

Timera Media (2015), 'The Japanese Invasion Threat of Australia', in *War History Online*, Timera Media Inc, Irving, Texas, available at www.warhistoryonline.com/war-articles/the-japanese-invasion-threat-of-australia

Tourism NT, 'Up the Track—the Stuart Highway', www.northernterritory.com/articles/up-the-track---the-stuart-highway

Tracey, Rowan (2010), 'Conflict in command during the Kokoda campaign of 1942: did General Blamey deserve the blame?', Royal United Services Institute, available at https://blog.kokodatreks.com/2010/07/21/conflict-in-command-during-the-kokoda-campaign-of-1942-did-general-blamey-deserve-the-blame-2/

Trueman, C.N. (2015), 'The Attack on Malaya by Japan', in *The History Learning Site*, available at www.historylearningsite.co.uk/world-war-two/the-pacific-war-1941-to-1945/the-attack-on-malaya-by-japan

Ungar, L.A. (1995), 'On the Home Front: A Personal Memoir', Parkes & District Historical Society

Vanovac, Neda and La Canna, Xavier (2017), 'Bombing of Darwin veterans commemorate the time World War II came to Australian soil', ABC News Online, available at www.abc.net.au/news/2017-02-19/bombing-of-darwin-remembered-75-years-on/8282024

Veterans of South Australia (2017), '75th Anniversary of the Battle of Gemas', available at www.anzaccentenary.sa.gov.au/2017/01/75th-anniversary-of-the-battle-of-gemas

Warland, Andrew (2018), 'The Battle of Bakri, Malaya: 17-20 January 1942—And the aftermath', in *Andrew Warland*, available at http://www.andrewwarland.com.au/bakribattle17-20Jan42.html

Warner, Denis (1946), 'Jap Invasion Plan For Australia', *The Herald*, Melbourne, p. 1

Wells, Kathryn and Mulholland, Jack (2015), 'The Japanese bombing of Darwin, Broome and northern Australia', available at www.australia.gov.au/about-australia/australian-story/japanese-bombing-of-darwin

Wheeler, Kristi (2003), 'Between Hitler and Stalin: Ukraine in World War II, the Untold Story', The Ukrainian Canadian Research & Documentation Centre, Toronto, available at www.ucrdc.org/Film-Hitler_annotated

Wikipedia, a range of articles, too numerous to list individually

Wilcock, Roy (2016), 'Archive Report: Allied Forces', in *Aircrew Remembered*, www.aircrewremembered.com/ramshaw-john-1

Wilcox, Craig (2006), 'The *Sanyo Maru* and Japanese Pearling in the Arafura Sea, 1934–1938', *The Beagle*, Supplement 2, Museum & Art Gallery of the Northern Territory, Darwin

Wilkinson, Stephen (2017), 'Australia's Pearl Harbor: Darwin', in *Historynet*, available at www.historynet.com/australias-pearl-harbor-darwin

Wintringham, Tom (1942), 'How to train citizens for a People's Army', *Daily Telegraph*, Sydney, 2 February 1942, p. 4

Wong Heng and Lay Tin Koh (2002), 'Sir Shenton Thomas', in *Singapore Infopedia*, National Library Board, Singapore, available at www.infopeia.nlb.gov.sg/articles/SIP_557_2005-01-09

Wood, James (2002), 'Sturdee, Sir Vernon Ashton Hobart (1890–1966)', in *Australian Dictionary of Biography*, vol. 16, Melbourne University Press, Melbourne

Wood, Richard (2017), 'Bombing of Darwin', in *Australian National Maritime Museum*, available at https://www.sea.museum/2017/02/19/bombing-of-darwin

Wright, Dr R.D. and Hogbin, Dr Ian (1943), 'Civilian Morale in North Queensland', report to Chairman, Prime Minister's Committee on National Morale, NAA A816, 37/301/199

Wright, Ken (2010), 'Coastwatchers—Thank God Such Men Lived', *Naval Historical Review*, Naval Historical Society of Australia, Sydney, March 2010, www.navyhistory.org.au/coastwatchers-thank-god-such-men-lived

Zakaria, Faizah bte (2011), 'Sembawang Naval Base', in *Singapore Infopedia*, National Library Board, Singapore, https://eresources.nlb.gov.sg/infopedia/articles/SIP_1771_2011-02-28.html

ORAL HISTORIES AND DIARIES

Acland, Bruce (1993), interviewed by Francis Good, Northern Territory Archives Service, NTRS226, TS677

——, diary, National Archives of Australia, M431, 1 & 2

Brown, Robert (2014, 2017), interviewed by the author, Melbourne

Burton, J.F., diary, Northern Territory Archives Service, NTRS2924, PB273

Clements, Josie (2017), interviewed by the author, Sydney

Daniel, Ivy, Australians at War Film Archive (UNSW), 1445

Frost, Alan, diary, Northern Territory Archives Service, NTRS1355, PB268

Johnstone, Robert, Australians at War Film Archive (UNSW), 2221

Lockwood, Douglas (1980), interviewed by Pat Rhode, Northern Territory Archives Service, NTRS226, TS264

Luke, Hylton, diary, Northern Territory Archives Service, NTRS319, PB201

Mofflin, Alfred 'Dave' (1983), interviewed by Ronda Jamieson, Northern Territory Archives Service, NTRS226, TS94

Oakley, Reg (1984), interviewed by Alan Powell, Northern Territory Archives Service, NTRS226, TS412

O'Hara-Close, Yvonne (2018), interviewed by the author, Sydney

Robb, Francis, Australians at War Film Archive (UNSW), 0140

Rogers, Ron (1983), interviewed by Alan Powell, Northern Territory Archives Service, NTRS226, TS390

Singe, Dorothy, Australians at War Film Archive (UNSW), 563
Talbot, Hannah (1984), interviewed by Helen Wilson, Northern Territory Archives Service, NTRS226, TS393
Vane, Maurice (1983), interviewed by Alan Powell, Northern Territory Archives Service, NTRS226, TS133
Vose, Dudley (1992), interviewed by Francis Good, Northern Territory Archives Service, NTRS226, TS703
Webber, Joel, notes, Northern Territory Archives Service, NTRS1360, PB268
Weston, Reginald (1983), interviewed by Wendy James, Northern Territory Archives Service, NTRS226, TS138
Wilkshire, John, diary, Northern Territory Archives Service, NTRS1483, PB352

EMAIL COMMUNICATIONS

Clark, Yang Jiang (2020), identifying Mandarin characters
Professor Rebecca Suter, Department of Japanese Studies, Sydney University (2020), examining for *kanji* text

INDEX

4th Independent Company 243–4, 246, 251
22 Mile 121
1937 federal election 9
1940 federal election 18, 245
1942 federal election 220–21

Abbott, Aubrey 94–8, 106, 113, 115–19, 122–3, 127, 209
Abbott, Hilda 106, 118–19
ABC 32, 78, 124, 236
ABDA Command 49, 100–1, 137, 148, 152
Aboriginal people 178–9, 225–7, 238–41, 247, 249, 257–8, 338
Acland, Bruce 34, 91, 94, 104, 107, 111, 113–14, 121–2, 331
Adams, Ray 304
Adelaide 146, 156, 179, 183
Adelaide River 116, 118–19, 121–22
Admiralty 19, 33, 58–9, 142, 334
Advisory War Council (Australia) 61, 124, 137, 141–2, 144, 158, 210, 304, 308, 320
AIF (Australian Imperial Force) 12, 134–6, 300
  6th Division 13, 17, 19, 135–7, 145, 214, 300
  7th Division 124, 135, 137–41, 145, 214, 309, 315
  8th Division 18, 24, 44–6, 55, 64–6, 76–7, 80, 85–6, 88–9, 137, 191, 214
  9th Division 135, 140, 305
  22nd Brigade 44–6, 50, 59, 65–73, 76, 80
  23rd Brigade 93
  27th Brigade 44, 50–5, 60, 65, 73–5
  Indian Ocean crossing 134, 137–46, 214
  Northern Territory Force 300
Air Flash 183–4
Air Raid Precautions (ARP) 14–15, 34, 54–5, 164–6, 175, 203, 327
Alamo Force 329
Alexandra Hospital 82
Albury 166–7
Alice Springs 92, 110, 116, 119–20, 123, 155, 178–9, 190, 192, 215
Allied aircraft
  Airacobras 197
  B-17 Flying Fortresses 150–1, 153–4, 300
  Brewster Buffalos 38–9, 53, 59, 61
  Catalinas 26, 61, 102, 229, 235, 247, 324
  Douglas A-24s 110
  Grumman Wildcats 312
  Hurricanes 47, 67, 85
  Lockheed Hudsons 24–5, 28–9, 31, 62, 93, 102, 110, 113, 228
  P-40 Kittyhawks 99–101, 103–6, 128, 316
  Spitfires 59
  Tornados 59
  Wirraways 92–3, 101, 110, 228, 267, 338

Allied Works Council 192–3
Alor Setar airfield 200
Ambon 99, 102, 111
American Civil War 3
American 'invasion' 147–8, 162, 194–7, 267, 345–6
Anderson, Charles 45–6, 52–3, 64
Anderson, Major 123
Anderson, 'Tubby' 272–3, 277, 279
Andrew, Bob 111–12
Andrew, Reg 284–7, 293–4
Aola 237, 247–8
Aravia 236
Argyll & Sutherland Highlanders 17, 56
Arnhem Bay 242
Arnhem Land 177, 225–7, 238–44, 246, 251
Arnold, General 321
Aroetta 241–4, 253–55
Australian Labor Party (ALP) 7, 9, 21, 95, 134, 209–11, 219
Australian newspapers/magazines
  Advertiser 126
  Age 10, 13, 33, 126
  Argus 10, 167, 186, 216
  Australasian Post 339
  Australian Women's Weekly 46, 55, 166
  Border Morning Mail 166
  Bulletin 22, 184–5
  Courier-Mail 125–7, 157, 185. 202, 307
  Daily Mirror 35, 40, 292, 296
  Daily Telegraph 180–1, 187, 219, 290, 297
  Herald 48, 125–6, 131, 337
  Newcastle Herald 126
  Pacific Islands Monthly 236
  Smith's Weekly 292–3
  Sun 185
  Sydney Morning Herald 33, 36, 40, 90, 126, 157, 166, 181, 185–6, 202, 207, 219, 291, 296–7, 308, 319, 327–8
Australian Women's Land Army 183

Bachelor airfield 101, 110, 153–4
Bakri 52, 54
Bald, Hurtle 97–8, 106–7, 110
Bald, Iris 97, 107, 110
Ballinger, Judy 182
Baltic Fleet 6, 16
Bambi 195
Ban, Katsuhisa 274, 277–8, 282, 284
Barkly Highway (see East-West Road)
Barwon Heads 208
Bataan Peninsula 150–2
'Bataan gang' 159, 320
Batavia 77, 140
Bathurst Island 97, 102–3, 105, 208
Bean, Charles 44–5
Beardsley, Eileen 176
Beasley, Jack 124
'beat Hitler first' 41, 137, 147, 158, 161, 301, 327
Bedell, Patrick 26
Benham, Greg 228–9
Bennett, General 13, 44–5, 50–1, 53, 55, 59–62, 64–8, 72–6, 78, 80–9
Bentson, Bill 195
Berrimah120–1
Betts, Ted 107, 122
Bickerton Island 227
Birdum 190–1
blackout/brownout 147, 168–9, 276, 327
Blake, General 101, 113, 119, 121, 123, 243
Blamey, General 13, 19, 22, 88, 90, 135, 139, 159–60, 189, 217, 301, 305, 310, 318–22, 328–9
Blesser, Florenz 123
Blyth River 242
Boardman, Anne 175
Bode, Captain 269, 273–4, 276, 278–9, 285, 313
Bombay 138–9
Bondi 172, 208
Bougainville 70, 233–7, 311, 314, 323–4
Braddon, Russel 14
Brereton, General 146, 151
Brett, General 100, 147, 149, 153–4, 215, 319
Brisbane 164–5, 168, 176, 196, 213, 256
Brisbane Line 212, 216, 218–21, 308, 330
British Army 76, 78
  18th Division 52–3, 62, 64, 136–7, 143
Broken Hill 179
Brooke-Popham, Air Chief Marshal 25–6, 35, 49, 59–61
Brooks, Louise 150
Broome 129–30, 182, 215
Brown, Charlie 281
Brown, Robert 15–16, 34, 54, 128, 183, 331
Bruce, Stanley 7, 142
Bruche, General 8
Buin 238, 311, 323–5
Buka Island 235–6, 238, 311, 323

Bukit Timah Road 73, 83–4
Bullard, Lance 269, 288
Buna 309–10, 313–14, 316, 323, 326, 328, 343
Burdekin River 182
Burma 69–70, 124, 138, 140–3, 145, 160, 317
 Railway 29, 89
 Road 15, 141–2
Burnett, Air Chief Marshal 125
Burns, Trooper 104

Cairns 167, 169, 232
Caldwell-Smith, Don 264
Caledon Bay 240, 242, 254
Callaghan, Brigadier 86
Calwell, Arthur 190
camouflage 99, 169–72
Cape York Peninsula 226, 238, 246
Cargill, Jimmy 260–2, 271, 280, 289, 293
Casey, General 208
Casey, Richard 13, 141, 147
cattle drive, northern Australia 209
Celebes 111
censorship 125–7, 130–1, 185–6, 290
Central Defence Camouflage Committee 170, 183
Chamberlain, Neville 9, 58
Changi Prison 89, 91
Chapman, Phil 104–5
Chifley, Ben 88
Chuma, Kenshi 271–4, 280, 282, 289
Chungking map 336–7
Churchill, Winston 16, 19, 22, 41, 47–9, 58–9, 63, 69–70, 76, 82, 124, 134–8, 140–5, 147, 158, 160, 301
'Churchill supplies' 201
Citizen Military Force (militia) 12, 18, 45, 60, 93, 136, 182, 210–11, 309, 314
Civil Collaboration Column 204
Civil Construction Corps 170
civilian invasion precautions 172–9, 198, 203–5
Clare, Captain 223
Clark, Alice 177
Clark Field 151, 153
Clemens, Josie 91
Clemens, Martin 237, 247–8, 314
Cloncurry 252
coast watchers 102, 223–5, 228–38, 241, 247–9, 253, 302, 310–12, 314, 323–6
Coast Watching Organisation 223–5, 237, 246, 255, 326
code breakers 248, 302, 305–7, 316, 326, 331
Collins, Lieutenant-Governor 2
Colombo 138–9, 144–5
Conlon, Alf 187–90, 259
conscription 211
Coomalie Creek 121
Cooper, Isabel 150
Coral Sea 215, 248, 259, 268–9, 291, 298, 302–5, 307–8, 313, 323, 326, 330, 332, 337, 343
Corregidor 152–3, 156
Crace, Admiral 303
Creswell, Captain 6
Crimean War 3–4
Croker Island 177
Cumming, M.N. 279–80
Curtin, Elsie 135, 137
Curtin, John 21–2, 31–3, 41–2, 47–9, 61, 69–70, 124, 126, 130–1, 133–47, 149, 154–5, 158, 160–1, 184, 187–90, 194, 209–11, 213–6, 218–21, 301, 303–5, 308, 310, 315, 318, 321, 326–30, 334, 337, 343, 346
 in Opposition 9, 20, 59
 statements 1, 32–3, 41, 48, 90, 124, 137, 138, 142, 144–5, 318, 326–7, 330
Cutler, Roden 180

Dakin, Bill 170
Dangerfield, Grace 174
Dark, Eleanor 187
Darwin 34, 41, 44, 92–7, 162, 167, 192, 215, 240, 243–4, 331
 air attack 101–12, 124–31, 142, 162, 163–4, 166, 172, 184, 214–5, 290, 328, 344
 bank managers 119–20
 Chinatown 93–4
 civil defence 96, 98, 109, 115, 117–19
 evacuation 96–8, 115–19
 exodus 114–17, 122, 125, 128, 131–2
 hospitals 109, 112, 120–21
 looting 118, 121–5, 127, 131
 military police (Provost Corps)117–18, 122–3, 127
 police 117, 119, 122
 rescue work 109–12,
 wharf labourers 34, 94–6, 105, 122
Davies, Natalia 183
Defence Act 211
Defence Committee (Australia) 202, 206, 208, 212, 218–19, 221

Defence Society 183
deGaris, Ren 11
Delissaville 178
Deniliquin 147
Denison, Governor 3
Department of Civil Aviation (DCA) 110, 113–14, 122, 124, 331
Department of Home Security 170
Department of Information 186–7, 189
Derwent River 2
Dhakiyarr 240
Dobbie, General 57–8
Dobell, William 170–1
Doig, Barbara 174
Doig, Ralph 304
Doolittle raid 342
Dowie, Don 28–9
Doyle, Captain 280
Drakeford, Arthur 124–5
Dripstone Caves radar post 128–9
Dubbo 171
Dulhunty, Robert 285
Dunkirk 15, 89–90, 184
Dunkley, Donald 281
Dupain, Max 170

East-West Road 191–2, 244, 251
Eastforce 50, 55
Eather, Brigadier 320, 322
Eichelberger, General 328–9
Eisenhower, General 146, 148, 152
Eleven Mile 114, 122, 124
Elkin, A.P. 187–8, 207
Elkington, Tom 241–2, 254–5
Empire Star 77–8
European War 9–13, 15, 22, 163, 180, 184, 201–2, 327
evacuations 175–8
Evatt, Bert 70, 138, 142, 301
Eveleigh Rail Yards 165
Ewing, T.T. 6, 33
Exmouth Gulf 130, 164
Eyers, Harold 261–2, 272–3, 287, 293–4

Fadden, Arthur 20–1, 59, 136, 210, 213, 219
Fannie Bay 102
Far East Command 25–6, 30–1, 35, 49
Feldt, Eric 223–5, 228–30, 237–8, 247, 255
'Ferdinand' 225
Fewtrell, General 207
First Fleet 2
First World War 8, 10, 13, 34, 44–5, 78, 149, 180–1, 184, 187, 211, 223, 246, 250, 269
Fletcher, Admiral 312
Flinders Street railway station 10, 169
Flying Doctor 244, 246–7
Force Z 37–40
Forde, Frank 70, 88, 157, 181, 210, 212–4, 218–19, 244–5, 320
Forgan Smith, Bill 186
Fort Canning 82–3
Fort Denison (Pinchgut) 3–4, 275
Fort Scratchley 295–6
fortifications, Hobart 2
  Melbourne 4
  Sydney 2–4
Fraser, Hugh 83–4
Fremantle 78, 121, 146, 214, 336
Fuchida, Commodore 102, 131
Fujita, Nobuo 263–5

Galbraith station 338
Gallipoli 7, 44, 89, 182, 333
Garbutt Air Base 198
Garden Island 263–8, 272–4, 276–81, 283–5, 288
Gardner, Jack 281
Gemas 50–1, 65
Gemencheh Bridge 50–1, 54
Georges Heights 265–6
'Gibraltar of the East' 16, 69, 163
gold rush 3, 5
Gorgon 78
Graf, Dick 154
Graham, Bill 16
Greater East Asia Co-Prosperity Sphere 23–4
Greece 19, 47, 62, 135, 160, 322
Green, Frank 133–4, 145
Gregory Downs 252
Gribble, Jack 102
Griffin, Alan 334
Griffith, Sturt 100, 113–14
Groote Eylandt 227, 242, 339
Guadalcanal 218, 233, 237, 248–9, 259, 309–14, 317, 322, 324–6, 344
  Japanese assaults 311–14, 317, 322–5
Gulf country 226, 252, 258, 338
Gulf of Carpentaria 227, 246, 253
Gulnare Bluff 244, 253

Halsey, Admiral 326, 329, 345
Hankey, Sir Maurice 8
Hanlon, Ned 218

Harney, Bill 257–8
Harris, Len 227, 339
Hart, Admiral 25–6, 151
Hashida, Sei 335
Hasluck, Paul 131–2
Hawke, Harry 110, 124
Hawkesbury River 182, 208
Heath, General 50, 60, 64, 76, 81, 83
Heffron, Bob 165
Helm, Margaret 185
Henderson Field 313–14, 322, 324–5
Heppel, Bob 94, 109
Herring, General 243–5, 247, 300–1
Higgins, Ernie 281
Hinde, John 161
Hinder, Frank 171
Hirsch, Ernest 295
Hitler, Adolf 136, 202
Hobart 2, 179, 209–10
Hogbin, Ian 198
Home Guard (UK) 181
Horii, General 314–15, 317, 322–3, 343
Horner, David 41
House of Representatives 133, 301, 303
Howroyd, Leonard 269, 281–2
Hughes, Billy 48, 210
Hurley, Patrick 184
Hyakutake, General 313, 317, 322

Idriess, Ion 182
Imperial Japanese Army (IJA) 23, 61–4, 82, 200–1, 340–3
  17th Army 313
  25th Army 24–31, 36, 40, 42, 44, 49–55, 67–73, 76
  Darwin air attack 111–12
  Ichiki Detachment 313
  Imperial Guards 52, 74–5
  South Seas Force (*Nankai Shitai*) 310, 314, 317, 322–3, 325–6, 328–9, 338, 344
Imperial Japanese Navy (IJN) 259, 305–6, 324, 340–2
  Awagisan Maru 26–9
  Darwin air attack 101–2, 104–9
  floatplanes 102, 236, 262–6, 335
  Hiryu 306–7
  I-class submarines 263–6, 269–71, 284, 294–6
  Ibuki 7
  invasion fleet, Malaya 24–30, 36, 38
  midget submarines 261–4, 269–80, 282–94, 297–8, 307, 335
  Shoho 248, 303
  Shokaku 303
  Zuikaku 303
Indian III Corps 17, 50–4, 60, 64, 75
  9th Infantry Division 24, 26–8, 35–6, 42, 44
Ingleburn 249–50
Inouye, Admiral 302
Inus plantation 236
Ioribaiwa Ridge 319–20, 322–3
Iron Chieftain 294
Iron Crown 294
'Islanders' 224, 229
Isurava 310, 314
Ito, Susumu 265–6
Ivanhoe 252
Iwasaki 265–6

Japan, as pre-war threat 6–9, 12–13, 15–16, 20–21
Japanese
  air attacks 228, 230, 237–8; *see also* Broome, Darwin, Guadalcanal, Singapore
  espionage/patrols 225–7, 229–30, 235–6, 259, 334–5, 339–40
  manufactured goods 16, 21, 36–7, 115
  internees 34, 97
  invasion banknotes 335–6
  occupation of China 6, 9, 15
Java 49, 77, 79, 83, 100–1, 126, 128–30, 139–40, 151, 185
Jeanneret, Yve 11, 16, 128, 161–2, 174–5, 280–81, 331–2
Jensen, Ossie 123–4
Jerilderie 179
Johnston, George 216
Johore 44, 49–50, 55, 58, 61, 69, 80
  Municipal Building 67
  Strait of 16, 64, 67, 70–2, 74–6
  Sultan of 61, 67, 86–7
Johore Bharu 61
Johore Volunteer Engineers 80
Joint Chiefs of Staff (US) 147–8, 152, 161, 305, 308–9
Jones, Air Commodore 99
Jones, Roger 194
Jurong line 66, 73, 76

Kahili airfield 324
Kalang 267
Kallang airfield 67, 85

Katherine 121–2, 125, 130, 246, 250–1, 253, 257
Kavieng 311
Kawasaki 31
Keating, Paul 333
Kedah 23, 42
Keep 'Em Flying 267
Kellogg's cereals 175, 183
Kelsall, Captain 2
Kenney, General 319–20
Key, General 75–6
Kieta 235–6, 238
Kimberley 246, 252
King, Admiral 301, 307–8
King George VI Dock 16–7
Kingsford Smith (Mascot) Airport 10, 208, 263
'Know Your Enemy' 186
Kokoda Track 218, 259, 309–10, 314–15, 317–20, 322–3, 326–8, 333, 338, 343–4
Kota Bharu 23, 25–37, 40, 54, 61–2
Kranji oil tanks 67, 74–5
Kranji River 64–6
Karnji-Berih line 66
Kreuger, General 329
Kuala Lumpur 201
Kuantan 38–40
Kyle, Bill 228–9

Lambing Flat 5
Larrakeyah Barracks 92, 96, 101, 120–1
Larrakia 225
Larrimah 116–17, 119, 191–2
Lavarack, General 8, 139–40
Lawson, Murry 114
Lazzarini, Bert 177
Leighton-Jones, John 28–9
Lend-Lease 194–5
Lennon's Hotel 147, 310
Leonski, Eddie 168, 195–6
Lettow-Vorbeck, Paul von 246
Ligertwood, Justice George 88
Littleby, Petty Officer 280
Lloyd, General 189
Lockwood, Douglas 125–6
Long, Commander 224, 292
Longmore, Cyril 130
Loughry, Brian 37
Lowe, Justice 131, 220–21
Lugsdin, Edith 331
Luna Park (Sydney) 165
Lunga 237, 248, 310–11, 313–14
Luzon 150–1
Lyons, Joe 9

MacArthur, Arthur 150, 153–5, 157
MacArthur, General 148–62, 206, 210–11, 215–17, 220–21, 233, 291, 301–5, 307–10, 315–21, 326, 328–31, 343–4
MacArthur, Jean 150, 153, 155, 157
Macarthur-Onslow, Sergeant Major 117–18
Macfarlan, Don 237, 248, 255, 324
Mackay, General 212–14, 218–22, 300
Mackenzie, Hugh 228, 230, 235, 255, 314
Maginot Line 15, 80
Majura hills 144
Makin, Norman 289–90, 292–3
Malacca 61, 87
Malaita Island 237
Malayan Volunteers 87
Manly ferry 261, 271, 274–5, 287, 291
Manpower Directorate 13, 188, 192
Manunda 109, 112, 121
Marshall, Dick 156
Marshall, General 141, 146, 148, 153, 159, 301, 308, 317–19, 321
Martin, Daisy 106, 122
Mason, Paul 233, 236–7, 311–12, 314, 323–6
Mataranka 178–9
Matsu Kikan 339
Matsuo, Keiu 282–3, 285–6, 288–9, 293, 298
Maxwell, Brigadier 60, 65, 73–6
Maxwell, Margaret 11, 127
McAdam, Bill 258
McCarthy, Keith 230–2
McColl, Albert 240
McDonald, Sergeant 104
McEachern, Mrs 295
McGrath, Father 102–3
McInerney, Admiral 290
McKell, Bill 203, 205, 290
McKernan, Michael 147
Mecklenberg, Commander 275–6, 279–80, 284
Melbourne 4, 10, 14, 33–4, 147, 155–7, 165–9, 176, 179, 196, 213, 263
Melville Island 102
Menzies, Pattie 13
Menzies, Robert 12–13, 18–22, 47–8, 58–9, 136, 210, 218
Menzies Hotel 157, 159

Merrylees, J.J. 235–6, 238
Midway Island 259, 298, 305–8, 326, 328, 342–3
Mikawa, Admiral 312–13
militia (see Citizen Military Force)
Milne Bay 215, 315–17, 322, 326, 334, 344
Mindanao 153–4
Ministry of Munitions 207, 209
Mizuno, Suzuhiko 339–40
Mooy, Toni 99
Moses, Charles 78, 85–8
Mount Isa 191–3, 251
Mount Vernon 139, 145
Muar River 51–2
Muirhead-Gould, Admiral 266, 269, 273–4, 276–7, 279–80, 283–4, 289, 293–4, 297–8
Murray, K.D. 187

Nackeroos 250; *see also* North Australia Observer Unit
Nagano, Admiral 341
Nagumo, Admiral 306
National Security Regulations 202–3
Neptuna 108–10, 125
New Britain 228–32, 314
New Guinea 1, 146, 158, 176, 197, 223–5, 235, 300, 308–9, 325–6, 329, 336, 342
New Guinea Force 217, 309, 314–15, 321
New Ireland 228–30
New Ways of War 180, 204
Newbigging, Brigadier 83–4
Newcastle 295–6, 334
Newcastle–Sydney–Port Kembla hub 164, 203, 206, 212–13, 221
night-time radio silence 169, 198
Nimitz, Admiral 301–2, 306, 308, 326, 329, 345
Noble, Wing Commander 30
North Africa campaign 19
North Australia Observer Unit (NAOU) 245–7, 249–53, 255–9, 338
  'A' Company 251–3, 255–6
  'B' Company 252
  'C' Company 252
North Australia Workers' Union (NAWU) 95–6
North-South Road (see Stuart Highway)
North-Western Area Command 100, 103–4, 113
Northern Territory Special Reconnaissance Unit (NTSRU) 238, 241–4, 246, 251, 253–5
NSW Maritime Services Board 260, 289, 293

Oakley, Reg 258
Oatley sewer tunnel 165
Oenpelli 177–8
Oestreicher, Robert 105, 125
Okuda 263
Operation Matador 24–6, 35–6
Oranje 271
Orcades 138–40
Orchard Road 77, 81
Oscar 258
Otford 178
Owen Stanley Range 309–10, 319, 343
Ozatwar.com 338
Ozawa, Admiral 38

Pacific Council (UK) 140
Page, Con 228–30
Page, Earle 69–70, 138, 140–2
Palau 101
Palembang 201
Palmer, 'Ernie' 241, 243, 254
Papuan Infantry Battalion 309–10
Parap 122
  airport 92, 104, 107, 110–11
  railway station 115–17
Parit Sulong Bridge 52–4
Parkes, Sir Henry 5
Parkhill, Sir Archdale 8
Parliament House (Canberra) 158–9
Pattani 23, 29–30
Patterson, Mary 169
Pearl Harbor 23–4, 26–7, 32–5, 101–2, 136, 151, 164, 262, 300, 302, 307, 344
pearlers 93, 225–6, 334
Pell, Floyd 100, 105
Penang 200
People's Army 179–81
Percival, General 42, 49–50, 55, 58, 60–70, 73–6, 79–86, 88, 300
Phibun 24, 29
Philippine Islands 22, 32, 48, 97, 148–53, 155–6, 158, 217, 310, 319, 328–9
Phillip, Governor 2
Phillips, Admiral 19–20, 25–6, 37–40
Piesse, Edmund 8
Pine Creek 178

Pollard, Jack 172
Pondo plantation 230–2
Port Jackson (see Sydney Harbour)
Port Moresby 41, 162, 214–5, 217–8, 223–6, 233, 236, 247–8, 300, 302–4, 309, 315–17, 319–20, 323, 327–8, 343–4
Port Phillip Bay 4, 263
Port Tewfik 138
Port Vila 225
Powell, Alan 132
President Grant 97
President Hoover 150
Prime Minister's Committee on National Morale 188–90, 198, 207, 216, 256
Prime Minister's War Conference 160, 310
Purvey, Betty 177, 179
Pye, Lieutenant 117–18

Queen Mary 44

Rabaul 41, 70, 99, 212, 216–7, 224–6, 228, 230–3, 235, 302–3, 308–9, 311–15, 321, 323–6, 329, 338, 342–3
Raffles Hotel 44, 63, 73
Raiwala 242–3
Ramshaw, Johnny 24, 28–9
Rangoon 140–5
Rape of Nanking 174, 292
RASC 87–8
Rattley, Reg 106
Read, Jack 233–7, 311–12, 314, 323–6
Reader's Digest 174
recruitment 13–14, 66
Reed, Mrs 296–7
Rhoades, 'Snowy' 248, 314, 324
Richardson, General 319
Richmond Air Base 264, 266
Riley, Fred 107
Riordan, Bill 180
Robinson, Horace 190
Roddick, 'Rod' 253
Rogers, Don 32
Rogers, Keith 250
Roosevelt, Franklin D. 19–20, 48–9, 141, 143–4, 147, 152, 154–6, 301
Roper Bar 251, 254–6
Roper River 227, 242–4, 251
Rowell, General 215, 314–15, 320–2
Royal Air Force (RAF) 140
  in Malaya/Singapore 26, 30, 39, 53, 59, 61, 67
Royal Australian Air Force (RAAF) 14, 136, 140, 237–8, 247, 319, 338
  at Darwin 92–3, 98–9, 102, 108, 110–11, 113–14, 122, 125, 128–9
  Fighter Command, Sydney 264–6
  in Malaya/Singapore 24–6, 28–32, 38–40, 53, 62, 85
  radio intercept units 99, 103, 171
Royal Australian Navy (RAN) 136
  HMAS *Canberra* 266, 268, 285, 313
  HMAS *Gunbar* 104
  HMAS *Kuttabul* 268–9, 278–81, 283, 288, 291
  HMAS *Lauriana* 282–3
  HMAS *Lolita* 272–3, 277, 279
  HMAS *Platypus* 111
  HMAS *Samuel Benbow* 288
  HMAS *Sea Mist* 284–6, 293–4
  HMAS *Steady Hour* 286–7, 293
  HMAS *Swan* 108
  HMAS *Vampire* 37
  HMAS *Wyalla* 274–5
  HMAS *Yandra* 273, 282–3
  HMAS *Yarroma* 261–2, 271–3, 277, 287, 293–4
royal commissions
  Darwin 131
  General Bennett 88
  Ward/Brisbane Line 220–21
Royal Navy 33, 37, 40
  Eastern Fleet 9, 17–18, 37
  HMS *Durban* 77–8
  HMS *Express* 39
  HMS *Indomitable* 37
  HMS *Prince of Wales* 37–40
  HMS *Repulse* 26, 37, 39
Royle, Admiral 294, 304
RSL 181, 334
Russia 3–4, 6, 20, 60, 136, 180, 201–2, 207, 299, 343–5
Ruwoldt, Rex 129
Ryan, Mick 95

Samuels, Alan 339–40
Santa Isabel Island 247
Sasaki, Captain 263, 265, 269, 294
Sato, Ken 337
Savage, Russell 85
Savo Island 248, 313
Scherger, Group Captain 100, 103, 109–10, 113
Schroeder, Leif 248, 314, 324
scorched earth 201–9, 215, 219

'Scorched Earth Code ' 205–6
scorched earth subcommittee 205
Scott, Colonel 241
Scratchley, Peter 4
Selman, John 123
Shedden, Frederick 13, 21, 31–2, 48, 160, 218–20
Shortland Islands 238
Singapore 63, 69, 73, 79–81, 85, 99, 137, 140–1, 143, 212–3, 267, 334
  air attacks 36, 46, 62, 78–9, 85
  Cathay building 84
  deserters 73, 77–8, 80
  evacuation 63–4, 69, 77, 138
  Ford motor factory 81, 84
  Naval Base (Sembawang) 6–8, 16–17, 26, 57, 64–5, 211
  Special Branch 61
Singapore strategy 9, 16–17, 19, 47, 54, 57–62, 90, 211, 222
  'period before relief' 58
Singapore Times 51
Singe, Dorothy 332
Skrine, Cynthia 187
Skudai River 70, 74
Smith, Joshua 170, 332
Sneath, Gladys 173
Sneath, Jim 174
Soldiering On 130
Solomon Islands 223, 233, 237–8, 247, 249, 302, 309–10, 323–4, 329, 343–5
Songkhla 23, 26, 29–30, 35, 38
South Head 264, 268, 271–4, 282–3
South Pacific Area 301, 308–9, 329
South West Pacific Area (SWPA) 148–9, 154, 159–61, 206–7, 217, 290, 301–2, 304, 307–10, 319, 328–9, 331
Spanish Civil War 180
Spencer Street railway station 31, 156–7
Spender, Percy 21, 220, 245
St James railway station 165
St Vincent's Hospital 124, 141–2
Stalin, Joseph 201
Stanley, Peter 334
Stanner, Bill 238, 244–7, 249–52, 255–7
Stantke, Brigadier 188
Stewart brothers 191
Stone, Meryl 196
Stuart Highway 190–2, 244, 300
Stuart Creek 171–2
Sturdee, General 44, 60–1, 139–40, 212–3, 218, 220
Sugiyama, General 341, 343–4
Sumatra 87–8, 139–40
Sutherland, Brigadier 245
Sutherland, General 151, 153–4, 156, 320, 329
Swain, Harold 203–7
Sydney 165, 167–70, 172, 177, 179, 181, 185, 196, 263–9, 275–82, 285, 288–92
  Eastern suburbs 294–6
  North Shore 181
Sydney Camouflage Group 169–70
Sydney Harbour (Port Jackson) 2–4, 10–11, 260–94

Tabar plantation 228
Takumi, General 28–9
Talasea 230–2
Tanaka, General 341
Tanglin Barracks 80
Taplin, James 282–3
Tate, Sylvia 185
Taylor, Brigadier 45, 65–6, 68, 72–3, 76, 80
Taylors Bay 285–90, 293
teleradios 228–30, 236–7
  FS6 field radio 253
  Type 3B 224
  WS133 253
Terowie 155–6, 217, 329
The Causeway, 44, 55–6, 64–5, 74, 80
The Corsican Brothers 267
The Lodge 133–4
The Mikado 185
The Overlanders 209
The Times 90, 245
The Warning 10
Thomas, Penry 100–1
Thomas, Governor 16, 58
Thomson, Donald 238–44, 246–7, 251, 253–5
Thursday Island 92, 97
Thyer, Jim 66, 74, 85
Time 148
Timor 41, 99, 101–3, 126–9, 339–40
Timor Sea 100–1, 110
Toberoi plantation 235–6
Tobruk 135–6
Tōgō, Admiral 6
Tojo, Hideki 342
Tomioka, Captain 341
Torrance, Brigadier 84
Tortoise Society 24

'Total War–and Total Civilian Collaboration' 203–5
Townley, Athol 285–7, 293
Townsville 130, 147, 153, 162, 164, 171, 176, 196–9, 213–14, 217, 224, 254, 300, 309
  air attacks 197
  civilian complaints 197–9, 216
  Ford Street 197
  US Navy hospital 196
Trapping the Jap 182
Travers, Jack 250
'Tresco' 269, 273–4
Trollope, Anthony 4
Truk 302, 313, 345
Tucker, Alan 167
Tulagi 224, 237–8, 247–8, 302–3, 305, 309–12
Turner, Admiral Kelly 312–13

Ubin Island 67
Ukraine 201
United Australia Party (UAP) 18, 95, 210, 245
US Army 147
  41st Division 148, 162, 214, 300
  Engineers 192
  transport unit 192, 251, 253
US Army Air Force 100–1, 103–6, 146, 153, 319
US Hospitality Bureau 195
US military camps (Australia) 147–8, 162, 196
US Navy 25–6, 32, 153, 307
  Asiatic Fleet 25, 151
  USS *Chicago* 264–9, 274–80, 283–5, 313
  USS *Enterprise* 305
  USS *Hornet* 305
  USS *Houston* 99, 101
  USS *Lexington* 300, 302–3
  USS *Peary* 99, 101, 108
  USS *Perkins* 264, 268, 276, 283–4, 290
  USS *Yorktown* 248, 300, 302–3, 305–6

Varley, Brigadier 80
Vasey, General 217
Veitch, Gerald 50
Vestey's meatworks 92, 121
Victoria Palace Hotel 32
Vigors, Tim 40
Volunteer Air Observer Corps 183–4
Volunteer Cadet Corps 175
Volunteer Defence Corps (VDC) 115, 181–2, 206, 246, 304, 338

Wainwright, General 153
Waldie, John 109
Walker, Gordon 78, 85–8
War Cabinet (Australia) 20, 31–4, 41, 59–60, 70, 88, 96, 137, 142–4, 155, 159–60, 180, 189, 206, 211, 214
War Office (UK) 4, 58, 60
Ward, Eddie 96, 209–11, 218–21
Warner, Denis 337
Washington Conference (1941) 146–7
Washington Naval Conference (1922) 7
Watson, Walter 295
Wavell, General 49, 55, 64, 67, 69, 76, 79–82, 138–40, 148, 160
Wellen 266–7
Wells, Judge 117–18, 240
Westforce 50–5
Weston, Reg 98, 115
White, General 18, 44
White, Max 250, 259
White Australia 5–6
Whittaker, Howard 269, 281
Wild, Cyril 83–4
Wilkes, Charles 2–3
Willcock, John 208
Wilson, Air Commodore 100–1
Wilson, Mrs 296
Wilson, Percy 265, 276–7, 284
Wintringham, Tom 180–2, 204
Witu Island 232
Wonggu 242
Woodah Island 240
Woodward, Barbara 296
Wright, R.D. 198
Wyett, John 55–6, 86–7
Wyndham 182, 209, 252
Wynter, Henry 7

Yamada, Admiral 311
Yamamoto, Admiral 263, 305–7, 342
Yamashita, General 24, 63, 67, 73, 75, 79, 81, 84
Yang, Admiral 336
Yokohama Specie Bank 34
Yolngu people 225–7, 238–43, 251, 253–5
Yong Peng 52–3
Young Malays Union (*Kesatuan Melayu Muda*) 24

Zealandia 97